THE
FLOWER
GARDEN

Originally published in France
as *Fleurs et Jardins* in 1988
First published in 1989 by Century Hutchinson Ltd,
Brookmount House, 62–65 Chandos Place, Covent Garden,
London WC2N 4NW

Century Hutchinson Australia Pty Ltd, 89–91 Albion Street,
Surry Hills, Sydney, New South Wales 2010, Australia

Century Hutchinson New Zealand Limited, PO Box 40–086,
Glenfield, Auckland 10, New Zealand

Century Hutchinson South Africa (Pty) Ltd, PO Box 337,
Bergvlei, 2012 South Africa

Photoset in Baskerville by Deltatype Ltd, Ellesmere Port
Printed and bound in France

British Library Cataloguing in Publication Data

Pereire, Anita
    The flower garden.
    1. Gardens. Annual & biennal flowering plants. Cultivation.
    Manuals   I. Title
    653.9′31

    ISBN 0–7126–1874–0

PUBLISHER'S NOTE
In the A–Z section, beginning on page 49, the UK
common name is followed by its US equivalent.

I should like to thank all those who have
contributed to this work:

Jean-Paul Collaert and Patricia Beucher for their
research on plants,
Philippe Bonduel who computerized this
information and Guy Loriot who did the
original typesetting so well.

My thanks, too, to Arnaud Descat for the plant
photographs

Philippe Ferret, Valérie Finnis, Philippe
Perdereau, François Rodrigues for garden and
landscape photographs

and Alain Meilland and Ernest Turc.

THE
FLOWER
GARDEN

Over 2000 Flowering Plants
for Every Situation

ANITA PEREIRE

CENTURY

London Sydney Auckland Johannesburg

So many books have been devoted to gardens and flowers that you may well ask, why do we need another one? The idea of writing this book came to me one day when a friend asked me to create a uniformly blue flowerbed for her, with no other colours except for the foliage. I am familiar with hundreds of plant species and varieties, but I was really quite embarrassed when I attempted to draw up a list of those which would flourish in the dry soil of the shady corner in question! I consulted huge botanical encyclopaedias to find flowers which would fulfil her wishes and, during my research, it occurred to me that enthusiasts or not, we all have similar problems when we set about establishing a garden or creating a flowerbed.

Garden centres, nurseries and, indeed, catalogues provide temptations that we gardeners can rarely resist. We will fall in love with a plant's appearance while perhaps being ignorant of its life rhythm and its requirements. How then do we introduce it comfortably into our gardens?

I don't believe in green fingers, but I do believe that if you love plants, you will be sensitive to their needs. It's a question of knowledge and love. In the following pages I will tell you all you need to know to succeed. As for love . . . I am sure it is already there between you and your flowers.

anita Pereire

The Art

and

Craft

Knowing the soil
Cultivation
Leaves
Flowers
Flowering through the year
Details that make all the difference
Special needs
Problems and difficulties

Planning the layout of a garden and the various elements that will bring it to life requires a little forethought. There are a few factors that should be taken into consideration: the soil and its characteristics, the area where the garden is located and its climate, your own taste and the amount of time you have to spare. I have looked at all the situations you could be confronted with and tried to answer the questions you might be asking. In that way, you will be able to avoid plants that could pose problems and choose instead those which, being easy to grow, require minimum attention or indeed simply ones that suit your colour scheme.

With a little shade, plenty of moisture and an acid soil
your ferns, primulas, meconopsis
and rhododendrons will thrive!

KNOWING THE SOIL

Flowers, like all other plants,
draw from the soil the nutrients that they need to sustain them.
Soils, however, vary even within a single garden,
and each type has different implications for the gardener.
If you don't know what type of soil you have or if you are in any doubt,
buy a soil-analysis kit from your local garden centre.

Peaty Soil

This soil is spongy and almost black. It is to be found mainly where marshes have been drained or forests cleared, or on the sites of ancient peat bogs. Here, vegetation has decomposed over long periods of time resulting in a humus-producing soil. However, nutrients in such soils are usually slow-acting, so it may be necessary to add fertilizer. If the soil is too acidic the addition of lime will help, though this should not be done at the same time as an application of fertilizer since a chemical reaction might result.

If your neighbours grow azaleas and rhododendrons and there are plenty of oaks and chestnut trees around, there is every chance that you will have this characteristically acid soil. Another indication is the natural growth of broom, heathers, thistles, daisies and creeping buttercup.

Even if your garden soil falls into a different category, you can still grow plants that need a humus-rich soil. Dig a trench and line its floor with a polythene sheet which has been perforated to allow drainage. Fill it with leafmould from hornbeam, chestnut, maple or oak. Alternatively, you could buy packs of compressed peat. It will also be important to choose the situation with care. Most plants that appreciate this type of soil do not enjoy direct sun or a ground that dries out quickly, so they must be kept in the semi-shade.

My choice: *Asclepias tuberosa, Cypripedium, Erica vagans, Erythronium, Gentiana sino-ornata, Lewisia, Lithospermum, Lupinus, Meconopsis betonicifolia, M. integrifolia, Primula acaulis, Sanguinaria, Trillium grandiflorum, T. ovatum.*

Wet Soil

Rather than going to all the trouble of improving the drainage for a very wet soil, by means of a soakaway or tile drain, it may be a good idea instead to treat the moisture content as a bonus and create a water garden or simply grow plants that appreciate damp situations. Arums and astilbes, for example, reach greater heights and produce more spectacular flowers than they would in a normal soil.

With water gardens, however, there is always the problem of staying dry while pruning and dead-heading. The answer is to set out stepping stones here and there which will also prevent the soil from becoming compacted.

If you are subject to hard frosts in winter, this can be catastrophic for your plants. For protection, therefore, lay down a thick mulch of straw, peat or any bulky organic matter towards the end of autumn. This can be dug into the soil when spring arrives.

Apply another generous mulch every spring to get new plantings off to a good start, and prevent soil becoming too mushy in heavy rain.

My choice: *Aconitum, Astilbe, Astrantia, Cimicifuga, Crocosmia, Dicentra, Fritillaria meleagris, Hemerocallis, Hosta, Iris sibirica, Ligularia, Lobelia cardinalis, Lythrum, Primula japonica, Zantedeschia.*

*Yellow **Arctotis** and blue **Felicia**, growing almost wild, form beautiful ground cover on a lakeside dune.*

Limy Soil

Limy soil is light in colour, hot during the summer and cold in winter, and the topsoil is thin. In the wild, it is home for clover, red poppy, corn crowfoot, old man's beard and viburnum. Many undemanding cultivated plants manage to thrive in this type of soil—bergenias, alchemillas, euphorbias and most geraniums.

New houses often seem to have gardens with a dry stony soil that may be even worse than the limy variety. If you cannot change it, there are still ways of growing flowers. Dig pockets five times the circumference and five times the depth of the plant's root system (ask a specialist if you are not sure) and fill with a mixture of ⅓ peat, ⅓ sand and ⅓ leaf-mould. Eventually, though, the lime will infiltrate again.

In extreme cases, first enrich the soil by growing manure crops (mustard, lupin, phacelia or buckwheat) which have the additional advantage of being decorative. Simply let them grow and later dig them into the ground for a richer soil

14

As the soil is cold and damp in winter, it is sensible to wait until the ground warms up in spring before planting and when supplements of peat, compost and sand will give them a better start.

Though clay soil is not poor, it needs to be lightened and aerated with straw manure, leaf-mould, peat and the like.

Two tips: as the soil hardens quickly in the sun, make a little channel around plants to allow them to get the most from watering, as slugs are fond of clay, keep them at bay by surrounding the collar of young plants with a few handfuls of coarse sand or wood-ash.

My choice: *Aconitum, Anemone nemorosa, Camassia, Crinum, Heracleum, Hyacinthus, Iberis, Macleaya, Monarda, Narcissus, Paeonia, Polemonium, Solidago.*

the following spring. Finally, there is always the consolation that this type of ground, with its mixture of stone and gravel, poses no drainage problems.

My choice: *Acaena, Acanthus, Asphodeline, Ballota, Dictamnus, Echinops, Erigeron karvinskianus, Eschscholzia, Lavandula, Oenothera, Onopordum, Salvia sclarea, Thymus, Vinca.*

Clay Soil

Clay soil is easily recognized as it is heavy and sticky when worked after a shower, and obstructs the passage of air to the roots. In fine dry weather, on the other hand, it is dry, hard as a brick and starts to crack. In other words, it is an inhospitable environment for many plants. Fortunately, however, there are certain plants that are at home in clay soils.

Sandy Soil

This is a porous, light, acidic soil, often leached by the rain. Though easily workable it has no food value. It can be recognized from the presence of plants such as chickweed, digitalis, common broom and wild sorrel.

Sandy soil must be provided with organic matter to enrich and stabilize it; add chopped straw compost, leaf-mould and peat. Chemical fertilizers should be avoided as they go through this soil as if it were a sieve. Clover, mustard or annual lupins sown in early August and dug into the soil before winter will enrich it.

Bulbs need well-drained ground and thus flourish in sandy soil, which is why tulips do so well in Holland. Ground-cover plants should also be grown as their root system helps to retain the soil. With these, therefore, it is possible to have a bright garden despite a poor soil. One final point in its favour is that sandy soil does warm up rapidly after the cold of winter.

My choice: *Allium, Alstroemeria, Arctotis, Dierama, Epilobium, Galega, Galtonia, Incarvillea, Lupinus, Nepeta, Nicotiana, Tulipa.*

15

*A typical temperate coastal scene with **Agave**,
Pelargonium and **Arctotis** flourishing in sunshine
and dry soil.*

SITUATIONS

Before anything is planted,
it is essential to know whether it should be placed in the sun,
in shade or in semi-shade. If, for example, you plant most cyclamens
and some fuchsias in full sun or cosmos and rock alyssum in the shade,
the results will be disappointing, to say the least.

Shade

Gardeners are forever complaining that there is too much shade in their garden. What they should remember is that some most attractive plants do perfectly well out of the sun and it is a pity to neglect an area with so many possibilities. Many plants that first grew in forests appreciate the semi-shade of deciduous trees.

There is, however, shade and shade!. The most difficult area to stock is under trees where all the moisture and nourishment is snapped up by old roots. In such conditions it is virtually impossible to grow large plants that require a rich soil. The shallow-rooted ground-cover plants, on the other hand, have no problems. If the shade derives from buildings or from a northerly or east-west aspect, there is no serious difficulty. Indeed, quite the opposite, as this part of the garden may become one of the most interesting areas! For maximum effect, use several species of each genus recommended to avoid monotony, especially those with unusual foliage and form as well as a variety of shades of green.

My choice: *Acanthus, Anemone hupehensis, Brunnera, Chelone, Fuchsia, Helleborus, Hosta, Impatiens, Lamium, Primula japonica, Pulmonaria, Ruscus, Tiarella.*

Sun

It might be thought that given sun there would be no need to do anything but sow, and growth and flowering would follow automatically. The sun, it is true, may be the source of life but, during planting, even the hardiest sun-lovers need protection between sowing and the appearance of the first shoots. If transplanting is necessary, it must take place in the evening after watering. Unless this is done, the plantlets fare badly. Should the ground be very exposed, they need to be screened with conifer branches or foliage.

As sunny conditions lead to rapid drying of the soil, it is a wise precaution to place a well-watered mulch in the base of planting holes. The result is more vigorous vegetation from the first year.

My choice: *Agapanthus, Anaphalis, Anthemis, Artemisia, Campanula, Delphinium, Dierama, Freesia, Galega, Helianthemum, Iris germanica, Lavandula, Phlox paniculata, Salvia.*

Dry and Hot

Most plants that enjoy sunny situations fare badly in dry soil and so many of them have developed natural protection. Some have a thick foliage that retains moisture and thus prevents dehydration; others have a velvety foliage which also offers some protection.

It is important to follow all the advice given for sunny gardens. It should further be noted that plants which manage in a dry climate need to be sheltered from heavy rains, particularly if there is

Primula japonica *and ferns enjoy the cool shade under large deciduous trees.*

any drainage problem. Panes of glass or sheets of clear plastic will act as a roof.

My choice: *Ceratostigma, Euphorbia, Helianthemum, Lavandula, Osteospermum, Romneya, Sedum acre.*

Temperate Coastal Garden

Hot and dry in summer, mild and wet from October to March, temperate coastal gardens provide a home for many delightful and spectacular plants, some retaining their foliage throughout the year. The period from the end of March to the end of May is when nature is at its most bountiful.

During the summer months, the plants slow

My choice: *Agapanthus, Althaea, Arctotis, Artemisia, Ceratostigma, Claytonia, Dianthus, Dierama, Galega, Iris bucharica, Lantana, Salvia, Sisyrinchium, Zinnia.*

The Seaside Garden

A seaside garden is going to be subjected to harsh light, salt-spray, gusting winds and a soil that is often stony or sandy. Plants, therefore, must be given protection from the moment of planting, using permanent wind-breaks in the form of trees and shrubs or temporary screens until they are well-established. As the soil will probably be dried out by salty winds, nourishment must be provided from whatever is locally available: seaweed, leaves, manure, humus, straw, grass-cuttings, peat.

If the ground is sloping, heavy rains will cause gullying, so rendering life difficult for any plants. The solution here is to grow alongside them ground-cover plants which are effective allies.

For plants that are difficult to establish, here is a simple remedy that has been tried and tested. Remove the bottom from as large a plastic pot or tub as you can find and place it in the ground, filling with best compost. Once inserted, your plant will benefit during its first years and will also derive the maximum from watering, a particularly important point where there is competition from tree roots. If necessary, the pot can be removed later. Then water thoroughly, filling the planting hole to the top and allowing it to drain through.

Before setting any containers in place, check the state of the roots: if they are tightly intertwined, use a sharp spade edge to trim off the dried roots from the sides and bottom and carefully tease out a few of the outer roots so as to ensure a good start. Once again, it is essential to see that the plants are properly watered, especially during the first years. Scoop out a shallow basin around each stem and spread gravel or pebbles in it together with twigs or chopped straw to conserve moisture.

My choice: *Althaea, Arabis, Bergenia, Campanula, Dictamnus albus, Hesperis, Lavatera trimestris, Lychnis, Malva, Nepeta, Osteospermum, Phormium, Salvia.*

down, particularly if water is in short supply, and the strong drying winds become an enemy to be reckoned with. The soil, therefore, needs to be treated with both animal and vegetable matter: sheep and horse manure, moist and well-composted chopped straw, leaf-mould or peat soaked before use.

In winter, the soil around young plants should be covered with straw to protect them from any frost. In summer, to conserve as much moisture as possible, the soil should be mulched with pine needles, grass clippings and leaves. If they are nourished, protected and watered in this way, the plants will flower happily.

The younger a plant is when it is put into the ground, the better it will take root and grow. Planting young is also more economical but those who cannot wait can buy plants in containers from a good specialist. Many plants which are treated as annuals in more northerly climates become perennial in temperate costal areas.

Bergenia *produces its pink or white flowers*
from January to May, depending on the species. The large glossy leaves
give visual interest throughout the year,
though they can become bedraggled.

FOLIAGE

Foliage has an important role to play in the garden.
It not only serves as a setting for flowers in bloom but,
when these have faded, it remains behind to delight the eye
with an infinite variety of form, texture and colour.
Ovate and lobed, toothed and prickly, leaves and fronds
offer every shade of green as well as gold, silver, red and purple.

Silvery Foliage

Because many silver foliage plants originated in Mediterranean countries many gardeners believe that they are fragile but, in fact, they may be capable of resisting temperatures of −15°C (5°F) without losing their leaves.

Generally, such plants will make do with a poor, dry soil like that of their countries of origin and, for the most part, they keep their foliage throughout the year. The many species possessing these advantages make it possible to develop very attractive borders.

A wide range of shades is available, including steel grey, moon-silver, blue-grey, etc. Curiously, the great majority have yellow flowers which, though usually rather insipid, may be combined with yellow annuals or perennials, or even used to soften contrasts between brighter colours.

Many silver foliage plants can be trimmed to form 'balls', an effect that works well with *Ruta*, *Santolina* and *Lavandula*.

My choice: *Artemisia splendeus, Ballota pseudodictamnus, Convolvulus cneorum, Geranium renardii, Lavandula, Lychnis coronaria, Nepeta faassenii, Ruta, Salvia argentea, Santolina chamaecyparissus, Verbascum* 'Broussa' or *V.* 'Brusa', *Veronica incana.*

Golden Foliage

Golden foliage brings a feeling of sunshine to the dullest day. The category includes both deciduous and evergreen plants but, in either case, choose the situation carefully as some lose their colour if placed in the shade. In the semi-shade, however, they will light up that area of the garden. A very attractive border can be obtained with golden foliage plants and the whole range of yellow flowers (see pages 26–7). Yellow roses, which are often difficult to place, blend perfectly with ground cover provided by the golden foliage of *Lamium* 'Aureum'.

My choice: *Erica cilaris* 'Aurea', *E. cinerea* 'Golden Drop', *Filipendula, Hosta fortunei* 'Aureomarginata', *Phormium tenax* 'Variegatum', *Salvia officinalis.*

Variegated Foliage

Variegated foliage may be either streaked or mottled, green and white or green and yellow. Pink and white or purplish-red are more unusual combinations. A few years ago, no one would have anything to do with them, largely because of their over-use in public parks. Today, however, they have returned to fashion and deservedly so on two grounds: they are easy to grow and they brighten the garden.

Occasionally, you will find that a variegated plant begins putting out leaves that are entirely green. Whenever this occurs, always remove the stem in question from the base.

All types of variegated leaves are difficult to match with other plants. If they are green and white or green and yellow, place them with yellow, violet and orange flowers and with green foliage. If the combination is pink and white, they are best associated with bright flowers.

My choice: *Arum italicum* 'Pictum', *Cyclamen purpurascens, Hosta fortunei* 'Albopicta', *Pulmonaria officinalis, Salvia officinalis* 'Tricolor', *Saxifraga stolonifera, Trillium sessile.*

Purple Foliage

Purple foliage plants will blend in with almost any flowers, even reds and oranges, without clashing. However, to set off the purple to best effect, plants should be placed in the open against the blue of the sky, their natural warmth of tone enhanced by pastel flowers around them.

My choice: *Ajuga reptans* 'Atropurpurea', *Foeniculum, Lobelia fulgens, Rheum palmatum, Rodgersia pinnata* 'Superba', *Salvia officinalis, Sedum maximum* 'Atropurpureum'.

Autumn Foliage

Though it is mostly trees and shrubs which change with the season, there are also fine autumnal shades to be found among annuals and perennials, providing a bonus at a time when garden flowers are beginning to fade.

The most common are the ground-cover plants whose coloured foliage is best seen in large patches or in the foreground of borders.

My choice: *Bergenia* 'Evening Glow', *Ceratostigma plumbaginoides, Epimedium* × *rubrum, Erica carnea, Geranium macrorrhizum, Geranium dalmaticum, Kochia scoparia, Lysimachia clethroides, Polygonum affine, Tiarella wherryi.*

This eye-catching border is composed of cushions of **Santolina** *and* **Lavandula**, *the deeply cut silvery foliage of* **Artemisia**, **Ruta** *and the velvety leaves of* **Stachys lanata**.

Evergreen Foliage

Many plants which keep and renew their foliage through the year came originally from hot, humid countries but have adjusted to European climates. Their principal advantage is that they retain their foliage in winter and so the garden is never bare.

As there are evergreen plants for every type of soil and situation, at least half of the space available should be devoted to them.

My choice: *Bergenia, Erica, Helleborus niger, Lamium galeobdolon, Lavandula, Phlox douglasii, Ruscus, Ruta graveolens, Salvia officinalis, Santolina, Sedum spurium, Sempervivum, Stachys olympica, Tiarella.*

*A dazzling border of primrose-like **Verbena hybrida** and showy, many petalled **Dahlia**,*
if it is to be properly appreciated, needs to be seen from a distance,
preferably against the background of an evergreen hedge.

FLOWERS

*Whether as the inspiration of poets or as a token of love,
flowers are for every occasion. Whether neatly arranged in beds
or scattered in grass, whether perfumed or without fragrance,
they are all, from the humblest violet to the majestic rose,
the gardener's reward for his work.
They are the colours for your palette and it is for you to compose
the canvas according to your own vision.*

— *White and Green Flowers* —

The number of species and varieties with white and green flowers is so great that without difficulty you will find a plant for every season and for many different arrangements. Blended with silver foliage plants, white and green flowers make elegant borders for any garden.

The neutral shades provided by this group have a significant role in all floral compositions—and bouquets—since they serve to separate flowers of contrasting colours. This is a point that should be borne in mind when planting.

For a successful white border, select species that vary widely in form, texture and size. At the same time, try to ensure that the border will remain in flower for as long as possible rather than just a few weeks. If this is not done, there will be unattractive empty periods.

White borders begin to make a show in April with the bulbs, reach a high point in summer with the roses and delphiniums and then finish with the glory of the asters and chrysanthemums in August and September.

My choice: *Anthemis cupaniana, Campanula latifolia* 'Alba', *Chrysanthemum maximum, Crambe cordifolia, Dahlia, Delphinium elatum* 'Icecap', *Filipendula, Gaura, Gypsophila, Helleborus niger, H. Foetidus, Iris, Lavatera, Libertia, Lychnis coronaria, Narcissus triandrus* 'Rippling Waters', *Penstemon, Phlox maculata* 'Miss Lingard', *Tulipa, Viola cornuta* 'Alba'.

Blue, Mauve, Violet or Black Flowers

The elegance of blue is never out of place no matter what the company. Moreover, as blues often flower late, they can mingle with the asters, adding further tones of mauve and violet. If you have not already thought of it, lay out a corner of your garden with blue and white flowers and you are guaranteed success.

Certain flowers gain from being placed in direct sunlight and the blues, mauves and violets belong in this category. If they are given a green hedge as a background, then place them in company with silver, apricot, yellow or pink. The darker the flower, the more it needs paler neighbours to bring out its qualities.

The principle just stated applies in particular to black flowers, which give an uncommon charm to any composition provided they are set off by white, pale yellow or pale pink. The black of these flowers is not at all funereal but tinged with brown or violet and it is particularly effective in the smaller garden.

My choice: _Agapanthus orientalis, Anemone coronaria_ 'Mr Fokker', _Aster × frikartii, Callistephus chinensis, Campanula allionii, Delphinium grandiflorum, Erigeron speciosus, Galega officinalis, Gentiana, Geranium ibericum_ 'Johnson's Blue', _Lobelia vedrariensis, Meconopsis betonicifolia, Nepeta × faassenii, Scabiosa caucasica, S. atropurpurea, Stokesia laevis, Veronica gentianoides, Viola cornuta._

Orange and Yellow Flowers

The majority of flowers in this group bloom in spring, arriving like a burst of sunshine after the cold, grey days of winter.

While it is easy to match yellows and apricot, the same is not true for orange which may appear

Nothing brightens a garden more than a yellow border as here with **Hemerocallis**, **Allium moly** _and_ **Alchemilla mollis**. _The flowers are set off perfectly by the green hedge._

26

rather 'loud' in the company of pink and red. On the other hand, you could take the opposite approach and decide to have multi-coloured beds, though in this case, it is worth taking the trouble to plan the distribution on paper beforehand. These brighter colours can then be situated at some distance or placed in the shadier parts of the garden.

My choice: *Alyssum saxatile, Cheiranthus cheiri, Coreopsis verticillata, Digitalis grandiflora,* syn. *D. ambigua, Eremurus robustus, Gerbera jamesonii, Heliopsis scabra, Iris, Lysimachia punctata, Oenothera fruticosa.*

Pink Flowers

Not only is there an enormous number of pink flowers but there is also an infinite range of tones from the very palest pink to raspberry verging on red.

These soft shades blend well with violet and mauve but should not be mixed with red or orange-yellow unless you are creating a multi-coloured border with no intention of seeking colour harmonies. Such arrangements can be very successful, especially with annuals, but do not settle for half measures. Either go for a pastel setting in which pink is an important element or compose a very variegated scene with all sorts of colours, forms and species.

My choice: *Althea rosea, Cleome spinosa* 'Pink Queen', *Cosmos bipinnatus, Diascia rigescens, Geranium endressii, Helianthemum* 'Wisley Pink', *Lathyrus latifolius, L. odoratus, Paeonia* 'Lady Alexander', *Penstemon barbatus, Phlox paniculata, Sidalcea malviflora, Tulipa* 'Clara Butt' (Div. 6).

Red Flowers

Whether red is a plus or a minus in any bed depends very much on the surrounding colours. For a border of red plants, there is no better example than Hidcote in Gloucestershire where masses of different forms and shades of red are blended with evergreens.

Beds of red flowers can also be enriched by providing a background of foliage plants in raspberry, garnet and plum.

If your reds are to appear only briefly, they should be situated at the back of the border with a foil of green that will set them off. They should not be near loud yellows as they often are in public gardens since this is never a happy combination except when it occurs by chance in nature. A bold but successful border combination is copper, red and orange.

My choice: *Aster novi-belgii* 'Crimson Brocade', *Bergenia cordifolia* 'Perfecta', *Cosmos, Helenium* 'Coppelia', *Heuchera, Lupinus, Malope trifida, Monarda didyma, Penstemon davidsonii, Phlox paniculata, Pulsatilla vulgaris* 'Rubra', *Sedum spectabilis.*

Cut Flowers for Bouquets

In the past, flowers for cutting were always grown separately, often near the kitchen garden, in straight rows without regard for any aesthetic considerations. Now that properties are far more modest and labour scarcer, these flowers have to be integrated into beds and borders artfully so that cutting does not diminish the general effect. One way to do this is by planting substantial groups of flowers in blocks rather than waves. Flowers are then cut from the centre so that the overall effect is not unduly impaired.

For the flowers to last as long as possible, they should be picked before they are fully open, if possible before sunrise or, if not, after sunset. They should be laid flat in a basket as they are being picked and then in a bucket of cold water up to the top of the stem. Remove all the foliage from the stems and leave them in the water until they are ready to be arranged in vases. Check the water level every day and, if the weather is particularly hot, add an ice-cube to the vase and spray the plants. Remove flowers and leaves as they fade.

My choice: *Agapanthus, Antirrhinum, Artemisia, Aster, Campanula latifolia, Cimicifuga, Cosmos, Diascia, Eremurus, Gaura, Iris, Lavatera, Liatris, Lilium, Malva, Paeonia, Penstemon, Sidalcea, Sisyrinchium, Veronica, Zantedeschia.*

Scented Plants

Many plants are slightly scented but to obtain a richly perfumed garden, a special selection must be made. Fragrances are also very much a matter of personal taste: some would say that *Ruta graveolens* (rue) stinks or that *Fritillaria imperialis* is pungent and foxy while others might find them pleasant.

Garden scents are inconsistent since the perfumes vary with the weather, the temperature and even the time of day. The first flowers of spring are among the most scented, for example *Cheiranthus* (wallflower) and *Narcissus jonquilla*. Also, do not assume that all plants of a genus such as *Lilium* are scented. Always check before buying! To obtain the maximum benefit, plant them close to windows, garden doors or pathways.

My choice: *Asclepias douglasii, A. quadrifolia, Cheiranthus cheiri, Dianthus barbatus, Freesia, Hyacinthoides non-scripta, Fritillaria imperialis, Iris germanica* 'Fascination', *I. g.* 'Moonbeam', *I. graminea, I. pallida, Lathyrus odoratus, Lilium amabile, L. hakerianum, L. candidum, Lupinus, Matthiola odoratissima, Monarda didyma* 'Adam', *M. d.* 'Blue Stocking', *Phlox paniculata, Verbena teucrioides*.

Long Flowering Plants

Some plants have much longer flowering seasons than others. The basic reason for this is that some produce no seed and others very little, so little or no energy is diverted from the flower to the formation of seed. Spread judiciously through your beds and borders, these long-flowering plants will provide weeks of pleasure.

For those with little spare time for gardening, it might even seem pointlesss to grow any other types but this would be to ignore the powerful effects and beauty of the short-lived flowers, and, of course, their seeds. As usual, a compromise is best.

My choice: *Agapanthus, Althaea, Anthemis, Campanula, Dicentra, Galtonia, Kniphofia, Nepeta, Nicotiana, Osteospermum, Veronica*.

Annuals to Sow in Place

For annuals, the cycle of growing from seed, flowering, setting seed and dying all takes place within the same year.

Sowing seeds *in situ*, that is to say sowing where they are to flower, in late March or early April is the simplest method but not invariably the most successful. There can be many problems, such as ground not properly prepared and dressed according to the requirements of the chosen plants, or not brought to a fine tilth just before sowing; seeds not sterilized—or sown when there are still hard frosts about; seeds watered irregularly.

The soil must be lightly watered before sowing and allowed to drain through, or the seeds will float. Seeds should be sown in shallow drills and not buried deeper than their own diameter. Sow very fine seeds on the surface of the tilth and lightly cover with soil shaken on to them through a fine sieve.

After sowing, the soil must not be allowed to dry out—but neither should it be too wet—and it must be kept weed-free. As the seedlings appear, thin them out to give those remaining room for development. Tie black thread in the form of a grid about 20cm (8in) above the area sown to prevent birds from enjoying your seed.

My choice: *Antirrhinum, Coreopsis, Cosmos, Delphinium* (annual), *Echium, Lathyrus, Lavatera, Limnanthes, Linum, Myosotis alpestris, Nigella, Phlox drummondii, Silene pendula, Viola cornuta*.

Half Hardy Annuals to Sow and Transplant

Half-hardy annuals can be sown indoors, under glass, during March, into thoroughly clean clay or plastic pots or trays filled with moist John Innes seed compost or soilless compost. When the tiny seedlings start to show, tilt the glass slightly to give more ventilation for a few days; then remove it completely. When the first pair of true leaves develop, carefully prick off into other boxes or pots

where they have more space and a richer growing medium. Label them! Pinch out growing tips periodically for a bushier habit. About two weeks before they are ready for planting out, gradually harden them off.

When planting out, it is important that the young plants have good soil in which to grow — remember that they have only a short lifespan. Prepare the soil in advance, raking in a good general fertilizer.

Once planting is complete, water thoroughly using a fine rose so that the spray will not damage the young plants and then water as necessary to keep the soil moist. Most annuals also benefit from regular feeding. Remove weeds whenever sighted.

My choice: *Browallia, Cleome, Dianthus chinensis, Impatiens* (hybrid), *Matthiola, Nemesia, Nicotania sylvestris, Rudbeckia, Salvia farinacea, Schizanthus, Zinnia.*

Self-seeding Plants

The seed is sown in place and the flowers appear at the end of the season. When they wither and die, the seeds fall to the ground and the cycle is then repeated the next year. When the new seedlings appear, thin them out, in the process removing any that look weak. It would be possible simply to leave all the dead flowers but, in fact, it is better practice to remove those that die earlier in the season so as to maintain the appearance of the bed. For seed, rely on those that die later. At the end of the season, lightly rake the ground over to remove fallen leaves and other debris. Then spread a mulch of organic matter to protect and nourish the seeds until spring.

My choice: *Dicentra eximia, Digitalis, Crambe, Echium, Eschscholzia, Hesperis, Limnanthes, Meconopsis cambrica, Nemophila, Verbascum, Viola.*

Calendula, Cosmos and **Lavatera** *scatter sown to create a scene as natural as wild flowers.*

29

*Spring arrives with the welcome flowering of **Narcissus**, **Primula**
and **Tulipa**, here close-planted and sheltered
by the house wall.*

FLOWERING THROUGH THE YEAR

*In a garden that has been well thought out,
there is no dead season. Flowers bloom throughout the year
and those that shun the cold give way to species that defy the frost,
such as* Eranthus hyemalis, *some of the winter-flowering heathers,*
Erica carnea *(now correctly* E. herbacea), Iris unguicularis,
and the Christmas Rose, Helleborus niger.
Don't leave them out of your plans.

Flowers for December and January

Having flowers ready to pick for Christmas is a feat that any gardener can be proud of. Plant the species or variety recommended close to the window so that they can still be enjoyed when it is too cold to go out.

My choice: *Crocus imperati, Cyclamen coum, Erica carnea, Galanthus nivalis, Helleborus niger, H. corsicus, Iris unguicularis, Liriope, Narcissus.*

Flowers for February and March

The emergence of the first bulbs shows that the soil, though still cold, is beginning to stir with the first signs of spring. Remember to mark the position of your bulbs, which will lose their flowers after two or three weeks, so that they are not damaged during later plantings. Let the foliage die back naturally.

My choice: *Anemone blanda, Bellis perennis, Crocus balansae, C. biflorus, C. fleischeri, Cyclamen persicum, Iris reticulata, Narcissus cyclamineus, Viola odorata.*

31

Flowers for April and May

Spring has begun and if some of your perennials are looking haggard after the winter, this is only natural—do not be in too much of a hurry to get rid of them. Remove any black or withered stems and wait patiently for the first signs of new growth. This is also the time to sow or plant for the summer season.

My choice: *Aquilegia alpina, A. vulgaris* hybrids, *Bergenia cordifolia, C. purpurascens, Cheiranthus cheiri, C. semperflorens, Dianthus × arvernensis, Euphorbia griffithii, Galega, Geranium cinereum, G. renardii, G. sylvaticum, Nepeta × faassenii, N. nervosa, Saxifraga, Tulipa.*

Flowers for June, July and August

This is the period when there is the most work but also the greatest rewards in the garden. To keep your flowers in bloom for the longest period possible, there are two necessities: regular watering and prompt removal of dead flowers. Many plants will continue to flower if not allowed to run to seed.

At the beginning of the season, fertilizer must be added regularly as plant metabolism is in high gear; always follow the pack instructions and never add extra fertilizer for good measure.

Take the opportunity to cut flowers for indoor display now as many plants will flower again at the start of autumn. With so many choice species and varieties available now, I give only the genera below.

My choice: *Acanthus, Agapanthus, Aquilegia, Calamintha, Crambe, Delphinium, Diascia, Filipendula, Gilia, Hemerocallis, Lathyrus, Lupinus, Lythrum, Phlox, Phlomis, Salpiglossis, Sedum, Thalictrum.*

Flowers for September, October and November

Though this is the end of the year, there is still a rich variety of flowers to enjoy. As it is cooler, they fade more slowly but the dead blooms must still be removed regularly to encourage further flowering. When flowering has finally ceased, they should be cut back to the ground as a start to the autumn clean-up.

Autumn-flowering genera can be planted either as groups, placed here and there in the beds to preserve overall colour, or they can all be massed together in the centre as a final flourish to the season. Keep up the regular watering.

In the case of Chrysanthemums and Dahlias, there are so many good species and varieties that it is impossible to list them here!

My choice: *Anagallis arvensis* 'Caerulea', *Anemone hupehensis, Aster × frikartii, A. novi-belgii, Chrysanthemum, Dahlia, Iberis umbellata, Salvia splendens, S. neurepia, Sedum spectabile.*

Bending the Seasons

It is certainly possible to have a regular progression of flowering through the year but many factors can intervene, some more controllable than others: the weather at the correct time for planting, the time when planting actually takes place, whether you choose a suitable site for the plants in question, your assiduity in watering and feeding . . .

If seeds are planted late, flowering will not be in jeopardy but will simply come later and therefore last for a shorter period.

If the winter has been exceptionally hard, plants start later than the dates nominally assigned to them in gardening calendars. And, of course, spring comes to some regions of the country earlier than to others.

At the end of May or beginning of June, depending on the weather, begins the flowering of the short-lived **Hesperis**, *the* **Papaver** *behind the* **Stachys lanata**, *with the border edge of clumps of* **Bergenia** *and* **Veronica**.

The spectacular **Gunnera manicata** *likes the water's edge,*
where its gigantic leaves may exceed
1 metre (3 ft) in diameter.

THE DETAILS THAT MAKE THE DIFFERENCE

*Anyone who wants a garden that is not merely well kept
but out of the ordinary needs to know what to plan under the rose bushes
or the trees, how to bring colour to areas of grass,
how to fit pampas grass into a small garden. . .
these options are open to every gardener who would like his garden
to be a little out of the ordinary and successful in every detail.*

Ground-cover Plants for Rose Bushes

In the past, the ground in rose gardens was kept scrupulously clear and regularly weeded by light hoeing. Nowadays, time is scarcer and it is also more unusual for a single variety of rose to be massed in borders unaccompanied. It is for these reasons that ground-cover plants have become so popular. Not only do they create a harmonious link between the roses and neighbouring shrubs but they also keep weeds at bay.

Though ground-cover plants are both useful and attractive, it is important to ensure that those chosen do not have extensive root systems that compete heavily with the roses for water and nourishment.

My choice: *Anaphalis margaritacea, A. triplinervis, Arabis fernandi-coburgii, Geranium farreri* 'Album', *G. sanguineum* 'Album', *Myosotis sylvatica, Nepeta nervosa.*

Plants to Naturalize in Grass

Because of the problems of maintenance, many people today prefer to put part of the garden to rough grass rather than having a formal lawn. This area can, nevertheless, be planted with a range of flowers for spring, summer and autumn.

To allow plants to develop properly, the ground must be prepared first by cutting clearings and pathways through the grass—setting the mower blades very low—and then removing all weeds. It is worth while taking this trouble as the plants will propagate better if they do not have to struggle against such competition to survive their first year. Bulbs positioned along the pathways will appear all the better in spring.

Bulbs should be planted in autumn and at greater depth than in a border, roughly three times the diameter of the bulb. Seed, on the other hand, should be sown at the beginning of spring in the same way as perennials that you might wish to plant. To prevent the seedlings from being choked, first remove about 20cm² (8sq in) of grass from wherever the seed is to be sown.

My choice: *Alchemilla mollis, Camassia leichtlinii, Centranthus ruber, Filipendula ulmaria, Impatiens roylei, Leucanthemum vulgare, Lythrum salicaria* 'Lady Sackville', *Malva moschata* 'Alba', *Sidalcea, Thalictrum, Zantedeschia aethiopica.*

Plants to Naturalize in Woodland Areas

Everything depends on the types of trees. With deciduous trees, sun and air can penetrate more easily in spring than with evergreens so that growth is facilitated and the choice of plants not so restricted. If the majority of the trees are deciduous, the soil will also be richer and easier to work thanks to the humus produced from fallen leaves every year. Whatever the case, this is not a formal area and planting should produce scattered groups as in nature.

Bulbs are useful to add a touch of colour in spring. As the edges of the wooded area will usually receive more light, use them for plants that will create an effective transition between the natural and the formal elements of the garden. Before planting, clear the ground, but not to the point of removing all the natural humus, and do remove any weeds to give your plants the best start.

My choice: *Anemone, Astrantia, Cardiocrinum, Cyclamen, Digitalis, Erica, Hosta, Hyacinthoides, Iris, Meconopsis, Primula, Pulmonaria, Tellima.*

Giant and Spectacular Plants

Plants of this sort make ideal 'specimen' plants and are, of course, no problem in large gardens but, even in quite small areas, they can be effective provided that they are correctly situated. Crambe, for example, is very decorative in the corner of a tiny lawn among some large stones whereas, in the centre, it could be rather overwhelming.

My choice: *Althaea ficifolia, Cardiocrinum giganteum, Crambe cordifolia, Eremurus elwesii, E. bungei, Gunnera manicata, Macleaya cordata, Rheum palmatum, Ricinus communis, Verbascum bombyciferum.*

Plants for Drying

The vast range of plants suitable for drying extends from grasses to ornamental fruit and includes many flowers, providing they are dried head downwards out of the sun.

My choice: *Anaphalis yedoensis, Cortaderia selloana, Echinops ritro, Eryngium* sp., *Helichrysum angustifolium, H. bracteatum, H. italicum, Limonium dumosum, L. latifolium, Pennisetum, Physostegia virginiana.*

Ornamental Fruit Plants

It is worth planting these species where they can be seen from the window because not only do they flower but also they produce brightly coloured fruit later in the year.

My choice: *Actaea asiatica, A. pachypoda, A. rubra, Arum italicum, Iris, Papaver orientale, Physalis alkekengi, Ruscus aculeatus, Solanum capsicastrum.*

Terraces in the Sun

It is all too often said that terraces do not give much scope for gardeners, and that plants tend to be puny and short-lived with a very brief flowering season. However, with a few elementary precautions this need not be the case. To protect flowers from hot sun, shade them with plastic or cane screens, or trellises for appropriate climbers. If there is no suitable wall for support, fix trellising between two tubs, or to the back of a large one. Shrubs and conifers are also good for keeping off fierce sun, but take care that they do not provide too much shade. The mainstay of such areas is an attractive assortment of containers—small ones can be moved around to suit your whim—and if containing tender plants they can be moved indoors later in the year. The size of the containers used should always be appropriate to the size of the plants. For instance, hedges of conifers will not thrive in 40cm (16in) boxes although many people try to make them. For both tubs and pots, the key factor is drainage and here small pebbles or shards of pottery are useful. Sieve the soil and lighten with a third part of peat or, alternatively, buy ready-mixed compost. For positions that are not very dry or particularly sunny, add a fourth part of sand to the soil to improve drainage.

The vital factor for success is watering, which should be done with a fine rose or spray in the evening after sunset. If bulbs have been planted, they should be kept separate so they can be watered only when they are in flower, otherwise they will rot.

Fertilizers should be used strictly according to the instructions on the pack at the beginning of the flowering season or in spring and their application should cease as soon as the flowering season is over. Care must be taken to avoid direct contact with the foliage or flowers, unless using a type sold as a foliar-feed.

Also keep a watch for any pests and diseases; take prompt action at the first signs. Given care, a great variety of plants, but especially the annuals, will flourish on balconies and terraces. It is even possible to create a kitchen garden there. In winter, however, temperatures must be monitored, as plants in tubs are more likely to freeze than those in the garden. Earthenware pots, moreover, are in danger of cracking unless protected from frosts by straw, polythene or some other insulating material.

My choice: *Agapanthus* (hardy hybrids), *Artemisia glacialis, Chrysanthemum frutescens, C. hosmariense, Cleome spinosa, Crinum × powellii, Datura ceratocaula, D. sauveolens, Echium, Geranium sanguineum, G. endressii, Iberis, Ipomoea coccinea, Lavandula nana atropurpurea, Petunia.*

Terraces in the Shade

It may be a truism but the problem here is the lack of light. To mitigate this disadvantage, mirrors can be fixed to the wall facing the sun.

The choice of container is important. Painted wood is brighter than stone for pots but there are problems of upkeep and durability. If the choice does fall on stone, it can be faced with trellis-work or painted. Earthenware, bowl-shaped containers are also very effective and add a Mediterranean touch.

To obtain the effect of grass, *Helxine* can be planted in window-boxes or between floor tiles. This mini-lawn is resistant to frost and grows well in the shade.

Plants should be protected from severe cold by sheets of glass fibre and a 20cm (8in) basal layer of peat.

It is not the absence of sun that kills off terrace plants but rather draughts or cold wind. If a shaded terrace or balcony is exposed to the wind, it must be sheltered with screen walling.

My choice: *Anemone, Aquilegia, Bergenia, Brunnera, Hosta, Impatiens, Hypericum, Lilium, Primula, Tellima, Trillium.*

The delicate blooms of **Nepeta** *will blend harmoniously with all kinds
of perennial flowers and roses. But if you are not a cat-lover, beware:
this sun-loving ground cover plant has a silvery foliage that,
when rubbed, gives off a perfume that cats find most attractive!*

SPECIAL CASES

*Perhaps you have a garden that you would like to see filled
with flowers but you can only get there at the weekend.
You may like aquatic plants but have no pond,
you would like to cover a bank or conceal an old tree stump
and you are impatient to see the results. Dilemmas such as these
can easily be resolved provided that you know the right plants.*

Ground-cover Plants for the Shade

There is no reason to leave bare earth in those shady parts of the garden where it seems that nothing will grow. Certain ground-cover plants actually appreciate these cooler spots, the only problem with them being a voracious root system that takes over all available nourishment and moisture. To start them off, they should be planted in pockets of humus-rich soil. A mixture of equal parts loam, sand and peat will ensure that they take root properly. If the roots of neighbouring trees are numerous and close to the surface, the ground level should be raised by adding a 15cm (6in) layer of soil. This will enable the ground-cover plants to establish themselves before the tree-roots once more reduce the fertility of the soil.

My choice: *Ajuga reptans, Alchemilla mollis, Asarum canadense, Bergenia, Geranium sanguineum, Hosta, Lamium, Polygonatum, Pulmonaria, Saxifraga umbrosa, Tellima grandiflora, Tiarella, Vinca.*

Ground-cover Plants for Sunny Sites

To reduce labour while at the same time enjoying a long flowering season, the gardener can do no better than try ground-cover plants that appreciate the sun. Most varieties require no more than a little attention during the first couple of years, such as weeding around the young plants and removing dead flowers to maintain vigour.

At the beginning of spring or in autumn, lift any plants that have become weed-infested. Soak them in a bucket to remove soil and then pick off the intruders from the roots. They should then be replanted, not in the former position but in freshly dug soil. Planting should take place after sunset in soil watered beforehand and afterwards.

My choice: *Acaena, Alchemilla, Arabis, Calamintha, Campanula portenschlagiana, Diascia cordata, Helianthemum nummularium, Iberis, Mesembryanthemum (Dorotheanthus), Myosotis alpestris, Nepeta × faassenii, Phlox subulata, Polygonum affine, Sedum spurium, Stachys olympica.*

Ground-cover Plants for Slopes and Banks

Because of the access problem, slopes and banks are always difficult to cover. Rather than grassing them, with all the difficulties of watering and mowing, use ground-cover plants which help to retain the soil in the face of heavy rains. In order to avoid crushing the plants and compacting the soil, an access path can be made with gravel, wood chippings or large flat stepping stones. Clearly, non-slip surfaces are essential in such locations.

If a slope is so steep that planting is virtually impossible and gulleying almost equally inevitable, the ground can be covered with coarse-mesh wire netting held in place by 20cm (8in) lengths of baling wire twisted into a hairpin shape. Plant inside the mesh and the netting will soon be covered with vegetation. Steps of some kind will also be needed.

To channel away rainwater, there are two solutions: either create terraces held in place by dry stone walls, or construct paths or ramps shallow enough to negotiate with a wheelbarrow. Even if you use fine gravel and flat stones here, run-off channels for rainwater will also be helpful. Whatever the case, the work must be done thoroughly if it is not to need continual maintenance.

Direction is extremely important: a southerly slope will be dry and baked while a northerly one will receive little sun and freeze easily. An easterly outlook receives early morning sun and then suffers from cold in the evening, a baneful combination for many plants. The best orientation is westerly since the plants are not exposed to great variations in temperature. Unfortunately, however, orientation is a factor over which one has little control.

My choice: *Acanthus, Arabis, Campanula portenschlagiana, Cerastium, Geranium macrorrhizum, Hypericum calycinum, Lysimachia, Polygonum affine, Sedum, Tellima grandiflora, Vinca major.*

Rockeries, Paving, Walls and Crevices

Rockeries, which have been fashionable since the nineteenth century, depend for their charm on a natural appearance. Whether on the flat or in the form of a mound, the stones must lie weathered side outmost as they would in nature. Slope each stone slightly backwards towards the centre of the site.

A minimum of soil is sufficient to fill the area available with varied and colourful plants. Pockets of soil can be distributed to create a free-draining alpine habitat in which roots find moisture without stagnating in water. The best composition is two parts garden soil to one part coarse river gravel, one part peat or leaf-mould and one part well-rotted manure (if possible) or compost. Cover with fine gravel to improve drainage and keep out weeds. The composition of individual pockets of soil can be modified to suit the needs of different plants (see page 13).

As attractive stone for terraces and walls is often hard to come by and extremely expensive, it may be necessary to make do with cement. A cover of vegetation, however, will give a presentable aspect within one or two years. During construction, cracks should be left open to provide a dry surface on which plants can take root and spread their foliage and flowers. If possible, sow directly in position or plant root cuttings.

When laying down paving in a garden or terrace, remember to leave a few spaces for carefully selected plants.

My choice: *Alchemilla mollis, Alyssum saxatile, Androsace cylindrica, Aubrieta, Campanula carpatica, C. cochlearifolia, Crocus aureus, C. sieberi, Diascia barberae, D. rigescens, Epimedium, Erigeron karvinskianus, Gaura lindheimeri, Muscari, Phlox subulata, Prunella grandiflora, Pulsatilla halleri, Stokesia laevis, Tanacetum corymbosum (Chrysanthemum corymbosum), Tulipa biflora, T. tarda, Verbena peruviana.*

Climbing Annuals for Sowing

Climbing annuals provide cover for arbours, for walls, for bare tree trunks and the like. Though the blooms are ephemeral, they will continue until the frosts if dead flowers are regularly removed. They grow prodigiously and flower without pause through the summer if given sufficient sunshine. Some can even reach heights of several metres (6ft or more) within a season, a talent that must be put to use. They do not need a rich soil, which would encourage foliage rather than flowers, but regular watering in summer is essential.

My choice: *Cobea scandens, Ipomoea purpurea (Convolvulus major), Lathyrus odoratus, Thunbergia alata, Tropaeolum majus.*

Bulbs to Leave in the Ground

As bulbs do equally well in the garden, in boxes on a balcony or in pots in the house, they are of great value to the gardener. Nevertheless, there are many who waver, thinking of the chores of digging up in winter, checking, storing, replanting. . . .

This is a mistake, however, as most of the hardy bulbs can be left in the ground provided that they are deep enough not to be disturbed by other garden work during the year.

Though the flowers produced over successive years may not always be the finest, this is not an unpardonable sin. Remember not to trim or cut back the foliage before it dies back as it provides the bulb with the nourishment necessary for flowering in the following year. Similarly, do not tie the leaves together in an attempt to tidy them; this can be detrimental.

My choice: *Camassia leichtlinii, Cardiocrinum giganteum, Cyclamen hederifolium (C. neapolitanum), Dierama pulcherrimum, Fritillaria meleagris, Galtonia candicans, Iris danfordiae, I. reticulata, Narcissus bulbocodium, Nerine bowdenii, Scilla sibirica, Tulipa clusiana, T. kaufmanniana.*

Old Favourites

As horticulturalists go off in pursuit of new varieties that are hardier or more abundant, seeking the unusual in form and colour, a number of old favourites are dropping from their catalogues. Fortunately, these plants continue to be cultivated by enthusiastic amateurs who are happy to maintain a tradition. These plants are close to the wild species and form a link between nature and man's designs. They can be planted without ceremony and will flower abundantly over the years in any corner of the garden with a minimum of attention, apart from cutting down the stems of dead flowers.

My choice: *Althaea, Calamintha, Campanula, Centranthus, Galega, Malva alcea, M. moschata, Myosotis alpestris, Paeonia lactiflora.*

The Weekend Garden

The garden should not be a place of drudgery, where precious 'leisure' hours are spent weeding, pruning, hoeing, mowing and all the other tasks associated with keeping it under control.

For the weekend gardener, bulbs are ideal if

they are used properly. Some people advocate simply dropping them and planting them where they fall to give a natural appearance but once the foliage withers this leaves a very untidy aspect. It is much more effective to plant them in groups of three, five or nine, set tightly together but with a spacing of 1–2m (3–6ft) between groups. Dead flowers should be removed but the foliage should be left to die back; if the bulbs are naturalized in grass, delay the first mowing to give them as much time as possible (you could mow around them). Ground-cover plants are also useful, for keeping weeds at bay.

Even the most rudimentary automatic watering system will also lighten the burden considerably, especially in dry summers.

My choice: *Alchemilla, Campanula, Chelone, Crambe, Erica, Geranium, Helleborus, Iris, Muscari armeniacum, Phlomis, Phygelius, Tellima, Tulipa, Vinca.*

Water Gardens

Not everyone has a lake, pond or stream in their garden but, for most people, it is perfectly possible —and simple—to introduce a small pool for aquatic plants. In fact, starting from scratch makes it all the easier as the ideal location can be chosen. This should be in an open, sunny situation and, to avoid an accumulation of fallen leaves, not too close to any trees.

Pre-formed glass fibre pools can be bought ready for installation or a hole can be dug to the required shape and then lined with either concrete, heavy-duty polythene sheeting or rubber and PVC liners. The lining is easily concealed by covering the essential overlap with flat stones. The depth should be at least 60cm (24in) and the sides gently shelving.

Stagnant water, of course, produces unpleasant odours and attracts parasites, both of which the gardener must combat by using oxygenating plants together with fish and molluscs which help to keep the habitat clean. If a water supply is fitted, the delivery and drainage holes must be at opposite ends, the latter being covered with a filter to prevent blockages.

Stones or bricks can be used to create platforms inside the pool at depths appropriate to the plants selected which can then be lowered into place so that their pots or baskets are completely immersed. For certain varieties of *Nymphaea*, floating baskets can be used. Other plants, of course, enjoy a marginal location.

My choice: *Iris laevigata, I. kaempferi, Lythrum salicaria, Nelumbo, Nymphaea laydekeri, N. marliacea, N. odorata, N. pygmaea, Pontederia cordata, Sagittaria japonica, Typha.*

A Habitat for Birds, Bees and Butterflies

Nothing could be easier than to encourage birds, bees and butterflies into your garden. There is a good choice of attractive plants to entice these welcome visitors. Also, during the winter, a bird-table can provide water and food in the form of bacon rind, stale cheese, or a mix of seeds and nuts.

My choice: *Calluna, Dictamnus, Heracleum, Hesperis matronalis, Lilium, Matthiola, Nepeta, Nicotiana, Sylibum, Thymus.*

Carnivorous Plants

It is fascinating to observe the different techniques used by insectivorous plants in catching their prey. Generally, the insect alights in the hollow of a leaf and is trapped either by a sort of liquid or by sticky secretions. The leaf then closes around the victim for digestion to take place. Certain aquatic plants, on the other hand, are equipped with tiny suckers along their stems to ingest the unwary. Others have sensitive hairs on the inside of the leaf which close to form a cage, preventing exit. *Dionaea muscipula*, Venus's Fly Trap, uses this method. However, it is susceptible to frost and must be brought inside during the winter.

My choice: *Dionaea, Drosera binata, Pinguicula grandiflora, Sarracenia purpurea.*

This mass-planting of golden **Narcissus** *needs no upkeep as the bulbs remain in the ground all year.*

42

This pretty scene is composed of **Hosta**, **Rodgersia**,
Dodophylla, *with its sprays of creamy flowers, and* **Crambe**. *The large leaves
must be protected against slugs.*

PROBLEMS AND DIFFICULTIES

*Looking out from your window, you smile
at the rabbits scampering on the lawn and only later discover
that they have been dining off your young plants!
The slugs, meanwhile, have been turning the leaves of your nasturtiums
into dainty lacework. As frost has already decimated
your rose bushes, you are getting somewhat discouraged. Don't give up!
For every gardening problem, there is a solution!*

Rabbits

The diet of rabbits is varied and if there is nothing better, they will try plants that they are supposed not to like. The only way of successfully protecting young plants until they are established is to use netting.

My choice: *Aconitum, Allium, Euphorbia, Fritillaria, Hyacinthus, Narcissus, Ruta, Salpiglossis, Solanum.*

Slugs

Nothing is uglier than foliage mutilated by slugs but, as usual, prevention is better than cure. Anti-slug pellets should be put down and sheltered from the rain by flat tiles. Wood-ash also makes an effective barrier with which to surround plants. Hedgehogs, toads and blindworms all prey on slugs and can provide added protection for plantlets and seedlings.

Slugs' choice meal: *Cardiocrinum giganteum, Dahlia, Delphinium, Dicentra, Hosta, Iris, Lilium, Omphalodes.*

Pollution

Pollution is a problem not only in towns but also for gardens that are close to main roads. There are, however, plants available that are remarkably resistant.

The worst time is in spring when, with the first heat and moisture, young shoots are at their most vulnerable. The leaves should be cleaned once a week, using a watering can or a hose for larger plants. This work should be done in the evening after sunset.

My choice: *Alchemilla, Artemisia, Aster, Callistephus, Camassia, Cimicifuga, Delphinium, Erodium, Geranium, Heliotropium, Lychnis, Silene.*

Invasive Plants

Plants that grow and spread rapidly are often put in with the intention of establishing a garden while waiting for trees to grow and shrubs to fill out. However, it is all too easy for them to get out of hand and invade every available area. Nevertheless, they are very useful plants if you know how to exploit them effectively: they must be carefully sited and planted with discretion. They are ideal for the ground under large trees where grass will not grow, for mounds with difficult access and for soils that are too dry, too moist or too poor for more choosy plants! They are similarly useful when it is necessary to cut down on labour soil or when improvements are problematic, for example at a holiday home. Such plants have the twin advantage of ousting any weeds while, at the same time, producing very attractive flowers.

My choice: *Campanula porscharskyana, Impatiens balfourii, Lysimachia nummularia, L. punctata, Oenothera biennis, Solidago canadensis, Stachys spicata, Viola odorata.*

Frost

Plants that originated in milder climates need to be protected against the rigours of winter, a mulch of straw being a simple and effective solution. This is laid after the plants have been cut back. The most economical mix is a base of straw, hay or grass cuttings but the result is hardly aesthetic. Leaf-mould is preferable or a 10cm (4in) layer of moist peat which, though more costly, is more efficient. In areas where really hard frosts are likely, this protective blanket should itself be covered with plastic sheeting pierced here and there for ventilation. This will guard against moisture retention and prevent rot. To protect the crowns of herbaceous plants, don't cut back the dead flowering stems until spring.

The grafting point of standard rose bushes is very sensitive to cold. Cover it with a few handfuls of straw held in position by a plastic bag attached to the stake rather than the bush.

My choice: *Agapanthus, Anemone, Dierama, Felicia, Gunnera, Romneya, Zantedeschia.*

Allergies and Poisons

If you experience itching after a walk in the garden, it is likely that you are allergic to certain plants growing there. Everyone knows that pollen can cause hay fever but few are aware that some foliage produces outbreaks of urticaria. The culprit must be sought out and removed.

Poisonous plants should not be grown where there are children and pets, and neither should they be grown in the kitchen garden borders. If there is any suspicion of poisoning by a garden plant take a sample and head for the nearest hospital with a casualty department, or your doctor. With such cautions very much in mind, the following plants are nevertheless lovely additions to most gardens.

My choice: *Althaea, Convallaria, Delphinium, Euphorbia, Primula, Thalictrum.*

Primula japonica *is a great favourite of flower-lovers but can produce allergic reactions.*

ACAENA
TO
ZINNIA

Acaena

ACAENA/SHEEPBURR

Rosaceae

These little mat-forming plants from New Zealand are very vigorous. Rising to no more than a few inches in height, they can form an excellent ground cover of dense foliage in just a few years. Undemanding and tolerant of dry conditions, they flourish in the poorest soils. Certain varieties are prized mainly for their fruit but all are valued for their fine foliage.

Useful hints

— Although *Acaena* will keep out many weeds once it is established, it needs support against such competition during the first year. To prevent the weeds getting a stranglehold, the soil must be kept clear after planting.

— Intersperse small spring bulbs among clumps of *Acaena*.

Recommended

— *Acaena buchananii* is noted for its bluish foliage while that of *A. novae-zelandiae* is russet.

— *A. microphylla* owes its reputation to the abundance of tiny crimson fruit that ripen in July.

Height: 2–3 cm (¾–1 in).
Spacing and planting distance: from 45–50 cm (16–20 in).
Soil: all soils, even poor ones, provided they remain healthy in winter.
Cultivation: full sun.
Propagation: by division in early spring.
Flowering season: July.
Type: perennial.

◁ *Acaena mycrophylla*
△ *Acanthus spinosus*
▽ *Acanthus mollis*

Acanthus

BEAR'S BREECHES

Acanthaceae

The acanthus is hardier than you might think. Ideally, it should be placed at the foot of a south-facing wall where its spikes will grow to over 1 m (3 ft) and remain decorative even after the flowers have faded.

Useful hints

— Plant in autumn or, better still, in spring. Prepare a pocket of coarse sand or gravel to keep the base of the plant dry over winter.

— Leave the clumps undisturbed for at least five years to allow them to develop. As slugs are very fond of the handsome leaves, put down anti-slug pellets.

— It is possible to grow the plant from seed but the results take a long time to appear. An easier method is by division and replanting at the end of the summer. It is also possible to propagate from root cuttings.

Recommended

— *Acanthus mollis*, the non-spiny variety is to be preferred. The glossy leaves are large, smooth and elegantly divided.

— *A. spinosus* differs from the preceding example by its spines and a darker foliage. It can be used to provide low, protective hedging.

Height: from 80–120 cm (32–48 in).
Spacing and planting distance: 60 cm (24 in).
Soil: ordinary, with good drainage (add sand if necessary).
Cultivation: must be placed directly in the sun if it is to flower.
Propagation: from seed or, better, by division.
Flowering season: July to August.
Type: perennial.

Achillea

YARROW

Compositae

These superb perennials are unbeatable for their brilliant flowers and for the ease with which they can be grown. On top of that, they blossom for three or four months continuously. Usually yellow but occasionally red or white, they are the queens of the summer garden.

Useful hints

— In a rich soil, don't forget to stake the larger varieties and, in particular, *Achillea filipendulina*.

— Where possible, plant in the spring, especially if your soil is wet and heavy.

— With the exception of *A. aurea*, the achilleas are very hardy. Nevertheless, they do require a healthy well-drained soil.

Recommended

— As far as the yellows are concerned, *A. aurea* and *A. filipendulina* lead the field.

— For a white flower, the choice falls on *A. ptarmica*. Here, 'The Pearl' grows quickly and makes a good cut flower.

— Less vigorous but, nevertheless, very robust is *A. millefolium* with its delightful little flower cups that are a pale red.

Height: 130 cm (50 in) for *A. filipendulina*, 80 cm (32 in) for *A. ptarmica*, 45 cm (18 in) for *A. aurea* and *A. millefolium*.
Spacing and planting distance: 50 cm (20 in) *A. filipendulina* and 30–40 cm (12–16 in) in all directions for the other varieties.
Soil: all soils, even poor ones, provided that they are well-drained.
Cultivation: full sun.
Propagation: by division in the spring.
Flowering season: July to October.
Type: perennial.

◁ ***Achillea filipendulina***
▽ ***Achillea ptarmica***

Acidanthera murielae △

Aconitum

MONK'S HOOD

Ranunculaceae

If they weren't so poisonous, the aconites would find a home in every garden. They are robust and their elegant palmate foliage is among the finest of the perennials. The blue of the flowers is of a rare intensity but unfortunately the sap is extremely toxic. For this reason, it is too dangerous to keep in gardens where children are around and, even for adults, strict precautions must be taken when handling the plant or cutting flowers.

Useful hints

— Plant in autumn or spring in a rich soil that remains moist in summer. Mulch the soil in May with lawn-cuttings or peat. Water once a month with liquid manure.

▽ *Aconitum napellus*

Acidanthera

ETHIOPIAN GLADIOLUS/DARK-EYE GLADIXIA

Iridaceae

If you like strong heady scents then *Acidanthera* is for you. Each bulb will yield a miniature 'gladiolus', the white flowers bearing a brown spot in the centre. As these open one by one, they have a noticeable perfume that is easily recognized even at about two metres away. Since they are not exactly graceful, plant them next to a neighbour with a compact outline, e.g. *Pelargonium*.

Useful hints

— Plant in April and May after the frosts are over. The bulbs should be at a depth of about 10 cm (4 in) and are best suited to a light soil.

— To extend the flowering season, water once a week and give liquid manure every fortnight. The appearance of a second spike is by no means uncommon.

— Once the foliage has dried, but before the hard frosts of autumn, dig up the bulbs and store them e.g. in a cellar out of the cold. To protect against parasites, remove leaves and clean before putting away to dry.

Height: from 40–80 cm (16–32 in).
Spacing and planting distance: 15 cm (6 in) in all directions.
Soil: rich and well-drained.
Cultivation: full sun.
Propagation: from offsets.
Flowering season: a good month during July–August.
Type: bulb.

— When fewer flowers are forthcoming, divide the clumps with an edging spade and replant only cuttings that have at least two or three shoots.

— Wash your hands well each time you handle this plant.

Recommended

— The best-known aconites are those that flourish at the end of spring, especially *Aconitum napellus* with the 'Blue Sceptre' improvements (purplish blue) and 'Bicolor' (blue and white). White flowers are also to be found.

— Though as yet relatively unknown, the autumn aconites are very valuable since they flower at the same time as the asters. *A. arendsii*, dark-blue in October–November and *A. wilsonii*, amethyst-blue and slightly earlier, reach heights of up to around 1.8 m (6 ft).

Height: from 100–180 cm (40–72 in).
Spacing and planting distances: 40 cm (16 in).
Soil: rich and moist.
Cultivation: at least 6 hours sun per day.
Propagation: by division as growing starts.
Type: perennial.

Actaea

BANEBERRY
Ranunculaceae

Some plants are a treat in themselves and this is the case with *Actaea rubra*. Though the flowering spikes do not last long, the tallish stature and elegant foliage make it a favourite for the wilder corners. The beautiful red berries prolong visual pleasure for the rest of the year. Beware, however, as the fruit is highly toxic.

Useful hints

— Plant from pots at any time but otherwise in autumn. Dig the ground over well as the roots go deep. Mulch the soil at the end of spring. Water thoroughly during the first year and in periods of great heat.

— Propagate by division as soon as you notice the plants becoming less vigorous but change their location as they exhaust the soil.

Height: from 1–2 m (2½–5 ft).
Spacing and planting distance: 60 cm (24 in).
Soil: ordinary, preferably slightly moist in summer.
Cultivation: half-shade.
Propagation: by division in autumn.
Flowering season: July.
Type: perennial.

Adiantum

MAIDENHAIR/MAIDENHAIR FERN
Polyprodiaceae

With its shiny mahogany stems and tapered undulating fronds, *Adiantum pedatum* is a charming little fern that should be found more often in the undergrowth of natural gardens. Being hardy, it flourishes in cool shady gardens to which it adds a rare touch of refinement. In more formal settings, it can be placed alongside helxine and the most elegant of decorative mosses.

Useful hints

— Plant in spring, either in April or May. Choose a shady bed and enrich the soil with two shovelfuls of leaf-mould or peat per square yard.

— When the clumps have grown to a good size after four years, divide them and plant in shady parts of the garden.

— This little fern loses its leaves in winter so don't worry if it turns brown in December.

Height: from 15–30 cm (6–12 in).
Spacing and planting distance: 30 cm (12 in).
Soil: rich in humus.
Cultivation: semi-shade.
Propagation: by division.
Type: perennial.

Adianthum pedatum ▷

▽ *Actaea rubra*

Adonis

PHEASANT'S EYE

Ranunculaceae

The cheerful yellow of this little plant is one of the earliest signs of life returning to the garden. The finely divided almost feathery foliage is a delight to see. Intersperse with early bulbs such as crocus or scilla for a charming scene. Alternatively, to obtain continuity, plant some hostas which will flower in the space during summer when the foliage of the adonis has died.

Useful hints

— Plant at the beginning of autumn in the half-shade at the foot of a deciduous tree. Mark the position with twigs as there are no leaves for a good part of the year.

— Mulch the soil in February using pine needles, leaf-mould or peat.

Recommended

— While *Adonis amurensis* comes from Manchuria, where the Amur river marks the border with the USSR, it also has a well-known European cousin, *A. vernalis*, also with foliage finely divided.

Height: 20–30 cm (8–12 in).
Spacing and planting distance: 20 cm (8 in).
Soil: ordinary; add a little leaf-mould.
Cultivation: needs at least 6 hours of sunshine per day for the flowers to open.
Propagation: by division at the end of the summer or from fresh seed in May–June (they take a year to germinate).
Flowering season: February, March.
Type: bulb.

Aethionema

AETHIONEMA/STONECRESS

Cruciferae

If you need to fill a dry corner of a wall, you can rely on *Aethionema*, a plant close to the alyssums which likes a sunny well-drained position. Given the right conditions, a single pot will produce a clump of spectacular grey-green foliage that remains covered with deep pink flowers for more than six weeks. They blend happily with tulips or, better still, with white decorative *Allium*.

Useful hints

— If possible, plant in autumn so that they become well-established before the

◁ *Adonis amurensis*

△ *Aethionema* 'Warley Rose'

Agapanthus 'Headbourne' △

worst of the cold. Place a handful of gravel around the neck to keep it dry.

— Prune after flowering in May to avoid seed formation.

Recommended

— While the hybrid 'Warley Rose' is the best known, *Aethionema grandiflorum* may also be found in catalogues. Its flowers are lighter.

Height: from 15–20 cm (6–8 in).
Spacing and planting distance: 20 cm (8 in).
Soil: light; leaf-mould and coarse sand.
Cultivation: full sun.
Propagation: relatively difficult, from root cuttings in spring or seeding in May.
Flowering season: June to August.
Type: perennial.

Agapanthus

AFRICAN LILY/LILY-OF-THE-NILE

Liliaceae

Once a familiar sight, agapanthus has now all but disappeared from our gardens and is more commonly seen in pots. The different varieties keep their fine strap-like foliage from one end of the year to the other except for *Agapanthus campanulatus* which tends to be deciduous.

Useful hints

— Plant the large tuberous roots of *Agapanthus umbellatus* in March, placing them in pots with a diameter of 30 cm (12 in) filled with a mixture composed half of leaf-mould and half of compost.

Agapanthus does not tolerate frost and in this way you can bring them in for the winter.

— Place *Agapanthus campanulatus* in pots with a diameter of 20 cm (8 in) or directly in the ground. In the latter case, don't forget to protect them in winter with peat or leaves. Avoid moving this variety if you would like to see it flower and multiply.

Recommended

— *Agapanthus umbellatus* has china-blue umbels which go very well with the fine dark blue of the hardy Headbourne hybrid.

— *A. campanulatus* has a superb blue which is ideal for bordering a gravel path or brightening a shady corner.

55

— *A. campanulatus* 'Albus' is a very pretty white variety. 'Isis', on the other hand, has a subtle, lavender-blue flower which is slightly larger than that of the species type.

Height: 50–70 cm (20–28 in).
Spacing and planting distance: 30 cm (12 in).
Soil: rich and light (*A. umbellatus*) ordinary and well-drained (*A. campanulatus*).
Cultivation: semi-shade to sunny.
Propagation: by division.
Flowering season: August and September (*A. umbellatus*), July to October (*A. campanulatus*).
Type: bulb.

Agathaea coelestis

see *Felicia amelloides*

Agave americana

AMERICAN ALOE/CENTURY PLANT

Amaryllidaceae

The agave is found only in warm climates. Suitable as a bedding plant in summer, at around 50 years it begins to flower in enormous stems with the strangest inflorescences, flat and round, rising one above another.

Useful hints

— Away from warm and temperate climates, the agave is more usually to be found in glass-houses although it is rather hardier than you might expect.

— To propagate, remove the young rosettes and leave to dry for three or four days before replanting in any ordinary sort of soil. It goes without saying that these sun-loving plants are not too fond of cold, damp soils.

Recommended

— Much more modestly proportioned than its American cousin, *A. victoriae reginae* has a height and circumference of some 15–20 cm (6–8 in). This is also a more elegant plant with pointed white-edged leaves. Watch out for those points, however, as they are every bit as sharp as those of the larger variety.

Height: 70–120 cm (28–48 in).
Spacing and planting distance: 50 cm (20 in).
Soil: ordinary.
Cultivation: sunny.
Propagation: division of rosettes.
Flowering season: July to August.
Type: perennial.

Agave americana ▷

56

Ageratum

AGERATUM

Compositae

Though somewhat out of fashion, the *Ageratum houstonianum* are really quite indispensable in a summer garden, their soft violet counter-balancing the loud yellow and orange of marigolds and carnations. Though seeding can be a problem because of the need for a little heat, the growing stage is easy. A few bunches placed around the edge of your beds will add a certain country vicarage charm to your garden.

Useful hints

— Seeding should take place out of the cold in April. Transplant once before finally planting out at the end of May. If you buy the plants, nip the flowers to get them to ramify.

— Watering at least once a week will help to get rid of the mites which swarm in hot weather and cause severe loss of moisture. Feed with liquid manure every fortnight.

Recommended

— All the F¹ hybrids are good. They come in a range of colours, the soft shades of pink being particularly attractive. Beware of white, however, which fades very rapidly and is always disappointing.

Height: from 15–25 cm (6–10 in).
Spacing and planting distance: 15 cm (6 in).
Soil: ordinary, enriched with a little peat or compost.
Cultivation: at least 6 hours sun per day.
Propagation: from seed, indoors in April.
Flowering season: throughout the summer from July to October.
Type: annual.

Ajuga

BUGLE

Labiatae

This is one of the best plants of all for ground cover. *Ajuga reptans* is ideal for the foot of shrubs or the front of flower beds. The plant is very robust and its stolons spread rapidly. It flowers in summer with small blue spikes and the brilliant foliage stays all through the year, including winter.

Useful hints

— Don't plant too close together: four or five laid down in the spring will be more than enough to yield a good carpet by the end of the year.

— Propagation by division is very easy and can be done at any time of year.

— A covering of peat spread between the young clumps at the time of planting will help the stolons to take root.

Recommended

— The most soberly coloured is *Ajuga reptans* 'Atropurpurea' which has a deep purple foliage. The most striking — though certainly not the most attractive—is *A. reptans* 'Multicolor' with leaves mottled pink, bronze and yellow.

Height: 15 cm (6 in).
Spacing and planting distance: from 30–40 cm (12–15 in).
Soil: moist in summer.
Cultivation: preferably shaded or semi-shaded (also in the sun if the soil is damp).
Propagation: by division at any time of year.
Flowering season: June, July.
Type: perennial.

Ageratum houstonianum △
Ajuga reptans ▽

57

Alchemilla mollis △

Alchemilla

LADY'S MANTLE

Rosaceae

There is room in every garden for this little plant with its pink-spangled foliage. Lady's mantle gives excellent ground cover both in shade and semi-shade. The elegant foliage is soft to the touch and, in summer, the yellowish-green calyx blends harmoniously with roses, lilies and many other perennials. Nothing can compare with *Alchemilla* to soften the line of a new path and, as it grows in very little soil, it will flourish among stone flags or in walls and steps.

Useful hints

— Being hardy, *Alchemilla* enjoys the half-shade where its foliage develops to best effect.

— Ideally, soils should be moist at all times. If it's not possible to water, leave a covering of peat or grass cuttings around plants at the beginning of summer.

— *Alchemilla* should be provided with twiggy sticks for support.

Recommended

— The best-known is *Alchemilla mollis* which forms well-rounded clumps. Less common is *A. alpina* which has a bluish foliage and is less invasive. It is sometimes confused with *Alchemilla conjuncta* which has dark green leaves divided into seven lobes that are rimmed with silvery leaves.

Height: from 15–40 cm (6–16 in).
Spacing and planting distance: 30 cm (12 in).
Soil: ordinary, preferably moist.
Cultivation: semi-shade, avoid direct sunshine.
Propagation: by division or from seed in spring.
Flowering season: June to August.
Type: perennial.

Allium

DECORATIVE ONION/ ORNAMENTAL GARLIC

Liliaceae

The onion has lost none of the charm of a wild plant. Compared to many other bulbs, onions have an elegant foliage though, if you don't like the smell of onion, you should avoid bruising it. They make very fine cut flowers.

Useful hints

— They should be planted in September or October after digging over the bed thoroughly. Add a barrow-load of compost if it is a thin soil. The small bulbs should be planted at a depth of 5 cm (2 in) by hand while large bulbs should be planted at 15 to 20 cm (6–8 in), using a dibble so as not to damage them.

— Check that the bulbs are in good condition by removing the outer skin. If there is any trace of rot, treat them with a thirame-based powder.

— Water regularly from April onwards to build up strength for later in the year and to avoid yellowing of the foliage that might come with temporarily dry conditions.

— Most of the decorative onions/ornamental garlics can be left in the ground for one year to another and, indeed, this is how the best clumps are formed. It is not uncommon for seedlings to appear naturally under trees and this is especially the case with *Allium ursinum*.

— Dwarf species (*A. moly*, *A. karataviense*, *A. cirrhosum* and *A. oreophilum*) can be grown very successfully in pots.

Recommended

— *Allium christophii* which flowers in June with balls of blossom some 25 cm (10 in) in diameter on stems that rise from 40–50 cm (16–20 in).

— *Allium caeruleum* is a smaller plant that flowers in June and July with a brilliant, almost electric, blue.

— *Allium cowanii* (formerly *A. neapolitanum*) has larger pure white flowers that are scented and somewhat less densely aggregated. Under glass, it can be made to flower as early as April.

— *Allium giganteum* is appropriately named, growing to a height of 1.5 m (5 ft) and producing heads that are around 20 cm (8 in) in diameter. They can be grown together with a shrub artemisia (*Artemisia arborescens*) which will serve as a support.

— *Allium moly* reaches a height of almost 20 cm (8 in) and so is almost a miniature compared to the preceding example. The bright yellow flowers are not dense but the clumps develop very rapidly and guarantee cover after a few years. Ideal for the wilder corners of a garden or for the edges of permanent beds.

— *Allium oreophilum*, which is still sold as *A. ostrowskianum*, produces a bright pink flower at the same time as the preceding example (May, June) and similarly grows to about 20 cm (8 in). The two go very well together and blend in perfectly with myosotis.

— *Allium schoenoprasum* is, of course, chives which, apart from providing flowering borders in summer, are also the essential ingredient for any vinaigrette. They can be planted in herb gardens, rockeries or even your window-box.

— *Allium schubertii* is expensive but impressive. The clump is relatively short with a rather elevated umbel. The metallic-red blooms are borne on 15 cm (6 in) stems and they are well worth keeping for arrangements of dried flowers.

Height: from 15–100 cm (6–40 in) depending on the variety.
Spacing and planting distance: 20 cm (8 in).
Soil: ordinary.
Cultivation: at least 3 hours sun per day.
Propagation: separation of bulblets in autumn.
Flowering season: March to July, depending on the variety.
Type: bulb.

Allium cowanii ▽

△ *Allium caeruleum*
◁ *Allium moly*
▽ *Allium christophii*

59

Alstroemeria aurantiaca **'Orange King'** △

Alstroemeria

PERUVIAN LILY

Amaryllidaceae/Alstroemeriaceae

The alstroemerias are very temperamental plants that can either spring up like weeds or show no progress at all for years. The fleshy root is very sensitive to transplantation.

Useful hints

— Planting should be very shallow and should take place preferably in spring. The soil should be deep and light.

— Water as the foliage develops. As the stems are delicate, they can be either supported with canes or allowed to grow through clumps of lavender or rosemary.

— When the foliage disappears in September or even later, note the position of the clumps and cover them with a handful of straw or coarse pine bark.

Recommended

— *Alstroemeria aurantiaca* spreads rapidly once it is established. The flowers range from pure yellow to orange, the best-known varieties being 'Lutea' and 'Orange King'.

— *Alstroemeria ligtu* is a hybrid and slightly less hardy. It is often sold as a cut flower for bouquets. The flowers are pink, lilac or white and are streaked with purple.

Height: from 40–90 cm (16–36 in).
Spacing and planting distance: 30 cm (12 in).
Soil: well-drained in winter. Add sand if necessary.
Cultivation: fully exposed to the sun but sheltered from dry spring winds.
Propagation: from seed *in situ* or by division.
Flowering season: June to August.
Type: bulb.

Althaea

HOLLYHOCK

Malvaceae

They should be placed at the back of a border, slightly in the shade. Though often considered to be perennial, they flourish in some regions only as biennials. Their charm and grace is to be admired in many gardens of note.

Useful hints

— When sowing, space the seeds well and use a rich soil. Once their leaves are touching, replant them about 15 cm (6 in) apart.

— They should be planted out finally in autumn, before 15 October, and should then be watered a few times to help them to take.

— In spring, water from time to time and make sure that they are treated against rust every month, using a triforine-based product.

Recommended

— Although the single flower is very attractive, it is more and more the case that *Althaea rosea* seeds are doubles or semi-doubles. The variety 'Chater' with its powder-puff flowers is very widespread but is suitable only in gardens that are very well cared for.

Height: 1.5–2 m (60–80 in).
Spacing and planting distance: 30–50 cm (12–20 in).
Soil: rich and fairly moist.
Cultivation: sun or semi-shade.
Propagation: from seed in spring or by division in winter.
Flowering season: July to September.
Type: perennial or biennial.

Alyssum

ROCK ALYSSUM/BASKET-OF-GOLD

Cruciferae

In April, the grey-green carpet of this alyssum suddenly blazes bright yellow, flowering at the same time as the tulips and only just after the forsythias. It is also very easy to grow: a clump the size of a fist planted in autumn will be larger than a dinner plate within 6 months. Be careful, however, or they will soon take-over.

Alyssum saxatile ▷
◁ *Althaea rosea*

Useful hints

— Protect the young plants against slugs and snails but they are so vigorous that this is not necessary for long.

— Grow from seed in trays and then plant out in a sunny spot. The only soil requirement is good drainage.

Recommended

— *Alyssum saxatile* 'Compactum' and 'Citrinum' are two good varieties. The former has bright yellow flowers, the latter an acid yellow that goes well with tulips. *Alyssum argenteum* also has bright yellow flowers with grey-green leaves.

Height: from 15–30 cm (6–12 in).
Spacing and planting distance: 15 cm (6 in).
Soil: ordinary.
Cultivation: sunny.
Propagation: from seed or cuttings.
Flowering season: April to June.
Type: perennial.

Amaranthus

AMARANTH/LOVE-LIES-BLEEDING
Amaranthaceae

Amaranthus caudatus produces a fountain of blossom. At the end of the summer, its drooping crimson tassels reach almost to the ground and provide fine decoration for a terrace. They can be combined with field daisies to form large bouquets.

Useful hints
— The seeds germinate easily and it is best to wait till April or May before sowing.

— Transplant the young growths at least once in a pot or forcing frame to get the roots to spread.

— Select the best and place them in a sunny spot. Water well at least once a fortnight during the summer. The addition of special flower nutrient in high summer will produce truly enormous blooms.

— Just before the frosts come, root out and burn the plants to prevent an invasion of self-sown seeds in the following year.

Recommended
— Love-lies-bleeding comes in two colours, the classical crimson and a greenish-white variety. They mix well with rudbeckias and tobacco plants.

Height: from 100–200 cm (40–80 in).
Spacing and planting distance: from 60–80 cm (24–32 in).
Soil: ordinary, rather rich.
Cultivation: sunny.
Propagation: from seed in spring.
Flowering season: from August until the first frosts.
Type: annual.

Amaryllis (Hippeastrum)

AMARYLLIS
Amaryllidaceae

When *Amaryllis belladonna* puts out great clusters of pink, scented, trumpet-like flowers at the end of August, the effect is so splendid that it is easy not to notice the absence of the foliage which does not appear until later. Because of this unusual feature, it's a good idea to plant three or four together as they will compose fine clumps from the very first year.

△ *Amaranthus caudatus*

Useful hints
— They should be planted by the beginning of September: any later and they may refuse to display a single leaf for a year. It is preferable to choose a southerly aspect as they like the sun.

— Provide a covering of leaves to protect them against heavy frosts.

Height: 70 cm (28 in).
Spacing and planting distance: 20 cm (8 in).
Soil: rich and deep.
Cultivation: sunny.
Propagation: from seed or by division of bulbs.
Flowering season: August, September.
Type: bulb.

Anacyclus

ANACYCLUS
Compositae

This little daisy-like plant is free-flowering over several weeks in spring

△ *Amaryllis belladonna*

and is an adornment for any rockery. The stems are covered with grey leaves and terminate in white flowers with pink on the outside of the ray florets. *Anacyclus depressus* can be recommended as a pot plant as it looks good close up.

Useful hints
— Plant the small pots in autumn with a handful of round gravel to protect the collar from any winter rot.

— If you decide to have it as a pot plant, choose a container that is more wide than tall, covering the soil with gravel to set off the foliage.

Height: 10 cm (4 in).
Spacing and planting distance: 15–20 cm (6–8 in).
Soil: leaf-mould and coarse sand.
Cultivation: full sun.
Propagation: from cuttings in summer or from seed in spring.
Flowering season: April to June.
Type: perennial.

Anacyclus depressus △
Anagallis linifolia ▷

Anagallis

ANAGALLIS/SCARLET PIMPERNEL, POOR MAN'S WEATHERGLASS

Primulaceae

A cousin of scarlet pimpernel, *Anagallis linifolia* has bright blue flowers with a purplish reverse side. They make an eye-catching decoration for balconies in summer.

Useful hints

— In warm and temperate climates, *Anagallis* is perennial but further north it must be treated as an annual since it does not tolerate frosts.

Height: 20 cm (8 in).
Spacing and planting distance: 20 cm (8 in).
Soil: ordinary.
Cultivation: sunny.
Propagation: from seed.
Flowering season: June to September.
Type: annual.

△ *Anaphalis triplinervis*

Anaphalis

PEARL EVERLASTING/PEARLY EVERLASTING
Compositae

This little perennial is a must, above all for white gardens. The display lasts for nearly nine months, beginning with the silvery-grey of the new foliage in spring. The plant gradually fills out and then, from mid-August to September, takes on a covering of innumerable, creamy-white heads. They are commonly used in floral arrangements.

Useful hints

— Like other silvery foliage plants, *Anaphalis triplinervis* cannot stand the water-logged soils of winter. Make sure that it is placed in a well-drained bed.

— To set pearl everlasting off to the best effect, it should be planted in groups of about 180 cm (6 ft) surrounded by bright red or blue flowers.

Height: 30 cm (12 in).
Spacing and planting distance: 30–40 cm (12–16 in).
Soil: any, even poor, provided that it is well-drained.
Cultivation: sunny or semi-shade in dry soil.
Propagation: by division in April.
Flowering season: August to October.
Type: perennial.

Anchusa

BUGLOSS
Boraginaceae

The tiny flowers are a dazzling blue but they are more commonly seen in the country than in town gardens. Like wild borage, a distant relation, it is easy to grow. Similarly, it likes a heavier soil in which it will spread rapidly, forming large clumps that, unfortunately, do not last for many years. They are best associated with other undemanding plants such as phlox, sweet-william or Aaron's rod.

Useful hints

— Place in a sunny bed.

— Any reasonable garden soil will do but it should not be loose.

— Because it spreads so rapidly, it should be divided every three years in the autumn.

— To ensure flowering throughout the summer, any withered stems should be removed.

Recommended

— The blues are all dazzling whether pure, as with *Anchusa azurea* 'Loddon Royalist', or tending towards violet, as with *A. azurea* 'Dropmore'.

Height: from 100–120 cm (40–48 in).
Spacing and planting distance: 5 cm (2 in).
Soil: ordinary.
Cultivation: sunny.
Propagation: by division.
Flowering season: July to October.
Type: perennial.

***Anchusa azuera* 'Loddon Royalist'** ▷

Androsace

ANDROSACE/NORTHERN FAIRY CANDELABRA

Primulaceae

Androsace is a firm favourite of lovers of Alpine plants but it is far from easy to manage. A cushion-forming plant of the high mountain screes, it requires a soil that is moist but never water-logged. It needs to be exposed but at the same time needs protection against winter damp, a condition to which it is never exposed in its native habitat. Nevertheless, when success comes, the proliferation of tiny vivid flowers makes it all worthwhile.

Useful hints

— Plant in spring either directly or, better still, in well-drained pots filled with a humus-rich mixture: e.g. leaf-mould and light-brown peat with lime stone chippings.

— For the first winter, keep them under shelter in a frame and then bring them out to the chosen spot in the rockery some time in March or April. Take great care not to damage the root clump.

— Cover the soil in the pots with gravel to facilitate the drainage of surplus water.

— Trim the clumps after flowering and keep some of the fruit to have enough seed for future sowing.

— Put the new seeds into a pan which should be left outside for the fresh air to stimulate germination. Lift in the following spring and after transplanting protect against winter damp.

Recommended

— *Androsace carnea* is one of the easiest. It flowers at the beginning of spring, producing very fine shades of pink. A northerly aspect is required.

— *Androsace sarmentosa* (now correctly *Androsace primuloides*) can grow to a good size but mostly remains about the diameter of a dinner-plate. In winter, it shrinks in the dry cold and appears greyer because of the 'hair' that covers its leaves. Flowering comes a little earlier than with the previous example but again the colour is pink.

Height: from 5–10 cm (2–4 in).
Spacing and planting distance: 20–40 cm (8–16 in).
Soil: rich and light.
Cultivation: north side of a rock.
Propagation: from fresh seeds.
Flowering season: April to July.
Type: perennial.

△ *Androsace sarmentosa*

Anemone

WINDFLOWER

Ranunculaceae

For the connoisseur of perennials, the anemone offers a wealth of variety. The year opens with the little *Anemone nemorosa* whose pure white flower shines out from beneath the trees. This is soon followed by the blue, pink and mauve of *A. blanda*. Neither of these species grows to over 15 cm (6 in). Twice as big, *A. coronaria* blossoms in mid-April, blue, pink, white and sometimes even scarlet. Finally, at the end of the year, it is the turn of *A. hupehensis* (Japanese anemone) whose elegant pink flowers can easily reach a height of 120 cm (48 in).

Useful hints

— With the exception of *A. coronaria*, which prefers direct sunlight, all anemones are most at home in the cool of semi-shade. The small varieties of early spring, in particular, need the cover of deciduous trees and shrubs.

— Where the climate is mild, *A. coronaria* can be made to flower throughout the year if planted at three month intervals.

Recommended

— Woodland varieties: *A. nemorosa* 'Robinsoniana' has marvellous blue

△ *Anemone coronaria* 'De Caen'
Anemone blanda ▽
▽ *Anemone nemorosa*

flowers although the species type has white.

— Species for direct sunlight: the *A. coronaria* 'De Caen' and 'St Brigid' are recommended for their bright colours.

— Late-flowering species: *A. hupehensis* 'Praecox' blossoms in mid-summer.

Height: 15 cm (6 in) (*A. blanda* and *A. nemorosa*), 30 cm (12 in) (*A. coronaria*), 120 cm (48 in) (*A. hupehensis*).
Spacing and planting distance: 40–50 cm (16–20 in).
Soil: well-drained and, if possible, moist.
Cultivation: semi-shade (direct sunlight for *A. coronaria*).
Propagation: by division in spring.
Flowering season: March–April (*A. blanda* and *A. nemorosa*), April–May (*A. coronaria*) and August–October (*A. hupehensis*).
Type: bulb and perennial.

△ *Angelica archangelica*

Angelica

ANGELICA

Umbelliferae

Angelica is incomparable for wet ground, a simple drainage channel allowing the development of impressive clumps. The roots can be used as tonics or aids to digestion. *Angelica archangelica* is a magnificent plant, yielding a smooth odour from all its parts. It develops best when cultivated as a biennial, i.e. the seedlings that appear naturally during the summer are taken for replanting in autumn and will be ready to flower the next summer. Massed on either side of a doorway, angelica will create the entrance of your dreams.

Useful hints

— Sow the seeds in spring and transplant carefully twice before finally planting in rich moist soil in autumn.

— Water regularly as soon as it starts to get hot, adding liquid manure or a handful of dried blood every month.

— If the clumps do not seem to be well developed, remove the floral spikes as soon as they appear to force the plant to produce more leaves. The following year, they will flower abundantly and then wither away.

Height: up to 3 m (10 ft).
Spacing and planting distance: from 60–80 cm (24–32 in) in all directions.
Soil: very rich and moist at all times.
Cultivation: at least 6 hours of sunshine per day.
Propagation: from seed in spring.
Flowering season: summer.
Type: biennial and perennial.

Antennaria

CAT'S FOOT/PUSSYTOES

Compositae

Taking the common name 'cat's foot' because of the shape of its infloresence, *Antennaria dioca* is one of the easiest Alpine plants to grow. It quickly forms a dense ground cover adorned with pink flowers through a good part of the spring. It serves well to conceal the joints between paving slabs or to cover the soil in tubs around the foot of a shrub. Regular watering is important as the grey foliage does not, in this case, indicate resistance to dry conditions.

Useful hints

— Always buy in pots, preferably in the spring. When planting, be careful not to bury the collar which, as with many tussock-forming plants, is prone to rot.

— Add a layer of coarse sand to the surface every spring and then pat down the foliage to help with rooting.

Height: from 5–10 cm (2–4 in).
Spacing and planting distance: 15 cm (6 in).
Soil: leaf-mould and sand.
Cultivation: sunny.
Propagation: by division in spring.
Flowering season: May, June.
Type: perennial.

Antennaria dioica ▷

Anthemis

ANTHEMIS/CAMOMILE

Compositae

The *Anthemis* genus contains a hundred species which are to be found in all kinds of beds and borders, rockeries and cut flower gardens.

Useful hints for *Anthemis cupaniana*

— It can be grown in any soil, even chalk, provided that it is well-drained. They must be planted out early in spring.

— To ensure a rapid take-off, add half a shovelful of compost to the soil on planting. When the plants have reached a height of 20 cm (8 in) nip off a few centimetres from the ends to get them to fill out.

— During the first year, remember to water regularly.

— If faded flowers are removed, new flowers will return all the more vigorously.

Useful hints for *Anthemis tinctoria* (golden marguerite)

— The only requirement is for a good well-drained garden soil (a heavy soil would choke them in winter).

— Though often considered to be perennial, it is safer to treat them as bi-annuals since, like antirrhinum and sweet-william, they lose vitality after a couple of years.

Recommended

— *Anthemis cupaniana* has a charming silvery-grey foliage that is velvety and finely divided. This delicately scented plant forms large rounded tussocks in dry mountainous country and these go well on a terrace, steps or the bends of paths in steeply sloping gardens. As it prefers sunshine and a dry climate, it makes an ideal plant for rockeries and, once established, makes few demands.

— *Anthemis nobilis* (common camomile) is a dwarf variety with white daisy-like flowers. It is a hardy plant that will grow on any exposed ground and is useful for covering slopes.

— *Anthemis nobilis* 'Treneague' is also good for ground cover. It doesn't flower but forms a soft carpet with tiny leaves.

— *Anthemis tinctoria* (Ox-eye camomile) is as easy to grow as common camomile and is covered with yellow daisy-like flowers throughout the summer. It goes

◁ *Anthemis cupaniana*

△ *Antirrhinum majus*

well with grey foliage plants and other perennials such as old roses.

— *Anthemis tinctoria* 'Kelwayi' is lemon-yellow and bushy.

Height: 25 cm (10 in) (*A cupaniana*), 15 cm (6 in) (*A. nobilis*), 60 cm (24 in) (*A. tinctoria*).
Spacing and planting distance: 15 cm (6 in).
Soil: ordinary, well-drained.
Cultivation: sunny.
Propagation: (*A. cupaniana*) by division in spring, (*A. nobilis*) from seed or cuttings, (*A. tinctoria*) from cuttings.
Flowering season: June to September.
Type: perennial.

Antirrhinum

SNAPDRAGON

Scrophulariaceae

Familiar to all of us from childhood memories, the snapdragon with its velvety snout and soft perfume is a flower that everyone, even the beginner, has to grow. Whether they are annual or perennial depends very much on the soil and the region. In northern Europe and in heavy soils they are annual. Whatever the case, they flower endlessly from spring to autumn as soon as they have been sown. There is a great variety of size and colour, except for blue, so that they can be used in any part of a border.

Useful hints

— It is best to sow in a frame by March, providing a good rich soil that is light and in a sunny position.

— When the plants have reached about 5–6 cm (2 in), nip the ends to ensure a stronger growth.

— If they are stopped from running to seed, they will flower for several years.

— In autumn, cut off the bare stems and then cover with dead leaves.

Recommended

— Traditional varieties like *Antirrhinum majus* 'Maximum' have a good smell but the F^1 hybrids such as 'Rocket' or 'Madame Butterfly' are better for cut flowers.

Height: from 25 cm (10 in) for the dwarf varieties; up to 100 cm (40 in) for the giants.
Spacing and planting distance: 20 cm (8 in) in all directions.
Soil: ordinary.
Cultivation: sunny.
Propagation: from seed.
Flowering season: June to September.
Type: annual and perennial.

Aponogeton

APONOGETON/CAPE POND WEED

Aponogetonaceae

This water plant deserves to be better known as it is one of the few that will flourish in the shade where water-lilies will produce no more than leaves. The white flowers of *Aponogeton distachyus* are strongly perfumed.

Useful hints

— Wait until May before planting either directly in the bottom of the pond if it is not cemented and has at least 20 cm (8 in) of good soil or in perforated baskets filled with heavy soil.

— In regions where the water does not freeze over in winter, *Aponogeton* is hardy but elsewhere it should be kept in a greenhouse. Problems usually occur if the pond is too shallow, a minimum of 30 cm (12 in) being recommended.

–– Plant in semi-shade if possible.

Height: 15 cm (6 in) above the surface of the water, 30–60 cm (12–24 in) below.
Spacing and planting distance: from 40–60 cm (16–24 in).
Soil: clay soil with fertilizer granules.
Cultivation: semi-shade (at least 6 hours of sunshine per day).
Propagation: by division in May.
Flowering season: all summer and sometimes even to Christmas.
Type: perennial.

Aquilegia

COLUMBINE

Ranunculaceae

The columbines are great favourites, coming in singles and doubles, one or two colours and a great range of attractive tones.

Useful hints

— If *Aquilegia vulgaris* is sown in March, it will flower the following spring.

— *A. flabellata* should be planted in leaf-mould with a north-westerly aspect.

— *A. vulgaris* likes a moist soil and can tolerate both shade and direct sun.

— *A. flabellata* should be kept out of direct sunlight but needs light to flower.

Recommended

— The dark-blue hoods of *A. vulgaris* are a common sight in country gardens,

◁ *Aponogeton distachyus*

△ *Aquilegia flabellata*

△ *Arabis*   *Arabis albida* △

where the deeply divided blue-green leaves are elegant until the frosts arrive.

— *A. flabellata* with similarly rounded foliage and tiny corollas has traditionally been classified with the Alpine plants. It makes a pretty sight in a rock garden together with primula and heathers.

— *A. flabellata pumila* is a dwarf variety, reaching barely 12 cm (5 in). Its light magenta is tinged with soft yellow.

Height: 50 cm (20 in) *A. vulgaris*, 15 cm (6 in) *A. flabellata*.
Spacing and planting distance: 20 cm (8 in) in all directions (*A. vulgaris*), 15 cm (6 in) in all directions (*A. flabellata*).
Soil: ordinary, well-drained (*A. vulgaris*), rich leaf-mould (*A. flabellata*).
Cultivation: anywhere (*A. vulgaris*), semi-shade (*A. flabellata*).
Propagation: from seed or by division.
Flowering season: May, June.
Type: perennial.

Arabis

SHEPHERD'S PURSE/ROCK CRESS
Cruciferae

Arabis can be used to adorn walls or as an excellent source of ground cover, capable of carpeting large areas within a few years and keeping out weeds. Though too invasive for most rockeries, it goes well at the foot of shrubs or hedges where the only other competition is moss. The downy carpet of shepherd's purse flowers every year at the same time as tulips.

Useful hints

— Plant in any season, though preferably in September, October or March, in semi-shade and well-drained soil, and water regularly.

— If planting takes place in spring, a large number of plants will normally be produced.

— After flowering, trim with shears to get them to spread and fill out.

Recommended

— *Arabis albida* (synonym: *A. caucasia*) and *A. albida* 'Variegata' which has very decorative mottled-white foliage. Apart from these, the double, *A. albida* 'Flore Peno' which has flowers like lily-of-the-valley.

Height: from 10–20 cm (4–8 in).
Spacing and planting distance: from 20–30 cm (8–12 in).
Soil: any kind, even poor.
Cultivation: sun and semi-shade (in the shade it will grow but will not flower).
Propagation: from seed or by division in any season.
Flowering season: April, May.
Type: perennial.

71

Arctotis grandis △
Arctotis grandis ▷

Arctotis

AFRICAN DAISY

Compositae

If a dry slope exposed to the sun is causing a problem, *Arctotis grandis* could be the solution. Even at 30°C (85°F) or more, it will flower all through the summer. The only difficulty will be in finding seed or a few plants as *Arctotis* seems to be in an undeserved limbo.

Useful hints

— Sow the seeds early, in February, in a frame or in a sheltered spot. Put out the young plants in individual pots and keep them sheltered until May when they can be planted out in their final position.

— A month after planting, nip the stems about half way up to force them to spread. In a warm and temperate climate, the plant will last for years and end up as a shrub.

— The flowers can be used in bouquets but they close at night.

Height: from 30–50 cm (12–20 in).
Spacing and planting distance: 30 cm (12 in).
Soil: light, add sand if necessary.
Cultivation: 6 hours of sun per day.
Propagation: from seed or, in warm and temperate climates, by division.
Flowering season: from July to the first frosts.
Type: annual and perennial.

Arenaria caepitosa aurea ▷

Arenaria

SANDWORT

Caryophyllaceae

Arenaria balearica, a relation of pearlwort, came originally from Corsica and the Balearic Islands. It rapidly forms a carpet that is used to best effect on paving or to conceal the bare soil in rockeries. Though they cannot withstand hard winters, it is easy to keep a small quantity on hand under a frame.

Useful hints

— Plant in April between the cracks of paving or in tubs at the foot of a shrub. Place a handful of sand around the plant to help it to take root.

— Every winter, take a clump and keep under frame even without heat. Divide into dozens of plants in March, placing them in a sandy soil in a pan. Rooting takes place quickly and the new growths can be planted out at the end of May.

— Little bulbs (squill, pushkinia, muscaris etc.) can be planted in autumn to produce a fine effect in spring.

Height: barely 2 cm (1 in).
Spacing and planting distance: 20 cm (8 in).
Soil: ordinary, not too heavy.
Cultivation: anywhere.
Propagation: from seed and by division in spring.
Flowering season: March to June.
Type: perennial.

Argemone mexicana △

Argemone

PRICKLY POPPY

Papaveraceae

Argemone mexicana is perfect for dry sunny gardens. The foliage, silvery with a milky tinge, is divided like that of eryngium. The flowers are large and silky like the red poppy but scented and with yellows and orange as well as red. The one problem is finding a nursery that stocks them.

Useful hints

— Plant in April either directly or from pot plants. This must be done with care as most members of the *Papaveraceae* are sensitive to transplantation.

— Place in a dry light soil in direct sunlight.

Height: 70 cm (28 in).
Spacing and planting distance: 40 cm (16 in).
Soil: light.
Cultivation: sunny.
Propagation: from seeds.
Flowering season: July to August.
Type: perennial.

△ *Arisaema candidissimum*

Arisaema

ARISAEMA/DRAGON ROOT
Araceae

Like all the *Araceae*, arisaema has a delicate trumpet, the corolla pink and striated like convolvulus and the spathe veined pink and green. A plant of the semi-shade, it has a shiny foliage like that of the arums. It is unlikely to appear before the beginning of summer. As the arisaema is a plant that is both expensive and difficult to find, the following advice is particularly important.

Useful hints

— Plant in semi-shade in a bed of leaf-mould in light sub-bush or fresh, shady area. The soil must remain moist until the end of June, the beginning of the flowering season, and must not be allowed to dry out thereafter.

— Bulbs bought over the counter often take a long time to flower. This is because they are from the Far East and need time to adjust.

Recommended

— *Arisaema sikokianum* is purplish brown and delicately veined with white. The cream-coloured spadix is curiously flattened like a golf club.

— *A. candidissimum* is pure white and slightly perfumed.

Height: 40 cm (16 in).
Spacing and planting distance: 30 cm (12 in).
Soil: rich moist leaf-mould.
Cultivation: semi-shade.
Propagation: by division.
Flowering season: June.
Type: perennial.

Armeria

THRIFT
Plumbaginaceae

This hardy little plant scarcely needs introduction as, with the garden pink, it is the most popular inhabitant of borders. And with good reason as it is very easy to cultivate and seems to flower forever. The foliage is as fine as that of grasses and the compact tuffets stay green even in winter.

Useful hints

— After flowering, cut back the faded cushions with shears. This shock treatment will give renewed vigour to the foliage through the winter.

Recommended

— *Armeria maritima* (synonym: *Statice armeria*) has pink flowers. Some may prefer the white of 'Alba' or the deep red of 'Splendens'.

Height: from 15–25 cm (6–10 in).
Spacing and planting distance: 30 cm (12 in).
Soil: good, well-drained garden soil.
Cultivation: sunny.
Propagation: by division in spring.
Flowering season: May to August.
Type: perennial.

△ *Armeria maritima*
▽ *Artemisia* '**Lambrook Silver**'

Artemisia

ARTEMISIA/ABSINTHE, WORMWOOD

Compositae

This is a plant for connoisseurs and the garden of tomorrow. The flowers are of little interest and the beauty of this plant lies in the blue-green and warm grey, aromatic foliage that brings interest to 'white' gardens. Ranging in size and form from tiny cushions to magnificent shrubs, they cater for every taste and the foliage is almost always fragrant.

Useful hint

— Have no qualms about cutting back the flowers as it is only the foliage that is decorative.

Recommended

— Tarragon (*Artemisia dracunculus*) with its aromatic green leaves is widely known but there should also be greater recognition for *A.* 'Lambrook Silver' (silvery-grey) and *A. ludoviciana* (off-white). The best of all is probably the finely spun silver of *A. schmidtiana* 'Nana'. *A. cupaniana* has strongly-scented white flowers. Plant it in poor dry soil and cut back flush with the ground at the end of the season.

Height: from 70–100 cm (28–40 in) (*A.* 'Lambrook Silver' and *A. ludoviciana*) 50 cm (20 in) (*A. dracunculus*), from 5–10 cm (2–4 in) (*A. schmidtiana* 'Nana').
Spacing and planting distance: from 30–40 cm (12–16 in).
Soil: light and well-drained.
Cultivation: full sun.
Propagation: from cuttings in a cold frame at the end of spring and in summer.
Flowering season: summer.
Type: perennial.

△ *Arum italicum* 'Pictum'

Arum

ARUM

Araceae

This is by far the most decorative of the genuinely hardy arums, a relative of the lords-and-ladies whose tiny red fruit brightens our undergrowth. The foliage is a finely marbled white. As the leaves appear in autumn and last until the end of spring, *Arum italicum* 'Pictum' is an ideal plant to enliven the garden during the dead season.

Useful hints

— The fruit which ripens in summer after the leaves have gone is very poisonous and should be removed if you have young children.

— The leaves are particularly fine in winter and are useful in bouquets.

Height: from 30–40 cm (12–16 in).
Spacing and planting distance: 40 cm (16 in).
Soil: any.
Cultivation: sun in winter, shade in summer (e.g. under deciduous trees).
Propagation: by division of tubers at the end of the summer.
Flowering season: March and April but the flowers are insignificant.
Type: perennial.

Aruncus sylvester ▷

Aruncus

GOAT'S BEARD

Rosaceae

Aruncus dioicus has different forms for the male and female: the male is more beautiful than the female though it is the latter which is most commonly sold by specialists. A mass of feathery foliage is formed rather like that of ferns and in summer this is covered with creamy white plumes. As they grow to over 2 m (80 in) and occupy a lot of ground, they are suitable for anyone with plenty of space and a small budget.

Useful hints

— Plant in spring and mulch the soil well in May and June with pine bark and grass cuttings.

— Propagation, which is by division in spring, is simple to carry out.

— Put together with the large *Fuchsia magellanica* and Japanese primulas to create a magnificent display. They are, however, very thirsty so do not forget to water regularly in the summer.

Height: 2 m (80 in).
Spacing and planting distance: 50 cm (20 in).
Soil: rich in humus and very moist in summer.
Cultivation: anywhere, even in the shade.
Propagation: by division in spring.
Flowering season: June to September.
Type: perennial.

Asarum caudatum △
Asarum europaeum ▷

Asarum

CANADIAN SNAKE ROOT/LONG-TAILED WILD GINGER

Aristolochiaceae

Originally a native of Canada, this little creeper gives off a strong scent of ginger from its large fleshy tubers. Though it can be situated in borders, it comes into its own as a ground-cover plant in moist and shady parts of the garden. The flowers are a fine deep red but even more important are the silky leaves that cover the soil throughout the year, even in winter.

Useful hint

— *Asarum canadense* dislikes dry conditions so take care in summer.

Height: 10 cm (4 in).
Spacing and planting distance: 30 cm (12 in).
Soil: any, provided that they are kept moist in summer.
Cultivation: shade and semi-shade.
Propagation: by division in spring.
Flowering season: April, May.
Type: perennial.

Recommended

— Apart from *Asclepias cornuti*, an attractive plant is *A. tuberosa* which has pale orange umbels.

Height: 1 m (39 in).
Spacing and planting distance: 40 cm (16 in).
Soil: ordinary.
Cultivation: sunny.
Propagation: from seed.
Flowering season: June to August.
Type: perennial.

△ *Asclepias tuberosa*
◁ *Asclepias currasavica*
▽ *Asperula odorata*

Asclepias

MILKWEED

Asclepiadaceae

Asclepias cornuti is commonly termed swallow-wort. It produces bunches of orange flowers on long stems. Hardy in warm and temperate climates, it is a perennial that goes well with hollyhocks, tobacco plants and phlox.

Useful hints

— Gather the pods in October and remove the seeds the following spring, stripping away their silky covering before planting. Usually, they grow very easily and flower the next summer. They should, however, be supported.

— In colder areas, protect in winter with a covering of leaves.

Asperula

ASPERULA/WOODRUFF

Rubiaceae

If you are tired of mosses under your trees and between the shrubs, *Asperula odorata* will solve the problem. Even in the shade of trees as difficult as the beeches, it will prosper, forming cushions of tender, green leaves that are finely divided. At the end of spring, asperula produces thousands of white flowers. These are odourless until dried when, in Germany, they are used to give a bouquet to white wines. Asperula are divided into three species: alpine, annual and herbaceous.

Useful hints

— If possible plant in autumn and mark the spot as the foliage disappears in winter. Intersperse with bulbs such as jonquils or the tulip *sylvestris*.

— To keep the soil moist in summer, mulch with peat, rotted compost or dead leaves.

— Do not bother to divide for propagation. Simply separate the rooted portions and plant out immediately.

Height: from 15–20 cm (6–8 in).
Spacing and planting distance: 20 cm (8 in).
Soil: ordinary.
Cultivation: shade.
Propagation: by division.
Flowering season: May, June.
Type: perennial.

Asphodeline lutea ▷

Asphodeline

ASPHODELINE/JACOB'S-ROD

Liliaceae

Rather ungainly in its appearance, *Asphodeline* flourishes on stony sun-drenched slopes. The erect leafy stems with their gold-flecked flowers sit well among cistus, rosemary and thyme. Like them, *Asphodeline* can withstand the worst drought but can be killed off with one cold wet winter.

Useful hints

— Plant in autumn so the roots are well set before winter comes. A rosette of leaves will develop flush with the ground.

— Cut the floral spikes after flowering to prevent the formation of seed pods which weaken growth.

— For use as dried flowers, cut right at the end of the flowering season.

Recommended

— Yellow asphodel (*Asphodeline lutea*) or Jacob's staff is the best known. A smaller variety, also yellow, is *A. liburnica*, a native of the Mediterranean.

Height: 90–120 cm (36–48 in).
Spacing and planting distance: 20 cm (8 in).
Soil: ordinary, slightly stony and well-drained.
Cultivation: sunny.
Propagation: by division in September or from seed in March.
Flowering season: June, July.
Type: perennial.

△ *Asplenium trichomanes*

Asplenium

ASPLENIUM/SCALY SPLEENWORT, RUSTY-BACK FERN

Polypodiaceae

These undemanding ferns are often to be seen growing on dry stone walls. In the garden, they are well-suited to paved areas or to some shady corner of a rockery. They can withstand ordinary frosts, suffering only a temporary drying of their foliage.

Useful hints

— Plant in spring, providing a pocket of good soil between two stones. The spot must be well-drained.

— Plant masses of them around your shrubs where the soil tends to be sandy. They will provide good support for your dwarf rhododendrons and kalmias.

Recommended

— *Asplenium adiantum-nigrum* is like a dwarf female fern and is most often found in dry places.

— Easily recognized from the round scales edging its lizard-tail fronds, *A. trichomanes* is a regular sight in wells and on mossy north-facing walls.

Height: 10–20 cm (4–8 in).
Spacing and planting distance: 20 cm (18 in).
Soil: leaf-mould and sand.
Cultivation: shade.
Propagation: by division in March.
Type: perennial.

Aster

ASTER

Compositae

The colourful shades of autumn would not be the same without the asters and it is hard to imagine a garden without their violet star-shaped flowers in the border. It is all too easily forgotten that they begin to bloom at the beginning of summer and last until December. All of them, moreover, are robust and can adapt to poor soils.

Useful hints

— Plant in spring or autumn and do not worry if the plants seem small in their pots. Keep an average distance of 30 cm (12 in) between them in all directions as they grow very rapidly.

— Mulch the soil in June and water in hot weather. This will help to prevent attacks of oidium which show up as a felty white on the leaves and should be sprayed with triforine.

— Divide every three years or flowering will suffer. Do not replant the cuttings in the same place but give them a good rich soil.

Recommended

— Asters deriving from mountain regions are the earliest. *Aster alpi us*, for example, grows to no more than 25 cm (10 in), the blooms being violet blue ('Triumph'), bright pink ('Happy End') or white ('Albus'). *A. farreri* is another, this time with a yellow heart that can be clearly seen whether in the lilac blue of 'Berggartenzwerg' or the mauve blue of 'Berggarten'.

— These are followed in summer by *A. tongolensis* which are generally violet with an orange heart. Examples are 'Leuchtenburg' or 'Wartburgstern'. Similar to these are *A. yunnanensis*, 'Napsbury' giving a bright heliotrope blue.

— Towards the end of summer, it is the turn of *A. amellus* which have very fine flowers. The best are 'Lac de Genève', 'Praecox Sommer Gruss' and 'Rudolf Goethe' for the blues, 'Pyreneus' for the mauves.

— Autumn is on its way when hybrid asters start to bloom. These are usually divided into *A. novae-angliae* and the slightly later *A. novi-belgii*.

— Among the dwarf varieties, those recommended are 'Alice Haslam', cherry red; 'Lady in Blue', violet blue; 'Marjorie', pink; 'Rosebud', cool pink; 'Professor A. Kippenberg', blue, semi-double; and 'Snow Sprite', pure white. Good varities of *A. novae-angliae* are

△ *Aster amellus* **'King George'**
▽ *Astilbe* **hybrid**

'Alma Pötschke', cherry red; 'Madame Loyau', soft pink; 'September Ruby', vermilion red.

— Of the *A. novi-belgii*: 'Patricia Ballard', luminous pink; 'Juliae', pinky white with strong development and rather late flowering; 'White Ladies', white, semi-double; 'Winston Churchill', plain red; 'Fellow Ship', pink, the large flowers making excellent bouquets; 'Royal Ruby', bright red.

— A final group consists of the **botanic asters**. *A. diffusus var. horizontalis* flowers at the same time as the chrysanthemums, in the form of a little pinky-white bush. *Aster ericoides, datschii* and *tradescantii* form clouds of tiny white flowers, somewhat reminiscent of gypsophila.

Height: 20–150 cm (8–60 in).
Spacing and planting distance: 30 cm (12 in).
Soil: ordinary, somewhat rich and remaining moist in summer.
Cultivation: at least 6 hours sunshine per day.
Propagation: by division in spring.
Flowering season: June to December, depending on the variety, but predominantly autumn.
Type: perennial.

Astilbe × *arendsii*

HYBRID ASTILBE
Saxifragaceae

It is useless to try to plant them in dry or even ordinary soil. They need plenty of water and, beside a pond or stream, they flower sumptuously with bright plumes like ostrich feathers rising from a fernlike foliage.

Useful hints

— If possible, plant in autumn, having first added lots of peat to the soil to hold water through the year.

— Water abundantly and regularly, especially at the beginning of the flowering season.

— Divide every three years as, with age, they produce fewer flowers.

Recommended

— Among the many hybrids, frequently of German origin, the best are: 'Koblenz', 'Rheinland' and 'Cattleya' for the pinks; 'Fanal' and 'Amethyst' for the reds; 'Gladstone' and 'Bergkristall' for the whites.

△ *Astilbe* hybrid

Height: 70–100 cm (28–40 in).
Spacing and planting distance: 30 cm (12 in).
Soil: rich in organic matter, moist at all times.
Cultivation: semi-shade (the colours fade in the sun).
Propagation: by division in autumn or spring. Divisions should be provided with shade during hot weather and liberally watered when dry.
Flowering season: July, August.
Type: perennial.

Astrantia

MASTERWORT/PINK MASTERWORT

Umbelliferae

Like borage, mountain primrose, pheasant's eye and other native wild flowers, *Astrantia major* has such natural charm that it has become very popular with gardeners. Its pink tinged with green will blend perfectly with the pastels in your flower beds. It flowers from July and August in any situation except for deep shade.

Useful hints

— Very little work is needed: it will flourish wherever you put it, whatever the soil.

— Propagate by division of roots in autumn or early spring, or gather the heads to seed in April.

— They last well as cut flowers which is an additional bonus.

Recommended

— For those who prefer something a little more exotic, a multi-coloured variety, 'Sunningdale Variegated', has been invented.

Height: 30 cm (12 in).
Spacing and planting distance: 20 cm (8 in).
Soil: ordinary.
Cultivation: sun or semi-shade.
Propagation: by root division or from seed.
Flowering season: June to August.
Type: perennial.

Athyrium

FEMALE FERN/LADY FERN

Polypodiaceae

Athyrium can be found in woods everywhere and is an ideal companion, in shady spots, for your conifers, fuchsias and hortensias. Clumps form from a central point which makes it easy to distinguish *Athyrium* from its invasive cousin, bracken.

Useful hints

— Plant at any time of year, having first watered the soil thoroughly. The foliage withers from November onwards but must not be cut as it protects the root.

— Every five years, divide clumps where they have grown too dense and replant at 30 cm (12 in) intervals in all directions.

Recommended

— *Athyrium filix-femina*, the true female fern, includes a number of varieties with foliage more finely divided than the species type but they are difficult to buy. The male fern is a *Dryopteris*.

— *A. goeringianum* is less hardy and needs to be kept under a bell-glass or brought in under a frame. Its mottled silver makes it a good pot plant for the terrace.

Height: 30 cm (12 in) (*A. goeringianum*) up to 100 cm (40 in) (*A. filix-femina*).
Spacing and planting distance: 30 cm (12 in).
Soil: preferably rich in humus (leaf-mould).
Cultivation: shade and semi-shade.
Propagation: by division in spring.
Flowering season: August, but fairly insignificant.
Type: perennial.

Aubrieta

AUBRIETIA/PURPLE ROCK CRESS

Cruciferae

The aubrietias are often to be seen cascading from walls or bordering steps and no rockery should be without *Aubrieta deltoidea*. Though some gardeners consider them vulgar or strident, this is only true of certain seed plants and cannot be said of the beautiful blues and violets of selected varieties. To obtain the best effect, they should be scattered here and there with tulips of pastel shade. Avoid clashes with yellow alyssums.

Useful hints

— Plant in winter with a handful of sand around the collar to avoid rot.

— After flowering, cut off all the dead heads with shears to force the foliage to thicken out. In this way, it is possible to obtain superb trails of soft grey-green leaves. Spray the foliage from time to time in summer.

Recommended

— The range of colours runs through the spectrum from red to purple, starting with 'Royal Rouge' and passing from 'Leichtlinii', 'Vesuvius' and 'Dr Mules' to 'Magician'. Pale blue is represented by 'Graeca', deep blue by 'Greencourt Purple' and 'Royal Blue'. For these

△ *Astrantia major*
Aubrieta deltoidea ▷
▽ *Athyrium filix-femina*

varieties the only satisfactory means of propagation is by division.

Height: from 10–15 cm (4–6 in).
Spacing and planting distance: 30 cm (12 in).
Soil: ordinary but not waterlogged in winter.
Cultivation: sunny (it flowers less in the shade).
Propagation: from seed or by division in spring.
Flowering season: April, May.
Type: perennial.

Lodged in dry stone walls, aubrieta and corydalis, both of which seed themselves in profusion, create a very colourful spring display.

84

Ballotta

BALLOTTA

Labiatae

Perfectly at home in stony ground and hot sun, the ballottas (*Ballotta pseudodictamnus*) produce one of the best of all silver-grey foliages. They are best used to set off other plants, especially bulbs with thin foliage, such as the dieramas and crocosmias or other perennials like penstemons, the pasque-flower or the nudicaul delphinium. To keep the profile of the clumps, it is necessary to cut the purple and white flowers but these are not really suitable for display.

Useful hints

— Plant in spring, preferably in a thin to stony soil. Water for the first year but after that they can be left. Prune every spring to remove shoots that have been frost-damaged.

— Propagate by taking the tips of the stems from June to September. During the first winter, keep the young plants inside under a cold frame.

Height: 60–80 cm (24–32 in).
Spacing and planting distance: 40 cm (16 in).
Soil: very light.
Cultivation: full sun.
Propagation: from cuttings, in summer.
Flowering season: June to September.
Type: perennial.

Baptisia australis △
Begonia **tuberous** ▷

▽ *Ballota pseudodictamnus*

Baptisia

BAPTISIA/BLUE WILD INDIGO

Leguminosae

Having kept the elegance of a wild plant, *Baptisia australis* is ideal for bringing colour to a grassy patch where it will emerge every spring to display fine lupin-like flowers.

Useful hints

— Plant in the middle of a bed of perennials or in a lawn after cutting out a 30 cm (12 in) square.

— Set up a triangle of bamboo canes or hazel twigs to stake the plants.

— Strip the foliage at the end of July to encourage new growth and to avoid the formation of seed.

Height: 60–100 cm (24–40 in).
Spacing and planting distance: 30 cm (12 in).
Soil: ordinary, preferably a little chalky and remaining moist in summer.
Cultivation: full sun.
Propagation: by division in April or September.
Flowering season: June.
Type: perennial.

Begonia

BEGONIA

Begoniaceae

Three groups of begonias are of interest to the gardener: the annuals obtained from seed in winter for flowering in beds the next summer; the tuberous begonias which are grown like dahlias and are excellent for shaded areas; and, finally, the perennial begonias which, though few in number, are very useful for those parts of the garden that are in semi-shade.

Useful hints

— Sow **begonia annuals** (*Begonia semperflorens*) in February using a pan placed

on a radiator. Prick out twice in pots and finally plant out in May. Alternatively, you can buy them in pots and plant them out at the same time after pinching the flowers to force new growth. Water at least once a week and trim the clumps in mid-August with hedging shears to induce new vigour.

— To get the **tuberous begonias** to germinate, set them hollow upwards in individual pots around mid-March. Do not plant out until mid-May when the soil has warmed up. Mulch the soil with peat or grass cuttings. Water once a week and add liquid fertilizer once a month. In November, pull up the clumps and leave them to dry in a warm place. Remove the tubers and keep in a warm dry place until March.

— Plant **perennial begonias** in April/ May in the semi-shade. Put down anti-slug pellets and water well throughout the summer. Once the first frosts have come, the foliage will fall. Cover the stems with 15 cm (6 in) of straw or dead leaves until spring when you can propagate by division.

Recommended

— **Begonia annuals** are grouped together under the name *Begonia semperflorens* and they include a large number of F^1 hybrids that have a dust-like seed. The varieties are forever changing but, at the present time, the reds 'Mizar' and 'Vision Rouge', the pinks 'Venus', 'Olympia Rose' and 'Vision Rose', and the white 'Athena' and 'Viva' are all enjoying well-deserved success and are easily available.

— The **tuberous begonias** are divided into two groups: varieties with large flowers (doubles, like pinks, 'Non Stop'); and varieties with small flowers, including the superb 'Pendula' which is indispensable for shaded gardens. The 'Bertini' variety is reasonably successful in the sun. The most widely known tuberous begonia is *Begonia evansiana* which produces pink flowers for a good part of the summer.

Height: 15–30 cm (6–12 in).
Spacing and planting distance: 15 cm (6 in) for the dwarf varieties, 25 cm (10 in) for the tuberous varieties.
Soil: rich and moisture-retaining.
Cultivation: full sun for the annuals, shade and semi-shade for the rest.
Propagation: from seed for the annuals, division of the tubers for tuberous varieties, and by division of the stems for perennials.
Flowering season: all summer, from June to the first frosts.
Type: annual, bulb, perennial.

Bergenia

PIG SQUEAK/LEATHER BERGENIA
Saxifragaceae

Borders of bergenias have become so common that the sight of their large leathery leaves and ruby flowers is not always a joy to the eye. For the gardener, however, there is the consolation that they will grow where many others will not and will keep their appearance throughout the year if tended.

Useful hints

— Plant at any season after first digging over the ground thoroughly. Enrich the soil with leaf-mould or peat.

— In March, remove dead leaves to allow new growth and to make way for the flowers that are beginning to show. Plant botanic tulips and ferns around them so that there will be some colour and foliage all year round.

Recommended

— *Bergenia cordifolia* is the most common whether in the red varieties or the bright pink. *B. cordifolia* 'Undulata' has a leaf with wavy edges that is more decorative than the species type.

— The best for borders is *B. purpurascens* 'Ballawley' which produces a fuchsia-red flower and has relatively tight foliage.

◁ *Bellis perennis*
◁ *Bellis perennis* 'Pomponnette'

Beta vulgaris 'Rubricaulis' ▷
Bergenia purpurascens ▽

Bellis

DAISY/ENGLISH DAISY
Compositae

The unsophisticated charm of *Bellis perennis* is apparent in all varieties from the simple meadow daisy on the lawn to the pink and red pompons of large display plants.

Useful hints

— Plant in October/November or at the beginning of spring. They are very resistant to cold but it is worth while watering them after long periods of frost.

— They can also be sown in June in a shaded spot and then transplanted about two months later. In fact, the daisy is more truly biennial than perennial, especially in varieties with large flowers.

Recommended

— The most outstanding are the 'Pomponette' doubles which form a magnificent carpet under tulips and among myosotis. Lovers of the unusual can sow 'Monstreuse', one of the Chevreuse strains, though this can look rather stark in display beds.

Height: 5–20 cm (2–8 in).
Spacing and planting distance: 15 cm (6 in).
Soil: ordinary, preferably clay.
Cultivation: at least 3 hours sun per day.
Propagation: from seed in spring and, for the meadow daisy, by division in autumn.
Flowering season: from March to September but mainly spring.
Type: biennial, perennial.

— *B. stracheyi* has given rise to some popular hybrids. 'Abendglut' has leaves that are bronze red in winter and fiery red flowers. 'Silberlicht' marries white with pink in flowers that stand out well above the foliage.

— Still relatively unknown is *B. ciliata*, one of the few varieties to have deciduous foliage. The leaves are similar to those of the saintpaulias but larger while the soft pink flowers are the finest of the whole genus.

Height: 30 cm (12 in).
Spacing and planting distance: 30 cm (12 in).
Soil: rich in humus.
Cultivation: semi-shade.
Propagation: by division after flowering or in autumn.
Flowering season: March to May.
Type: perennial.

Beta vulgaris

DECORATIVE CHARD/ ORNAMENTAL CHARD

Chenopodiaceae

It may seem strange to include a vegetable among the flowers but the beet 'Ruby Chard' is well worth it, producing a red to compare with many blooms. It is easy to grow and comes into its own during the autumn when the rest of the garden is beginning to look a little drab. It is also edible.

Useful hints

— Do not sow too early: the best time is mid-April or the beginning of May. Put three or four seeds in a pot and place directly in the ground at the spot of your choice. They can be transplanted a month later.

— Water once a week in the hot weather and mulch the soil. Liquid manure or dried blood are welcome additions.

— The chards can be cut in November for eating. When cooked, they lose their colour.

Recommended

— The best of all is 'Ruby Chard' which is sometimes offered in catalogues as red chard beet.

Height: from 100–120 cm (40–48 in).
Spacing and planting distance: 40 cm (16 in).
Soil: as rich as possible.
Cultivation: full sun.
Propagation: from seed at the end of spring.
Flowering season: summer of the second year but uninteresting.
Type: annual, biennial.

Bletilla

BLETILLA

Orchidaceae

Bletilla hyacinthina grows so easily and so vigorously that it is hard to remember that this is an orchid. The delicacy of the flowers and the elegant pink are certainly a reminder but otherwise it is more comparable to the tulip. The foliage is identical to that of gladioli.

Useful hints

— Plant the rhizomes in spring in ordinary well-drained soil.

— Cover with a thick layer of dead leaves or ferns and this will preserve them through the coldest of winters.

— Every three years, dig them up and divide, preferably in September.

Height: 30 cm (12 in).
Spacing and planting distance: 15 cm (6 in).
Soil: ordinary, even a little limy.
Cultivation: semi-shade.
Propagation: by division at the end of the summer or in spring.
Flowering season: May to July.
Type: bulb.

△ *Borago officinalis*
◁ *Bletilla striata*

Bocconia

See Macleaya

Borago officinalis

BORAGE

Boraginaceae

Borage is more often to be found in kitchen and herb gardens than in the flower bed. However, they are easy to grow from seed and will produce masses of azure flowers in summer. They seed themselves with equal ease and soon

Brachycome 'Purple Splendour' △

Brachyome

BRACHYOME/SWAN RIVER DAISY
Compositae

Originally from Australia, these flowers are now very popular for the balcony or window-box. *Brachyome iberidifolia* forms magnificent cushions of blooms throughout the summer. At one time, they were only available in blues but now there are also dazzling yellows.

Useful hints

— Plant immediately after the frosts are over in a mixture of leaf-mould and peat. Although they are fond of the heat, they need to have plenty of water. If the pot is too small, they will fade during the day and only recover at night. In mid-summer, water regularly, at least once a day.

— Every fortnight, cut off the dead heads with scissors to prevent seed formation. Keep cuttings or a stem on your verandah or under glass. You can also sow the seeds in March in a hot-house.

Height: from 30–45 cm (12–18 in).
Spacing and planting distance: 25 cm (10 in).
Soil: leaf-mould and light peat.
Cultivation: sunny.
Propagation: from seed, in spring.
Flowering season: from June to the frosts.
Type: annual, perennial.

become the established neighbours of your rose bushes.

Useful hints

— Sow in April/May, placing three seeds in 5 cm (2 in) holes spaced at 20 cm (8 in) intervals.

— Water well during the hot weather or cover the soil with grass cuttings.

— After flowering, cut the stems back flush with the ground. Remove all the old foliage and put it on your compost heap or you will have lots more borage in the same place the next year.

Height: from 40–80 cm (16–32 in).
Spacing and planting distance: 20 cm (8 in).
Soil: ordinary, even poor and dry.
Cultivation: sunny.
Propagation: from seed, in spring.
Flowering season: 3 months after sowing.
Type: annual.

△ *Briza maxima*
▷ *Browallia speciosa*
Brunnera macrophylla ▷

Briza

QUAKING GRASS
Gramineae

A favourite for displays of dried flowers, this annual grass has hanging spicules that quiver in the least breath of air. *Briza maxima* should be sown in a corner of the herb garden together with everlasting flowers. They also go well in flower beds to soften the outline of zinnias or dahlias.

Useful hints

— Sow in April and then transplant the surplus a month later. Water regularly until the first spikelets appear and then leave to ripen.

— Briza should be cut in July when the ears have formed but have not yet opened. Hang in bunches in a cool place for the rest of the summer.

Height: from 20–40 cm (8–16 in).
Spacing and planting distance: 15 cm (6 in).
Soil: ordinary.
Cultivation: sunny.
Propagation: from seed, in spring.
Flowering season: June, July.
Type: annual.

Browallia

BROWALLIA
Solanaceae

Frequently on sale at florists from August onwards, *Browallia speciosa* looks delightful in the living room or on a balcony and also in a sunny flower bed where its soft blue will persist for weeks on end.

Useful hints

— Sow inside in March and then transplant in individual pots in April. The final planting out should be in mid-May. Pinch the stems half way up to get them to spread.

— Water once a week in summer, adding liquid manure once a month.

Recommended

— 'Blue Troll' does not exceed 30 cm (12 in) and spreads gracefully. 'White Bell' is also stylish if you can find the seeds.

Height: 30–40 cm (12–16 in).
Spacing and planting distance: 15–20 cm (6–8 in).
Soil: rich (leaf-mould and peat).
Cultivation: at least 6 hours sun per day.
Propagation: from seed, inside, in March.
Flowering season: all summer.
Type: annual, perennial.

Brunnera

BRUNNERA
Boraginaceae

Brunnera macrophylla (heart leaf brunnera) is a sad sight in winter, the foliage black and apparently dead. Nevertheless, do not remove the leaves as they protect the stem from the cold. If you are patient and wait until March, you will be rewarded two months later with an abundance of myosotis-like flowers. It flourishes in the shade where it reseeds naturally.

Useful hints

— Plant in autumn if possible. Mulch the soil with pine bark or peat. Water only in the hottest weather.

— Plant with the small-flowered narcissus or the yellow botanic crocus. The epimediums flourish in the same conditions and are set off by the blue of the brunneras.

Height: 40 cm (16 in).
Spacing and planting distance: 30 cm (12 in).
Soil: ordinary.
Cultivation: best in shade, though will cope with sun provided soil does not dry out.
Propagation: by division in autumn.
Flowering season: May to July.
Type: perennial.

Calamintha

CALAMINTHA

Labiatae

Calamintha forms a tight little bush about 30 cm (12 in) high, covered with soft lavender flowers. It will survive in the semi-shade but prefers the sun and a soil which is not too rich. It should be planted around rose beds.

Useful hints

— Plant in spring if possible, mulching the soil with pine bark or grass cuttings.

— Shortly before the worst frosts, cut the foliage and leave it where it lies to protect the root-stock.

Recommended

— A good variety for rockeries is *Calamintha alpina* which grows to only 15 cm (6 in) and has mauve blue flowers.

— A favourite with cats is *C. nepetoides* which flowers for a good part of the summer.

Height: 15–30 cm (6–12 in).
Spacing and planting distance: 20 cm (8 in).
Soil: ordinary.
Cultivation: at least 6 hours sun per day.
Propagation: by division in spring.
Flowering season: June to October.
Type: perennial.

▽ *Calamintha alpina*

93

△ *Calendriana umbellata*

Calandrinia

CALANDRINIA/ROCK-PURSLANE
Portulacaceae

Originally from Peru, *Calandrinia umbellata* is like our purslanes and thrives in the sun. It forms sturdy clumps that are entirely covered with flowers throughout the summer. The silky magenta-crimson blooms emerge as soon as there is any sunshine.

Useful hints

— In a warm and temperate climate, they should be sown in March or April, either in pots or directly into the ground. The seeds should be sown very shallowly and covered with sand.

— Transplant in May or thin out the seedlings. They go well in borders, in rockeries or on dry stone walls.

Height: 15 cm (6 in).
Spacing and planting distance: 15 cm (6 in).
Soil: ordinary.
Cultivation: in full sun or the flowers will not open.
Propagation: from seed in April.
Flowering season: all summer.
Type: annual and perennial.

△ *Calceolaria herbeo-hybrida*
◁ *Calceolaria darwinii*

△ *Calendula officinalis*

Calceolaria

CALCEOLARIA/SLIPPERWORT, POCKETBOOK PLANT

Scrophulariaceae

Calceolaria is a wonderful genus. Some species, with their yellows and pouch-like flowers, go well in beds or rockeries.

Useful hints

— In a warm and temperate climate they are hardy but, elsewhere, it is best to wait until spring before planting. Keeping them under a cold frame over the winter is a wise precaution.

— Give them a raised position and do not hesitate to pinch out stems that are too thin to encourage stronger growths.

— If there is any yellowing of the foliage, this could come either from asphyxiation caused by excessive watering or from greenfly swarming under the leaves. In the latter case, treat with a decamethrine-based insecticide or granules of some disulfoton-based product.

Recommended

— The hardiest of the calceolaria is the marvellous *Calceolaria darwiniai* which is the jewel of any rockery. It must be protected from slugs which consider it a delicacy.

— The hybrid calceolarias (*C. herbeo-hybrida*) are very decorative with spots and mottling. These are better suited to the veranda. They are grown as bi-ennials from seed in June and are kept in a cold frame over the winter.

— *C. rugosa* are the calceolarias that are to be seen in public parks, a single stem creating the effect of a whole mimosa bush. Propagate from cuttings taken in summer and kept under shelter through the winter. They can also be grown from seed and make good pot plants.

Height: 15–60 cm (6–24 in).
Spacing and planting distance: 25 cm (10 in).
Soil: rich and well-drained.
Cultivation: at least 6 hours sun per day.
Propagation: from seed at the beginning of summer or from cuttings in August.
Flowering season: June to September.
Type: annual, biennial, perennial.

Calendula

MARIGOLD

Compositae

One of the most engaging of the annuals, marigold produces large seeds that are easily grown, turning into robust plants that flower throughout the summer provided that faded blooms are regularly removed. It also reseeds without the least trouble.

Useful hints

— Sow *Calendula officinalis* in a cold frame in March or in position in April/May. Transplant a month later or thin out the seedlings to leave a spacing of 20 cm (8 in). Plant some in the kitchen garden as well since they cleanse the soil and can also be used for cut flowers.

— Water once a week, at the same time removing faded heads to prolong the flowering season. If a woolly white outbreak should appear on the leaves, spray with triforine.

Recommended

— For cut flowers, the best varieties are the large ones. The medium sizes, 'Fiesta Gitana', 'Corniche d'Or' or 'Orange Coronet' are perfect for beds and borders.

Height: 30–60 cm (12–24 in).
Spacing and planting distance: 20 cm.
Soil: ordinary, preferably moist in summer.
Cultivation: at least 6 hours sun per day in summer.
Propagation: from seed in spring.
Flowering season: from May until first frost.
Type: annual.

△ *Callistephus chinensis*

△ *Callistephus chinensis*

Callistephus

CHINA ASTER

Compositae

The china aster is not as popular as it once was and has become a less common sight in gardens but, even as a source of cut flowers for the end of the summer, they are well worth planting. Unfortunately, though, they have become susceptible to a fungus that can cut them down overnight even during flowering. For this reason, never leave them in the same place for two years running.

Useful hints

— Sow from mid-March to mid-May when the ground has warmed up again and cover the seed with 1 cm (½ in) of sand.

— A month later, thin out the seedlings to leave 15 cm (6 in) between them and transplant the surplus with the same spacing in your flower beds. Pinch them half way up.

— Dose the collar once with liquid Cryptonol.

Recommended

—The single flower varieties remain firm favourites and include the elegant 'Arc en Ciel' and 'Madeleine'. The dwarf varieties are like tiny cushions: 'Déesse', 'Pépite' and 'Pinocchio'. To create a little hedge around your kitchen garden, choose the double flower giants which will grow to 1 m (40 in) if staked: 'Beauté d' Amérique', 'Super Princess', 'Giant Ray' or 'Unicum'. They are good as cut flowers.

Height: from 20–100 cm (8–40 in).
Spacing and planting distance: 15–30 cm (6–12 in).
Soil: rich, add compost if necessary.
Cultivation: sunny.
Propagation: from seed in spring.
Flowering season: 2–3 months after sowing.
Type: annual.

Calluna

HEATHER

Ericaceae

A common plant in clearings, this heather can be recognized from the vertical spikes that appear from the end of summer to the beginning of winter. It creates a perfect scene when planted with grasses, dwarf conifers and other heathers at the foot of birches.

Useful hints

— Plant at any time of year in an acid soil, a mixture of sand, heath soil and peat being ideal. Mulch with pine bark.

— After flowering, the withered blooms remain decorative and should not be removed till March to keep the plants tightly bunched.

— If there is any sudden withering, treat three times with Aliette.

Recommended

— There are many: 'Alba Plena', white 'Goldsworth Crimson', deep red and 'H. E. Beale', silvery red being among the best. 'Blaze-away', 'Golden Feather' and some others have a golden foliage but are often frail.

Height: 15 60 cm (6–24 in).
Spacing and planting distance: 25–30 cm (10–14 in).
Soil: acid.
Cultivation: sunny, semi-shade for the golden varieties.
Propagation: by division in spring.
Flowering season: August to November.
Type: perennial.

▽ *Calluna vulgaris*

Caltha

MARSH MARIGOLD/KINGCUP

Ranunculaceae

Nothing is prettier than a clump of *Caltha palustris* covered with pure yellow flowers at the end of spring. They transform the damper regions of the garden before the arrival of the water-lilies. One variety has double flowers that are almost round. The glossy leathery foliage disappears in winter.

Useful hints

— Plant in spring into pockets of rich soil just at the edge of the water or even slightly below the surface.

— Divide in spring, keeping one bud per cutting, and replant immediately.

Height: 30–40 cm (12–16 in).
Spacing and planting distance: 30 cm (12 in).
Soil: rich in humus and moist at all times.
Cultivation: sunny.
Propagation: by division in March.
Flowering season: May, June and, sometimes, in September.
Type: perennial.

▽ *Caltha palustris*

△ *Camassia cusickii*

Camassia

CAMASSIA/COMMON CAMAS

Liliaceae

If you do not like bulbs that have little foliage, why not try the camassias. Within a few years, these robust plants will have formed solid bunches and they will have foliage that remains decorative up to the end of August. They flower in all shades of blue and go perfectly with pink peonies and yellow roses.

Useful hints

— Plant as early as possible in autumn. Put down anti-slug pellets in spring.

— Leave for at least four years before dividing. Continue watering right up until they wither.

— Removed dead flower heads unless seeds required.

Recommended

— *Camassia cusickii* bulbs grow to an impressive size, up to 1 m (40 in) once well-installed. The flowers are lavender blue.

— *C. leichtlinii* has white or blue floral spikes that rise well above the foliage and they do not require staking.

— *C. quamash* was once rooted up by North American Indians for food. Now, as a garden plant, it provides us with a rich variety of shades from white to violet blue.

Height: 60–90 cm (24–36 in).
Spacing and planting distance: 30 cm (12 in).
Soil: ordinary, rather rich and remaining moist in summer.
Cultivation: sunny.
Propagation: separation of offsets from bulbs in autumn.
Flowering season: June, July.
Type: bulb.

△ *Campanula latifolia*

△ *Campanula medium*
▽ *Campanula fragilis*

Campanula

BELL-FLOWER/BLUEBELL, HAREBELL, BLUEBELL OF SCOTLAND

Campanulaceae

This is a vast family ranging from dwarves of barely 10 cm (4 in) to the large herbaceous varieties which can easily exceed 2 m (80 in). The basic colour is blue but they incline also towards white and cool pink. Some favour dry soils, others moist. Some prefer the sun, others the shade. There is something here for everyone.

Useful hints

— Plant campanula in the spring if possible when roots are beginning to stir again or in September, to give them time to get started before the arrival of the frosts.

— Water regularly during the first summer and mulch the soil with peat or pine bark.

— Pinch out the faded stems to prevent seeding. This is one way to make the large campanulas flower again but it is necessary to pinch each flower one by one as the new blooms appear at the axilla of the previous ones.

— Divide just before flowering in spring. It is also possible to grow from seed with flowering coming, for the most part, in the second year and this is the only way to propagate the large-flowered bell-flower.

Recommended

— *Campanula alliariifolia* is very attractive in shape, the species type with its creamy white flowers in June being preferable to the larger flowered but less elegant 'Ivory Bells' variety.

— *C. carpatica* is often used to border rose-beds, the corolla being so broad and numerous that they hide the foliage in June and July. 'Turbinata', also blue and white, is somewhat more compact.

— *C. cochlearifolia* produces its tiny blue and white flowers in July/August and is

Campanula porscharskyana ▽ ▷

△ **Campanula mollis**

a favourite for rockeries and paved areas.

— *C. glomerata* is easily recognized from the tight clusters of flowers that appear at the beginning of summer. The 'Joan Elliott' and 'Dahurica' varieties are both of a very rich violet blue.

— The great bellflower, *C. latifolia*, flowers in July and August, providing good company for marshmallow, loose-strife and yellow pimpernel in wilder parts of the garden.

— The large-flowered campanula is more biennial than perennial. Sowing in June will produce plants with plenty of flowers a year later.

— A variety that never goes wrong is the peach-leaved bell-flower, *C. persicifolia*, which often reseeds in a wonderful mixture of blue and white.

— *C. muralis*, lamentably rechristened *C. portenschlagiana*, brings a vivid blue to May and June which can be employed both as wall cover or in borders. A more vigorous variety is *C. poscharskyana* which is ideal for paved areas.

— Unlike the preceding examples, the pyramid bell-flower (*C. pyramidalis*) attains a height close to 2 m (80 in) and its mid-summer flowering is a spectacular sight. Unfortunately, it is susceptible to winter rot and can only be relied on for one year.

— *C. trachelium*, which at a distance could be mistaken for a nettle, is often to be found growing wild along lanes. It produces long clusters of mauve blue flowers in mid-summer and grows well on the poorest soils.

Height: from 100–200 cm (40–80 in).
Spacing and planting distance: 15–30 cm (6–12 in).
Soil: ordinary, well-drained in winter.
Cultivation: sun and semi-shade.
Propagation: from seed or by division.
Flowering season: May to October, depending on the variety.
Type: annual, biennial, perennial.

△ **Campanula barbata**
▽ **Campanula carpatica**

△ *Canna* 'Lucifer'
▽ *Canna* hybrid

Recommended

— Green foliage: 'Centurion', bright orange; 'En Avant', yellow with red spots; 'Oiseau de Feu', scarlet; 'Soleil d'Or', majestic yellow; 'Talisman', golden yellow with a red heart.

— Purple foliage: 'Angèle Martin', soft salmon pink; 'Assaut', bright scarlet; 'La Gloire', carmine pink; 'Peau Rouge', copper red; 'Semaphore', orange yellow.

— Dwarf varieties: 'Clèopatre', bright orange with a golden edge; 'Lucifer', blood red with a yellow edge; 'Mistral', pink; 'Petit Poucet', yellow with red spots; 'Puck', yellow.

Height: 30–120 cm (12–48 in).
Spacing and planting distance: 30 cm (12 in).
Soil: as rich as possible.
Cultivation: sunny.
Propagation: by division of rhizome just before planting.
Flowering season: from July to the first frosts.
Type: bulb.

Canna

CANNA/CANNA LILY, INDIAN SHOT

Cannaceae

Though sometimes despised because of their overuse, often with discordant colours, in public parks, the cannas may well provide a touch of piquancy to your flower beds. They can, moreover, be grown by anyone.

Useful hints

— Start the rhizomes by placing in individual pots over a radiator in March/April. Let them adjust gradually and then plant out towards the end of May.

— Water at least once a week, adding liquid manure every second time. Dig up the tubers in October and allow to dry in a warm place.

Cardiocrinum

GIANT LILY

Liliaceae

There are few plants as impressive as *Cardiocrinum giganteum*, the stems of which can reach up to 3 m (120 in), each bearing a score or more of fragrant trumpet-shaped flowers. The sad thing is that the plant dies after flowering leaving behind offsets that take another six years before coming into bloom.

Useful hints

— A woodland plant, the giant lily appreciates rich soil and a shaded position.

— Plant as soon as you get them since the bulb must not be allowed to dry out. If the weather is still too cold, place the bulb in a pot of leaf-mould with just the tip showing.

— Put down anti-slug pellets immediately since that garden pest will devour the leaves and even the bulb.

— Straight after flowering, dig up the bulblets that appear around the principal stem and replant immediately at a suitable distance.

Height: 1.5–3 m (60–120 in).
Spacing and planting distance: 40 cm (16 in).
Soil: pure leaf-mould.
Cultivation: not more than 3 hours sun per day.
Propagation: from offsets.
Flowering season: July, August.
Type: bulb.

△ *Cardiocrinum giganteum*

△ *Catananche caerulea*

△ *Cataranthus roseus*
▽ *Cataranthus roseus* **hybrid**

Catananche

CATANANCHE/BLUE CUPID'S DART

Compositae

Catananche caerulea enjoys a somewhat dry position and is good company for grey foliage plants and at the front of a border. The paper-like bracts keep well if dried. In damp conditions, they tend to be short-lived but, just as often, they reseed spontaneously in another part of the garden.

Useful hints

— If possible, plant in spring or early in autumn, taking the precaution of placing a few handfuls of coarse sand around the collar as a protection against winter rot.

— Propagate by dividing the fleshy roots in December or, better still, from seed in spring. The plants will flower by the following year. The white variety, however, is not reliable when grown from seed.

Height: 50–70 cm (20–28 in).
Spacing and planting distance: 30 cm (12 in).
Soil: sandy, well-drained in winter.
Cultivation: must be sunny.
Propagation: by root division or from seed.
Flowering season: July to September.
Type: perennial.

Catharanthus

MADAGASCAR PERIWINKLE

Apocynaceae

Catharanthus roseus (synonym: *Vinca rosea*) is very different from our woodland periwinkles and its reputation has been based more on its medicinal properties than its beauty. It is, nevertheless, an excellent plant for the flower bed, easily sown in a hot frame and producing flowers throughout the year.

Useful hints

— Sow in February/March in pans placed either in the soil or on a radiator. Transplant into pots a month later and finally plant out some time in May. Take note, however, that the slightest frost is fatal.

— Remove the withered flowers once a fortnight. Water frequently, adding liquid manure every three weeks.

— The plant can be kept for a further year by bringing it inside in a pot but it quickly loses its foliage from the base upwards and the result is hardly pretty.

Height: 30–60 cm (12–24 in).
Spacing and planting distance: 25–30 cm (10–12 in).
Soil: somewhat rich, add leaf-mould if necessary.

Cultivation: sunny.
Propagation: from seed in hothouse, in February.
Flowering season: July to the first frosts.
Type: annual.

△ *Celosia* **'Cockscomb'**

Celosia

CELOSIA

Amaranthaceae

With their tiny corollas forming plumes or velvety caps and with their glowing colours, the celosias are the stuff of a gardener's dreams. However, they are very demanding and require a great deal of expertise if they are to give of their best. Because of their unusual appearance, it is also no easy task to match them with other plants. They do well in deep window-boxes and form excellent bouquets.

Useful hints

— The seeds, which are very fine, should be sown in March in a tray of leaf-mould kept in the warm. Prick out three weeks later and finally plant out in May.

— Add plenty of fertilizer and well-rotted manure to the soil. Water regularly, adding liquid manure every second time.

— To get long-lasting bouquets, cut the stems as soon as the first flowers open. To dry them, hang upside down in a dark room for two months.

Recommended

— The 'Cockscomb' variety has an enormous head that is full of dense curls. 'Coral Garden' reaches a height of no more than 25 cm (10 in). The flowers are bright red, scarlet, golden yellow and 'Modern Style' pink.

— The plumed celosias explode in every colour, 'Apricot Brandy' being a soft orange. 'Plume Naine' is very bushy. 'Triomphe de l'Exposition' is very large and looks every bit a prize-winner.

Height: 25–80 cm (10–32 in).
Spacing and planting distance: 20–30 cm (8–12 in).
Soil: very rich and always moist.
Cultivation: sunny.
Propagation: from seed, in hothouse, in March.
Flowering season: from July to first frosts.
Type: annual.

Centaurea

KNAPWEED/CORNFLOWER, BACHELOR'S BUTTON

Compositae

Centaurea provides a delightful splash of colour in any flower bed. Of the 600 or so species, the best-known is the cornflower (*C. cyanus*) which brings rustic charm to city gardens. They combine well with *Nepeta*, *Echinops* and *Godetia*.

Useful hints

— Sow the annuals in position either in autumn or at the beginning of spring. Those planted in autumn need protection during the winter.

— Sow the perennials in a cold frame in April. Transplant into trays and then put in place at the beginning of autumn.

— If the withered flowers are removed, there is a good chance that they will flower again.

— Divide the perennials every four years or so.

Recommended

— The best-known annuals are the cornflowers (*C. cyanus*) whose petals look as if they had been cut out of crepe paper. Among the vivid colours available are striking blues and pinks. The 'Impériale' strain tend to pastel shades and have a rich, musky fragrance.

— Among the perennials *C. dealbata* is worth noting. It reaches a height of 60 cm (24 in) and has foliage that is grey-green above and silvery on the underside. The large pink flowers have white hearts and appear from May to August.

Height: 25–60 cm (10–24 in).
Spacing and planting distance: 10 cm (4 in).
Soil: ordinary, preferably light, even dry.
Cultivation: sunny.
Propagation: from seed.
Flowering season: June to September.
Type: annual and perennial.

▽ *Centaurea cyanus*

△ Centaurea dealbata 'Stenbergii'

▽ Centaurea montana

Centaurea macrocephala △
Centaurea cyanus hybrid ▷
Centaurea pulcherrina ▽

103

△ *Centranthus ruber*

Centranthus

VALERIAN/RED VALERIAN
Valerianaceae

An often uninvited but always welcome guest, valerian can transform garden walls where it will flourish and bloom for a good three months from June to the end of summer. Whether white or purplish pink, as in the standard variety, the clusters of flowers are perfectly set off by the abundant, slightly bluish foliage.

Useful hints

— Any packet of seeds will provide you with more than enough young growths that should be planted out in September. They are then guaranteed to flower the next summer.

— Clean up the old valerians in March to let new vigorous growths come through.

— If the soil is acid, add a little chalk or slaked lime before planting. Water only during prolonged hot weather.

Height: 40–60 cm (16–24 in).
Spacing and planting distance: 25 cm (10 in).
Soil: ordinary, preferably limy.
Cultivation: at least 6 hours sun per day.
Propagation: from seed in March/April.
Flowering season: progressively through the summer.
Type: perennial.

△ *Cerastium biebersteinii*

Cerastium

**MOUSE-EAR CHICKWEED/
SNOW-IN-SUMMER**
Carophyllaceae

Though virtually a weed, *Cerastium* is an attractive sight and a single root stock will provide a mat almost 1 m (40 in) in diameter within a month. The fine silvery foliage of *Cerastium tomentosum* is covered with thousands of tiny white stars at the end of spring. As it is somewhat invasive, it should not be placed in company with fragile plants. It provides excellent ground cover under conifers and rose bushes or can be grown in large patches interspersed with irises.

Useful hints

— If possible, plant in September to give it time to get established before the arrival of winter frosts. Space widely as they spread rapidly.

— Cut back to a height of 5 cm (2 in) in March, using shears or even a mower.

— Plant botanic tulips among *Cerastium* to obtain a pretty effect in spring.

Height: 10 cm (4 in).
Spacing and planting distance: 30 cm (12 in).
Soil: any, even poor.
Cultivation: any, except dense shade.
Propagation: from cuttings or by separation.
Flowering season: May, June.
Type: perennial.

Ceratostigma

**PLUMBAGO/BLUE
CERATOSTIGMA, FALSE
PLUMBAGO**
Plumbaginaceae

Ceratostigma plumbaginoides is not a name that trips lightly off the tongue but it is a first-class ground-cover plant which, contrary to popular legend, is perfectly hardy and will add colour to the garden at a time when few flowers are in evidence. The sky-blue flowers begin to appear in September just before the foliage, which thrives in the cold, turning fiery red. It combines well with sternbergias and white colchicums.

Useful hints

— Plant in spring, having first added a little peat and compost to the soil. Mulch the ground in June and water regularly throughout the first summer. Every spring, add a little peat to encourage new root production.

— It is possible to leave the plant intact for up to 10 years but division and replanting can also be carried out in March. Beware of couch-grass which will try to insinuate its way into the densely packed mass.

Height: 25 cm (10 in).
Spacing and planting distance: 30 cm (12 in).
Soil: ordinary, preferably well-drained.
Cultivation: at least 6 hours sun per day.
Propagation: by natural layering or by division in spring.
Flowering season: September to October.
Type: shrub.

Cheiranthus

WALLFLOWER

Cruciferae

Though somewhat stiff in appearance, *Cheiranthus cheiri* possesses an irresistible fragrance and, for that reason, it should be planted close to the house. Bees swarm to it to enjoy the first nectar of the season. In warm climates, the wall-flower may become perennial.

Useful hints

— Sow in July, spacing the seeds out well and barely covering them with peat or compost. At this time of year, a simple unprotected seeding tray will be quite sufficient.

— When the young plants have reached 8–10 cm (3–4 in), they can be transplanted but care must be taken not to damage the sparse root system. Once the stems have reached 20 cm (8 in), pinch them half way up.

— If the autumn is dry, water them and fill in the gaps that invariably occur.

— When the flowers fade, cut off the whole floral stem to encourage the appearance of new ones.

Recommended

— Dwarf varieties like 'Tom Thumb' are common and very effective on walls or in rockeries. The taller yellow varieties such as 'Buisson d'Or' are worth trying, not to mention the violet and carmen shades and the blends of pastel colours which contain a soft beige.

Height: 30–60 cm (12–24 in).
Spacing and planting distance: 20–40 cm (8–16 in).
Soil: ordinary.
Cultivation: sunny.
Propagation: from seed in spring.
Flowering season: March to June.
Type: biennial.

Ceratostigma willmottianum △
◁ *Cheiranthus cheiri*
Cheiranthus **'Buisson d'or'** ▽

Chelone

TURTLEHEAD

Scrophulariaceae

Chelone obliqua is perfect to cover the transition between the summer flowers and the asters. A cousin of the penstemons, it blooms at the end of summer, opening out in flowers that are like miniature foxgloves. The colours range from pink to white.

Useful hints

— Plant in October or March and, as *Chelone* makes great demands, the soil must be dug over deeply and enriched with leaf-mould.

— Mulch the soil in June so that there is no danger of drying out in summer.

— Leave the dead stems where they are during the winter and do not remove until spring. Divide every three years when the growths become too dense.

— Chelones may need twiggy sticks for support in exposed positions.

Height: 50–60 cm (20–24 in).
Spacing and planting distance: 20 cm (8 in).
Soil: rich and moist in summer.
Cultivation: sun and shade.
Propagation: by division in spring.
Flowering season: August, September.
Type: perennial.

△ *Chelone obliqua*
▽ *Chionodoxa luciliae*

△ *Chionodoxa gigantea*

Chionodoxa

CHIONODOXA/GLORY-OF-THE-SNOW

Liliaceae

Chionodoxa is very easy to cultivate and deserves to be more widely appreciated. As with the crocus and the snowdrop, the flowering season, two weeks in April, is short but the light or luminous blue star-like flowers are worth the trouble. They can be grown in short grass, at the front of borders or on rock gardens.

Useful hints

— Plant the tiny bulbs in groups of from 5–7 into a rich light garden soil. For window-boxes, use a rich mixture of garden soil and compost.

— They combine perfectly with cornute violets and pansies.

Recommended

There are two species: *Chionodoxa gigantea* is bright blue and fairly tall (30 cm – 12 in); *C. luciliae* is a lighter shade. *C. sardensis* has blue flowers with white centres.

Height: 20–30 cm (8–12 in).
Spacing and planting distance: 10 cm (4 in).
Soil: preferably rich and light.
Cultivation: sunny.
Propagation: by division.
Flowering season: April.
Type: bulb.

Chrysanthemum/ Chrysanthemum × Hortorum

CHRYSANTHEMUM

Compositae

Chrysanthemums, ever popular with gardeners, are available in a vast range of brightly coloured annuals and perennials.

Useful hints

— Sow the annuals in April or May either in a cold frame or directly into the ground. Prick out or thin out a month later, leaving intervals of 30 cm (12 in). At the same time, pinch the main stem. Water regularly and position a few hazel branches to give support. Extend the flowering by removing dead heads from time to time.

— Plant the perennials in spring or even in June and July if they have been in pots waiting for their turn to come. Water a few times to help them to get started. Once the stems have reached a height of 40 cm (16 in), pinch the stems half way up. Should white patches appear on the foliage, treat with a triforine-based anti-oidium product. When the foliage dies in winter, protect the roots with a few armfuls of straw which can then be removed in spring. The white Shasta daisy is perfectly hardy.

— Chrysanthemums are suitable for growing as pot plants outside, in the greenhouse or in the home, on rock gardens or amongst mixed borders.

Recommended

— **annuals**: Carinatum hybrids which have flowers in the form of concentric circles of contrasting colours, 'Burridge' being the most popular at the moment. Alternatively, the chrysanthemums double, still referred to as 'Korean', are excellent for bouquets. Also of note are the small *Chrysanthemum paludosum* which is white with a yellow heart and its cousin, *C. multicaule*, which is pure yellow. These go particularly well in borders.

— **summer-flowering perennials**: feverfew (*C. parthenium*) which is better for bouquets than the flower bed; the Shasta daisy (*C. maximum*) which is still labelled *Leucanthemum* in quite a few nurseries. Cultivars include: 'Wirral Supreme' with very large double flowers; 'Petite Princesse d'Argent' which is only 30 cm (12 in) high; 'Etoile d'Anvers' an old favourite that is still in fashion; *C. haradjanii* with fern-like

△ *Chrysanthemum frutescens*
◁ *Chrysanthemum* hybrid
▽ Naturalized chrysanthemums

Florists' chrysanthemum △
Chrysanthemum frutescens ▽

△ *Chrysanthemum maximum*
◁ *Chrysanthemum* hybrid
◁ *Chrysanthemum uliginosum*
Chrysanthemum carinatum ▽

△ **Chrysanthemum** hybrid
▽ **Chrysanthemum** rubellum

silvery grey foliage; finally, *C. parthenium*, also with decorative silvery grey foliage but growing to twice the height of the previous example.

— **autumn-flowering perennials**: *C. rubellum* forms whole cushions of flowers: 'Clara Curtis', pink; 'Lady Brockett', apricot; 'Mary Stoker', soft yellow. *C. coreanum*, the Korean chrysanthemums, are slightly later: 'La Perle', pure white; 'Isabella', beige; 'Red Velvet', a purplish-blue double. Also noteworthy is *C. uliginosum* which grows to over 2 m (80 in), forming a cloud of white flowers. Then there are the large-flowered hybrids so often seen in cemeteries, but that's another story... Some anemone-flowered types together with others as finely petalled as the florist's 'Spider' are worth lifting in November and replanting the following year. The florist's varieties need to be grown in a frame but it is difficult to force them to flower outside their normal autumn season.

Height: 20–200 cm (8–80 in).
Spacing and planting distance: 20–50 cm (8–20 in).
Soil: rich and moist.
Cultivation: sunny.
Propagation: in spring from seed or cuttings, or by division.
Flowering season: June to December.
Type: annual and perennial.

Cimicifuga

BUGBANE
Ranunculaceae

Cimicifuga flourishes in the wilder parts of the garden. Its flowers are reminiscent of the astilbes but are always pure white. Planted together with fuschias, hortensias and ferns, they create an atmosphere of freshness.

Useful hints

— Plant widely spaced in spring.

— Mulch the soil at the beginning of summer with grass cuttings or well-rotted dead leaves.

— Divide every five years when the growths become too large.

Recommended

— *Cimicifuga dahurica* flowers at the beginning of autumn with long thin spikes.

— *C. racemosa* is somewhat larger than the previous example and the fuller plumes bend gracefully. The odour is somewhat unpleasant.

Height: 80–150 cm (32–60 in).
Spacing and planting distance: 40–50 cm (16–20 in).
Soil: deep and moist in summer.
Cultivation: semi-shade, sun if the soil is damp.
Propagation: by division in spring.
Flowering season: July to October.
Type: perennial.

Cimicifuga dahurica ▷
Cimicifuga racemosa ▽

Clarkia

CLARKIA/GODETIA

Onagraceae

Direct sowing produces masses of flowers. Each plant forms a little pyramid terminating in silky spikes of pink, white or red. *Clarkia elegans* are magnificent in combination but, as they do not last for very long, they need to be mixed with earlier plants like oriental poppy and later ones such as aster.

Useful hints

— Sow directly in April, having first loosened up the soil and spread a 2 cm (1 in) layer of good compost. Tap down the soil with the back of a rake just after sowing.

— Thin out a month later, leaving 20 cm (8 in) intervals and transplant any surplus growths into another bed.

— They can also be sown in September, October with the plants being kept in a frame over the winter period. When planted out in March, they will flower a month earlier than the others.

Height: 40–50 cm (16–20 in).
Spacing and planting distance: 20 cm (8 in).
Soil: ordinary.
Cultivation: sunny.
Propagation: from seed in spring or autumn.
Flowering season: from June to the first frosts, for a good month.
Type: annual.

Clarkia elegans **hybrid** ▷
Cleome spinosa ▽

Cleome

SPIDER FLOWER

Capparidaceae/Capparaceae

One of the most beautiful of the annuals, *Cleome spinosa* has prominent corollas crowned throughout July with tufts in every shade of pink. It has a slightly disagreeable smell but this should not prevent its use in combination with decorative tobacco plants and old-fashioned varieties of rose.

Useful hints

— Sow under cover in trays at the beginning of March, using a light compost. Transplant the young growths in May.

— Water regularly during the hot weather.

Height: 70 cm (28 in).
Spacing and planting distance: 20 cm (8 in).
Soil: ordinary.
Cultivation: sunny.
Propagation: from seed.
Flowering season: June to the end of September.
Type: annual.

Clivia

KAFFIR LILY/NATAL LILY

Amaryllidaceae

With lustrous green foliage, the bearing of a giant leek and spectacular flowers, *Clivia* is extremely decorative. It flowers very early in spring and requires only little attention. *Clivia miniata* needs a milder climate to survive in the garden and so, as with the agapanthus, is generally best kept as a pot plant.

Useful hints

— Plant in good garden soil to which two spadefuls of well-rotted compost have been added per plant.

— Water well during the hot weather but not at all in winter. This is the secret for successful flowering every year.

Height: 40 cm (16 in).
Spacing and planting distance: 30 cm (12 in).
Soil: ordinary.
Cultivation: sunny.
Propagation: by division.
Flowering season: April.
Type: perennial.

▽ *Clivia miniata*

Cobaea

COBAEA/CUP-AND-SAUCER PLANT
Polemoniaceae

Although *Cobaea scandens* has fine colours and forms, germinates easily and grows vigorously over everything within reach, it is in some ways a disappointment. Rare indeed are the occasions when it is in full bloom and, even then, the flowers start off green and do not open until September just before the frosts that will sound their death knell. As a plant for the veranda, however, they are first rate. The white variety is not recommended as the flowers do not stand out against the foliage.

Useful hints

— Sow in March or April in pots and then plant out in May, taking care not to damage the roots.

— Water regularly in summer. Add a little liquid manure but not too much as *Cobaea* does not require too rich a nourishment.

— Once fully grown, the plant is supported on its own tendrils. Up to a height of 50 cm (20 in) or so, however, it should be staked.

— As a verandah plant, it should be pruned every spring to renew the foliage. Better still, however, is to grow again from seed each year as it prospers better when cultivated as an annual.

Height: up to 6 m (20 ft).
Spacing and planting distance: 1 m (40 in) or in pots of 30 cm (12 in) diameter.
Soil: moist in summer.
Cultivation: sunny (will grow but not flower in the shade).
Propagation: from seed in spring.
Flowering season: end of summer.
Type: annual.

Cobaea scandens ▷

Codonopsis

CODONOPSIS

Campanulaceae

To see inside the tiny bells of this flower, you really need to get down to ground level. The creamy background is splashed with violet like certain types of Chinese porcelain. Unfortunately, the foliage of *Codonopsis clematidea* gives off a foxy odour if bruised.

Useful hints

— Plant in spring if possible, marking the spot carefully with a durable label. If not, there is a danger that this late starter will fall victim to a misplaced stroke of the hoe.

— Every year, add a handful of good compost to the root. Water in hot weather. As it is a semi-creeper, codonopsis likes to entwine itself in other plants such as lavender, *Santolina* or even a dwarf rose bush.

Height: 60–80 cm (24–32 in).
Spacing and planting distance: 20 cm (8 in).
Soil: leaf-mould and coarse sand.
Cultivation: semi-shade.
Propagation: by division in spring.
Flowering season: June, July.
Type: perennial.

Colchicum speciosum **'Waterlily'** ▷
Colchicum autumnale ▷
▽ ***Codonopsis clematidea***

112

Colchicum

COLCHICUM/NAKED BOY, SHOWY AUTUMN CROCUS, MEADOW SAFFRON

Liliaceae

A plant of lawn and meadow, colchicum flowers in the autumn. As all varieties are very poisonous, they are not recommended for growers with children.

Useful hints

— They will grow in any good garden soil but much prefer moist ground.

— Plant in April or May for autumn flowering.

Recommended

— *Colchicum autumnale* is a native of our water meadows and it exists in lilac pink and white varieties. *C. bizantium* originates from Turkey and produces more flowers per bulb *C. cilicium*, also from Turkey, has a darker colouring.

— The hybrids are numerous: 'Lilac Wonder', very late amethyst flowers; 'The Giant', with appropriately large corollas; 'Violet Queen', bright violet; 'Waterlily', with soft pink double flowers like those of the nymphœas.

— Among its many peculiarities, *C. luteum* is the only yellow colchicum and the only one to flower in spring. People usually prefer to grow it in pots as it is not reliably hardy. It is, however, a valuable rarity.

Height: 15 cm (6 in).
Spacing and planting distance: 20 cm (8 in).
Soil: ordinary but moist.
Cultivation: sunny.
Propagation: division of offsets.
Flowering season: autumn.
Type: bulb.

▽ *Colchicum speciosum 'Album'*

△ *Colchicum* 'Lilac Wonder'
▽ *Convallaria majalis*

Convallaria

LILY OF THE VALLEY

Liliaceae

Convollaria is most at home in deep, moist, slightly clayey soils, forming easily managed displays together with columbines, peonies and snowdrops.

Useful hints

— To be sure of flowering by 1st May, plant fist-sized clumps in flower pots filled with well-rotted compost and then water regularly.

— Every three years, divide the growths which otherwise are too invasive.

Height: 20 cm (8 in).
Spacing and planting distance: 20 cm (8 in).
Soil: ordinary, tending to clay.
Cultivation: semi-shade.
Propagation: by division of rhizome.
Flowering season: April, May.
Type: perennial.

Convolvulus mauritanicus △

Convolvulus cneorum △

Convolvulus

BINDWEED/GLORYBIND

Convolvulaceae

There is a vast difference between the common bindweed and the marvellous *Convolvulus cneorum* and *C. mauritanicus*. The former develops into a small grey bush studded with white flowers throughout the summer while the latter is a ground creeper that dons a mantle of sky-blue corollas. Being semi-hardy, they need protection from winter rains.

Useful hints

— Plant in April, May into a pocket of good well-drained soil to which sand may be added.

— Water once a week through the summer, stopping in October to slow down their metabolism.

— Cuttings taken in July and rooted in sand take off very quickly and can easily be kept in a frame through the winter.

Recommended

Morning glory (*C. tricolor*) can be grown by any beginner. The large seeds grow rapidly to form clumps that are covered with flowers arranged in contrasting concentric rings, the blossoms opening in the morning and closing in the afternoon. All varieties have a yellow throat. If possible install with a south-westerly aspect.

Height: 50 cm (20 in) for *C. cneorum*, 15 cm (6 in) for *C. mauritanicus*.
Spacing and planting distance: 25 cm (10 in).
Soil: light and well-drained.
Cultivation: direct full sun or the flowers will not open.
Propagation: from cuttings in summer.
Flowering season: from June to the first frosts.
Type: perennial.

Coreopsis

TICKWEED/COREOPSIS

Compositae

For anyone who likes pure yellow, the coreopsis are indispensable. Some are annuals (*Coreopsis tinctoria* and *C. drummondii*) while others are perennial (*C. grandiflora* and *C. verticillata*). The former are delicate and short-lived while the latter are more robust. All varieties appreciate deep soils that remain moist in summer.

Useful hints

— **annuals**: sow in March, April either directly in place or in a pan for planting out a month later. Pinch the young plants half way up the stem during May to force them to fill out. Remove the dead flowers as the large seeds will soon drain the plant of all vigour.

— **perennials**: plant in spring after enriching the soil with leaf-mould. Leave the dead foliage during the winter and do not remove until the following April.

Recommended

— *Coreopsis drummondii* has given rise to some interesting varieties, including 'Couronne d'Or' which has a maroon heart.

— The most elegant is *C. tinctoria* which carries its flowers very high on fine stems and can be dispersed in beds to lighten the general effect.

— *C. grandiflora*, though well-known, is somewhat disappointing, producing so many flowers that they die off very quickly towards the end of summer. Do not use with a soil too rich in humus or the leaves will be disproportionately large.

Coreopsis drummondii △
Cortaderia selloana **'Pumila'** ▷

— *C. verticillata* has none of the disadvantages of the previous examples and should find a place in any garden. Even without flowers, it has a pleasing aspect though this period is itself short since few plants bloom so abundantly.

Height: 40–60 cm (16–24 in).
Spacing and planting distance: 30 cm (12 in).
Soil: ordinary to fairly rich.
Cultivation: full sunlight
Propagation: from seed in spring for the annuals and by division at the same time for perennials.
Flowering season: from June to the first frosts.
Type: annual, perennial.

Cortaderia

PAMPAS GRASS

Graminaceae/Gramineae

The creamy plumes of pampas grass (formerly *Gynerium*) have now been popular in gardens for over three decades. Make any decision carefully because once installed, it is there to stay.

Useful hints

— It is not fussy about soil or climate and will flourish in any garden.

— After three years, use a sharp spade to divide the growths which will otherwise grow too large.

— Cut the plumes in autumn to make bouquets that will keep for a long time in a cool room.

— Cover the root stock with a sheet of plastic in October, having first pruned the stems. Remove in April.

Height: 1.5 m (60 in).
Spacing and planting distance: 1.5 m (60 in).
Soil: ordinary.
Cultivation: any.
Propagation: by division of root stock.
Flowering season: July to November.
Type: perennial.

Corydalis

FUMITORY/CORYDALIS, FUMEWORT

Papaveraceae/Fumariaceae

A few handfuls of soil in some crevice of a dry stone wall or flight of steps will be enough for these two varieties of fumitory. The yellow is almost a weed but its cousin, *cashmeriana*, is a jewel that requires endless effort.

Useful hints

— Pick a few stems of yellow corydalis during the summer and then replant carefully, watering regularly. Spontaneous reseeding will occur, the seedlings then being planted out as required. Take care, however, as they are very invasive.

— *Corydalis cashmeriana* should be planted in spring in the semi-shade and provided with a pocket of good sandy soil. During winter, protect with a pane of glass or a plastic sheet. As a precaution, take some seed that can be sown in October and left in a cold frame through the winter. The plants can then be lifted in spring and planted out in May.

△ *Corydalis lutea*
▽ *Corydalis cashmeriana*

Recommended

— *Corydalis lutea* flowers for nine months out of twelve in successive waves and the blooms are beautifully set off by fine blue-green foliage.

— The blue flowers of *C. cashmeriana* can only be described in superlatives and are a rarity that marks the grower as an expert.

Height: 15–20 cm (6–8 in).
Spacing and planting distance: 20 cm (8 in).
Soil: rich and well-drained.
Cultivation: at least 6 hours sun per day.
Propagation: from seed.
Flowering season: April to December.
Type: perennial.

115

Cosmos bipinnatus △

Cosmos atrosanguineus △
Crambe ▷

Cosmos

COSMEA/COSMOS

Compositae

This is a summer-flowering annual whose plumed foliage sets off flowers in primary colours from purple to pure white. The delicate fragrance comes from the foliage. As almost nothing can go wrong, they are a good flower for beginners.

Useful hints

— Sowing is easy because the seeds are so large – space them a couple of inches apart as growth is rapid. Sow in April using either a frame or the corner of a radiator. Prick out a month later either in pots or directly in place into ordinary soil that has been well dug over. Water plentifully and remove any dead leaves to promote healthy growth.

— Yellow cosmos is more tricky, needing a little heat at the moment of sowing or requiring a wait until May to sow directly in place. Thin out a month later, pinching the stems half way up to get the plants to fill out.

Recommended

— The best known is *Cosmos bipinnatus* of which 'Sensation Mixed' displays a single line of petals while 'Sunset' has a single deep red colour on semi-double flowers.

— Yellow and orange are to be found in the flowers of *C. sulphureus* which is more open and less hardy than the previous examples. The semi-doubles 'Bright Lights' and 'Klondyke' are the most popular.

— Still a rarity is *C. atrosanguineus* which looks more like a single-flowered dahlia than a cosmos. The brownish flowers smell of chocolate. They have to be cultivated like dahlias, i.e. the tuberous root must be brought inside during the winter.

Height: 60–140 cm (24–56 in).
Spacing and planting distance: 30 cm (12 in).
Soil: ordinary.
Cultivation: sunny.
Propagation: from seed or by division of rhizome (*C. atrosanguineus*).
Flowering season: June to the frosts.
Type: annual and perennial.

116

Crambe

CRAMBE

Cruciferae

A rare and spectacular plant, *Crambe* brings a cloud of thousands of tiny delicate flowers to any bed of perennials. Though difficult to find in nurseries, it is by no means difficult to grow. Despite its height, *Crambe* needs no staking but stands solidly on its own stem. It is ideal for use as a specimen plant, or ringed by much smaller plants.

Useful hints

— It needs a sunny situation and is ideal for seaside gardens.

— Place in a well-drained bed enriched with well-rotted compost. A sandy soil is almost certain to succeed.

— As it can also tolerate limy ground, any soil type will do provided that it is light.

— In a small garden, it is spectacular enough to be given the place of honour. Otherwise, ensure that the bed or border is at least 1 m (40 in) wide.

Height: 120 cm (52 in).
Spacing and planting distance: 1 m (40 in).
Soil: ordinary.
Cultivation: sunny.
Propagation: by division.
Flowering season: June and July.
Type: perennial.

Crepis

HAWK'S BEARD

Compositae

Looking rather like a weed, *Crepis aurea* may well be relegated to some dry corner where the soil is poor. However, it is there that it will flourish and, if the flowers resemble small orange dandelions, they are still a better sight than bare earth.

Useful hints

— Dig over the ground before planting in spring to allow the roots to go deep.

— In summer, cut back flush with the ground to force new stems to emerge. At this time, cover with straw and well-rotted compost, this mixture removing the chore of watering.

— Beware of self-seeding, as *Crepis* is very invasive.

△ *Crepis incana*

Height: 15–35 cm (6–15 in).
Spacing and planting distance: 20 cm (8 in).
Soil: any, rather poor but well-drained.
Cultivation: sunny.
Propagation: by division in March or from seed in spring.
Flowering season: summer.
Type: perennial.

Crinum × powelli

CRINUM

Amaryllidaceae

Like agapanthus and *Clivia*, *Crinum* loves mild climates. It will, however, survive the winter if covered with an armful of dead leaves in autumn. *Crinum* will provide good company for climbing roses, Californian lilacs and a number of perennials since its delicately scented flowers are a delight with clusters of trumpets like tiny pink lilies.

Useful hints

— Plant at least 15 cm (6 in) under a good garden soil enriched with two spadefuls of leaf-mould.

— Protect in autumn by covering with dead leaves and placing a plank on top.

Height: 30 cm (12 in).
Spacing and planting distance: 30 cm (12 in).
Soil: ordinary, rich.
Cultivation: sunny.
Propagation: bulb separation.
Flowering season: July, August.
Type: bulb.

Crocosmia ▷
Crinum × powelii ▽

Crocosmia

CROCOSMIA

Iridaceae

Crocosmia (synonym: *Montbretia*) has become naturalized in mild climates. The flowers are a gaudy orange or red and the plant spreads with great rapidity. Crocosmia are particularly good for use as cut flowers.

Useful hints

— Plant the bulbs, which resemble a miniature gladiolus, in autumn, giving them a good, preferably sandy, garden soil.

— For the first year, protect them with a layer of dead leaves.

— Plant in groups of 10–12 for a spectacular effect.

Recommended

The best known is *Crocosmia × crocosmiiflora* which has orange or sometimes yellow flowers. A more imposing variety is *C. masonorum* which is reddish-orange.

Height: 60 cm (24 in).
Spacing and planting distance: 15 cm (6 in).
Soil: light and well-drained.
Cultivation: sunny.
Propagation: division of bulbs.
Flowering season: June to October.
Type: bulb.

118

Crocus

CROCUS

Iridaceae

Everyone is familiar with the spring crocus which breaks the monotony of winter and heralds the return of life. A place must also be reserved, however, for the autumn crocuses which are an even deeper mauve than the colchicums with which they are sometimes confused. Plant them by the dozen as they require massing to show up to good effect. They are perfect company for *Iris reticulata*, primula and the small botanic narcissi.

Useful hints

— Plant in good ordinary garden soil that has been enriched with a handful of general purpose fertilizer per square metre or square yard. Place the bulbs gently at a depth of 5 cm (2 in) and at intervals of 10 cm (4 in). This must be done before the end of December which is when their growth begins. Crocuses bought later than this are often hollow.

— Autumn crocuses are planted in August, September for flowering in the following year. Water the soil the night before to loosen it. During the summer, the crocus is at rest and loses its foliage entirely. They can be placed to good effect in rockeries or among spring flowers such as spreading phlox for example.

— Allow crocuses to become well-established, not dividing the patches unless flowering appears to weaken.

Recommended

— **Spring crocuses**: there are three main groups: *Crocus chrysanthus* blooms very early with small flowers and is resistant to bad weather. 'Advance' (cream and violet), 'Blue Pearl' (blue and silver) 'Zwanenburg Bronze' (golden yellow and brown) are the best varieties. The second group, *C. vernus*, is more popular, having larger flowers. Good varieties include: 'Yellow Giant', 'Pickwick' (white with a blue stripe) and 'Vanguard' (light blue) which opens at the same time as 'Yellow Giant' and combines well with it. The third group includes many botanic species (i.e. ones that have retained their natural characteristics). The flowers are generally average to small while the colours are bright. They are often sold in mixtures.

— **Autumn crocuses**: the flowering season is from September to December. The best known varieties include *C.*

Crocus sativus △
***Crocus* hybrid** ▷

ochroleucus (creamy white), *C. pulchellus* 'Zephyr' (white tinged with pearly grey) and *C. sativus* (pinky white to pale lilac) the pistils of which are used to produce the spice saffron.

Height: 10–15 cm (4–6 in).
Spacing and planting distance: 10 cm (4 in).
Soil: ordinary, preferably well-drained.
Cultivation: at least 6 hours sun per day.
Propagation: separation of corms in summer.
Flowering season: September to April.
Type: corm.

119

△ *Cucurbita pepo*

△ *Cuphuea cyanea*

Cucurbita pepo

COLOCYNTH/ORNAMENTAL GOURDS

Cucurbitaceae

These annuals are so easy that children will enjoy growing them. Like its cousins, the edible gourds squash and pumpkin, *Colocynth* needs only sunshine and a good rich soil to produce its large and curiously striped or bossed fruit.

Useful hints

— Sow in May in a tray of compost shielded with a pane of glass. Transplant a month later into a pocket of well-rotted manure next to a trellis or railing in some sunny spot. Water thoroughly during the summer.

— Gather the ripe fruit and leave to dry in a cool dark place. They can be waxed to make interesting compositions.

Height: 2 m (80 in).
Spacing and planting distance: 50 cm (20 in).
Soil: rich.
Cultivation: sunny.
Propagation: from seed.
Flowering season: autumn.
Type: annual.

Cuphea

CUPHEA/CIGARFLOWER

Lythraceae

Though still relatively unknown, *Cuphea cyanea* makes a splendid summer-flowering addition to the garden with its tubular-shaped blooms a mixture of scarlet and violet blue. It can be used to good effect in window-boxes.

Useful hints

— Plant in mid-May when there is no longer any danger of frost. A rich light soil (half sand, half leaf-mould) is required.

— Add liquid manure every three weeks and remove the dead flowers regularly.

— During the summer, take cuttings from the base of the stem and place in sand. They can be kept over winter in a warm well-lit place. This is more effective than bringing in the parent plants which quickly degenerate.

Height: 30–40 cm (12–16 in).
Spacing and planting distance: 25 cm (10 in).
Soil: light and fertile.

Cultivation: at least 6 hours sun per day.
Propagation: from cuttings in summer.
Flowering season: all summer.
Type: annual, hardy in warm and temperate climates.

Cyclamen

CYCLAMEN

Primulaceae

For ground cover in semi-shade, there is nothing better than the star-like foliage of cyclamens that is often edged with silver. With a careful choice of varieties, there will be something to see from spring to autumn. The flowers are as light as butterflies and their fragrance bears a hint of violet. This should be some consolation for the long months when there is nothing to be seen above ground but dead foliage and the bare spires from the base of the flowers. Combine white-flowered periwinkles and lamiums with your cyclamen to make the best use of space.

Useful hints

— Plant in a soil enriched with leaf-mould and perhaps two spadefuls of well-rotted compost per square metre or yard. Leave them for years without hoeing as spontaneous seeding is common. If the carpet becomes too thick, remove a few bulbs while they are at rest and replant elsewhere in the garden. The curved face of the bulb should be facing downwards.

— Sowing is possible with fresh seed, the first flowers appearing after two years.

Recommended

— Cyclamens flower, for the most part, at the beginning of September. *Cyclamen hederifolium* and *C. purpurascens*, however, both flower from summer to autumn in pale pink or carmine against foliage like that of the splashed ivies. Their bulbs may grow to the size of a plate. *C. hederifolium* and *C. cilicium* both naturalize very easily.

— Less well-known than the previous examples are the spring cyclamens which are the rivals of the violet. Here, the most common are *C. coum* and *C. repandum*. The source of all the florist's cyclamens, *C. persicum*, has larger leaves than the others and these are often slightly silvery. Their fragrance recalls that of lily-of-the-valley.

— In warm and temperate climates, miniature cyclamens can be grown outside in pots. They are very close to the botanic cyclamens and bear numerous tiny flowers. The seeds, however, are

△ *Cyclamen repandum*
▽ *Cyclamen coum*

very expensive and take two years to come into bloom.

Height: 10–40 cm (4–16 in).
Spacing and planting distance: 20 cm (8 in).
Soil: rich in humus.
Cultivation: semi-shade.
Propagation: from seed in autumn.
Flowering season: in every season if full range of species is grown.
Type: bulb.

△ *Cynara carduncullus*

Cynara carduncullus

CARDOON

Composaceae/Compositae

The cardoon or edible thistle makes a fine plant as well as a traditional meal. They can be planted at the back of a bed or even in front of a hedge where the almost metallic foliage will show off to good effect. The flowers are like those of the artichoke and go well in bouquets of both fresh and dried flowers. The soil must be rich and well-drained in a sunny and sheltered position. A pretty combination is a mixture of cardoon and 'Queen Elizabeth' roses.

Useful hints

— In spring, sow the seed in fives in a warm place. Transplant a month after shoots appear or leave in place and get rid of any sickly plants. Protect from the cold by earthing up in November.

— Water in hot weather and treat against greenfly.

Height: 1.5–2 m (60–80 in).
Spacing and planting distance: 1 m (40 in).
Soil: very rich, dry in winter.
Cultivation: sunny, foot of south-facing wall.
Propagation: from seed or by division in spring.
Flowering season: from summer to autumn.
Type: annual.

△ *Cynoglossum*

Cynoglossum

HOUND'S TONGUE/CHINESE FORGET-ME-NOT

Boraginaceae

Cynoglossum is very like a giant myosotis, having the same slightly rough leaves and the same china blue colour. The only difference is the larger size and a later flowering, right at the beginning of summer. This timing allows some excellent combinations, notably with montbretias.

Useful hints

— Plant *Cynoglossum nervosum* in autumn or spring, preferably in the semi-shade. Place a dozen together to form a solid patch.

— After flowering, cut back with lawn shears to encourage new foliage.

— In September, divide any growths that are too large and replant the excess elsewhere.

Height: 40–60 cm (16–24 in).
Spacing and planting distance: 25 cm (10 in).
Soil: humus-rich and moist in summer.
Cultivation: semi-shade.
Propagation: by division in autumn.
Flowering season: June, July.
Type: perennial.

Cyperus

PAPYRUS

Cyperaceae

At the water's edge, *Cyperus* produces long supple stems that are green and topped with radiating leaves. In warm climates, it is the perfect companion for Siberian iris, arums and bamboo. In colder regions, it must be kept inside during the winter if it is to survive.

Useful hints

— Although *Cyperus* grows readily from cuttings, a leaf cut off flush with the stem will take root in a glass of water. It is recommended, however, to propagate by division which is easy and much quicker.

Recommended

— Though there are over 550 species of *Cyperus*, few are hardy enough to last through moderate northern winters. One example is *Cyperus eragrostis* which looks very like the popular indoor 'papyrus' (*C. alternifolius*) so beloved of cats. *C. longus* forms dense metre-high (40 in) colonies with reddish brown flowers and dangerously sharp leaves.

Height: 60–120 cm (24–48 in).
Spacing and planting distance: 30 cm (12 in).
Soil: ordinary, wet.
Cultivation: sunny.
Propagation: from cuttings and by division.
Flowering season: from summer to autumn.
Type: perennial.

◁ ***Cyperus***
▽ ***Cypripedium calceolus***
Cypripedium reginae ▷

122

Cypripedium

LADY'S SLIPPER

Orchidaceae

Lady's slipper is customarily the sign of refinement in a garden since growing requires care and assiduity. Unless, of course, conditions are ideal and then they can be quite invasive. In this case, you will be enchanted every spring by the sight of these slipper-like flowers with their strange waxy texture.

Useful hints

— Only buy plants raised in pots and not with bare roots. Plant out in spring as soon as the first shoots appear. Provide a humus-rich soil, pure leaf-mould if possible.

— Put down anti-slug pellets in April and May.

— Water at least once a fortnight in summer and allow the dead flowers to seed.

— After a few years when the growths have become very thick, they should be divided carefully in March/April.

Best varieties

— *Cyprepedium calceolus*, a native plant facing extinction, is a mixture of yellow and brown. It appreciates a slightly limy soil and can tolerate a sunny position.

— *Cypredium reginae* originally came from North America and it prefers acid woodland soils that are a reminder of its native forests. It can reach and, indeed, exceed 60 cm (24 in).

Height: 30–60 cm (12–24 in).
Spacing and planting distance: 15–20 cm (6–8 in).
Soil: rich in humus.
Cultivation: semi-shade under deciduous trees.
Propagation: by division in spring.
Flowering season: June, July.
Type: perennial.

Daboecia cantabrica ▷

Daboecia

DABOECIA

Ericaceae

The daboecias are related to the heathers and differ from them chiefly in terms of their flowers which are like little rugby balls in varying shades from white to violet. Not quite hardy, they need a maritime climate to flourish. Give them a good covering of dead leaves or coarse pine bark to protect the root.

Useful hints

— Plant in September or March and water regularly during the first year. Put down a 5 cm (2 in) layer of peat before the mid-summer hot weather.

— Every spring, clean up the plants by removing withered stems.

— Combine the daboecias with other autumn-flowering heathers.

Height: 40–60 cm (16–24 in).
Spacing and planting distance: 30 cm (12 in).
Soil: rich in humus and without lime.
Cultivation: sunny.
Propagation: tricky, from cuttings in winter.
Flowering season: from May to September in successive waves.
Type: perennial.

Dahlia

DAHLIA

Compositae

There is a patronizing attitude in some quarters to dahlias but what other plant can boast such a variety of forms and flowers with a robust constitution? They should be given a place not only in principal beds to balance the effect of gauras and cleomes but also in the kitchen garden where, in good soil and in the company of vegetables, they stand out like giants.

Useful hints

— Start them in March, placed in pots over a radiator and in direct light. Otherwise, wait until May before planting according to the orientation of the buds. Dahlias are not worth buying after May because they seldom prosper. Check that there are living buds on the remaining parts of the previous year's stems.

— Mulch the soil in June and water well, putting down anti-slug pellets from time to time. The addition of liquid manure will help to promote generous flowering.

— When the foliage turns colour after the first frost, dig up the root together with a little soil and leave to dry in the cellar until the next spring. In this way, it will be possible to sow single-flowered dahlias and then collect tubers for the colours that are the most pleasing. Sowing takes place in March in a warm place.

Recommended

— Dahlias are classified according to form and flower.

— **Decorative dahlias**: The flowers are flat, double and often very large. Our choices are: 'Arc de Triomphe', orange yellow; 'Banquise', pure white; 'Brazil', orange and white; 'Deuil du Roi Albert', violet and white, a very old favourite; 'Le Nil', superb yellow; 'Londres', shocking pink; 'Tropique', vermilion red.

— **Cactus dahlias**: The flowers end in points. The large-flowered varieties went out of fashion but are making a come-back with: 'Cithare', salmon pink; 'Le Niger', mahogany black; 'Folies de Dentelle', mauve pink; 'Cheerio', red with white spots. The 'Princess' series is also worthy of note with very light flowers on a fairly small plant. 'Park Princess' is bright pink and there are also reds and oranges.

△ *Dahlia* 'NS merveilles'
◁ *Dahlia* pompon 'Eclaireur'
Dahlia pompon miniature ▷
▽ *Dahlia* mignon

△ *Dahlia* **nain**

— **Pompon dahlias**: These are superb for bouquets where they will last for a week if the water is changed every day. Among the best are: 'Chopin', mauve violet; 'Liszt', dark red; 'Valencia', coppery orange; 'Kochelsee', scarlet red.

— **Double-flowered dwarf dahlias**: They are lighter than the decorative types and the flowers are similar to those of the rudbeckia doubles. Those preferred are: 'Cosette', salmon pink; 'Fanny', bright yellow; 'Perle des Jardins', pink; 'Petit Pierre', red with bronze foliage.

— **Single-flowered dwarf dahlias**: As flowering continues over several months, they are indispensable for display beds. Good varieties are: 'Chaperon Rouge' and 'Etoile d'Or', both bright yellow; 'Féerie', pink; 'Roxy', fluorescent lilac against a bronze foliage

— **Anemone-flowered dahlias**: The heart is tightly ruched. The most common in the catalogues are: 'Guinea', pure yellow; 'Inca', ruby-red and silver; 'Roulette', soft pink with a yellow heart.

— The 'Topmix' dahlias are robust and, as they are available in all the main colours, can be used to good effect in window-boxes or at the edge of beds.

— There is an almost endless list of other varieties with such names as: camellia-flowered dahlia, water-lily dahlia, giraffe-dahlia and even orchid-dahlia. In general, their appearance is disappointing.

Height: 30–160 cm (12–64 in).
Spacing and planting distance: 20–50 cm (8–20 in).
Soil: rich and moist at all times.
Cultivation: sunny.
Propagation: by division in spring.
Flowering season: June to the first frosts.
Type: annual, bulb.

125

Datura metel △   *Delphinium* 'Cliverton Beauty' △

Datura

DATURA
Solanaceae

The exotic perfume and vast trumpets of the datura evoke the tropical jungles which were its original home. There are arborescent varieties but we will look only at the annuals and one near perennial. In the garden, they can be displayed in large earthenware pots or placed together with banana and castor-oil plants. One note of caution: the foliage is extremely poisonous.

Useful hints

— They should be sown, like tomatoes, in a heated greenhouse in March. Let them adjust to the outside temperatures gradually and avoid planting out until May. They need a very rich soil with frequent watering and liberal additions of liquid manure.

— As soon as the flowers have faded, cut the prickly fruit unless they are wanted for displays of dried flowers.

Recommended

— The so-called Egyptian datura (*Datura metel*) in fact comes from India. It will readily grow to 1.20 m (48 in) in a season and bears creamy-white flowers that are nearly 20 cm (8 in) across. More common is the double-flowered 'Fastuosa' which has a strong scent and purple on the underside of the petals.

— *D. meteloides* is almost hardy and will flower from the root-stock in spring if it has been covered with 20 cm (8 in) of straw and a plastic sheet. It reseeds freely in the surrounding area. The flowers are white with a suggestion of pink and they remain for much of the summer.

Height: 60–120 cm (24–48 in).
Spacing and planting distance: 30 cm (12 in).
Soil: rich in humus and always moist.
Cultivation: sunny.
Propagation: from seed in March, under glass.
Flowering season: July to October.
Type: annual.

Delphinium

DELPHINIUM/LARKSPUR
Ranunculaceae

The highly characteristic silhouette of the delphinium brings substance to any flowerbed. The annuals make delightful cut flowers reminiscent of bouquets composed with wild plants. The perennials, on the other hand, are more majestic and can be used to create settings in company with various rosebushes. The beauty, however, has to be earned as they are relatively demanding plants to grow.

Useful hints

— **annuals**: Also called larkspur, they should be planted directly in position during March, April. Thin out the seedlings a month later, ensuring that they are always well watered. Flowering begins in June and lasts for six weeks. Sowing is also possible in September, at the foot of a wall exposed to the sun. The young plants will tolerate moderate

126

△ *Delphinium* 'Tessa'

△ *Delphinium cardinale*

△ *Delphinium zalil*
◁ *Delphinium* 'Giant Pacific'
▽ *Delphinium* hybrid
Delphinium 'Summer Skies' ▽

frosts and they develop quickly in spring.

— **perennials**: Plant in September or March, April. Raise for a year in the kitchen garden until they are sufficiently developed to be bedded out. Put down anti-slug pellets regularly in the period from March to May but after that they have nothing to fear. Cut the floral spikes at the end of their season to avoid exhausting the plant.

— The best means of propagation is by division in March, April. They can be grown from seed in the same months but the colours cannot be guaranteed. Flowering occurs after a year.

Recommended

— **annuals**: The hyacinth-flowered doubles, generally dwarf, are good. 'Giant Imperial' makes an interesting cut flower with varieties like 'Blue Spire' (deep blue) and 'Blue Bell' (azure). The flowers are simple but adorned with an upturned spur like that of the columbine.

— **perennials**: Best of all is the 'Pacific' series, bearing the names of figures from the Round Table: 'Black Knight', deep blue; 'Guinevere', mauve pink; 'Galahad', pure white; 'King Arthur', violet . . . All of these examples are over 1.5 m (60 in) whereas the 'Fountains' series offers the same range of colours in plants under that height.

— **hybrids**: The *belladonna* range are more graceful and do not require staking. The slender spikes, moreover, continue to be produced right up to the end of summer. The most common are: 'Lamartine', violet blue; 'Cliverton Beauty', light blue; 'Casa Blanca', white.

— Unlike the preceding examples, the red delphiniums are fussy and do not enjoy sandy soils. They tend to be short-lived. *Delphinium nudicaule* and *D. cardinale* barely reach 60 cm (24 in). *D. zalil* has a beautiful soft yellow but it also does not last for long. The finest of the blues is *D. grandiflorum* (or *D. chinense*). It is a wise precaution to keep seeds on one side in case the plant dies.

Height: 30–180 cm (12–72 in).
Spacing and planting distance: 20–50 cm (8–20 in).
Soil: rich and well-drained.
Cultivation: at least 6 hours of sun per day.
Propagation: from seed or by division in spring.
Flowering season: May to October.
Type: annual and perennial.

127

△ *Dianthus gratianopolitanus*
Dianthus ▷

Dianthus plumarius △
Dianthus alpinus ▷
Dianthus deltoides ▽

Dianthus

PINKS

Carophyllaceae

The pinks seem to have nothing but virtues: bright colours, a rich spicy scent, attractive blue-green foliage and a robust constitution that means they can be grown by beginners. A border of garden pinks alongside some peonies and old roses brings back to mind the gardens of yesteryear.

Useful hints

— Sow in March or April. The annuals will flower immediately but the perennials will often need a whole year to bloom. Sweet-william is sown in June or even in August as this gives better resistance to frosts.

— Garden pinks are best sown in autumn unless the soil is very wet in winter in which case they are best sown in spring. Every spring, bank up the earth around them by adding a few handfuls of compost which helps creepers to root. Immediately after flowering is over, propagate from these rooted creepers or from tip cuttings placed in a sandy mix.

— To produce carnations, remove the lateral buds leaving only the terminal. Stake the stems and water regularly.

Recommended

— **annuals**: China pinks form a carpet of dazzling colours but are completely odourless. Preferable to these are the selected multi-coloured Chabaud pinks or, better still, the classic Marguerite pinks whose flowers do not go too quickly. Sweet-william is more biennial than annual. The doubles last a little longer than the singles. Superb bouquets can be made from the large 'Robustus'.

— **perennials**: The best known are the garden pinks (*Dianthus plumarius*) which are available both as singles and doubles, the fragrant flowers ranging through all shades of red, pink and even bright orange ('Glory'). The deltoid pinks are slightly later and do not exceed 20 cm (8 in), making an excellent border plant of an intense red well exemplified by 'Vampire'. Catalogues still suggest rockery pinks such as: *D. gratianopolitanus*, light pink; *D. alpinus*, pink with carmine centre; *D. arenarius*, white; *D. knappii*, sulphur yellow. Another that is worth noting is *D. superbus*, still fairly common in meadows, with flowers that are slashed with bright pink.

Height: 15–70 cm (6–28 in).
Spacing and planting distance: 15–30 cm (6–12 in).
Soil: well-drained and somewhat limy.
Cultivation: sunny.
Propagation: from seed or by division.
Flowering season: April to August.
Type: annual and perennial.

△ *Diascia cordata*

Diascia

DIASCIA/TWINSPUR

Scrophulariaceae

Diascias are becoming more readily available from nurseries specializing in perennials and they are splendid in rockeries and on paved areas. It is a pity that they are not hardy enough to be used everywhere.

Useful hints

— Plant in spring if possible in company with campanula. The soil should be enriched with peat.

— After the first flowering, cut back to allow a second some two months later.

— Protect from the cold with a pane of glass and a few handfuls of coarse pine bark or rock wool. To be on the safe side, put aside a few cuttings taken in summer and keep in a frame over the winter.

Recommended

Diascia cordata has been eclipsed by 'Ruby Field', a hybrid obtained from itself and *D. barberae*. The colour is a very warm pink.

Height: 15–20 cm (6–8 in).
Spacing and planting distance: 25 cm (10 in).
Soil: ordinary, fairly well drained.
Cultivation: sunny if possible or semi-shade.
Propagation: from cuttings in summer.
Flowering season: from May to the end of the summer.
Type: perennial.

Dianthus 'Waithmans Beauty' ▽

Diascia regescens ▽

129

△ *Dicentra spectabilis*

▽ *Dicentra eximia*

▽ *Dichelostemma ida-maia*

Dicentra

BLEEDING HEART

Fumariceae

Together with the peony, bellflower and myosotis, bleeding heart (*Dicentra spectabilis*, synonym: *Dielytra*) belongs to that indispensable group of plants that is both graceful and uncomplicated. They either like your garden or they don't and there are no two ways about it. They are ideal plants for borders, and the smaller species are good for rockeries.

Useful hints

— For real success, the soil should be rich in humus and fairly moist though exposed to the sun for at least half the day.

— Plant either early in autumn (September) or early in spring (March) and then leave undisturbed.

Recommended

— As well as the very popular *Dicentra spectabilis* which is pink, we would also advise the white June-flowering variant, *D. spectabilis* 'Alba'.

— The *D. eximia* are also worth trying. The pink or white flowers appear in July on plants that reach about 20–30 cm (8–12 in).

Height: 20–60 cm (8–24 in).
Spacing and planting distance: 30 cm (12 in).
Soil: rich and light.
Cultivation: sunny.
Propagation: by division.
Flowering season: June to August, depending on the species.
Type: perennial.

Dichelostemma

CALIFORNIAN FIRE-CRACKER/ FIRECRACKER FLOWER

Liliaceae

Dichelostemma ida-maia deserves to be more widely publicized. Hardy in warm and temperate climates, it produces very elegant flowers clustered on the end of long spikes and these make fine and unusual bouquets. For the garden, they should be placed among low grey foliage plants such as lavender or wormwood.

130

Useful hints

— Plant in September and mark the spot carefully so that it can later be covered with a 10 cm (4 in) layer of crushed pine bark. This should be topped with a cloche or simply a sheet of transparent plastic to avoid excess water. The covering is removed in spring.

— Water regularly until August and then let the foliage dry out naturally.

Height: 60 cm (24 in).
Spacing and planting distance: 15 cm (6 in).
Soil: light and sandy.
Cultivation: sunny.
Propagation: bulb separation in September.
Flowering season: June, July.
Type: bulb.

Dictamnus

BURNING BUSH/GASPLANT

Rutaceae

Though *Dictamnus* is sometimes a slow starter in the first year, it very quickly forms solid growths crowned with pink flowers on spikes. The whole plant secretes an essence that will give an explosive crack if approached with a flame. This is harmless and may amuse children. *Dictamnus* is a good candidate for long term residence in gardens that are somewhat wild or even dry.

Useful hints

— Plant in spring after digging over the soil thoroughly to allow for the deep roots. Add a little lime if the soil is acid.

— Cover the ground with a thick layer of straw or grass cuttings to retain moisture. Mark the position of the plants carefully to avoid accidental damage while hoeing in spring.

— Every five years, divide growths that have become too dense and replant immediately.

Recommended

— The usual burning bush (*Dictamnus albus*) is salmon pink streaked with violet. There is also, however, an extremely fine white variety (*D. albus* 'Albiflorus') which is all too rare in the catalogues.

Height: 50–100 cm (20–40 in).
Spacing and planting distance: 40 cm (16 in).
Soil: fairly compact, well-drained and preferably chalky.
Cultivation: sunny.
Propagation: from seed or by division in spring.
Flowering season: June, July.
Type: perennial.

△ *Dictamnus albus purpurens*
▽ *Dierama pulcherrimum*

Dielytra

see *Dicentra*

Dierama

DIERAMA

Iridaceae

Dierama is the pride of the garden with its long strap-like leaves and slender arching stems from which hang bells of pink or white or purple. It must, however, be carefully protected against frost.

Useful hints

— Plant in September, October into pockets of rich leaf-mould.

— The plants are very sensitive to transplantation and should be moved as little as possible.

— Every year, at the beginning of October, cut the stems flush with the ground and protect the root-stock with two spadefuls of dead leaves.

Recommended

— Apart from wand flower (*Dierama pulcherrima*), you can also choose *D. pendula* but this is even less hardy. The plant grows to about 40 cm (16 in) and its flowers are mauve or white.

Height: 40–90 cm (16–36 in).
Spacing and planting distance: 30 cm (12 in).
Soil: rich and light.
Cultivation: sunny.
Propagation: by division.
Flowering season: August to October.
Type: bulb.

131

△ *Digitalis purpurea*

△ *Dionaea muscipula*

△ *Dodecatheon meadia*

Digitalis

FOXGLOVE

Scrophulariaceae

When the purple foxgloves (*Digitalis purpurea*) appear suddenly in June, the shade under chestnut trees is transformed into a carpet of pink. The first flower to re-emerge after undergrowth has been cleared, the foxglove is ideally suited to gardens with a moist, slightly acid soil. They blend well with ferns, columbine, meadow-rue and bleeding heart.

Useful hints

— Plant in September for flowering in the following spring.

— If they are prevented from running to seed, they will survive for many years. Otherwise, they are exhausted after two seasons.

Recommended

— The foxgloves are better cultivated as biennials. The purple foxglove (*Digitalis purpurea*) has been improved to give horizontal rather than hanging flowers. The most common variety is the 'Excelsior' range.

— Not quite hardy, *D. ambigua* (or *D. grandiflora*) produces a dazzling yellow on somewhat small plants of 60 to 100 cm (24–40 in). It is wise to take precautions against sudden death of the plants by keeping seed in reserve. *D. ferruginea* is copper-coloured and reaches a height of 90 cm (36 in). *D. mertonensis* has a strawberry pink flower that will delight the connoisseur.

Height: 60–130 cm (36–52 in).
Spacing and planting distance: 20 cm (8 in).
Soil: ordinary, moist.
Cultivation: semi-shade to sunny.
Propagation: from seed.
Flowering season: June, July.
Type: biennial, perennial.

Dimorphotheca

see *Osteospermum*

Dionaea

VENUS'S FLY-TRAP

Droseraceae

Everyone must have been tempted at one time to try growing this insect-eating plant. However, though *Dioneae* can last for years, there may be disappointments unless certain precautions are taken.

Useful hints

— Buy a well-developed plant and not some leafless starter. The best time for replanting is between April and August, using pure light peat and a pot that is wider than it is tall. Water thoroughly and place the pot on a saucer that will be kept filled with water from April to winter.

— Place the *Dioneae* in the open, directly in the sun. Water once a week without adding fertilizer. If a fly lands or is placed on a leaf, it will close up and the prey will be digested in the course of a week.

— When winter approaches, empty the saucer and place the pot in a corner or in a cold frame. *Dionaea* can survive temperatures of −5°C (23°F) or even lower. Flowering is usually the sign that the plant is about to die so gather the seed and germinate in peat from the pot.

Height: 20 cm (8 in).
Spacing and planting distance: 20 cm (8 in).
Soil: pure peat moss.
Cultivation: full sun.
Propagation: from seed.
Flowering season: summer, not spectacular.
Type: perennial.

Dodecatheon

SHOOTING STAR

Primulaceae

A *Dodecatheon* in bloom is a veritable firework display. The shape of the flowers, their subtle colours, the way in which they nod on the end of their long stalks, all adds to the spectacle. But there are problems involved in cultivating them. Their life cycle is incredibly short: often, less than three months pass from when the first shoots appear until the entire plant has faded. This is a plant for passionate, experienced gardeners. But be warned, it dies off completely in winter.

Useful hints

— Before planting, enrich the soil with peat and leaf-mould. The soil must be capable of holding enough water to feed the plant right through the spring.

— Plant in early autumn and March. Let clumps fill out before dividing them.

— Sowing fresh seeds can give good results: the plants will shoot in spring.

Recommended

— It's easy to lose your way among the different species of *Dodecatheon*. The best one is *D. meadia*, sometimes known as *D. pauciflorum* or *D. paucifolium*.

Height: 45 cm (18 in).
Spacing and planting distance: 20 cm (8 in).
Soil: rich in organic matter.
Cultivation: semi-shade.
Propagation: from seed or by division in September.
Flowering season: May, June.
Type: perennial.

Doronicum

LEOPARD'S BANE

Compositae

It looks like the first shafts of sunlight in spring. Devotees of marguerites owe it to themselves to include March-flowering leopard's bane in their gardens. Combined with tulips and myosotis, it brightens up the slopes by its lightness and the brilliance of its colours. In summer, create lovely carpets around your bushes and trees with this hardy plant, which likes the shade.

Useful hints

— Best planted in autumn, turning over the soil a little. Make up the soil with a little peat if it is too light.

— Water from April onwards if the rain is late in coming: this plant likes a certain amount of moisture.

— Cut the plants to ground level in autumn.

— Divide the clumps every 4 years to preserve their strength. Replant the roots immediately.

— Watch out for snails.

Recommended

— The most widespread is *Doronicum caucasium* or Caucasian leopard's bane: the variety 'Finesse' has very elegant yellow flowers.

— More lavish, *D. plantagineum* 'Excelsum' quickly forms 80 cm (32 in) high, wide clumps, and has golden yellow flowers. The variety 'Miss Mason' has striking bright yellow flowers, which look very nice as cut flowers for the home.

Height: 50–80 cm (20–32 in).
Spacing and planting distance: 30–40 cm (12–16 in).
Soil: quite deep, moist even in summer.
Cultivation: semi-shade or gentle sun.
Propagation: by division at the end of summer.
Flowering season: March–May.
Type: perennial.

▽ *Donoricum caucasicum*

Draba

WHITLOW GRASS

Cruciferae

In March, this yellow flower is often found in seed merchants' stalls. It owes its charm to its appearance, reminiscent of the mosses of the forest, and to its yellow flowers. It's tricky to keep in good condition for long, though, since it wilts quickly. A well-drained corner of your rockery would be ideal for *Draba aizoides*.

Useful tips

— Plant the flowering pots in spring in a pocket of sandy soil. Cut down the stems after flowering to prevent seeds forming, and sprinkle the clumps with a little handful of sand at the end of winter to help surface rooting.

— You can also cultivate them in pots, along with early bulbs like crocus or *Iris reticulata*.

Height: 5–10 cm (2–4 in).
Spacing and planting distance: 15 cm (6 in).
Soil: well-drained, very sandy.
Cultivation: full sun.
Propagation: by division after flowering or from seed in spring.
Flowering season: March, April.
Type: perennial.

▽ *Draba*

Dryas

D. OCTOPETALA/MT. WASHINGTON DRYAD

Rosaceae

This native of the tundra is not bothered by the cold. In your rockery, it will be one of the few flowers able to brighten up north-facing slopes, forming a deep green carpet dotted with white flowers in June. *Dryas octopetala* goes well with small conifers, heather and early spring bulbs, which will find it easy to cross the beautiful background of its foliage.

Useful hints

— Plant preferably in September/October or just after the first cold spells, in sandy pockets of peaty soil. Water regularly for the first year.

— Add some sand to the centre of the clumps at the start of each winter to avoid standing moisture. Don't cut off flowers once they have wilted, because the fluffy seed-heads are very decorative.

— At the end of winter, take cuttings and let them root right through the winter under a cold frame. Prick them out permanently in spring.

Height: 10 cm (4 in).
Spacing and planting distance: 30–50 cm (12–20 in).
Soil: acid, sandy (heath soil).
Cultivation: anywhere, even north-facing.
Propagation: from cuttings at end of winter.
Flowering season: June, July.
Type: perennial.

▽ *Dryas octopetala*

Dryopteris

BUCKLER FERN/SHIELD FERN

Polypodaceae

You will often have seen this in damp undergrowth, cascading down embankments along forest paths. It's an ideal plant for rapidly filling out new gardens, since it thrives on very little and keeps its foliage well. It makes an ideal companion for *Helxine, Eucomis*, hostas, hortensias and fuchsias. In winter, its leaves cut down and laid on the ground will protect the delicate plants pushing up between them.

Useful hints

— Plant it in spring, in moist soil rich in leaf-mould. It particularly likes damp corners.

— Cut away the faded fronds each spring.

Recommended

— Everyone knows buckler/shield ferns from the woods. In some places, they are very common, but equally—and surprisingly—they are absent from entire regions. Their light, semi-evergreen fronds are a pretty light green. They are completely separate from the female fern, which is an *Athyrium*.

— *Dryopteris dilatata* (or *D. austriaca*) has almost triangular fronds with very few incisions. It is frequently used in flower arrangements.

— Very finely sculptured, the foliage of *D. cristata* is reminiscent of Japanese paper cutouts. It loves damp places and goes marvellously with Candelabra primroses and astilbes.

Height: 40 cm (16 in).
Spacing and planting distance: 30 cm (12 in).
Soil: ordinary, moist.
Cultivation: semi-shade.
Propagation: from seed.
Type: perennial.

Eccremocarpus

CHILEAN GLORY FLOWER

Bignoniaceae

Few climbing plants can boast such a glorious red. Indeed, from July to October, this pretty annual creeper offers you tubular corolla in stunning coral, pink, red and yellow, with a little touch of gold at the edge of the throat.

△ *Dryopteris filix-mas*
▽ *Dryopteris pseudomas*

▽ *Eccremocarpus scaber*

But it's not easy to grow. Like cobaeas, *Eccremocarpus scaber* has a capricious streak, and has been known to drive the most patient gardener to despair. Perhaps that's why it's so popular! Try to bring your plant under glass at the end of summer: it will be bound to do well, since it is frost which kills it.

Useful hints

— To get all possible luck on your side, sow it early (from the end of February) under glass.

— Make up a rich porous mulch from peat, ripe compost and leaf compost in equal proportions.

— Once the plants are 10 cm (4 in) high, towards mid-April, plant them out in good, ordinary, well-exposed soil.

— As this is a spreading plant which puts out tendrils, provide it with a trellis or light stakes for support.

Height: 2 m (80 in).
Spacing and planting distance: 80 cm (32 in).
Soil: ordinary, well-drained.
Cultivation: sunny.
Propagation: from seed.
Flowering season: July–October.
Type: annual.

Echinacea

PURPLE CONE FLOWER

Compositae

It's not long since this big pink rudbeckia changed its name, and some people still call it *Rudbekia purpurea grandiflora*. This is one of the most familiar plants of our older gardens, which it decorates in autumn with its somewhat wistful pink stems crowned with 'daisy heads'. Brighten *Echinacea purpurea* up by planting it by your asters or heleniums, and don't let it take over—it is remarkably vigorous.

Useful tips

— Plant the clump divisions in October or the spring, in good common garden soil.

— Give it a well-shaded slope to show the flowers off to best advantage.

— Divide the clumps every three years.

Height: 1–1.5 m (40–60 in).
Spacing and planting distance: 40 cm (16 in).
Soil: ordinary.
Cultivation: sunny.
Propagation: by division.
Flowering season: July–September.
Type: perennial.

Echinops

GLOBE THISTLE

Compositae

Echinops is only really beautiful in large numbers, next to red campions (*Lychnis*) in a harmony of rather daring minor colours or, more classically, combined with phlox or climbing roses such as 'Cornelia' or 'Penelope'. These false thistles (thistles are in fact *Eryngium*, and therefore members of the *Umbelliferae*) show both a freedom of movement, and an evident rigidity in their dense clumps of flowers. This is one of the best summer flowers for low-maintenance gardens.

Useful hints

— Plant in autumn or spring, in any well-drained soil. Cut off faded stems in autumn.

— Don't overfeed, since the plants will bolt, without losing their spikes or getting more flowers.

Recommended

— *Echinops ritro* is a violet blue, and forms clumps 60 cm (24 in) high. The 'Veitch's Blue' variety is hardier, and its heads are a darker steel blue.

— *E. sphaerocephalus* gives a very decorative grey flower at the end of summer. It is a good idea to stake it, since it often grows over 1.5 m (60 in) high and may be flattened by storms.

Height: 90–160 cm (36–64 in).
Spacing and planting distance: 30 cm (12 in).
Soil: ordinary, but must be well-drained.
Cultivation: sunny.
Propagation: from seed or by division in spring.
Flowering season: June–September.
Type: biennial, perennial.

△ **Echinops ritro**
◁ **Echinacea purpurea**
▽ **Echium fastuosum**

Echium

VIPER'S BUGLOSS

Boraginaceae

On sunny roads or rocky paths, pushing up between the stones, you will find the pretty spikes of *Echium vulgare* speckled with an overwhelming pink; it is a little cousin of *Echium fastuosum* which is such a feature of Mediterranean gardens. It goes well in dry, shady gardens, next to *Verbascum* and agaves. But beware of winter: these pretty plants should only be used on favourable slopes and rockeries.

Useful hints

— Plant in spring, in rich soil, on a very sunny slope.

— Each year, reseed with the natural seeds which will appear on the slopes, because these plants don't live very long and are often biennial.

— Sow in spring: the plants will flower the following year.

Recommended

— As well as *Echium vulgare* and *E.* *fastuosum*, *E. lycopsis* will seduce you with its white, red or purple spikes like those of 'Blue Bedder'.

Height: 30–100 cm (12–40 in).
Spacing and planting distance: 30–70 cm (12–28 in).
Soil: ordinary, rich.
Cultivation: sunny.
Propagation: from seed.
Flowering season: July, August.
Type: annual, perennial.

△ *Epilobium angustifolium*

Epilobium

WILLOW-HERB/FIREWEED

Onagraceae

Rarely offered in catalogues, although very decorative and a native of our countryside, willow-herb works wonders in the slightly wilder corners of the garden, in large spreads next to groups of foxgloves. Its common name of willow-herb suggests a definite preference for moist locations. The common variety is a purple-pink colour, but there is also a very pretty white.

Useful hints

— Plant shoots in autumn or spring. Clumps can easily be separated from new plants. If in flower, don't hesitate to prune it to one-third of its height to make up for its losing its roots and to help it 'take'.

— Watch out for it spreading sometimes further than you would like. Cut back the rhizomes running along the ground with a spade.

Height: 1.5 m (60 in).
Spacing and planting distance: 50 cm (20 in).
Soil: any soil, but must stay moist in summer.
Cultivation: sunny or semi-shade.
Propagation: by division in spring or after flowering.
Flowering season: August, September.
Type: perennial.

Epimedium

BARRENWORT, BISHOP'S HAT

Berberidaceae

It's strange that barrenwort should still be so little known, since it is probably the best answer to unpromising situations. It prospers in the shade of trees just as well as ivy, and repays the investment in it many times over in its foliage which changes colour over the seasons and also offers a graceful bloom in early spring.

Useful hints

— Plant at any time of year, but don't forget to water it right through the first year. It grows very slowly at first, then the clumps fill out. By dividing them every three years, you will soon have a veritable carpet of several square metres from a single plant.

— At the end of winter, cut away the old growth to accentuate the blooms. Use this opportunity to add a well-rotted peat or compost mulch.

Recommended

— *Epimedium grandiflorum* has flowers of different colours, as large as (and looking like) columbines.

▽ *Epimedium rubrum*

— The leaves of *E. rubrum* take on magnificent colours in spring and autumn.

— *E. versicolor* 'Grandiflorum' has finely toothed leaves and ravishing pale yellow flowers.

Height: 20–30 cm (8–12 in).
Spacing and planting distance: 20 cm (8 in).
Soil: normal, preferably rich in humus.
Cultivation: shade.
Propagation: by division in September.
Flowering season: March, April.
Type: perennial.

△ *Eranthis hivernalis*

Eranthis

WINTER ACONITE

Ranunculaceae

Of a stunning yellow, *Eranthis hyemalis* blooms while the snow is still on the ground. Just like the snowdrop, this is a little plant which should never be picked, since it is only happy in the garden, a rockery or a rich soil slope.

Useful hints

— Plant in September, in little groups of 7 or 8, in humus-rich but very well-drained soil.

— These plants take easily: use them as undergrowth, in sparse clumps.

Height: 10–15 cm (4–6 in).
Spacing and planting distance: 15 cm (6 in).
Soil: rich and light.
Cultivation: semi-shade to sunny.
Propagation: by division or from seed.
Flowering season: January–March.
Type: bulb.

△ *Eremurus rubustus*
Eremurus himalaicus △
◁ *Eremurus stenophyllus bungei*

Eremurus

FOXTAIL LILY/DESERT-CANDLE
Liliaceae

This is undoubtedly one of the most stunning plants in summer. Give it the rich, deep soil that it likes, and *Eremurus* will think nothing of growing 2 m (80 in) high. Plant it close to foxgloves, delphiniums and *Heracleum*, and the display will be more than impressive.

Useful hints

— Plant large stripped roots in September, in pockets of light soil on a shady slope.

— Each autumn, cut away the dry stems and cover the roots with 10 cm (4 in) of mulch to protect them.

— Avoid planting eremurus in windy gardens, or be ready to use stakes.

Recommended

— The best-known and most graceful is *Eremurus stenophyllus bungei*, with its fine yellow flowers; it is not too overwhelming at 1 m (40 in) high. This has been used to create numerous hybrids, such as 'De Ruiter' or 'Oasis' (pink) or 'Romance' (salmon).

— The giant *E. himalaicus* reaches 1.2 m (48 in), and is pure white, while the even larger *E. robustus* at 3 m (120 in) is a lovely peach yellow.

Height: 1–3 m (40–120 in).
Spacing and planting distance: 50 cm (20 in).
Soil: rich, well-drained.
Cultivation: sunny to semi-shade.
Propagation: from seed.
Flowering season: June.
Type: perennial.

Erica

HEATHER/HEATH

Ericaceae

Heather is something you either love or hate. Its supporters love its soft colours and natural appearance, its detractors denigrate its squat profile and gloom in winter. We can reunite the two camps by finding it a little spot in company with a few grasses to lighten it. Avoid large, monotonous groups and disperse it in shady corners.

Useful hints

— Plant in September, October or March, April in a low lime soil which keeps slightly moist even in summer.

— Prune the clumps to half height with a pair of hedging shears just after flowering. This will make the clumps much more dense and long-lasting.

— Keep the soil clear for the first few years, making sure above all to weed out couch grass. Once in place, heather will stop weeds from growing.

Recommended

— Winter heather (*Erica carnea*) braves bad weather to present us with its bells. Amongst the prettiest are 'Cecilia M. Beale' (white), 'Praecox rubra' (pink), 'Springwood' (white with violet tips or pink), and 'Winter Beauty', carmine pink. The last is one of the heathers best able to tolerate lime soils. 'Aurea', a variety with golden leaves and pink flowers, does not always thrive in them.

— Bell heather (*E. cinerea*) is common on our heaths and clearings. Its loose racemes of flowers on the end of its stems herald the end of summer. The prettiest are 'C. D. Eason' (dark pink), 'Cevennes' (a curious lavender colour) and 'Pallida', light pink with many flowers.

— *E. darleyensis* is the result of a cross between the winter heather and a Mediterranean species. It tolerates lime relatively well, but flowers a little later. Varieties are rarely named but are offered by colour.

— Easy to recognize by its little rugby balls of flowers in tight clusters on the end of its stems, *E. tetralix* flowers just after *E. darleyensis*, at the start of summer. The varieties 'Rosea' (pink) and 'Con Underwood' (speckled red) are the most common.

— Linking these and the winter heathers, Cornish heath (*E. vagans*) quickly forms a dense carpet. The stems are sometimes split by hard frosts but

△ **Erica vagans**

△ **Erica carnea 'Springwood'**
▽ **Erica cinerea**

soon resprout from the base. 'Mrs D. Maxwell' (red) and 'Saint Keverne' (cerise) are well worth trying.

Height: 30–50 cm (12–20 in).
Spacing and planting distance: 30 cm (12 in).
Soil: acid, sandy.
Cultivation: sun, semi-shade.
Propagation: by division after flowering.
Flowering season: all year, depending on species.
Type: perennial.

Erigeron speciosus **hybrid** ▷

Erigeron

FLEABANE

Compositae

Aster lovers should like these: they are very similar, and have the advantage of flowering in summer when the prettiest asters aren't around. Use them to edge borders and low walls and don't forget to divide them each spring, as this makes them produce more flowers. They go well with *Viola cornuta*, *Cerastium* and alyssums.

Useful hints

— Best time for planting is April, May: young plants often prove vulnerable to heavy frosts.

— Divide clumps regularly in autumn to prevent them ageing and fading and prune the clumps down to ground level.

Recommended

— The earliest fleabanes are *Erigeron aurianticus*, whose orange flowers open in early summer, and *E. leiomerus*, pink and a prolific flowerer.

— The vast majority of fleabanes bloom from June to September. These are the famous hybrids *E. speciosus*. The best are 'Foerster's Liebling', double and deep pink, 'Rosa Triumph', brilliant red, or even 'Violetta', a very dark violet, one of the predominant fleabane colours taken to its limit.

— As for the others, *E. mucronatus* (or *Vittadinia triloba*) is in blossom in the frosts. Its very delicate daisies range from pink to white and give a dainty impression on low walls, which it colonizes readily. Protect in winter.

Height: 15–45 cm (6–18 in).
Spacing and planting distance: 15–30 cm (6–12 in).
Soil: ordinary, light, moist.
Cultivation: sunny.
Propagation: from seed or by division.
Flowering season: June–September.
Type: annual, biennial, perennial.

Erinus alpinus △

Erinus alpinus

ALPINE ERINUS/ALPINE LIVERBALSAM

Scrophulariaceae

Ideal for starting a rockery, it slides into the smallest crevices, reseeding itself as required, and forms dark green cushions which literally vanish under flowers for a good part of spring and summer. Its only drawback: it doesn't live very long.

Useful hints

— Plant in autumn or spring in crevices in low walls or pavements.

— Prune the clumps after flowering, leaving a few fruit to ripen and produce seeds. Sow these in a dish and leave them under glass over the winter. They will shoot the next spring.

Recommended

— There aren't many *Erinus alpinus* in the catalogues. The best known varieties are 'Coeruleus' (blue) and 'Dr Hanele' (carmine red).

Height: 10 cm (4 in).
Spacing and planting distance: 25 cm (10 in).
Soil: pebbly, on the dry side.
Cultivation: light sun.
Propagation: from seed or by division in September.
Flowering season: May–July.
Type: perennial.

Erodium

STORK'S BILL/HERONBILL

Geraniaceae

Not really easy to cultivate, the erodiums are the mountain equivalent of our hardy geraniums: the same very sound foliage in dense clumps and the same flowers with very simple corollas. They are less hardy, however, due to their dislike of too much water in winter.

Useful hints

— Plant in spring, preferably after having let them winter under glass away from too much rain. Give them a sunny spot and well-drained, even pebbly, soil.

— Water regularly until the flowers appear. Once they have passed, prune the clumps to make way for new foliage.

— They are propagated by taking cuttings in autumn and putting in sand to root.

Recommended

— *Erodium chamaedryoides* 'Roseum', with its slightly sad pink flowers, is the most widely grown although not the hardiest.

— Much more vigorous, *E. manescavi* forms a good clump of foliage which peaks at 45 cm (18 in). Its purple flowers can be seen from way off.

Height: 5 cm (2 in) (*E. chamaedryoides*) to 40 cm (16 in) (*E. manescavi*).
Spacing and planting distance: 25 cm (10 in).
Soil: pebbly, rather poor.
Cultivation: full sun.
Propagation: from cuttings.
Flowering season: June–August.
Type: perennial.

▽ *Erodium chamaedryoides* 'Roseum'

Eryngium

SEA HOLLY

Umbelliferae

Thistles: people love them or hate them, depending on whether they are already in their clutches or looking at them from a distance. In the former case, their formidable spines make us swear to root them out of our gardens mercilessly. The rest of the time, we can only admire their armour, worthy of the knights of old. The majestic sweep of their flowery stems is an unforgettable sight, and you never stop going each morning to see if their flowers have opened. Their steel blue colour is the only one which suits their dignity.

Useful hints

— Plant in spring, away from the edge of slopes. Combine them with some gramineas and yellow summer marguerites to give a vibrant display seen from afar. Cut off faded flowers to prevent seeds spreading over the entire garden. New young shoots are often found at the foot of the old plants.

— For drying under ideal conditions, cut the inflorescences when they are barely opened. Hang them head down in a dry, shady place for two months.

Recommended

— Although *Eryngium agavifolium* has very full rosettes of pink leaves and a flowering stem over 1.5 m (60 in) high, its relatively small violet blue flowers are a little disappointing.

— Hailing from the mountains, *E. alpinum* has much larger flowers in a magnificent steel blue in July/August.

— *E. bourgati* is smaller, but deserves to be cultivated just for its white- and silver-veined leaves. It is rarely more than 60 cm (24 in) high, and comes from the Pyrenees.

— Still common on some beaches, *E. maritimum* and *E. oliverianum* are some of the best flowers for dried bouquets.

— Very different in appearance, *E. variifolium* gives long-lasting white-veined leaves with few prickles. Its flowers are smaller, but come in extraordinary clusters, so heavy that the plant has to be supported to prevent it collapsing in the first storm. Mix with rosemary, cistus and euphorbia to give a Mediterranean appearance.

◁ *Eryngium bromliafolium*

140

Height: 60–140 cm (24–56 in).
Spacing and planting distance: 20–50 cm (8–20 in).
Soil: ordinary, well-drained, even pebbly.
Cultivation: sunny.
Propagation: from seed or by division.
Flowering season: July – November.
Type: perennial.

Erysimum

ERYSIMUM/WALLFLOWER

Cruciferae

A great lover of walls, the stock *Erysimum* delights owners of dry gardens. Indeed, this pretty hardy plant with the yellow flowers like those of an Indian pink, is only happy in dry soils, like its cousin *Cheiranthus*. Less fragrant than the latter, it can still offer a gentle scent. Its splendid colour thrives in the company of myosotis and late tulips, among dark colours like those of black parrot tulips or Triomphe 'Hans Anrud'.

Useful hints

— Sow in nurseries in September, then prick out in early spring, in March. The first flowers will survive until the following spring. You can also sow in May and prick out in September/October, and so see the plants flower the following May.

— Renew beds every other year: although hardy in sunny gardens with light soil, these plants lose their beauty from their second year onwards.

Height: 30 cm (12 in).
Spacing and planting distance: 30 cm (12 in).
Soil: ordinary.
Cultivation: sunny.
Propagation: from seed.
Flowering season: May, June.
Type: biennial, perennial.

△ *Erysimum* **'Bowles Variety'**

△ *Erythronium revolutum* **'White Beauty'**

Erythronium

ERYTHRONIUM/FAWN-LILY

Liliaceae

With their pale corollas, sometimes pink, sometimes yellow, and their cream- or brown-splashed foliage, erythroniums look good in the spring, especially planted in light, humus-rich undergrowth in clusters of five or six.

Useful hints

— Plant moist bulbs in early autumn in good humus-rich earth. They grow best in leaf mould.

— Watch out for fieldmice and frosts. In the first year, protect the bulbs you have planted 10 cm (4 in) underground with a 5 cm (2 in) coat of leaves, under which you put some poison.

Recommended

— *Erythronium dens-canis* (dog's tooth violet), with its pink flowers, is the best known.

— *E. tuolumnense*, with its beautiful lac-quered yellow flowers and glistening leaves, is the most graceful.

— *E. revolutum*, with its ivory flowers, is favoured by those with 'white' gardens.

Height: 10–25 cm (4–10 in).
Spacing and planting distance: 15 cm (6 in).
Soil: humus-rich.
Cultivation: semi-shade.
Propagation: by separating bulbs
Flowering season: April, May.
Type: bulb.

Eschscholzia californica △
Eucomis punctata ▽

Eschscholzia

CALIFORNIA POPPY

Papaveraceae

Owners of dry gardens despairing of ever seeing them produce flowers, and reluctant gardeners whose main aim is to avoid spending their weekends doing a thousand and one little jobs, should discover the California poppy (*Eschscholzia californica*). They don't come much tougher than this one! Give it a minimum of soil and a maximum of sun, and not only will it flower incessantly from June until the frosts come, but it will also reseed itself. Plant it with eryngium and marigolds for company and your garden will be a feast for your eyes.

Useful hints

— Sow directly on site in the second half of April, choosing sunny banks if possible.

— Thin out plants if too tightly packed after a little rain and try to prick out the surplus, watering well.

— Gather the seed pods in dry weather in September.

— Spontaneous seedings will revert to their original colour after some years.

Recommended

— There are singles and doubles, but our vote goes to the classic California poppy with its simple flowers, sold in a mixture of colours; it runs through all the yellows.

Height: 20 cm (8 in).
Spacing and planting distance: 15 cm (6 in).
Soil: normal.
Cultivation: sunny.
Propagation: from seed.
Flowering season: June–October.
Type: annual.

142

△ *Eschscholzia* (mixed)

△ *Eupatorium purpureum*

Eucomis

PINEAPPLE LILY

Liliaceae

For those lucky enough to have a well-watered garden in partial shade, and those who worry that their garden is too shady, the *Eucomis* is a godsend worth investigating. With its unusual delicate green violet-speckled inflorescence, resembling a pineapple, and its long ribbon leaves, it is not lacking in appearance. *Helxine*, columbines, ferns, foxgloves and violets keep it company, and, as the seasons pass, you will see it fill out and bloom lavishly.

Useful hints

— Plant the large bulbs, resembling those of hyacinths, in March, in deep moist soil, 10 cm (4 in) down.

— Where winter is likely to be harsh, mulch the clumps and protect them under a screen cloth.

— In heavy soil, plant in pockets filled with a very sandy mulch mixture.

Recommended

— There are two species, very similar: *Eucomis bicolor*, which grows to 30 cm (12 in) and has light green petals with purple edges, and the fragrant *Eucomis punctata*, taller at 50 cm (20 in) and with garnet-striped stems.

Height: 30–50 cm (12–20 in).
Spacing and planting distance: 20 cm (8in).
Soil: ordinary, moist.
Cultivation: semi-shade to shade.
Propagation: from seed or by separating bulbs.
Flowering season: June–August.
Type: bulb.

Eupatorium

HEMP AGRIMONY/BLUESTEM, JOE PYE WEED, WHITE SNAKEROOT

Compositae

While the most stunning *Eupatoriums* are those that come from Brazil, smelling of vanilla and flowering all year round on verandahs, let us not forget their domestic cousins which have no equals when it comes to natural decoration for the damper, wilder corners of the garden, or the North American species, which are are also very decorative.

Useful hints

— Plant in spring or autumn, first turning over the soil well and feeding it with peat to help it hold moisture.

— Water regularly and well for the first year. Mulch the soil with turf or lawn cuttings.

— When the flowers on the clumps dwindle, divide them just after they flower.

Recommended

— Perfectly at home among the bushes, the purple *Eupatorium* (*Eupatorium purpureum*) reaches the peak of its beauty in August, when its powerful stems are crowned with hundreds of purple-pink flowers.

— Not quite so tall, but forming larger clumps, *E. rugosum* looks like an enormous ageratum with its feathery white flowers.

Height: 1–2 m (40–80 in).
Spacing and planting distance: 50 cm (20 in).
Soil: rich, moist even in summer.
Cultivation: sun and semi-shade.
Propagation: by division in autumn.
Flowering season: August, September.
Type: perennial.

Euphorbia

EUPHORBIA/RATTLESNAKE WEED

Euphorbiaceae

There is a euphorbia suited to every nook of the garden, from shade to sun and dry to moist. Some are among the best space-fillers, while others have a majestic enough silhouette to allow them to stand alone at a turn in an avenue. Although most are hardy, there are even easily-sown annuals. The choice is really overwhelming.

Useful hints

— Plant in spring or early autumn (September/October) to allow them to put down good roots before winter. A light, fairly rich soil is what suits them best.

— Mulch the soil with peat at the end of winter. Lawn clippings or pine bark are suitable. This will prevent clumps being stripped by rain, exposing the main roots.

— Divide clumps every three years, cutting the fleshy roots cleanly. Prick them out in a mixture of sand and peat and let them spend their first winter under cold glass.

Recommended

— Very spectacular, *Euphorbia characias* grows over 1 m (40 in) high. Its bluish-leaved stems terminate in spikes of remarkably sulphur-yellow waxen flowers. It blooms at the same time as late tulips, in May.

— *E. wulfenii* looks very similar, but just a little bigger, and flowers later, in June. Plant in sheltered position.

— Pointed, often red-veined leaves, flowers in bunches with red bracts playing a starring role: this is *E. griffithii*, whose variety 'Fireglow' has the most brilliant shades of orange.

— Snow on the mountain (*E. marginata*) is often used as foliage in dainty bouquets. To seal the cuts and prevent the latex escaping, just soak the ends of the stems in hot water. Sow under glass in April, or directly into the vegetable garden in May.

— Very unusual, with geometrical interwoven leaves all the way up its towering stems, *E. myrsinites* works wonders in rockeries, low walls and dry stone steps. It blooms early, in April.

— One of our favourites is *E. polychroma*, whose stunning green leaves terminate in pale yellow flowers in April/May. Mix with white tulips for a really charm-

△ *Euphorbia characias*

△ *Euphorbia myrsinetes*
◁ *Euphorbia wulfenii*
▽ *Euphorbia marginata*

ing picture. Prune in June/July to ensure the new foliage will be perfect.

— *E. robbiae* is the queen of dry, shady spots. Its tough, dark green leaves are in themselves a guarantee of hardiness. It forms beautiful carpets, even at the foot of a weeping willow, and flowers at the end of spring in that green chartreuse colour which is such a feature of the euphorbiae.

Height: 10–120 cm (4–60 in), depending on variety.
Spacing and planting distance: 20–40 cm (8–16 in).
Soil: normal, on the moist side.
Cultivation: full sun to shade, depending on variety.
Propagation: by division after flowering.
Flowering season: spring.
Type: annual or perennial.

△ *Euphorbia graffithii* '**Fireglow**'

Euryops acraeus △

Euphorbia mellifera ▷

Euphorbia griffithii '**Dixter**' ▽

▽ *Euphorbia polychroma*

Euryops acraeus/Euryops

EURYOPS

Compositae

Its origins in the Drakensberg mountains of South Africa are no doubt the reason why this eternal patch of silver can withstand our average winters. Give it a sunny, well-drained corner in your rockery, and you will be rewarded with a cushion of delicate grey adorned with bright yellow flowers at the start of summer. You can also put it in large tubs in company with a dark-leaved conifer, like a yew or a mountain pine, or use it as the background for another delicate plant, the fabulous *Rhodohypoxis*, itself a South African exile.

Useful hints

— *Euryops* is best planted in spring, to save it having to go through a winter without good roots. Put it in a pocket of well-drained soil and cover the soil with a layer of fine gravel to keep the neck out of reach of moisture.

— Each spring, add a little leaf-mould to the heart of the clumps to help the twigs root. Cuttings taken in summer will also take root well in sand, but must be allowed to winter under glass.

Height: 25 cm (10 in).
Spacing and planting distance: 30 cm (12 in).
Soil: very well drained.
Cultivation: sunny.
Propagation: from cuttings.
Flowering season: June, July.
Type: perennial.

145

Felicia amelloides △

Felicia

FELICIA

Compositae

Anyone who likes cacti, little 'artichokes' of all kinds (the echeveria), agaves and sedums will like this little plant. There is the added advantage that *Felicia amelloides* flowers each year without fail and multiplies with ease. Its only shortcoming is its lack of hardiness apart from in warm and temperate climates, although it makes a good balcony plant elsewhere.

Useful hints

— Plant *Felicia amelloides* (syn. *Agathaea coelestis*) in April/May in a sunny corner of the garden or in tubs to decorate walls and paths.

— It is not very fussy, and will be happy with a good ordinary soil.

— Flowering abundantly, it propagates easily from seed, and is fun for children to try their hand at growing.

Height: 30–40 cm (12–16 in).
Spacing and planting distance: 30 cm (12 in).
Soil: ordinary.
Cultivation: sunny.
Propagation: from seed or cuttings.
Flowering season: June–September.
Type: perennial.

Festuca

FESTUCA/FESCUA
Graminaceae/Graminceae

This pretty blue herb is unusual in that it forms very dense round clumps and also in that it doesn't get everywhere. It is ideal for placid borders or for introducing a touch of calm in borders full of colour. Mix it with spring bulbs and wild flowers to create a natural little corner.

Useful hints

— Plant *Festuca glauca* in autumn or spring, first turning over the soil thoroughly. It's a very frugal plant, which even thrives on a little deprivation.

— Avoid soil which holds water in winter. Prune clumps at the end of summer when the flowers are no longer decorative.

— *Festuca* is easy to propagate, either by dividing the clumps in spring or sowing at the same time. The clumps look good from the second year onwards.

Height: 20–30 cm (8–12 in).
Spacing and planting distance: 20 cm (8 in).
Soil: ordinary, not too rich, but well-drained.
Cultivation: at least 3 hours of sun per day.
Propagation: from seed or by division in spring.
Flowering season: June, July.
Type: perennial.

◁ *Festuca glauca*
▽ *Filipendula rubra* 'Magnifica'

Filipendula

FILIPENDULA/MEADOWSWEET
Rosaceae

A godsend to gardeners with little time to spare who would rather keep their corner of a meadow as a wild garden rather than put the finishing touches to their borders, *Filipendula* needs no care whatsoever. Whether the 'queen of the meadows' (*Filipendula ulmaria*) or other members of this large family, these are plants which are happy with a moist, lightly-shaded soil and which, combined with *Lysimachias*, *Macleayas*, *Rodgersias* and ferns make banks that are as delightful as they are easy to maintain.

Useful hints

— Plant *Filipendulas* in March or September, in clean, moist soil, preferably in partial shade.

— Create pleasant splashes of colour by planting at least five or six plants side by side.

— Every three years, divide up clumps which are threatening to overrun.

Recommended

— As well as the queen of the meadows, deliciously scented, *Filipendula hexapetala*, with its pale rose blooms and incised leaves like those of a fern, and *Filipendula rubra* 'Magnifica' (deep pink) give the best effects.

Height: 60–90 cm (24–36 in).
Spacing and planting distance: 30 cm (12 in).
Soil: ordinary.
Cultivation: sun or semi-shade.
Propagation: by division.
Flowering season: June–September.
Type: perennial.

Foeniculum vulgare/ Foeniculum

FENNEL
Umbelliferae

The advantages of fennel are a very imposing bearing thanks to its soaring silhouette, surrounded by a cloud of very fine greyish-green leaves and graceful flowers of a very sweet chartreuse yellow, and a typical scent of aniseed which it releases at the slightest brush. Use it in abundance, in company with old-fashioned varieties of rose or to lighten over-heavy banks.

Useful hints

— Plant in springtime, putting a little pocket of sand around its base. Stake the

△ *Foeniculum vulgare*

main stem at the end of spring to help it stand up to gusts.

— Let the flowers go to seed, collect the seeds and sow them all at once at random. Some will come up and you will have the benefit of having them there without having to prick them out. Since fennel takes up little room in terms of width, you can leave plants right at the edges of banks.

Recommended

— There is a version with bronzes leaves (i.e. a sort of reddish brown) known as *Foeniculum vulgare* 'Atropurpureum'. It stays true to type.

Height: 1.5–1.8 m (60–72 in).
Spacing and planting distance: 30 cm (12 in).
Soil: ordinary, even dry.
Cultivation: full sun.
Propagation: from seed in autumn or spring.
Flowering season: July, August.
Type: perennial.

Freesia × kewensis △

Freesia × kewensis/ Freesia

FREESIA

Iridaceae

In June/July, the freesias are in bloom on sunny banks and in jardinieres, since they are quite happy to grow in pots. Spreading brilliantly coloured corollas along their delicate stems, they bring the surrounding area alive. It is when combined with *Eschscholzias*, oriental poppies and *Ceratiums*, which, like them, love the sun, that they make the most brilliant banks, leaving gardeners on holiday to enjoy their summer rest, since they need little care to thrive.

Useful hints

— In warm and temperate climates they can be planted in October to accelerate flowering. In areas where there is a risk of frost, plant them as early as possible in spring.

— Put your freesias in sandy soil. If your soil is heavy, plant them in 20 cm (8 in) pockets filled with a mixture of peat and sand in equal parts.

Height: 20 cm (8 in).
Spacing and planting distance: 10 cm (4 in).
Soil: ordinary.
Cultivation: sunny.
Propagation: division of corms.
Flowering season: June, July.
Types corm.

Fritillaria

FRITILLARY/GUINEA-HEN FLOWER

Liliaceae

Two fritillaries are familiar to all: *Fritillaria imperialis* (imperial fritillary), for its crown of bright yellow or orange bells, and *Fritillaria meleagris* (snake's head), a denizen of moist meadows.

The latter owes its common name to the mauve criss-cross markings on its wine-coloured blooms. Both are stars of spring. Plant them in company with pretty ferns, delicate-leaved arums, golden lady's mantle, and you will get enchanting banks.

Useful hints

— Plant your fritillaries in early autumn, in September. The bulbs *must*

△ **Fritillaria imperialis**
▽ **Fritillaria meleagris**

be fresh otherwise you'll never see a single flower.

— Give them a humus-rich but well-drained soil (stagnant moisture in heavy soils kills them off in winter).

— Don't plant imperial fritillaries too close to the house, because of their unpleasant smell.

Recommended

— As well as the two varieties mentioned, why not try *Fritillaria persica* (Persian fritillary) with its marvellous black flowers? This is a rare variety to which it is worth giving pride of place.

Height: 20–50 cm (8–20 in).
Spacing and planting distance: 30 cm (12 in).
Soil: permeable, humus-rich.
Cultivation: semi-shade to sun.
Propagation: by separating bulbs.
Flowering season: April, May.
Type: bulb.

Fuchsia

FUCHSIA

Onagraceae

Where would our shady garden nooks be without fuchsias and their charming, back-turned bells? In company with hostas and ferns, they bring colour to where few other flowers would survive. You can also cultivate them in hanging baskets, giving preference to varieties with a trailing habit or by cultivating them as bushes, i.e. selecting a stem which you then prune at 50 cm (20 in) height. Do this several times over two years and this method will give you superb-looking bushy plants.

Useful hints

— Don't plant them outside before May in the South or June in the North. Water regularly during heatwaves and mulch the soil with peat or pine droppings. Give them soluble fertilizer every month. If tiny white flies are in evidence, treat with a decamethrin-based insecticide, or take preventive action by putting two pinches of a disulphotone-based insecticide on each base before watering.

— In late autumn, shelter the plants in a cold greenhouse, just out of reach of the frost. Some fuchsias can stay outside providing they are covered with a good bed of straw and plastic sheeting to prevent them rotting. As a precaution, and to avoid overloading your greenhouse, take cuttings in August and keep the cuttings for the winter in little pots.

△ *Fuchsia boliviana*
▽ *Fuchsia magellanica*

Fuchsia magellanica **'Gracilis'** △
Fuchsia **'Ting-a-ling'** ▷
Fuchsia **'Leonora'** ▽

Recommended

— There isn't enough room to mention all the interesting hybrids. Just ask your grower how they stand: upright, trailing or prostrate. That will give you an idea of how to use them: on banks or in tubs.

— The only really hardy fuchsia is *Fuchsia magellanica*, which forms veritable hedges if a particularly hard winter doesn't raze them to the ground. If that happens, they just bounce back even better in the spring and before you know

it the clumps will be over 1.5 m (60 in) high. Best varieties are: 'Riccartonii', whose thousands of dainty flowers stir in the slightest breeze; 'Alba', not white in fact but a pale pink—this fuchsia, with its very green tender leaves, does not suffer frost damage, and is one of the hardiest around; 'Versicolor', a handsome fuchsia with leaves a mixed pink and cream, which looks like a mist of all different colours from a distance. It has

no equal when it comes to giving a sense of lightness to shady banks. Try it with hostas and *Thalictrum dipterocarpum*, and see what happens!

Height: 30 cm–1.8 m (12–72 in).
Spacing and planting distance: 30 cm (12 in).
Soil: rich in humus and always moist.
Cultivation: shade, semi-shade.
Propagation: from cuttings in summer.
Flowering season: from June to the frosts.
Type: annual, perennial.

149

Here is a spectacular herbaceous border! Stocked with perennial plants, it brings together day lilies, campion and coral flowers. At the back, goat's rue, campanula, delphiniums and lupins complete the display.

Gaillardia

BLANKET FLOWER/INDIAN BLANKET, FIREWHEEL

Compositae

With their starry corollas of large brown, red or golden yellow daisy-like flowers, always outlined in brown or a lighter shade, gaillardias are essential in banks of summer flowers. Just like marguerites, ornamental tobacco plants, zinnias and gauras, they are in flower all summer, filling the garden with colour.

Useful hints

— Sow the annual varieties in March in a cold frame filled with good light soil, and then prick them out in May on a sunny slope. They will flower all summer.

— Sow the perennial varieties in a nursery in June, prick them out in September on sunny slopes. They will then flower the following summer.

Recommended

— The annual Gaillardia, *G. aristata*, is especially pretty in a mixture of different tints.

— As far as *G. pulchella* is concerned, choose a mixture and then decide on which colours you like.

Height: 30 cm (12 in).
Spacing and planting distance: 20 cm (8 in).
Soil: ordinary.
Cultivation: sunny.
Propagation: from seed.
Flowering season: June–October.
Type: annual, perennial.

Galanthus

SNOWDROP

Amaryllidaceae

Each year, it's the same: when it's time to buy them, snowdrops are the last thing on your mind, and then, when February comes, you go wild over those that appear in the garden next door. One year, at least, get some bulbs and plant them near the house so you can have the pleasure of looking at them without freezing.

Useful hints

— Buy several dozen to give a mass effect. Plant before mid-December in soil to which some peat has been added, since they like a certain amount of moisture.

— Snowdrops settle in easily. Rather than waiting for their leaves to fade before dividing them when they get too tightly packed, do it just after they flower.

Recommended

— The best known snowdrop is *Galanthus nivalis*: a double-flowered version of this exists. It looks very good under deciduous trees, with its flowers breaking through the carpet of dead leaves.

— Slightly larger, *G. elwesii* has lovely bluish-green leaves. In the light soils it likes, it can almost become a weed.

Height: 15–20 cm (6–8 in).
Spacing and planting distance: 10 cm (4 in).
Soil: ordinary.
Cultivation: under deciduous trees or in sun.
Propagation: by division in April.
Flowering season: February, March.
Type: bulb.

Galega

GOAT'S RUE

Leguminosae

It flowers exuberantly, and must be staked. It owes its common name 'goat's rue' to its leaves, which have the same properties as those of rue and are much liked by goats. It does well in ordinary soils, and flowers for a long time. In ornamental gardens, its tendency to spread is not always welcome, but it is very good as a space-filler in less well-tended areas.

Useful hints

— Sow in springtime, first soaking the seeds in water overnight. As soon as three leaves appear, prick it out into pots before finally planting in place at the end of summer.

— Cut down the stems at the start of winter, then mark the location of the stems to avoid damaging them in spring.

— The leaves are an excellent raw material for compost or even for sheltering other plants from the cold.

Recommended

— The English cultivars, such as 'Lady Wilson' or 'Her Majesty', are preferable to the true breed, whose unrestrained growth is not always controllable.

Height: 1–1.5 m (40–60 in).
Spacing and planting distance: 50 cm (20 in).
Soil: ordinary, moist even in summer.
Cultivation: sunny.
Propagation: from seed in spring or by division in winter.
Flowering season: June, July.
Type: perennial.

△ **Gaillarda aristata**
▽ **Galanthus nivalis**

Galtonia

SUMMER HYACINTH
Liliaceae

Few bulb flowers bloom in summer other than the gladioli. Also natives of South Africa, *Galtonia candicans* shares this feature. It comes in very handy in brightening up banks of perennial flowers which are a little dull at that time of year and is very effective combined with little-flowered fuchsias or phlox.

Useful hints

— Plant in April/May in deep, fairly rich soil which stays moist in summer. Put the bulbs at least 15 cm (6 in) down, since the stem will later grow to over 1 m (40 in) high: they need to be well secured to stand up to storms without being flattened.

— Cut the flowering stems in September to prevent them going to seed. The seeds sometimes shoot of their own accord but the young plants must always be pricked out into rich soil if they are to grow at any speed.

— The simplest method of propagation consists of stripping the bulblets from around the main bulb and replanting them in a corner of the kitchen garden. They will flower in 2–3 years.

— In October, pull out the clumps with a little earth and let them dry in a cellar. Then clean the bulbs and store in a temperate place over the winter.

Height: 1.2–1.5 m (48–60 in).
Spacing and planting distance: 20 cm (8 in).
Soil: ordinary, rich in compost.
Cultivation: full sun.
Propagation: from seed or by separating young bulbs.
Flowering season: July–September.
Type: bulb.

▽ *Galega officinalis*

△ *Gaultheria procumbens*
▽ *Galtonia candicans*

Gaultheria

PARTRIDGEBERRY, WINTERGREEN/PEARLBERRY
Ericaceae

Partridgeberry, wintergreen or pearlberry, this is a plant with some pretty names. With its little round leaves and its pretty red berries, this space-filler which never grows higher than 20 cm (8 in) is not short of attractive features. It's also an undergrowth plant which makes beautiful carpets in carefully-tended clearings, and makes good company for *Filipendulas* and *Rodgersias*.

Useful hints

— Plant in early autumn or spring, in humus-rich, slightly acid soil (it likes moist soils).

— Divide the roots every three years.

Recommended

— *Gaultheria procumbens*, the most popular (this is the one most often called partridgeberry) has white or pink flowers.

— *G. shallon*, less well known, reaches 1.2 m (48 in) and flowers equally in pink or white before producing black berries.

Height: 15 cm–1.2 m (6–48 in).
Spacing and planting distance: 30–90 cm (12–36 in).
Soil: humus-rich, acid.
Cultivation: semi-shade.
Propagation: by division.
Flowering season: June, July.
Type: perennial.

Gaura lindheimeri/ Gaura

GAURA/WHITE GAURA

Oenotheraceae/Onagraceae

Little known, but very hardy, this plant rapidly becomes an essential when tried out for a year. It forms very graceful clumps, since each very fine stem carries just a few delicate leaves. Flowers appear along these stems throughout the summer, catching the eye by their resemblance to white butterflies. White with the merest wash of carmine pink, they flower in succession and are excellent flowers for quality bouquets.

Useful hints

— Plant in spring in any kind of soil, but preferably well-drained. Its place is the second row of mixed borders. You can also combine it with semi-dwarf dahlias or cosmos.

— Mulch the soil to help it stay moist in summer. Collect some seeds in September – the little seeds dotted around the stems – and sow them in spring under a cold frame. They shoot rapidly and the plants will flower the first summer.

Height: 0.9–1.2 m (36–48 in).
Spacing and planting distance: 30 cm. (12 in)
Soil: ordinary, on the light side.
Cultivation: at least 6 hours of sun per day.
Propagation: from cuttings in summer and from seed in spring.
Flowering season: all summer.
Type: perennial.

△ *Gaura lindheimerii*
▽ *Gazania* 'Sunbeam'

Gazania

GAZANIA/TREASURE FLOWER

Compositae

With its pretty silver-backed leaves, this is an ideal plant for beginners. Whether you treat it with care and sow it early in spring under glass or just scatter the seeds a little later, in April/May or September in a corner of the nursery, you're bound to succeed. And if you like the idea of yellow leaves crowned in brown, intense yellow, rust or red, don't delay. Gazania brightens up the garden right through summer. All it needs is watering—and there you are. It waits until the sun is right overhead before unfurling its corollas, but closes up as soon as the sun goes in.

Useful hints

— From sowing to flowering, all it needs is heat and sunlight. Don't plant gazanias in the shade, as they will not thrive there.

— You can grow them in open ground, in any soil as long as it is well-drained, as well as in pots. In these conditions they not infrequently last for several years.

Height: 30 cm (12 in).
Spacing and planting distance: 15 cm (6 in).
Soil: ordinary.
Cultivation: sunny.
Propagation: from seed or cuttings.
Flowering season: July–October.
Type: annual, perennial in warm and temperate climates.

154

Gentiana

GENTIAN
Gentianaceae

Gentians form an enormous group with a wealth of very beautiful flowers. The only problem is sorting out the varieties which will not thrive in anything but an upland climate from those which are happily at home in rockeries anywhere.

Useful hints

— Plant gentians in early autumn or spring, in fresh but well-drained soil. The addition of peat and coarse sand is recommended.

◁ *Gentiana acaulis*
Gentiana septemfida ▷
Gentiana sino-ornata ▷
▽ *Gentiana verna*

— Since these plants suffer in winter from excess moisture, which can lead to disastrous rot, surround their base with a layer of gravel at least 2 cm (1 in) thick.

— Gentians can be grown from seed if the seed is fresh, and they are sown in autumn and left to winter outside to undergo the effects of the cold and alternate frosts and thaws. Prick the young plants out in the spring.

Recommended

— Acaulous (i.e. stemless) gentian, is a little gem which flourishes in fresh sunny, humus-rich surroundings. Its stunning blue flowers are reminiscent of the azure blue of mountain skies. There is a number of different varieties, of which *D. acaulis* 'Dinarica' is the easiest to cultivate in the open, with larger, later flowers which appear in May–July instead of April–June.

— Completely different, with its stems with their willow-like leaves, willow gentian (*G. asclepiadea*) can reach 60 cm (24 in). It can be used in mixed borders but is undoubtedly prettier in slightly wild undergrowth.

— Farrer's gentian (*G. farrieri*) comes to us from China, and could easily take over from acaulous gentian in our gardens. Its sky-blue corollas, open wide against the clouds, are superbly enhanced by the stripes which form a kind of corset. It is late flowering, usually in September.

— The large gentian (*G. lutea*) certainly lives up to its name—it may reach over 2 m (6 ft 6 in) tall if it likes the soil. It flowers in late summer, even if grown in the open. Its roots are used in making a well-known aperitif.

— Of all the dwarf gentians, *G. septemfida* is the easiest to grow. It crawls across the soil with bunches of flowers on stems barely 15 cm (6 in) tall.

— You may sometimes have to wait until October to admire *G. sina-ornata* in flower. Its flowers, a stunning blue often with violet streaks, are one of the final flings of the rockery. It is relatively easy to grow in peaty, slightly sandy soil.

Height: 10–200 cm (4–80 in), depending on variety.
Spacing and planting distance: 15–30 cm (6–12 in).
Soil: Fresh *and* well-drained.
Cultivation: at least 3 hours of sun a day.
Propagation: by cold sowing or dividing clumps.
Flowering season: May–October, depending on variety.
Type: annual, perennial.

155

Geranium

GERANIUM
Geraniaceae

These hardy perennials, which must not be confused with the 'geraniums' at the florist's (which are in fact pelargoniums), are a real boon to lovers of mixed borders and gardeners in general. They literally come up all by themselves, quickly forming wide bands of flowers, usually in shades of pink, mauve or blue. Nor does their attraction end with their flowering, since they have very elegant, downy leaves running the whole gamut of green in nature. They are ideal for use with ancolias, poppies, lupins and even ferns, since they have no objection to growing in semi-shade.

Useful hints

— Plant early in spring, in fresh, humus-rich soil. Water regularly to help the clumps take. Cut away faded flowers to avoid sapping the plants' strength unnecessarily.

— Every three years, split the clumps into a dozen new specimens and replant immediately. Some, like *Geranium psilostemon*, form very dense roots. Split the clumps with a very sharp knife, preferably in September, and plant the shoots in sand enriched with peat. Bring in

◁ *Geranium platypetalum*
▽ *Geranium renardii*

under cold glass in the first winter. Each specimen must have a shoot if it is to survive.

Recommended

— Spring geraniums open the proceedings from May onwards: *Geranium macrorrhizum* is an excellent ground cover, with its quilted leaves with their rich autumn colours, particularly in the 'Spessart' variety; but don't overlook its delicate pink flowers either. *G. renardii* is ideal for rockeries, since it never grows over 30 cm (12 in) tall. Its white flowers with their streaks of violet are very delicate seen close up, and set off to perfection by silvery-green leaves. It contrasts well with *G. subcaulescens*, with stunning purple-red flowers.

— Early summer sees most geraniums flowering in profusion, such as *G. endressi*, mauve pink in the pure strain and pure pink (one of the prettiest in spring) in 'Wargrave Pink'. The real stars are *G. pratense* and its numerous hybrids, among them 'Johnson's Blue', a very delicate mauve blue, very much like the blue of *G. platypetalum*. Hybrid geranium genealogy is a highly complex subject, and the frequent changes of name mean that you would be well advised to consult your grower about the nature of the plants he is selling you. Species are often interbred.

— The geraniums which follow bloom in a succession of waves over most of the summer: these include the very pretty hybrid 'Russel Prichard', which never grows over 20 cm (8 in) high but forms dense carpets covered in vivid magenta flowers from June until the frosts. *G. sanguineum* is a purple red, but is also available in white. But the undoubted star of them all is *G. psilostemon* (formerly *G. armenum*), which from June onwards forms a majestic dome 1.20 m (4 ft) high and equally as wide, with so many magenta/purple black-centred flowers that even its abundant foliage almost disappears. It first flowers at the same time as roses, and has a second flowering at the same time as them, in August. You can then prune the foliage right back to ground level, allowing new, trim leaves to take over until the frosts: a flower you won't want to be without once you've tried it.

Height: 15–120 cm (6–48 in).
Spacing and planting distance: 20–50 cm (18–20 in).
Soil: ordinary.
Cultivation: semi-shade or sunny.
Propagation: by dividing clumps after flowering or in spring.
Flowering season: May–October.
Type: perennial.

△ *Geranium ibericum*
▽ *Geranium pratense* **'Johnson's Blue'**

△ *Geranium pratense* **'Mrs Kendal Clark'**
▽ *Geranium maculatum album*
Geranium subcaulescens ▽

▽ *Geranium endressii*
Geranium argenteum ▷

▽ *Geranium sanguineum*

Gerbera

GERBERA

Compositae

After gaining acceptance with our florists, *Gerbera jamesonii* are now making minor forays into our gardens. It has to be admitted, however, that its squat silhouette does not make it a good plant for slopes. The dwarf varieties, on the other hand, are ideal for tubs in temperate climates: they tolerate the coldest temperatures without complaining and flower throughout the summer.

Useful hints

— Plant your gerberas in spring, in rich soil which hasn't lost its freshness (equal amounts of leaf-mould and good garden soil). Water regularly, adding soluble fertilizer every month, or less often if the leaves turn yellow.

— Bring the pots inside in October: they will go on flowering over most of the winter on a barely heated veranda.

— Divide the clumps each spring: this will revive them.

Height: 30 cm (12 in).
Spacing and planting distance: 30 cm (12 in).
Soil: rich.
Cultivation: full sunlight.
Propagation: sowing in the warm in February or by dividing clumps in spring.
Flowering season: June–October.
Type: annual, perennial.

▽ **Gerbera jamesonii**

Geum × borisii △
Geum chiloense 'Mrs Bradshaw' ▷

Geum

AVENS

Rosaceae

Avens were very familiar plants to our grandparents. Their downy delicate green leaves, their vivid, almost enamelled flowers and their highly decorative fruit made them a popular choice. They are worth rediscovering for their resilience and simplicity.

Useful hints

— While at home in any type of soil, they prefer a well-drained soil slightly enriched with leaf-mould.

— Plant in autumn or spring. No protection needed in winter. Let the fruit develop, since it is usually pretty.

Recommended

— There are few summer hardy perennials which can rival *Geum × borisii* for length of flowering—from May to September, but admittedly only if well watered. Its large flowers are an attractive orange colour.

— Originally from Chile, *G. chiloense* has given rise to some excellent hybrids, of which the best known are 'Lady

Stratheden' (bright yellow), 'Mrs Bradshaw' (scarlet), 'Fire Opal' (flame red), 'Georgenberg' (orange-yellow) and 'Princess Juliana' (orange).

Height: 30–60 cm (12–24 in).
Spacing and planting distance: 25 cm (10 in).
Soil: ordinary, enriched with a little peat.
Cultivation: at least 3 hours of sun a day.
Propagation: by sowing or dividing clumps in April.
Flowering season: May–September.
Type: perennial.

Gilia capitata △
◁ *Gilia tricolor*

Gilia

GILIA

Polemoniaceae

We won't be far wrong in predicting a great future for gilias in weekend gardens: all you need to do is sow them, and success is assured. Nor is it unusual for them to reappear the following year, so well do they reseed themselves.

Useful hints

— Sow in March–April in warm, crumbly soil. Thin out the seedlings a month later, leaving 15–20 cm (6–8 in) between plants. Pinch off the main stems a little later.

— Water once a week in summer, adding a little soluble fertilizer every third watering.

Recommended

— The delicate feathery green leaves of *Gilia capitata* make an excellent background for its dense heads of violet/blue flowers. Sow generously to fill the space at the foot of old rose bushes or to go with gladioli or white tobacco.

— The flowers of *G. tricolor*, with their purple heart bordered in white which end in a delicate violet, give off a vanilla-like scent reminiscent of chocolate. They flower in succession over a number of weeks. Sow around the edges of beds or on both sides of a gravel path.

Height: 30–40 cm (12–16 in).
Spacing and planting distance: 15–20 cm (6–8 in).
Soil: ordinary, fairly cool in summer.
Cultivation: at least 6 hours of sun a day.
Propagation: by sowing in March–April.
Flowering season: from June until the frosts.
Type: annual.

159

Gladiolus

GLADIOLI (SWORD LILY)
Iridaceae

Everyone knows gladioli, with their long scapes of sometimes slightly outrageous-coloured flowers. While superb in bouquets, it is a different matter in the garden, where their slender silhouette needs the company of plants with generous foliage if it is not to look a little out of place. So plant them in groups on slopes of sage, tobacco, loose-strife or monardas to create wide swathes of colour; and, especially, don't forget the charming spring gladioli, which were once found in the wild and have retained an entirely natural grace.

Useful hints

— Plant spring gladioli in October – November in soil lightened with sand, scattering them amongst stocks and myosotis.

— Classical gladioli are planted in April–May, 10 cm (4 in) down with the point of the shoot upwards. If arranging in groups of three to five, train them inconspicuously with bamboo stakes.

— In the kitchen garden, if growing them for bouquets, plant them in rows, earth them up in June and train them by tying them to twine strung horizontally between two stakes.

— Water regularly, adding fertilizer once a fortnight. Cut off the floral scapes when the first floret opens; the bulbs will usually be exhausted afterwards.

Recommended

— There is a real surfeit of choice amongst the large-flowered species. Follow your seed merchant's advice and only buy the best quality to ensure good results. There are even green gladioli, not to mention the 'butterfly' or 'fantasy' varieties which are not to everyone's taste.

— *Gladiolus primulinus* flowers at the same time as those above, and offers less tightly packed flowers on scapes which are shorter and hence less vulnerable to wind. 'Anitra' is bright red, 'White City' is white and 'Yellow Special' a golden amber.

— The spring-flowering gladioli are less well known, the commonest being *G. byzanthinus*, with its purple red flowers, which may take if it likes the soil, and *G. colvillei* which never exceeds 60

◁ *Gladiolus* **hybrid**

△ **Yellow gladiolus**

△ **Pink gladiolus**
Violet gladiolus ▷

cm (24 in) in height and flowers in a variety of colours, usually marked by a handsome pink or red throat.

Height: 60–140 cm (24–55 in).
Spacing and planting distance: 15 cm (6 in).
Soil: rich and deep.

Cultivation: sunny.
Propagation: by separating new corms in November.
Flowering season: between May and October, depending on the species and when planted.
Type: bulb.

161

△ *Glaucium flavum*

Glaucium

HORNED POPPY

Papaveraceae

If you like walking in the countryside in May, you are bound to have admired the flowers of the horned poppy. Linked firmly to the soil by a massive root system, it unfurls a new flower each day, rather like its cousins the corn poppies. *Glaucium flavum* is a little gem, grown like a biennial or hardy perennial.

Useful hints

— Plant in autumn, in a pocket of sand or gravel, or wait until spring if your soil is heavy in winter.

— They can also be sown in May–June, in which case they will flower the following year. The main problem is finding seeds, so let your first specimens go to seed and harvest them at the end of the year.

Height: 30 cm (12 in).
Spacing and planting distance: 30 cm (12 in).
Soil: rather poor but well-drained in winter.
Cultivation: full sunlight.
Propagation: by sowing in late spring.
Flowering season: June–September.
Type: annual, biennial, perennial.

162

Gloriosa

GLORIOSA

Liliaceae

From the end of June onwards, *Gloriosa rothschildiana* bursts into a host of flaming orange butterflies, swarming up the slightest trellice if on a sunny wall. Grow them near your grey-leaved hardy perennials, such as sage or *Stachys olympica*, to temper the brilliance of their colour a little.

Useful hints

— Plant in September, in large tubs filled with leaf-mould mixed with compost in areas where the winters are cold; pot them out in their chosen positions in April. In places where the climate is mild, plant in the open along a well-exposed wall on pockets filled with the same compost.

— Protect the roots with a cover of dead leaves each autumn.

Height: 2–3 m (6–9 ft).
Spacing and planting distance: 50 cm (20 in).
Soil: rich in humus.
Cultivation: sunny.
Propagation: by separating rhizomes in spring.
Flowering season: July–October.
Type: bulb.

◁ *Gloriosa rotschildiana*
▽ *Godetia grandiflora* **'Whitney'**

Godetia

GODETIA

Onageaceae

There aren't many annuals with the spectacular colours of *Godetia grandiflora*: delicate pinks, subtle mauves, never-jarring reds. . . . Each plant is a bouquet in itself, since the flowers all unfurl at the same time. This firework only lasts three weeks, but what a beauty!

Useful hints

— Sow directly on the spot in April – May, once the soil has warmed up, first mixing the fairly fine seeds with sand to give a better distribution. Thin out the shoots two weeks later, leaving one plant every 20 cm (8 in).

— Pinch the plants off halfway up a month later. Water regularly, adding a little soluble fertilizer every other time.

Recommended

The 'Whitney' form often has single flowers on semi-dwarf plants. The double 'Azalea-flowered' form is better known, and is more compact (35 cm [14 in] on average). Some seed merchants sell colours separately, enabling you to paint a magnificent canvas.

Height: 35–45 cm (14–18 in).
Spacing and planting distance: 20 cm (8 in).
Soil: on the rich, fresh side.
Cultivation: full sunlight.
Propagation: by sowing in April–May.
Flowering season: May–August, for 3 weeks.
Type: annual.

Gomphrena

GOMPHRENA

Amaranthaceae

Gomphrena globosa has funny globulous inflorescences ranging from purple and carmine to charming pink. These plants look good in a bed of hardy perennials, lending it a hint of nostalgia at the end of summer.

Useful hints

— Sow in a sheltered spot in March, in a mixture of equal parts of peat and fresh earth, then prick out in place in May. The plants will flower from July to October.

— Best grown in the sun, but need generous watering.

— Very suitable for dried flower arrangements.

△ *Gomphera globosa*

Height: 30 cm (12 in).
Spacing and planting distance: 20 cm (8 in).
Soil: ordinary.
Cultivation: sunny.
Propagation: by sowing in March.
Flowering season: July–October.
Type: annual, biennial, perennial.

Gunnera

GUNNERA

Gunneraceae

Gunnera manicata is an ideal plant for filling out a wild corner of the garden in style, especially if it is crossed by a stream or is in a cool spot. Its enormous leaves usually unfurl some time between April and May, and then grow to a stunning size. The plant sometimes flowers in summer, in funny caviar-coloured heads. It belongs with the larger Caucasus heracleums, ornamental rhubarbs, water irises and arums.

Useful hints

— Plant in March–April by a body of water in well-enriched soil. Allow four spadefuls of manure compost per square metre/yard.

— Protect the roots each autumn with a cover of straw, since a cold winter may harm them.

— Plants are best bought bare-rooted, but plant them immediately.

Height: 1.50 m (5 ft).
Spacing and planting distance: 2.50 m (8 ft).
Soil: rich, humid.
Cultivation: sunny to semi-shade.
Propagation: by splitting clumps.
Flowering season: July–August.
Type: perennial.

Gunnera manicata △

Gynerium

See *Cortaderia*

Gypsophila **'Roseuschleier'** △
Gypsophila elegans ▷

Gypsophila

GYPSOPHILA/BABY'S-BREATH, GYSOPHILA

Caryophyllaceae

Also known as 'mist' because of its extraordinarily light flowers, it belongs on sunny, light-soiled, well-exposed slopes with salvias, old roses and robust perennials such as the oriental poppy or *Gaura*. It will flower throughout the summer, and can be used in dried flower arrangements.

Useful hints

— Sow both annuals and perennials in April under cover. When pricked out on to sunny slopes, the annuals will flower the same summer and the perennials the following one.

— Always plant gypsophila in light, humus-rich soil: it hates cold, damp clay soil.

Recommended

— One annual species, *Gypsophila elegans*, with flowers 1 cm (½ in) across, lightens up borders.

— Two perennials, *G. paniculata*, with its tiny flowers sometimes in pairs, and *G. repens*, are marvellous in rockeries.

Height: 10–60 cm (4–24 in).
Spacing and planting distance: 20 cm (8 in).
Soil: light, humus-rich.
Cultivation: sunny.
Propagation: from seed and by division in spring.
Flowering season: June, September.
Type: annual, perennial.

△ *Haberlea rhodopensis*

Haberlea

HABERLEA
Gesneriaceae

Your main problem will be tearing these plants away from their wonderful surroundings in the Balkans. You may have to join a rockery plant club, but it'll be worth it, since you'll then discover one of the joys of European flora. Looking somewhat like a miniature gloxinia, this plant forms a cushion of embossed leaves, with some rosettes of flowers in the spring. Their buds unfurl in orchid-pink corollas culminating in a yellow throat. It is certainly worth going to some trouble to obtain it.

Useful hints

— Plant in springtime in a corner exposed to the north and shelter under a pane of glass through the winter to prevent too much moisture.

— Put down anti-slug pellets and keep the soil moist through the summer. If mosses appear around the edges, that's a good sign. Collect the seeds and sow them nearby. They will come up the following year and you can prick out the young plants after a year.

Height: 15–20 cm (6–8 in).
Spacing and planting distance: 15 cm (6 in).
Soil: peat and sand.
Cultivation: sheltered, north-facing.
Propagation: from seed.
Flowering season: late spring.
Type: perennial.

Hedysarum

HEDYSARUM/SWEET VETCH
Leguminosae

These plants are at their best on sunny hillocks or surrounded by borders of hardy perennials, their compact flowers going well with achilleas or chrysanthemums.

Useful hints

— Sow directly on site in September or March if you want to treat them as annuals.

— Alternatively, layer long shoots in September, leaving the top 10 cm (4 in) above ground. Separate the new plant from the old a year later.

— Once established, don't disturb, but train if necessary.

— Cut the stems 5 cm (2 in) from the ground in November.

Recommended

— *Hedysarum coronarium* – sainfoin – can be used as a biennial or perennial, in which case its life will be short (3 to 4 years). The flowers are red and scented.

Height: 1 m (40 in).
Spacing and planting distance: 50 cm (20 in).
Soil: normal, well-drained.
Cultivation: sunny.
Propagation: from seed or by layering.
Flowering season: June–September.
Type: annual, perennial.

▽ *Hedysarum multijugum*

165

Helenium autumnale 'Chipperfield' △

Helenium

HELENIUM

Compositae

Heleniums belong on banks of perennials along with felty-leaved plants such as stachys, sage and autumn 'marigolds' such as asters, chrysanthemums or rudbeckias. They make delightful patches of warm colours which go superbly with the mauves, pinks and greys of their companions.

Useful hints

— Give *Helenium autumnale* a rich but well-drained soil, planting in 20 cm (8 in) wide pockets filled with rich, sandy loam.

— Sow in the nursery in May and prick out in September or even the March after sowing: they will flower in the summer after the one in which they are planted.

Recommended

Most are hybrids, like 'Coppelia' (toffee-coloured), 'Mahogany' (yellow with orange rings), 'Pumilum magnificum' (golden yellow, richer in colour than the true varieties).

Height: 60–80 cm (24–32 in).
Spacing and planting distance: 30 cm (12 in).
Soil: rich, light.
Cultivation: sunny.
Propagation: in spring, from seed or by division.
Flowering season: August–October.
Type: annual, perennial.

Helianthemum

ROCK ROSE/SUN ROSE

Cistaceae

Helianthemum is ideal for carpeting rockeries or the dry slopes often found bordering hillside gardens. *Helianthemum nummularium* insists on sunlight and very hot, dry soils, and goes marvellously with dainty or alpine marigolds whose massive cushions of delicate flowers match its exuberant sheets of flowers in delicate or brilliant colours.

Useful hints

— It should preferably be planted in spring to save the young plants from the summer rains, in ordinary but warm well-lit soil.

— Cut away shrivelled flowers to encourage new ones to appear.

— Divide major clumps every 3 years.

Recommended

— It is impossible to list them all: let's just mention 'Amy Baring' (yellow, golden bud); 'Ben Afflick' (delicate orange); 'The Bride' (white); 'Wisley Pink' (pink).

Height: 20–30 cm (8–12 in).
Spacing and planting distance: 50 cm (20 in).
Soil: ordinary.
Cultivation: sunny.
Propagation: in spring, from seed or by division.
Flowering season: June–October.
Type: perennial.

Helianthemum **'Wisley Pink'** △
Helianthus decapetalus ▷
Helianthus salicifolius ▽

Helianthus

SUNFLOWER/COMMON SUNFLOWER, MIRASOL

Compositae

Use sunflowers as a temporary hedge to screen off a new garden, or in imposing groups to light up a dull corner. But don't plant any of this family in your beds, because their greed is equal only to their thirst, and neighbouring flowers will suffer.

Useful hints

— Sow annual sunflowers directly on site in pockets of three seeds; later, space them out 30 cm (12 in) apart.

— Plant the perennials in spring.

— These plants prefer a rich soil—in fresh, dry soil, they will be somewhat stunted (although some would say a reasonable size!).

Recommended

— As well as the classic sunflower, *Helianthus annuus*, there are two perennial species: *H. salicifolius*, with long fringed leaves like a willow, reaches 2 m (80 in) high before unveiling its yellow flowers; *H. decapetalus* is a large double sunflower.

Height: 1–2.5 m (40–100 in).
Spacing and planting distance: 30 cm (12 in).
Soil: rich.
Cultivation: sunny.
Propagation: from seed or by division.
Flowering season: July, August.
Type: annual, perennial.

△ *Helichrysum petiolatum*

△ *Helichrysum bracteatum*

Helichrysum

EVERLASTING FLOWER/ STRAWFLOWER

Compositae

What a large variety there is to choose from – there are the annual varieties, which we know as 'everlasting', semi-wild ones and even shrubs. Their common characteristic is their stars of flowers and their incredible ability to withstand even the hottest ground. Sometimes they are enhanced by grey leaves which play a not unimportant role in their decorative effect. They are usually excellent for windowboxes, since they thrive on very little soil.

Useful hints

— Sow everlasting in the sun in spring, in the warm in March, under cold frames in April or directly in the ground in May, in a corner of your kitchen garden to give you dried flowers all year round.

— The only care needed is a little hoeing and watering. Tie the stems to prevent them collapsing in violent storms.

— Harvest them in late August/early September, when the flowers are well open but their hearts have not yet faded. Dry head-down in a dark place for two months.

— Little helichrysums for decorating slopes and windowboxes are planted in April/May in a rich, sandy soil. Pinch them out several times to give dwarf plants. Take cuttings in summer and keep them out of the cold in winter on a balcony or in a heated frame.

— The hardiest varieties can stay where they are, providing you shelter the base with straw or rock wool then cover the whole with plastic film.

Recommended

— 'Bracted' everlastings (*Helichrysum bracteatum*) are often sold mixed, which is a pity, since you can use specific varieties to greater effect. There is the 'Bikini' variety, most often available in fiery red, and slightly shorter at 35 cm (14 in).

— Also known as the curry plant, *H. angustifolium* (or *H. serotinum*) is one of the wildest of the shrub-like helichrysums. All its silvery-grey foliage gives off a very pronounced curry odour. It flowers in late summer in a strong yellow.

— *H. hybridi* (sulphur light) will enchant anyone who loves grey foliage. Its very soft mimosa yellow flowers are exactly what is needed to set off the blue of *Caryopteris* or lavender.

— A popular helichrysum for decorating balconies is still the *H. petiolatum*. It threads its way easily amongst more distinguished foliage like that of the pelargoniums and sets it off perfectly with its grey leaves. The species known as 'Limelight' will look quite startling in conjunction with yellow primulas.

Height: 30–120 cm (12–48 in).
Spacing and planting distance: 30 cm (12 in).
Soil: ordinary, even a little on the dry side.
Cultivation: full sun.
Propagation: from seed in spring or by taking cuttings in summer.
Flowering season: July, August.
Type: annual.

△ *Heliopsis scabra*

Heliopsis

HELIOPSIS

Compositae

With its double, warmly coloured flowers like large pompoms, some gold, some yellow, *Heliopsis scabra* is like a ray of sunshine bringing magic into a garden. It leaves you in no doubt that it's a hardy perennial: sometimes it even threatens to take over. Watch out for your less robust plants! Plant only in company with other outstandingly robust varieties such as tansies, heleniums, asters or even Chinese lanterns (*Physalis*).

Useful hints

— Sow in May in the nursery and then prick out in autumn or the next spring on well-exposed slopes.

— Any good garden soil will do.

Recommended

— There are giants such as 'Golden Plume', golden-yellow doubles which reach 1.2 m (48 in), and smaller varieties such as 'Summer Sun', only 50 cm (20 in) tall but semi-double and a butter-yellow colour.

Height: 50–120 cm (20–48 in).
Spacing and planting distance: 30 cm (12 in).
Soil: ordinary.
Situation: sunny.
Propagation: by division in autumn.
Flowering season: July–October.
Type: perennial.

Heliotropium

HELIOTROPE, CHERRY PLANT

Boraginaceae

Heliotropes have long been popular, both for their flowers, which come in shades ranging from mauve to blue with a few bursts of white and stand out well from their embossed, slightly coarse foliage and above all, for their scent, unique and captivating. It seems that over the years the heliotropes have lost this enchanting scent, and those we grow now just smell of vanilla. They form little shrubs in the warm and temperate climates to keep jasmins and aromatic plants company.

Useful hints

— Sow in March/April in little boxes filled with rich, light soil, sheltered under glass. Prick out on site in May.

— Outside warm and temperate areas, protect in winter or, better still, grow them in tubs which you can take indoors in winter.

Height: 30–50 cm (12–20 in).
Spacing and planting distance: 30 cm (12 in).
Soil: rich, well-drained.
Cultivation: sunny.
Propagation: from seed in March/April or from cuttings in spring.
Flowering season: June–September.
Type: annual.

△ *Heliotropium × hybridum*
▽ *Helipterum manglesii*

Helipterum

HELIPTERUM, RHODANTHE/ MANGLE SUNRAY

Compositae

These are the prettiest of the everlasting flowers. Each plant forms a bouquet of charming seersucker flowers in delicate colours. Very easy to grow in a corner of a kitchen-garden, *Helipterum manglesii* can also be used to decorate sunlit slopes where they will show to good effect for most of the year.

Useful hints

— Sow seeds on the spot in April, first adding a little sand if the earth is heavy. Thin the seedlings out in May, leaving just one plant every 20 cm (8 in). Water regularly, but don't add any fertilizer.

— Flowers can be harvested in September. Cut the whole stems and hang them head down in a dry, shady room for 2 months.

Height: 30 cm (12 in).
Spacing and planting distance: 20 cm (8 in).
Soil: any soil will do, preferably sandy.
Cultivation: full sun.
Propagation: from seed in spring.
Flowering season: July–September.
Type: annual.

△ *Helleborus lividus*
▽ *Helleborus orientalis*

△ *Helleborus corsicus*
▷ *Helleborus × sternii*
◁ *Helleborus niger*

Helleborus

HELLEBORE/CHRISTMAS-ROSE
Ranunculaceae

Plants with a great future, hellebores combine the beauty of flowers and an imposing silhouette. These are very robust plants which fit just as well in the slightly wilder corners of the garden as in the most formal beds. As if this were not enough, they also tend to flower in midwinter, when there aren't many flowers around.

Useful hints
— Plant in autumn to give them time to settle in before the frosts. If planting in pots, put the pots under cold frames since the roots are somewhat prone to freezing.

— Mulch the soil with pine bark or peat from May onwards. Let the fruit ripen, since this will give you a lot of natural seeds. In very hot weather, water now and again and watch out for swarms of greenfly on the ends of young stems.

— Every three or four years, rejuvenate by dividing them, preferably in September. Water generously to encourage the plants to take.

— *H. foetidus* will do much better in a shady position.

Recommended
— The best-known hellebore is undoubtedly the Christmas rose (*Helleborus niger*). The flowers sometimes appear at this time, but more often wait until January or even February. They are relatively large, white with a hint of green.

— If you like purple flowers, pick *H. atrorubens*, which has the same bearing as the one above.

— Taller and often darker, *H. orientalis* is truly fascinating. The colours vary widely, so we recommend buying them as flowering plants to avoid washed-out shades.

— Even if you're put off by the name stinking hellebore, leave room for *H. foetidus*. Its handsome palm leaves and its bouquets of a stunning pale yellow make it the star of January. It is a sight growing wild in the countryside. Its main stem droops sadly when the cold winds blow but it perks up as soon as it thaws.

— The undisputed queen, the Corsican hellebore (*H. lividus corsicus*), is very similar, but taller and with finely toothed leaves. Its lime-green flowers go superbly with mahonias, narcissi or golden variegated ivy.

Height: 20–70 cm (8–28 in).
Spacing and planting distance: 25–30 cm (10–12 in).
Soil: very rich in humus (leaf-mould or peat).
Cultivation: semi-shade.
Propagation: from seed or by division, in September.
Flowering season: December–May.
Type: perennial.

169

Helxine/Soleirolia

MIND YOUR OWN BUSINESS, BABY'S TEARS

Urticaceae

What could be prettier or more delicate than *Helxine*, a godsend to dark, damp gardens, one of the same family as the stinging nettle? Plant it in a town garden, in a windowbox in the shade or a pot, and it will always survive. Hide a few snowdrop, crocus or cyclamen bulbs in the soil beneath it to give a charming, ever-changing display through the seasons.

Useful hints

— It is best planted in spring: water generously.

— Watch out for frost in winter. It isn't very fragile, but droops sadly once the temperature falls towards −10°C (14°F). Don't water so much at this time of year, but remember to keep the earth a bit moist if growing it inside.

Height: 5–10 cm (2–4 in).
Spacing and planting distance: 10 cm (4 in).
Soil: light, rich in humus.
Cultivation: shade or semi-shade.
Propagation: by division in spring.
Type: perennial.

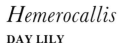

△ **Hemerocallis fulva**
◁ **Helxine soleiroleii**
Hemerocallis citrina ▷
▽ **Hemerocallis hybrid**

Hemerocallis

DAY LILY

Liliaceae

The Americans go wild over them (they even have their own shows), but they are used less in Europe despite their astonishing hardiness. With their corollas of little lilies running the gamut of yellows, oranges, pinks and reds, they have a lot of charm and ought to belong in all perennial beds. When they feel at home, they quickly form impressive clumps covered in flowers from July to September. But don't use them in flower arrangements, since they wilt very quickly. New flowers appear each day.

Useful hints

— Best planted in spring in good, ordinary soil on sunny slopes.

— Every three years, divide any clumps which have become invasive in spring.

Recommended

— *Hemerocallis citrina* has little star-shaped flowers of lemon yellow with a delicate perfume.

— *H. fulva*, very hardy and common, has orange flowers.

— As well as these two charming species, a number of hybrids with large waxen flowers have appeared, such as 'Autumn Red', 'Pink Prelude' and 'Bonanza'.

Height: 40 cm (16 in).
Spacing and planting distance: 40 cm (16 in).
Soil: ordinary.
Cultivation: sun or light shade.
Propagation: by division in spring.
Flowering season: June–August.
Type: perennial.

△ *Hepatica triloba*

Hepatica

HEPATICA

Ranunculaceae

Looking a lot like a blue wood anemone, *Hepatica triloba* are charming in spring alongside early bulbs such as *Eranthis*, crocus or *Iris reticulata*. They are also at home in undergrowth or in shady corners of rockeries and make delightful borders.

Useful hints

— Plant at any time of year, in groups of at least 6 to give a feeling of size. Mulch the soil with pine bark to show the flowers off better against a neutral background.

— Divide clumps every 3 years just after flowering, and water regularly to help them take. They are often self-seeding.

Height: 10 cm (4 in).
Spacing and planting distance: 15 cm (6 in).
Soil: ordinary, fairly rich in humus.
Cultivation: shade.
Propagation: by division in spring.
Flowering season: February–April.
Type: perennial.

Heracleum mantegazzianum △
Hesperis matronalis ▷

Heracleum

HERACLEUM/COW PARSNIP

Umbelliferae

Looking for an imposing, fast-growing plant to hide an unpleasant view or put life into a newly-planted garden? Then look no further, this is the one you need. Just over 3 m (120 in), *Heracleum* will produce increasingly impressive thickets as the years go by. Its only fault is that its leaves can cause terrible itching in people who are sensitive to it.

Useful hints

— Plant in autumn in well-turned-over soil with some peat and leaf-mould added. Water frequently and generously once the warm weather arrives. Use this period to add soluble fertilizer once a month.

— Once flowering is over, cut off a lot of the stems to avoid being invaded by self-seedings. (Use gloves.)

— You can cut the last scapes in October and dry them to give spectacular flower arrangements.

Height: 2–3 m (80–120 in).
Spacing and planting distance: 1.5 m (60 in).
Soil: rich, stays cool in summer.
Cultivation: at least 3 hours of sun per day.
Propagation: by division in March.
Flowering season: July, August.
Type: perennial.

Hesperis

HESPERIS/DAMES' ROCKET

Cruciferae

One of the old favourites, *Hesperis* enchants us with its delicate violet flowers and its bewitching scent of stocks in May, especially in the evenings. *Hesperis matronalis* seeds itself with ease everywhere, looks delightful with narcissi or tulips, and at the same time gives depth to slopes, since it grows just over 1 m (40 in) tall. There is a smaller white variety which flowers longer, and is not uncommonly found in bloom in July. This is what the artist Monet's famous garden at Giverny is based on.

Useful hints

— Plant in autumn, preferably away from the front of your beds, since this hides its inelegant foliage near the ground. Train the stems carefully in April to stop them collapsing in sudden showers.

— Gather the natural seeds appearing in summer and replant them at leisure. Generally speaking, the stems which flower profusely quickly wilt. The white variety is hardier.

Height: 60–100 cm (24–40 in).
Spacing and planting distance: 30 cm (12 in).
Soil: ordinary, on the rich, heavy side: likes chalk.
Cultivation: at least 3 hours of sun per day.
Propagation: from seed in June.
Flowering season: May, June, sometimes July.
Type: perennial.

Useful hints

— Plant in early spring or September/ October in good garden soil, in semi-shade or in sunlight. Heavy clay soils should be avoided.

— Every three years, divide the clumps in spring and use this opportunity to enrich the soil with four spadefuls of compost per square metre.

Recommended

The hybrids you often find under the name *Heuchera brizoides*: 'Bressingham Blaze' (orange) and 'Pearl Drops' (white).

Height: 30 cm (12 in).
Spacing and planting distance: 20 cm (8 in).
Soil: ordinary.
Cultivation: sunny.
Propagation: by division in spring.
Flowering season: June–August.
Type: perennial.

Heuchera brizoides △
Hieracum aurandiacum ▷

Heuchera

CORAL FLOWER/CORAL BELLS

Saxifragaceae

A native of village gardens where it is often found in company with violets, marigolds, bergenias and ancolias, *Heuchera sanguinea* needs no care since it grows in any soil, fills out over the years and flowers faithfully each year. It can also be grown in pots, in a shady court-yard where its delicate foliage and strands of coral flowers will look wonderful, as edging in borders or as ground cover underneath deciduous trees. The modern hybrids and varieties are more attractive than the species.

Hieracium

HIERACIUM/HAWKWEED

Compositae

The genus *Hieracium* includes a lot of weeds, some medicinal plants such as hawkweed and some very decorative plants, especially for the slightly wilder corners. They go well with Siberian iris, *Geum* and *Sedum spectabilis*.

Useful hints

— Plant at any time of year, even if in flower, but water them well afterwards. Weed the clumps carefully each spring and build them up with 2–3 cm (1 in) of leaf-mould or well-rotted compost.

— Every 3 years, divide the clumps and replant immediately, preferably in early spring.

Recommended

— *Hieracium aurandiacum* is a lively orange-red. This creeping plant forms borders resistant even to invasive plants.

— The hawkweed (*H. pilosella*) has lemon-yellow flowers. The leaves and flowers are used in herbal teas for the liver and for fevers.

Height: 10–30 cm (4–12 in).
Spacing and planting distance: 20 cm (8 in).
Soil: any soil, on the light side.
Cultivation: at least 6 hours of sun per day.
Propagation: by division in spring.
Flowering season: June–September.
Type: perennial.

Hosta

**PLANTAIN LILY/FRAGRANT
PLANTAIN LILY**

Liliaceae

Hostas prefer cool, shady gardens, where they show at their best, unfurling their sculptural, deeply veined, lacquered leaves, sometimes with splashes of cream or delicate rings of silver. In town, they can be used to good effect in gardens using just the outline of their leaves and the range of greens and whites. Put them with *Helxines*, ferns and *Eucomias*: the result will be elegant, surprising and will need no tending.

Useful hints

— Plant in spring, in humus-rich soil.

— Divide the clumps every third or fourth spring.

— Plant varieties with interesting flowers such as *Hosta plantaginea*, *H. fortunei*, *H. lancifolia* and *H. ventricosa* in semishade to make them flower better.

Recommended

— The most beautiful is *Hosta plantaginea* for its white lily flowers and its scent. *H. fortunei* and *H. lancifolia* have mauve flowers and *H. ventricosa* violet ones. *H. sieboldiana*'s foliage is the most seductive, since it is a velvety blue-green.

Height: 30 cm (12 in).
Spacing and planting distance: 30 cm (12 in).
Soil: humus-rich.
Cultivation: semi-shade.
Propagation: by division in spring.
Flowering season: July, August.
Type: perennial.

△ *Hosta*
◁ *Hosta fortunei*
Hosta sieboldiana ▷
▽ *Hosta lancifolia*

Houttuynia cordata △

Houstonia

BLUETS

Rubiaceae

Very little known, *Houstonia caerulea* (or correctly *H. serpyllifolia*) is a charming little American plant that looks like chickweed and forms a dense cushion of bright green leaves barely 15 cm (6 in) high, with flowers that start off blue and then turn pale and white. Give it room in your rockery in a sheltered corner away from the cold which can kill it. Its flowers, which last several months, stay longer if the earth is cool. Mix with *Phlox subulata* which has very similar shades.

Useful hints

— Plant in spring in a patch of good, humus-rich soil enriched with peat. Water regularly throughout the year. When winter draws near, cover with glass to drain off excess water.

— Collect some seeds and sow them in sand before winter. They will come up in spring. Or propagate by division.

Height: 12 cm (5 in).
Spacing and planting distance: 15 cm (6 in).
Soil: cool, humus-rich.
Cultivation: semi-shade.
Propagation: from seed or by division i.. spring.
Flowering season: May–July.
Type: perennial.

Houttuynia

HOUTTUYNIA

Saururaceae

If you like lacquered leaves, full of metallic-coloured sap, you'll like *Houttuynia cordata*. Often invasive in gardens with cool soil, it puts out new mahogany shoots every year before unfurling large, dark green leaves tinted with mahogany or slate blue. In early summer, white flowers appear, giving off a unique piquant scent. It is at home with *Arum italicum*, bamboo and water iris, rapidly forming great carpets of colour.

Useful hints

— Plant clumps in a moist soil or by a pond.

— Divide plants every 3 years to stop them growing too much.

— Plant young rooted shoots in shallow earth about 5 cm (2 in) down. In ponds, plant in a container with the soil just breaking the surface.

— Check growth if they flourish.

Height: 30 cm (12 in).
Spacing and planting distance: 30 cm (12 in).
Soil: clay, moist.
Cultivation: anywhere.
Propagation: by division in spring.
Flowering season: June, July.
Type: perennial.

△ Hyacinthoides hispanica
▽ Hyacinthoides non-scripta

Hyacinthoides

WILD HYACINTH

Liliaceae

At the end of April, just when the broom is in flower, the wood hyacinths, *Hyacinthoides non-scripta*, spread in large dark blue sheets in the shelter of the undergrowth or along cool banks. Whether the undergrowth is sparse or entangled with brushwood letting little light in, they return each spring. Plant them in large beds at the foot of your flowering cherry trees to give magnificent results at little cost.

Useful hints

— Plant the bulbs as soon as the flowers have faded, burying them 20 cm (8 in) deep in good, moist, humus-rich earth—then leave them alone.

— When you pick the flowers, leave the leaves to allow the plants to go on drawing nourishment and, above all, don't try to uproot them with your bare hands: they are so deeply rooted that you'll spoil them to no avail.

Recommended

— While *Hyacinthoides non-scripta* has a pleasant scent, and mainly blue flowers, with the very occasional white, the Spanish hyacinth, *H. hispanica*, is a pale blue and has no scent at all.

Height: 20–40 cm (8–16 in).
Spacing and planting distance: 15 cm (6 in).
Soil: cool and deep.
Cultivation: anywhere.
Propagation: by separating bulbs after foliage fades.
Flowering season: April, May.
Type: bulb.

Hyacinthus

HYACINTH

Liliaceae

The common hyacinth, *Hyacinthus orientalis*, is hardly ever grown now, which is a pity, because it was a treat for the eyes, blue and slight, growing even taller than its little hybrid sisters. Growers have now bred so many varieties that you can now have hyacinths from December to March. They grow happily outside and brighten up the first days of spring.

Useful hints

— Plant hyacinths in pots in a mixture of equal parts of peat and garden soil.

— Plant hyacinths in beds in large holes filled with porous compost.

— They withstand cold well, but in heavy earth they do better if you grow them in pockets of permeable soil.

— To make the bulbs in your pots flower again, put them in compost as soon as the flowers have gone, spreading their roots out well and watering them regularly until the leaves turn yellow.

Recommended

— 'White Pearl' (pure white); 'Anne-Marie' and 'Lady Derby' (pale pink); 'Amethyst' (dark mauve); 'Ostara', dark porcelain blue; 'City of Haarlem' (cream).

Height: 10–20 cm (4–8 in).
Spacing and planting distance: 10 cm (4 in).
Soil: rich and light.
Cultivation: sunny.
Propagation: by separating bulbils in summer.
Flowering season: April, May.
Type: bulb.

Hypericum

ST JOHN'S WORT/AARON'S-BEARD, ROSE OF SHARON, HYPERICUM

Guttiferae

It's difficult to decide the boundary between hardy and shrub varieties, since the latter have very tough roots. Their bright yellow flowers brighten up rockeries and dry stone walls. They were formerly mashed in olive oil to make a sovereign remedy for wounds and burns.

Hyacinthus orientalis △

Hypericum olympicum △
Hyssopus officinalis ▷

Useful hints

— Plant in autumn or spring in a pocket of good earth. Water regularly in the first summer: then let the clumps spread as they will but watch they don't invade less hardy plants.

— Remove dried leaves in spring to give squat clumps.

Recommended

— While *Hypericum calycinum* is popular for banks which it decorates with its tough foliage, it's difficult to get rid of it if you tire of its rather hundrum yellow.

— *H. olympicum*, yellow and dense, 'Citrinum', a lemon yellow, *H. patulum*, a golden yellow with deep green leaves, and *H. polyphyllum*, golden yellow with bluish leaves, are much to be preferred in rockeries since their clumps spread relatively slowly.

Height: 15–30 cm (6–12 in).
Spacing and planting distance: 20 cm (8 in).
Soil: on the light side.
Cultivation: sunny or semi-shade.
Propagation: by division in spring.
Flowering season: June–September.
Type: perennial.

Hyssopus

HYSSOP

Labiatae (family not confirmed)

If you are at your wits' end trying to think what to plant in a pebbly corner scraped bare of earth, here's one of the few plants that can help you out. Hyssop does not merely tolerate these conditions: this is where it reaches the peak of its beauty and scent. It would be impossible not to mention the impact of its violet blue flowers or their delicious scent, a mixture of thyme and camphor. They can be used to make delicious infusions for use against stomach or throat problems. So don't delay – there's room for hyssop in your garden.

Useful hints

— Plant in spring. It will be quite at home in poor soil if it is well-drained. Place it high up to let it trail down gracefully. Its stems will become erect when it flowers, bringing lots of bees and butterflies.

— As winter draws near, cover the clumps with plastic foil or glass to keep rainwater off. Hyssop is more vulnerable to excessive moisture than cold.

Height: 40 cm (16 in).
Spacing and planting distance: 60 cm (24 in).
Soil: poor and dry.
Cultivation: full sun.
Propagation: from seed or cuttings in spring.
Flowering season: June–September.
Type: perennial.

△ *Iberis umbellata*

△ *Impatiens* **hybrid**
◁ *Iberis sempervirens*
Impatiens balsamina ▷
▽ *Impatiens balfouri*

Iberis

CANDYTUFT

Cruciferae

A very attractive little plant in a garden or terrace, since it keeps its foliage in winter. Planted in a tub or low wall border, *Iberis* knows how to make a pretty trailing clump.

Useful hints

— Sow seeds in March or take cuttings in May. Plant in a mixture of equal parts of sand and peat. Plant out in September.

— Dead-head stems with a pair of scissors.

— For sturdy plants, remove 2 to 3 cm (1 in) of young shoots in April.

— To rejuvenate old plants and force new shoots, prune to 10 cm (4 in) above ground in March or April.

Recommended

Iberis amara flowers in white and the whole range of reds and pinks. Its leaves can be used in salads. *I. officinalis*, a hardy perennial, has mauve, pink or white flowers, the latter being the prettiest.

Height: 40 cm (16 in).
Spacing and planting distance: 20 cm (8 in).
Soil: normal.
Cultivation: sunny or semi-shade.
Propagation: from seed in March or cuttings in May.
Flowering season: July–September.
Type: annual, perennial.

Impatiens

BUSY LIZZIE/BALSAM

Balsaminaceae

Impatiens has become extremely popular in recent decades: it is difficult to imagine what our grandparents planted in the shade, where its little flowers work wonders. It has proved to be a marvellous garden plant, even tolerating the sun if it is watered regularly, i.e. once a day during a heatwave.

Useful hints

— Sow in March or April in the warm on a radiator shelf. They need light to germinate. Don't bury the seeds, but cover the seed trough with a layer of earth for the first 2 weeks. If you sow a mixture of colours, prick out all your

178

plants, including those that aren't thriving so well, since this will give you a wider selection and not just dark reds. Don't water too much, or the plants will die: and they must be aired regularly.

— Plant *Impatiens* out in May or until mid-June. Enrich the soil with peat or leaf-mould. Add soluble fertilizer once a fortnight when you water them.

— They can be taken indoors in October, where they will continue to flower, but then it is better to grow them in pots since no good ever comes of transplanting adult flowers.

Recommended

— Growers are always producing new varieties of *Impatiens* for beds. The fashion for super-dwarfs is currently on the wane, and medium-sized and tall plants are coming back, such as 'Futura' or 'Amazon'. The *Impatiens* of New Guinea are taller and generally have variegated leaves. They are grown for pots but do very well outdoors in shady beds.

— The balsamines (*I. balsamina*) have a different appearance, their flowers being shaped like a Greek helmet, or a cockade when double. They are a grand sight with leaves arranged like a little palm tree. They will give your garden a very marked turn-of-the-century look.

— Do not forget two almost wild varieties: *I. balfouri* will undoubtedly already have attracted your eye, since its gaudy two-tone purple and white flowers are a common sight in ditches. Their long fruit bursts open at the slightest touch (hence the name 'Impatiens'), spreading the seeds far and wide. Gather them and sow before winter: the plants will come up next year and reappear annually. *I roylei* is simply a giant version, nearly 1.5 m (60 in) tall, whose pale or dark pink flowers (or white in rare instances) smell of plums. Sown among *Macleya* and *Leycesteria* they make a grand show.

Height: 15–150 cm (6–60 in).
Spacing and planting distance: 15–50 cm (6–20 in).
Soil: cool and rich in humus.
Cultivation: shade or semi-shade.
Propagation: from seed in spring.
Flowering season: from June until the frosts.
Type: annual.

Incarvillea

INCARVILLEA/TRUMPET FLOWER

Bignonaceae

Bringing a touch of the exotic to a garden is child's play, thanks to the

△ *Incarvillea delavayi*

Incarvillea. The pink foxglove-like flowers and delicate leaves of this genus are in fact the perennial cousins of many tropical flowers. Use them in the second line of your herbaceous beds, since they can flower for only about 5 weeks and then just take up space.

Useful hints

— Plant in spring in humus-rich soil, well turned over since the carrot-shaped roots go down deep. Watch out for slugs or greenfly which often swarm on the young stalks in June.

— When the clumps are dense, separate the secondary roots with shoots at the start of autumn and replant immediately.

— You can also sow the seeds under glass in April, in which case they will flower the following year.

Recommended

— *Incarvillea delavayi* is the most common, with its divided leaves which develop after the brilliant purple-pink flowers with pink throat that unfurl at the start of summer. *I. mairei* (or *I. grandiflora*) is smaller, with undivided leaves. Its flowers are brighter, some even crimson.

Height: 30–60 cm (12–24 in).
Spacing and planting distance: 30 cm (12 in).
Soil: humus-rich.
Cultivation: semi-shade or sunny.
Propagation: in spring, by division or from seed.
Flowering season: May–July.
Type: perennial.

△ *Inula magnifica*

Inula

INULA
Compositae

If you like wild flowers, *Inula ensifolia* is for you. It has retained the elegance and harmony of roadside flowers: no over-grown corollas, no weighed-down stems which collapse at the first gust of wind, no perennially-infected or insect-ridden leaves—it can withstand anything.

Useful hints

— Plant in autumn or spring in well turned over soil, since the roots go very deep.

— Mulch the soil in spring with dead leaves from last year, pine bark or lawn trimmings.

— Divide the clumps every three years and cut down plants once they have flowered.

— Mix with *Eryngium*, pasque flowers and *Graminaceae* to give a very natural overall appearance.

Recommended

The most dwarfish is *Inula ensifolia* which is rarely more than 40 cm (16 in) high and flowers in early summer. *I. orientalis* and *I. hookeri* reach 80 cm (32 in). *I. magnifica* and *I. helenium* reach 2 m (80 in) by the end of summer.

Height: 40 cm–2 m (16–80 in).
Spacing and planting distance: 30–60 cm (12–24 in).
Soil: ordinary, deep, retaining some moisture in summer.
Cultivation: sunny.
Propagation: by division in spring or autumn.
Flowering season: June until the frosts.
Type: perennial.

◁ *Inula hookerii*
▽ *Inula ensifolia*

△ *Ipheion uniflorum*

Ipheion uniflorum

IPHEION
Liliaceae

Although a little sparse in early years, *Ipheion uniflorum* in time gives dense clumps with leaves exactly like grass. The surprise comes in May, when the flowers appear, one to a stem, a very pale violet blue. Scatter them over your rockery or use them to make very decorative tubs where they will be sheltered from the worst of the cold.

Useful hints

— Plant the bulbs in autumn 5 cm (2 in) down in relatively light earth. In tubs, mix with some yellow crocuses or *Iris danfordiae*.

— Guard the clumps from severe cold by covering with a layer of dead leaves in December.

— Divide the clumps every 3 years and replant the bulbs about 10 cm (4 in) apart. Do this when the leaves have dried back and replant straightaway if possible, or store the bulbs in a cool place.

Height: 15 cm (6 in).
Spacing and planting distance: 10 cm (4 in).
Soil: ordinary, lightened with a little sand or peat.
Cultivation: sunny.
Propagation: by separating bulbils in summer.
Flowering season: April, May.
Type: bulb.

Ipomoea tricolor ▷

Ipomoea

MORNING GLORY/BLUE DAWN FLOWER

Convolvulaceae

Ipomoeas have no rivals when it comes to decorating an old tree or wire fence and covering it with flowers in a variety of colours. One wire is all they need to climb several metres in just a few weeks. It is easy to create a tunnel with them.

Useful hints

— Soak the seeds overnight to moisten the very tough integument, then make light incisions with a knife before soaking them again in lukewarm water. They will then double in volume and the first roots will appear very quickly. You can sow them either under cold glass in April or directly on site in May.

— If cold, the leaves will turn yellow.

Recommended

— *Ipomoea purpurea* has red, white or purple flowers which fade after a few hours. The trumpets are of around average size (8 cm [3 in] across).

— The corollas of *I. tricolor* syn. *rubro-caerula* are bigger (10 cm [4 in] across) and have a yellow heart. They open in the morning and close in the afternoon.

Height: 2–3 m (6½–10 ft).
Spacing and planting distance: 30 cm (12 in).
Soil: rich, staying moist in summer.
Cultivation: north-east, east or south-east but not directly southwards.
Propagation: from seed in spring.
Flowering season: July–September.
Type: annual.

Iris

IRIS

Iridaceae

If you like irises – and who could resist their beauty? – you might like to know that you can enjoy them all year round, since the Algerian iris (*Iris unguicularis*) flowers right through the winter, and is then followed by *Iris reticulata*, Dutch and English irises. Once summer has arrived, there are the Siberian irises, the innumerable *Iris germanica* and *louisiana*, and *Iris spuria*, not forgetting the new remontant hybrids which come up in September. However, they don't all like the same conditions, so be careful when choosing and planting.

Useful hints

— Plant rhizomatous irises between the end of July and the start of September. They like well-drained soil and sun, except *Iris laevigata, pseudacorus, kaempferi* and *versicolor* which prefer moist soils. Cut the flowery scapes once they have faded to avoid beds looking dreary.

— Plant bulbous irises in September/October in a well-drained soil and watch out for fieldmice who will have a field day with the bulbs if they are not planted deep enough. Enrich the soil with well-rotted compost, five shovelfuls for each square metre. *I. bucharica must* be allowed to dry in summer.

Recommended

— **Bulbous irises**: *Iris danfordiae* and *I. reticulata* are the dwarves here, since they are scarcely 15 cm (6 in) high. The former often flowers from the end of summer in bright yellow, while the latter is later and often blue or mauve. Both have a pleasant scent—if you bend down to smell them. Grow them in pots and take them indoors when they flower.

— The English iris (*I. xiphoides*) and Dutch iris (*I. xiphium*) are frequently confused. The former's deep rich blue flowers appear from February onwards, and don't have the yellow tinge, while the second appears later and flowers in all colours including yellow and claret. They are the same shape and size, about 60 cm (24 in), and are excellent in flower arrangements. The leaves of *I.xiphiodes* do not overwinter.

— *I. bucharica* is still the easiest of this range to grow. Its leaves appear in March, curiously folded and waxed. The flowers bloom from the axil of the leaves, a sort of marriage of white and yellow which is very pretty. It goes

△ *Iris spuria* 'Premier'

△ *Iris xiphium* 'Wedgwood'

△ *Iris lavifolia*
◁ *Iris kaempferi*
◁ *Iris bucharica*
▽ *Iris pseudacorus*

land. Dig it up in November and keep it under cold glass over the winter. There are numerous hybrids, including 'Geisha Hiskiki' (deep purple), 'Gracieuse' (blue with white centres), 'Comtesse de Paris' (pure white, and with some variations in pink, blue and purple on generally flat flowers).

— Staying with moisture-loving irises, we come to *I. louisiana* and *I. spuria*, taller than those above since they grow to over 1 m (40 in) high. The former are only hardy to a limited extent in cooler climates. Their very varied colours include delightful pastel shades. *I. spuria* has flowers of blue-purple. 'Notha' has rich purple flowers while those of 'Custom Design' are purple-brown with a bright yellow patch.

— Almost the opposite, Siberian irises (*I. sibirica*) prefer a dry life. Their very delicate leaves lighten up beds and their stems are so thin the blue flowers seem to float in the air. Their leaves disappear in winter, so mark where they are so as not to upturn them accidentally. They are not easy to obtain.

— The best-known irises are still *I. germanica* and the thousands of hybrids. They run the whole gamut of colours from white to an almost black purple, and from yellow to pink, with only pure red missing. Often undulating and marked with rich patterns, their flowers follow in May or June at the same time as gloxinia, old roses and poppies. They are one of the stars of the garden. Grow them in large groups or mixtures, they are pretty either way. In large numbers, they give off a delightful violet scent. Note that there are now new remontant hybrids but they will not flower well a second time in autumn if the summer is too hot.

— The Algerian iris (*I. unguicularis*) flowers at the same time in lavender blue or lilac. Allow it time to settle in, and it will reward you with dozens of flowers over most of the winter. It takes a very severe frost indeed to kill its leaves, and even then it will still be back the next spring. Flowers taken for indoor decoration should be pulled gently at the bud stage. Once indoors, they will open in a matter of minutes.

Height: 10–120 cm (4–48 in).
Spacing and planting distance: 10–40 cm (4–16 in).
Soil: depends on species.
Cultivation: sunny.
Propagation: by dividing clumps or separating new bulbs a little while after flowering.
Flowering season: all year round, depending on variety.
Type: bulb and perennial.

△ *Iris unguicularis*
◁ *Iris danfordiae*

wonderfully in rockeries since it spreads rapidly when it feels at home.

— **Rhizomatous irises**: the corm iris (*I. foetidissima*) is rarely seen flowering en masse in nature and it is its curious half-open fruits and bright red seeds which draw our attention in dried flower arrangements. Its delicate mauve flowers appear discreetly in June but its elegant leaves make it worth placing by water along with marsh irises with yellow flowers (*I. pseudacorus*).

— Another star of damp corners is the Japanese iris (*I. kaempferi* and also *I. laevigata* and *I. ensata* which are very close). Unfortunately, it only likes the dry winters normally found in its home-

△ *Ixia*

Ixia

IXIA/CORN LILY

Iridaceae

The best thing you can do with ixias is to grow them in pots to make sure of not losing them: these bulbous plants from South Africa are not very hardy. They can also be used in flower arrangements, since their colours are very delicate.

Useful hints

— Plant the bulbs in autumn in groups of 8 or 10 in 15 cm (6 in) diameter pots filled with a crumbly mixture of sand and leaf-mould with one-third of peat. Put them under cold glass to keep the winter rains off. As soon as the shoots appear, put the pots in a light, cool room where the stems can unfurl.

— In warm and temperate climates, you can also plant ixias outside in a sunlit corner towards mid-November. Keep the cold off with a cover of dead leaves.

Height: 60 cm (24 in).
Spacing and planting distance: 5–10 cm (2–4 in).
Soil: light.
Cultivation: full sun.
Propagation: by separating bulbils.
Flowering season: June, July (outside), spring (inside).
Type: bulb.

Jasione

SHEEP'S-BIT

Campanulaceae

It would take a botanist's eye to tell that this plant was a cousin of the campanulas. In your mixed borders, *Jasione perennis* will add a dash of blue in midsummer. It makes pretty borders in front of your pink remontant rose bushes, or an excellent rockery plant.

Useful hints

— Plant in spring or autumn, adding a little peat. This plant does not like heavy, chalky soils.

— Trim the leaves in spring, but leave them on the clump all winter to protect the plant.

Height: 30–40 cm (12–16 in).
Spacing and planting distance: 30 cm (12 in).
Soil: ordinary.
Cultivation: full sun.
Propagation: from seed or by division in spring.
Flowering season: July–September.
Type: perennial.

▽ *Jasione heldreichii*

△ *Kniphofia* hybrid

Kniphofia

TORCH LILY, RED HOT POKER/ POKER PLANT

Liliaceae

This plant was very popular around twenty years ago, when it was known by the botanical name *Tritomia* and its curious orange spikes were to be seen in virtually every garden. Since then, possibly as a result of its new and unpronounceable name, only a few gardeners have discovered that it also comes in attractive yellow, pink and cream varieties. Yet this is a sturdy plant that causes few problems.

Useful hints

— This plant will grow in any well

△ *Kniphofia galpinii*

△ *Kochia scoparia* 'Tricophylla'

fertilized garden soil. When planting, allow one spadeful of compost per plant.

— Plant relatively deep, at a depth of 20 cm (8 in).

— To encourage flowering, avoid moving the plants if possible.

Recommended

— *Kniphofia galpinii* is a most attractive yellow species: some delightful varieties are 'Gloire d'Orléans', pure yellow, 'Luna', orange, and 'Alcazar', incandescent red.

Height: 60 cm (24 in).
Spacing and planting distance: 40 cm (16 in).
Soil: ordinary.
Cultivation: sun.
Propagation: by division in spring.
Flowering season: June, July.
Type: perennial.

Kochia

KOCHIA, FALSE CYPRESS/SUMMER-CYPRESS

Chenopodiaceae

If you are an impatient gardener, looking forward to a garden punctuated with carefully trimmed bushes and tired of waiting for your *Lonicera nitida* to fill out, sow some *Kochia scoparia*. In just 3 months, you will have delightful 'bushes' of pale green, fluffy foliage. In autumn they will turn a purplish red, then bright red, before the first frosts finally tinge them with beige. They only last one season, but what a picture they make!

Useful hints

— Sow early in April, in boxes filled with light compost. Plant out in May, preferably in soil that has been well fertilized over the winter, and in a sunny position. Support in windy locations.

— Plant out in rows, spaced 50 cm (20 in) apart, to imitate French-style gardens, or in groups of 3 to 5.

— When planted in rich soil in a sunny position, kochias will often reseed themselves. Collect the seeds by shaking the plants on to a sheet of newspaper in October.

Height: 30–60 cm (12–24 in).
Spacing and planting distance: 50 cm (20 in).
Soil: ordinary.
Cultivation: sun.
Propagation: from seed in early April.
Flowering season: insignificant flowers.
Type: annual.

185

Lagurus

HARE'S TAIL GRASS

Gramineae

Rarely has a plant been so aptly named. When you see the fluffy, rounded heads of this variety of grass, it is easy to imagine how it acquired its name. Grown mainly for dried flower arrangements, *Lagurus ovatus* gives attractive relief in a flower bed. Its slightly glaucous shade tones in beautifully with old roses, clarkias or agrostemmas.

Useful hints

— Sow in spring, or better still in autumn, when farmers are sowing their wheat. It will remain quite small over winter, forming large tufts in spring, before producing ears. Prick out the seedlings, leaving 15 cm (6 in) between stems, and plant clarkias, *Echium* and godetias in between. You could also plant a few wild gladioli, such as *G. bizanthinus*.

— Cut the flowering stalks in August and dry them, heads down, in a dry, well-ventilated area.

Height: 30 cm (12 in).
Spacing and planting distance: 15 cm (6 in).
Soil: ordinary, even clay.
Cultivation: sun.
Propagation: from seed in spring.
Flowering season: June to August.
Type: annual, biennial.

▽ *Lagurus ovatus*

Lamium

DEAD NETTLE/COMMON DEAD NETTLE, COMMON HENBIT

Labiatae Lamiacea

Few ground cover plants have as many qualities as dead nettles – to the extent that they have perhaps been over-used as uniform carpeting. They make a more interesting picture when mixed with other shade-loving plants, such as hostas, peonies or arum lilies, producing some very effective greenery patterns.

Useful hints

— Plant from October to March. Add a little peat, and cover the soil with pine bark to suppress weeds until the dead nettles have provided full cover.

— Propagate by separating rooted stems in spring: plant out immediately.

Recommended

— The most elegant of the lamiums is *Lamium maculatum*, its leaves marked with white in the case of 'Beacon Silver', or silvery green in the case of 'Chequers'. It has pink flowers.

— *L. galeobdolon*, which is extremely common, sometimes suffers from a bad reputation, as it tends to spread rampantly. The 'Florentinum' and 'Silver Carpet' varieties are rather less guilty of this. Both are plumed, with white flowers.

Height: 20–25 cm (8–10 in).
Spacing and planting distance: 25 cm (10 in).
Soil: ordinary, preferably rich in humus.
Cultivation: shade.
Propagation: by division in spring.
Flowering season: April to June.
Type: perennial.

△ *Lamium maculatum*
Lantana selloviana ▷
▽ *Lamium galeobdolon*

△ *Lantana camara*

Lantana

LANTANA

Verbenaceae

With the effective insecticides now available against whitefly, we can once again savour the charms of the lantanas. These tender plants, which should be grown in the same way as fuchsias, flower incessantly throughout the summer, and their domed flower heads, which frequently change colour as they age, are delightful to look at.

Useful hints

— Plant lantanas in relatively large pots (30 cm [12 in] in diameter) filled with rich, well-drained soil (half compost, half peat, enriched with fertilizer). Do not remove from the pots until mid-May. Pinch out the main shoots at half height to encourage side shoots. Remove dead flower heads and water frequently. It is useful to stake the plants.

— Apply preventive treatment against whitefly in the form of granules of a disulphoton-based insecticide which you should sprinkle on to the soil before watering. This will go into the sap and kill the insects.

— Take cuttings from the ends of shoots in August and over-winter in a cool, light room.

Height: 1.5 m (60 in).
Spacing and planting distance: 50 cm (20 in).
Soil: rich, cool in summer.
Cultivation: full sun.
Propagation: from cuttings in summer.
Flowering season: June to first frosts.
Type: annual.

△ *Lathyrus* **hybrid**

Lathyrus

SWEET PEA

Leguminosae

The incomparable sweet pea that provides us with such attractive bunches of flowers! They are just as charming in clumps, their stalks using other plants as climbing supports, unless they are true ground-cover varieties which the perennial types become after a few years.

Useful hints

— Sow annual sweet peas in March under a cold frame, or in April directly in the ground. Soak the seeds the night before sowing to soften their seed coats.

— Plant perennial varieties in spring or autumn and mark the sowing position with a tag to avoid the risk of hoeing them out inadvertently. The best supports are hazel twigs with side branches, or bean netting.

Recommended

— Among the **annual** varieties (*Lathyrus odoratus*), the most decorative for cutting still remain the 'Spencer' varieties with large, often highly fragrant flowers, or 'Cuthbertson', an earlier flowering variety. For growing in clumps: the semi-dwarf 'Knee-hi' varieties; 'Bijou', extremely free flowering; 'Patio', compact, and 'Buisson semi-dwarf mixture' which reaches a height of 60 cm (24 in) and requires no staking.

— Of the **perennial** sweet peas, *L. grandiflorus* and *L. latifolius* differ only in the size of their flowers, which are larger in the former, and the variety of shades, which is greater in the latter, offering purplish reds as well as classic purplish pink, and more especially a magnificent white. *L. vernus* is an earlier variety, beginning to flower in April/May. It is short-lived, and virtually non-climbing.

Height: 30–40 cm (12–16 in).
Spacing and planting distance: 20 cm (8 in).
Soil: ordinary.
Cultivation: sun.
Propagation: from seed in spring.
Flowering season: May to October.
Type: annual, perennial.

△ *Lathyrus grandiflorus*
▽ *Lathyrus latifolius*

188

△ **Lathyrus odoratus**
▽ **Lathyrus hybrid**

▽ **Lathyrus vernus**

△ *Lavandula*

Lavandula

LAVENDER

Labiatae

Can there be anyone who is not familiar with lavender? Perfect for dry gardens, for covering barren slopes with a frizz of silvery clumps, or for a border to a sunny path, lavender has the added virtue of providing fragrant bouquets of flowers that will leave a delicate scent in your linen cupboard.

Useful hints

— This is a southern plant, a lover of sun and well-drained soils. Avoid planting in the shade or in clay; compact soil will cause it to suffer in winter.

— Plant small clumps in spring in good, perfectly drained, garden soil.

— Remove dead flowers immediately to keep the clumps nicely rounded. Where necessary, cut down each spring, in April.

Recommended

Lavandula spica is the prettiest, with its violet blue, subtly fragrant, long-lasting flowers. Try the 'Hidcote' variety, in a darker blue. *L. stoechas* has a strange tousled outline, and is less fragrant than its cousin.

Height: 30–80 cm (12–32 in).
Spacing and planting distance: 50 cm (20 in).
Soil: ordinary.
Cultivation: sun.
Propagation: from cuttings in summer.
Flowering season: July, August.
Type: perennial.

△ *Lavatera trimestris*

Lavatera

MALLOW

Malvaceae

A single packet of *Lavatera trimestris* seeds will provide plenty of decoration, as each develops into a little bush covered with light flowers throughout the summer. But beware: if you apply too much high nitrogen fertilizer, you will have more foliage than flowers! The colours of *Lavatera*, which are always very fresh, bring beauty to the garden.

Useful hints

— Sow the large seeds in seed trays or pots under cover in April. Thin out one month later, or sow them directly into the ground like beans in May, provided your soil is crumbly, clean and on the dry side, as *Lavatera* dislikes moisture.

— Pinch back the main stalks to approximately half their height when they have reached 20 cm (8 in), to encourage them to send out side shoots.

— Keep well watered when in flower.

Recommended

The classic varieties such as 'Loveliness' have been superseded by two hybrids, 'Mont Rose' and 'Mont Blanc', which are pink and white respectively and have very much larger flowers.

Height: 60–120 cm (24–48 in).
Spacing and planting distance: 40 cm (16 in).
Soil: rich and cool in summer.
Cultivation: sun.
Propagation: from seed in spring.
Flowering season: throughout the summer.
Type: annual.

△ *Leucojum aestivum*

△ *Leontopodium alpinum*

Leontopodium

EDELWEISS

Compositae

No rockery is complete without an edelweiss. This symbol of the high mountains is rarely as silvery in colour as on its native scree, unless you choose the 'Mignon', a smaller, pure white variety.

You will have a succession of flowerheads all summer long, provided that there is plenty of sun.

Useful hints

— Wait for spring before planting in a hollow between two rocks. A crumbly, slightly chalky soil is ideal. Water regularly throughout the first summer to encourage the plant to become well established. In very rainy areas, protect in winter under a glass cloche.

— Sowing in a cold frame in spring is quite successful. Transfer the young plants into small pots and keep under cover for their first winter before planting them out the next spring.

Height: 10–20 cm (4–8 in).
Spread and planting distance: 20 cm (8 in).
Spacing: light, and slightly chalky.
Cultivation: full sun is essential.
Propagation: from seed in spring.
Flowering season: May to July.
Type: perennial.

Leucanthemum

See *Chrysanthemum*

Leucojum

SNOWFLAKE

Amaryllidaceae (family not confirmed)

A relatively uncommon plant in gardens, snowflakes make an enchanting picture in spring, with their gracious silhouette and the pure white of their corollas, the tips of the petals being tinged with green. These are marvellous plants for informal gardens.

Useful hints

— Bury the bulbs in autumn at a depth of 7.5 cm to 10 cm (3–4 in) in ordinary, ideally slightly heavy soil. Then allow

Lewisia cotyledon ▷

190

the bulbs to become naturalized, forming clumps of increasing size.

— Divide after five years, just after flowering, and replant immediately, spaced well apart.

Recommended

— Wrongly called the summer snowflake, since it flowers in April and May, *Leucojum aestivum* is particularly decorative in large clumps at the water's edge and in cool ground.

— Together with hepatica, *Iris reticulata* and snowdrops, *L. vernum* forms a wonderful carpet in the woods in February and March.

Height: 15–60 cm (6–24 in).
Spacing and planting distance: 15 cm (6 in).
Soil: ordinary, tending towards clay.
Cultivation: semi-shade and shade.
Propagation: division of bulbs after flowering.
Flowering season: February to May.
Type: bulb.

Lewisia

LEWISIA
Portulacaceae

Lewisia cotyledon, with their jewel-like flowers, are by no means easy to grow. Their main enemy is moisture around the collar in winter, which inevitably leads to rot. But their flowers provide supreme compensation with their extremely bright colours, particularly among the pinks. The abundance with which the flowers are produced is truly astonishing.

Useful hints

— Plant in spring in an almost vertical crevice between two rocks, or in a pot filled with a mixture of compost and coarse sand. Put some chippings in the bottom of the pot and around the collar to assist drainage. Leave these pots outside until November, then put into a cold frame, setting them at an angle, almost on their sides, to prevent water from stagnating.

— The best method of propagation is to sow seeds in spring in a cold frame. Thin out into pots and make sure to over-winter in a well-insulated cold frame. They will flower for the first time when a year old.

Height: 20–30 cm (8–12 in).
Spacing and planting distance: 25 cm (10 in).
Soil: very well-drained.
Cultivation: sun.
Propagation: from seed in spring.
Flowering season: May, June.
Type: perennial.

Liatris

**BLAZING STAR, GAYFEATHER/
DOTTED GAYFEATHER**

Compositae

The spikes of *Liatris* have an unusual feature in that the flowers open from the top. With its grass-like fine leaves and tuberous roots, it is difficult to place in the large family of *Compositae*, particularly since it has abandoned their typical yellow in favour of a gentle violet, pleasantly restful in high summer. It is excellent for cut flowers, which may last for over a week.

Useful hints

— Plant preferably in spring, in rich soil that remains fresh in summer. Put in at least 6 plants to obtain interesting clumps of flowers from the first year onwards, and leave to establish themselves: avoiding dividing too soon.

— They are best set against plants with broad foliage such as mauve hostas, bergenias or ornamental rhubarb. Their tender shade goes well with that of garden pinks or annual lupins.

Recommended

— *Liatris scariosa* can grow to a height of 90 cm (36 in) and are to be found in white, while *L. spicata*, the most common, is most popular in its 'Kobold' variety, growing to a maximum height of 60 cm (24 in), in an attractive lilac pink.

Height: 60–100 cm (24–40 in).
Spacing and planting distance: 20 cm (8 in).
Soil: well drained, but not dry in summer.
Cultivation: sun.
Propagation: by division in spring.
Flowering season: July to September.
Type: perennial.

◁ **Liatris spicata**

Libertia

LIBERTIA

Liliaceae

The silhouette of *Libertia formosa* is quite astonishing in mid-winter: its leaves are as green as those of holly. With its compact, neat habit, it is covered in pure white flowers in July and August, followed by orange fruits. Combine with plumed foliage leaves, against a background of everlasting shrubs and peonies.

Useful hints

— Plant in spring in a sunny position protected from cold winds. Water regularly and cover the soil with pine bark or dead leaves.

— Divide the clumps only when they have become too densely packed.

Height: 30–60 cm (12–24 in).
Spacing and planting distance: 30 cm (12 in).
Soil: rich and well-drained.
Cultivation: full sun only.
Propagation: by division in spring.
Flowering season: July, August.
Type: perennial.

Ligularia

SENECIO/GOLDEN-RAY

Compositae

Ligularias, which grow exceptionally vigorously in deep, humid soils, are useful for covering large areas. They blend well with ferns, *Meconopsis*, *Lysimachia* and *Lythrum salicaria* to decorate the edges of ponds etc.

Useful hints

— Plant in autumn or spring after digging the soil to a good depth and mixing in compost and peat to lighten and improve the soil.

— Protect from slugs by using slug bait, and water regularly over the first summer. Provided the soil remains cool at depth, the plants will thrive as they are easy-going by nature.

Recommended

— *Ligularia clivorum* is one of the most modest varieties in terms of size. It forms a dome, 1 m (40 in) in height. The 'Desdemona' variety has leaves with a purple underside.

— Somewhat taller is *L. przewalskii*, with its amazing denticulate leaves. Its flower spikes tower up to a height of 2 m (80 in).

— More vigorous still, *L. wilsoniana* is shrub-sized. Its big, rounded leaves show off its large golden yellow flower spikes beautifully.

— *L. japonica* will grow to an impressive size if placed in moist ground. It does, in fact, thrive on water.

Height: 100–150 cm (40–60 in).
Spacing and planting distance: 60–100 cm (24–40 in).
Soil: rich, always moist.
Cultivation: sun or semi-shade.
Propagation: by division in spring.
Flowering season: June to September.
Type: perennial.

△ **Libertia formosa**
Ligularia przewalskii ▷
▽ **Ligularia taponica**

Lilium

LILY
Liliaceae

Just a few lilies are all you need to give a corner of the garden a welcome touch of refinement. Lovers of soil rich in humus, they will flourish without much attention, provided you choose the more robust varieties.

Useful hints

— Plant preferably in spring with the exception of the Madonna lily, which has a growing period beginning in September and which should be planted in summer. Dig to a depth of at least 30 cm (12 in), and mix in plenty of compost. Bury the bulbs at a depth of 15 cm (6 in), and surround with a pocket of sand to prevent rotting and attack by slugs, and also assist their growth.

— Mark the planting site with a tag, as vegetation will only begin to appear in April. Surround with slug bait, and water regularly. When the stems reach a height of 30 cm (12 in), support them discreetly, either individually or with hazel tree branches. If any red insects should appear, treat immediately: these are *Crioceris*, and their larvae are liable to devour the entire foliage of the plant.

— After 3 years, you may dig up the bulbs in September, while the stems are still green. Split off the new bulbs and put into a tray filled with peat in a cold frame. Plant them out in March. Avoid leaving them in the open air, as they dry out very quickly.

Recommended

— The Japanese lily (*Lilium auratum*) has very large white flowers with brown spots. The flowers open wide, and the petals curl slightly outwards. This is a wonderful variety, but unfortunately one that is highly sensitive to viruses, which kill them off in a matter of just a few years. It should be grown in sandy leaf-mould.

— The Madonna lily (*L. candidum*) is extremely common in old gardens, where it forms large clumps. It flowers early, when its foliage is just beginning to dry out. It is a sun-lover, and likes plenty of heat.

— Relatively little known, *L. hansonii* deserves to be more popular. Its orange-yellow flowers, with their very thick petals, are reminiscent of our Turk's cap lilies. It should be grown in semi-shade to prevent its colours fading.

— One of the giants in the group is unquestionably *L. henryi*, of which the

△ *Lilium* hybrids

stem reaches heights of up to 2 m (80 in). It should be planted deep and carefully staked as its flowers are so numerous that their weight bends down the stem. It is tolerant of lime and can be planted in spaces between spring-flowering shrubs.

— The highly fragrant flowers of *L. longiflorum* are well known, taking pride of place in florists' shops. They are best planted in pots.

— Turk's cap lilies (*L. martagon*) originate from mountain regions. Although their flowers have little fragrance, they have an interesting turban shape and a purple red colour.

— In peaty, moist soil, *L. pardalinum giganteum* will quickly form tangled clumps, as it sends out rhizomes in all directions. It has relatively small but extremely numerous orange flowers dotted with purple and enlivened by a golden heart.

— If you want to be surrounded by fragrance without giving yourself a lot of work, plant some *L. regale*. This is one of the most robust of all lilies, flowering unfailingly year after year. And what a fragrance! There is a totally white variety ('Album'), but the flowers of the species type are shaded pink on the outside.

— *L. speciosum* does not really deserve the praise that is commonly showered upon it. It is susceptible to viruses and it is slightly out of proportion in view of the exceptional size of its flowers.

— The tiger lily (*L. tigrinum*) is easily

△ *Lilium candidum*

△ *Lilium regale*

increased by simply removing the bulbils that appear on the stem. They will flower in two years. Their wide open flowers are a virulent orange colour.

— There are numerous hybrid lilies. The most remarkable are 'African Queen', with an orange trumpet; 'Enchantment', nasturtium red; the 'Imperial' series with large, widely spread flowers dotted with gold; 'Moonlight', golden yellow; 'Pink Perfection', a purplish pink which is lighter in the centre.

Height: 30–200 cm (12–80 in).
Spacing and planting distance: 30 cm (12 in).
Soil: rich in humus and sand.
Cultivation: mainly semi-shade.
Propagation: separate new bulbs in spring.
Flowering season: June–September.
Type: bulb.

Limnanthes

LIMNANTHES/DOUGH'S MEADOW FOAM

Limnanthaceae

This plant is particularly popular with English gardeners. Sow it at least once, to enjoy the unique charm of its white flowers with yellow centres, giving rise to its nickname of 'poached egg'. Its deeply cut leaves are attractive in themselves, and this plant will reseed itself readily without need for protection. An ideal flower for weekend gardeners.

Useful hints

— Sow the large seeds in the flowering site in April, and thin out the seedlings a month later, leaving one plant every 20 cm (8 in).

— Water regularly until July. Flowering will then stop. Cut the foliage at mid height to encourage a second burst of flowers. Apply soluble fertilizer to sustain the vegetation.

— Collect the seeds at the end of the summer and sow at random, without bothering to cover them. Some of them will germinate immediately, and the remainder will do so in the spring.

Height: 15 cm (6 in).
Spacing and planting distance: 20 cm (8 in).
Soil: ordinary.
Cultivation: at least 3 hours sun per day.
Propagation: from seed, any season.
Flowering season: May–July.
Type: annual.

▽ *Limnanthes douglasii*

Limonium sinuatum △

Limonium

STATICE/SEA LAVENDER

Plumbaginaceae

The distinctive feature of statice flowers is that they are almost dry from the outset. This is why they are so often used in dried flower arrangements. In the garden, the perennial statice is a valuable asset, brightening up beds with its thousands of misty lavender flowers.

Useful hints

— Sow annual statice in April in a cold frame and in May in a corner of the kitchen garden. Hoe regularly and water until in flower. Then pick and dry in the shade.

— Plant perennial statice in spring. It dislikes over-frequent division. It loves watering in summer, and will grow in seaside areas.

Recommended

— *Limonium sinuatum* (annual) is commonly sold in mixtures for dried flowers. Nowadays it is possible to find *L. suworowii* with long, pale pink spikes.

— The common name for *L. latifolium* (perennial) is sea lavender. It is a worthy plant for the edges of rose beds, but its flowers can also be preserved in dried flower arrangements. *L. tataricum* is smaller and has a pale pink flower.

Height: 30–60 cm (12–24 in).
Spacing and planting distance: 20 cm (8 in).
Soil: slightly sandy.
Cultivation: sun.
Propagation: from seed in spring or by division in early autumn.
Flowering season: July, August.
Type: annual, perennial.

Linaria

TOADFLAX/BUTTER-AND-EGGS
Scrophulariaceae

With their miniature antirrhinum-like flowers, *Linaria* add a touch of brightness wherever they grow. They are so frugal that even the tiniest amount of mediocre

△ **Linaria maroccana**
▽ **Linum grandiflorum**

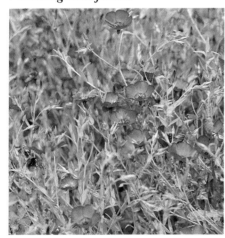

▽ **Linum narbonensis**

soil is sufficient for them to flourish. Make good use of them on dry walls, in the rockery, or in containers.

Useful hints

— Sow *Linaria* in spring. The annual varieties will flower three months later, and the perennials the next year. As the seeds are very fine, mix them with some sand: do not cover with soil. The stems branch out very quickly. Plant the perennial varieties in spring in a pocket of sandy soil.

— Water regularly in hot weather and cut back after flowering to encourage regrowth at the end of the summer.

Recommended

— Annual Moroccan *Linarias* (*Linaria maroccana*) are sold in a mixture known as 'Fairy Bouquet'. Each plant forms an individual clump studded with hundreds of flowers.

— The perennial *Linaria* 'Roman ruin' (*L. cymbalaria*) derives its name from the fact that it is frequently found in old walls. It has trailing stems bearing mauve flowers followed by fruits that crackle to the lightest touch. It can sometimes be rather invasive in rockeries, but it gives an attractive effect on dry stone walls, or on stone steps. A close relative, the perennial Alpine linaria (*L. alpina*) forms dense cushions covered with bluish-violet flowers with a bright orange centre. It tends to be a biennial rather than a perennial, and again will reseed itself quite readily.

— The purple *Linaria* (*L. purpurea*) is to some extent a purplish blue variation of our common yellow *Linaria*. It should be grown in slightly dry, informal areas of the garden, in the company of *Euphorbia polychroma*, horned poppies and pentstemons.

Height: 5–40 cm (2–16 in).
Spacing and planting distance: 20 cm (8 in).
Soil: ordinary, slightly sandy.
Cultivation: sun.
Propagation: from seed or by division of perennials.
Flowering season: June–September.
Type: annual, perennial.

Linum

FLAX/PERENNIAL FLAX
Linaceae

A common feature of all decorative flaxes is a certain elegance of line deriving from their long, thin stems. Their flowers appear to flutter in the air, and move at the slightest wisp of breeze.

They are unrivalled in their ability to brighten up flower beds and give a natural touch to highly sophisticated arrangements. Their only defect is their precarious health, which often causes them to disappear after only a few years, in spite of being classified as perennials. On the other hand, they are easy to propagate from seed.

Useful hints

— Sow in spring. Annual flaxes will flower 3 months later, while perennial flaxes will take a year to fill out. Shelter in a cold frame over the first winter.

— Combine annual flaxes with *Nigella*, cornflowers and marguerites for a charming rustic combination. Perennial flaxes go well with plants with grey foliage, such as *Senecio greyi* or the medicinal sages, which like the same dry, pebbly soil.

Recommended

— The best of the annual flaxes is *Linum grandiflorum*, of which 'Venise' is a stockier improved variety in a lovely bright red. The flax used in textiles (*L. usitatissimum*) has a pale blue flower.

— Of the perennial flaxes, we should mention *L. narbonensis* and *L. perenne*, which is bright blue and is also available in a dwarf form ('Heavenly Blue' or 'Sapphire'). The little *L. flavum*, which is pale yellow, is magnificent in rockeries, flowering in mid-summer.

Height: 30–60 cm (12–24 in).
Spacing and planting distance: 15 cm (6 in).
Soil: ordinary.
Cultivation: sun.
Propagation: from seed in spring.
Flowering season: June–September.
Type: annual, perennial.

Liriope

LIRIOPE/LILY-TURF
Liliaceae

Imagine a giant grape hyacinth that flowers at the end of summer, with striped foliage that is just as decorative as its lilac mauve flowers, and you have the *Liriope*. Use it in borders, mixed with nerines, colchicums and *Anaphalis* for a colourful autumn scene.

Useful hints

— Plant in spring in rather light, nonchalky soil. Water lightly in hot weather. At other times the plants will look after themselves, given their fleshy roots.

— Divide clumps when they become too tight, preferably in spring.

196

△ *Liriope muscari*

△ *Lithospermum diffusum* 'Heavenly Blue'

Recommended

— The best known is *Liriope muscari*: its long-lasting leaves provide an attractive background for its violet spikes.

— *L. spicata* is slightly larger than this last-named variety but otherwise is quite similar to it. Some plants may produce dark blue flowers, depending on the soil and position.

Height: 40–60 cm (16–24 in).
Spacing and planting distance: 40 cm (16 in).
Soil: ordinary, rather sandy, well-drained in winter.
Cultivation: sun and semi-shade.
Propagation: by division in spring.
Flowering season: September, October.
Type: perennial.

Lithodora

See *Lithospermum*

Lithospermum

LITHOSPERMUM/FRINGED GROMWELL, PULLOON, WAYSIDE GROMWELL

Boraginaceae

Although its name has recently been changed to *Lithodora*, the lithospermum is often still referred to in catalogues by its old name. The best known cultivar is 'Heavenly Blue'. This is one of the very best rockery plants for a sunny position. The deep blue of its flowers is renewed all summer long, looking equally attractive with helianthemums, broom and the early heathers.

Useful hints

— Plant in spring, in a pocket of acid soil (a mixture of leaf-mould, sand and peat).

— Take cuttings in summer and overwinter the young plants in a cold frame, as they are liable to be killed by heavy frost.

Height: 15–20 cm (6–8 in).
Spacing and planting distance: 30 cm (12 in).
Soil: light.
Cultivation: full sun.
Propagation: from cuttings in summer.
Flowering season: June–October.
Type: perennial.

197

Lobelia △

◁ *Lobelia cardinalis*
◁ *Lobelia lindblomii*

Lobelia

LOBELIA

Campanulaceae

If we are to judge by the intense blue of the annual variety 'Crystal Palace' or the flaming red of the perennial *Lobelia cardinalis*, lobelias come in bold colours. Use them sparingly next to grey foliage plants and pastel-coloured flowers.

Useful hints

— Sow in the warm, no later than April as their initial growth is slow. Carefully prick out before hardening them off. Plant out in May.

— Plant perennial varieties, preferably in spring, in fresh, deep soil. In June, fork in peat or pine bark. Water regularly, as the plants are very thirsty. In November, cover with a layer of straw

198

Lobelia erinus △
Lobelia vedariensis ▷

and a piece of plastic film to protect the roots from the cold and damp.

Recommended

— In the annual varieties (*Lobelia erinus*): 'Crystal Palace', dwarf, dark blue; 'Sapphire', a bright blue with a white eye.

— In the perennial varieties, *L. splendens* 'Queen Victoria', with scarlet flowers and bronze foliage. *L. splendens* is sold by the name of *L. fulgens*. Note also *L. siphilitica*, which is smaller, with soft blue flowers at the end of the summer, and *L. × vedrariense*, with a violet colour.

Height: 10–90 cm (4–36 in).
Spacing and planting distance: 10–30 cm (4–12 in).
Soil: permanently damp.
Cultivation: at least 6 hours sun per day.
Propagation: from seed in spring, from cuttings, or by division.
Flowering season: June–November.
Type: annual, perennial.

199

Lobularia maritima

ALYSSUM MARITIMUM/SWEET ALYSSUM

Cruciferae

Better known by the name *Alyssum maritimum*, *Lobularia maritima* is under-used in gardens. Its fine seeds produce tiny seedlings that initially look rather like weeds before developing into imposing clumps. These are covered in flower heads, at first insignificant, but ultimately covering the entire foliage. With the added benefit of a honey fragrance it is without doubt an excellent plant for growing in borders and containers.

Useful hints

— Sow in April or May in a cold frame after mixing the seeds with fine sand to avoid spreading them too densely. Prick out groups of 3 or 4 seedlings one month later, spacing them 20 cm (8 in) apart in all directions.

— Water regularly and hoe the soil. When the first flowering is over, cut back with scissors to prevent fruits from forming, and encourage a further show of flowers one month later.

Recommended

— Beside the classic 'Little Gem' and 'Snowcloth', in pure white, an even more dense variety 'Wonderland' deserves a special mention. The violet varieties 'Royal Carpet' and 'Violet Queen' go well with pastel roses.

Height: 7–15 cm (3–6 in).
Spacing and planting distance: 20 cm (8 in).
Soil: ordinary, even light soil.
Cultivation: sun.
Propagation: from seed in spring.
Flowering season: June–September.
Type: annual.

▽ *Lobularia maritima*

△ *Lunaria rediviva*
◁ *Lotus berthelottii*

Lotus

SWEET CLOVER/BIRD'S FOOT TREFOIL, CORAL GEM

Leguminaceae/Leguminoseae

These are cousins of the yellow sweet clovers that are found in the fields and not of the lotus flower, known to botanists by the name *Nelumbo*. While one is of interest in rockeries, the other is one of the most extraordinary plants of all for containers: imagine a trail of grey foliage speckled with intense red flowers of a strange shape, like partially opened lobster's claws.

Useful hints

— Plant yellow sweet clovers/bird's-foot trefoil in any season in a corner of the rockery or between two stones in a dry stone wall.

— Plant Berthelot sweet clover/coral gem in spring, and bring out only when all risk of frost is over. Water freely, from time to time adding soluble fertilizer. Take cuttings in summer and overwinter the young plants on the veranda or in a cold greenhouse.

Recommended

The perennial *Lotus corniculatus* is grown mainly for its bright yellow, double form. The annual, *L. berthelotti* (Berthelot sweet clover) is becoming increasingly frequently available in catalogues. Try them in hanging baskets, and you will be won over immediately.

Height: 15–30 cm (6–12 in).
Spacing and planting distance: 20 cm (8 in).
Soil: rich, well-drained.
Cultivation: sunny.

△ *Lunaria annua*

Propagation: from cuttings in summer.
Flowering season: June–September.
Type: annual, perennial.

Lunaria

HONESTY/DOLLAR PLANT

Cruciferae

Everyone knows honesty, a must in dried flower arrangements. We tend to forget that its deep purple flowers are not unattractive either. Plant them in the company of white fleur-de-lys tulips, yellow cornute violets or as a carpet at the foot of azaleas or magnolias, as they are tolerant of shade.

Useful hints

— Sow *Lunaria annua* seeds in June, in a shady position. Thin out once into pots, then transplant into their flowering site in autumn. They will flower the next spring.

— Allow the fruits to mature on the plant, then cut off the whole stem and dry indoors. Rub each fruit between the fingers to reveal the central pod.

Height: 100 cm (40 in).
Spacing and planting distance: 30 cm (12 in).
Soil: ordinary.
Cultivation: sun or semi-shade.
Propagation: from seed in June.
Flowering season: April–June.
Type: biennial.

Lupinus

LUPIN/LUPINE

Leguminosae

A pleasant green fertilizer in poor, excessively light soil, the annual lupin (*Lupinus tricolor*) will readily reseed itself in gardens where it feels at home, and will flower prettily in fragrant blue and white spikes at the beginning of the summer, while hybrid perennial lupins and the tree lupin will flower throughout the summer, playing with yellows and whites and a whole range of colours (blue, lilac, pink, red, violet). Lupins are happy in the company of peonies and hollyhocks, producing magnificent flowerbeds that give no trouble to the gardener.

Useful hints

— Their only weakness: they do not like lime. Don't try: the results are dreadful. They grow well in heavy, clay soils but last longer in light soil.

— Cut off dead flowers to extend the flowering season and propagate by taking cuttings: you will then be certain of your colours.

Recommended

— Of the annual lupins: in addition to *Lupinus tricolor* there is the Hartweg lupin, which reaches a height of 60 cm (24 in) and is enchanting with its flowers in extremely gentle colours.

— Of the perennial lupins: the Russell strain of lupins (*L. polyphyllus* hybrids), including 'La Châteleine', in pink and white; 'La Demoiselle' in white and cream; 'Le Chandelier' in pale yellow and gold; 'Le Gentilhomme' in blue and white, or 'Les Pages', bright crimson. The 'Minarette' strain has a similar number of variations in a plant that reaches a height of no more than 40 cm (16 in) i.e. half the height of those above. It is also an earlier strain, and flowers practically without fail from the first year if sown early in spring.

— Of the tree lupins: *Lupinus arboreus* with attractive silvery foliage and slender flower spikes, in gentle colours such as lemon and baby blue or white. Though short-lived, this species does well in seaside gardens.

Height: 70–80 cm (28–32 in).
Spacing and planting distance: 30 cm (12 in).
Soil: ordinary, non chalky.
Cultivation: sunny.
Propagation: from seed in March or April or by division.
Flowering season: June, July.
Type: annual, perennial.

△ *Lupinus* 'Misty'

△ *Lupinus lescensis*
▽ *Lupinus polyphyllus*

△ *Lychnis coronaria*
◁ *Lychnis alpina*
Lychnis chalcedonica ▷
▽ *Lychnis* × '**Arkwightii**'

Lychnis

CAMPION

Caryophyllaceae

The *Lychnis* genus is vast. It contains some plants which remain close to their wild appearance, providing a natural look that is attractive if you are trying to accentuate the 'country' aspect of a particular scene. *Lychnis* provide a very elegant accompaniment to old roses and aromatic plants.

Useful hints

— Plant preferably in spring as they do not like the cold if their roots are not well-developed. Give them a well-drained chalky soil and a sunny position.

— You can sow seeds in spring or propagate by dividing the clumps just after flowering. Over-winter young plants in a cold frame for the first year.

Recommended

— *Lychnis alpina* forms a low, tight mat covered with dense clusters of flowers in dark pink. It is in future to be known as *Viscaria alpina*.

— The red of *L. chalcedonica* (Cross of Jerusalem, or Maltese Cross) is so bright that few other colours can stand comparison with it, except for the white of peach leaved campanula and Madonna lilies.

— *L. coronaria* is a truly magical plant. The harmonious combination of the exceptionally bright magenta red of its flowers and the silvery velvet of its leaves is perfect. Use in large masses that will remain in flower from June right through to the first frosts. There is also a highly regarded white variety, although this is a little less vigorous.

— Allow *L. flos-jovis* to become naturalized in the garden, reseeding itself spontaneously. It will provide a framework for the garden, and will prosper at the foot of flowering shrubs such as mock orange, lilac and hydrangeas.

— *L. haageana* is a small hybrid. Its poppy red flowers are borne on purple tinted foliage – a combination that not all gardeners find pleasing! The 'Arkwrightii' hybrid is even more virulent, if that is possible.

Height: 20–120 cm (8–48 in).
Spacing and planting distance: 20–30 cm (8–12 in).
Soil: chalky, well-drained.
Cultivation: sunny.
Propagation: from seed in spring or by division.
Flowering season: May–October.
Type: perennial.

△ *Lysichiton americanum*

Lysichiton

LYSICHITON/YELLOW SKUNK-CABBAGE

Araceae

It is impossible not to be impressed by the giant arum-like yellow flowers of *Lysichiton americanum*. They appear at the beginning of spring, adding a touch of fantasy by the water's edge where this plant flourishes. Nevertheless, it has to be admitted that its leaves, rather like those of white beet, are not of the most attractive.

Useful hints

— These hardy plants will only grow in damp soil. Plant at the water's edge, by the side of a stream or pond. Avoid planting large numbers close to the house, as their flowers give off a slightly unpleasant scent.

— You can sow the many seeds that appear, preferably as soon as they ripen, by simply scattering them about. Divide clumps in early autumn.

Height: 1 m (40 in).
Spacing and planting distance: 60 cm (24 in).
Soil: very damp throughout the year.
Cultivation: sunny.
Propagation: from seed or by division in early autumn.
Flowering season: March–May.
Type: perennial.

△ **Lysimachia clethroides**
▽ **Lysimachia nummularia**

▽ **Lysimachia punctata**

Lysimachia

LYSIMACHIA/LOOSESTRIFE
Primulaceae

Lysimachia are the maids-of-all-work of the garden. Capable of flourishing in damp as well as dry locations, in full sun or in partial shade, less than a finger's height or growing to 1 m (40 in), these plants will give you no problems, as they are hardiness incarnate.

Useful hints

— Plant at any time in the season, providing them with deep soil as they have powerful roots. They prefer the cool, but they will be quite happy in soil that is slightly dry in summer. They will simply not grow quite as tall.

— Divide clumps when they begin to flower less abundantly, approximately every 3 years. By taking action as soon as flowering is over, you will gain a year and the plants will again be attractive the following summer.

— Combine with other flowers that like damp corners of the garden, such as purple loosestrife, marsh mallows, meadow sweet or hostas.

Recommended

— The most curious of the *Lysimachias* is, without question, *Lysimachia clethroides*. Its white flower heads bend over, like huge commas. The autumn foliage colours are glorious.

— The little known *L. ephemerum* bears its white spikes above delicate grey-green foliage. In spite of its name, its flowers last for many weeks.

— A dwarf in comparison with the previous varieties, *L. nummularia* forms a very dense carpet sprinkled with hundreds of bright yellow flowers in early summer. Use as ground cover at the foot of conifers. The 'Aurea' variety has yellow-green foliage. It is superb in hanging baskets and containers.

— *L. punctata*, which is recognizable at the first glance, has whorls of yellow flowers in 15 to 20 cm (6–8 in) spikes. Extremely hardy, this variety will succeed in all types of soil and is even resistant to damage caused by dogs.

Height: 5–100 cm (2–40 in).
Spacing and planting distance: 30 cm (12 in).
Soil: ordinary, preferably cool.
Cultivation: at least 3 hours sun per day.
Propagation: by division in September.
Flowering season: July, August.
Type: perennial.

△ **Lythrum salicaria**

Lythrum

LYTHRUM/PURPLE LOOSESTRIFE
Lythraceae

You will be familiar with *Lythrum salicaria*, having picked it a thousand times on holiday from the damp ditches that it populates in the company of golden *Lysimachia* and marsh mallow. Sadly, its pretty magenta spikes soon fall as fine grain, but it is an ideal plant for growing in a corner of the garden near a pond or ditch. Alongside rodgersias, bocconias and *Filipendula* it makes a wonderful show.

Useful hints

— Plant in 20 cm (8 in) deep, wide holes in cool soil treated with compost, in a moist position.

— Divide any overgrown plants every 3 years.

Height: 60 cm (24 in).
Spacing and planting distance: 30 cm (12 in).
Soil: damp, ordinary.
Cultivation: sunny.
Propagation: by division in spring or autumn.
Flowering season: July–September.
Type: perennial.

Macleaya cordata △
Macleaya microcarpa ▷

Macleaya

PLUME POPPY

Papaveraceae

This plant's time of glory was around the year 1900! Nevertheless, it provides an attractive means of decorating wilder corners of the garden, with its tall silhouette and its magnificent white or unusual pink spikes throughout the summer. Like ferns and purple loosestrifes, it likes cool soil. Plant as an accompaniment to rodgersias, gunneras or Caucasian heracleums and your garden will quickly become spectacular.

Useful hints

— Plant early in spring in March or September, in holes 20 to 30 cm (8–12 in) wide, filled with well-rotted manure.

— Always plant in deep, cool soil.

— Allow plants to fill out for 3 years before dividing.

Recommended

— The best known is *Macleaya cordata*, a giant plant with a pinkish white flower. *M. microcarpa* has a smaller pink flower.

Height: 1.5–2.5 m (60–100 in).
Spacing and planting distance: 1 m (40 in).
Soil: ordinary, deep.
Cultivation: sunny.
Propagation: by division in spring.
Flowering season: June–August.
Type: perennial.

△ *Malope trifida*
▽ *Malcolmia maritima*

Malcolmia/Malcomia

VIRGINIAN STOCK/VIRGINIA STOCK

Cruciferae

In years when you fail to sow any of your annual flowers in spring, remember *Malcolmia maritima*. Sown in May or June, they will flower reliably in less than 2 months. Their flowers will not, of course, last for 3 months, but they are more attractive than bare soil. Mix Virginian stocks with clarkias and annual alyssums to give fresh-looking borders.

Useful hints

— Sow seeds directly in the flowering site, in crumbled soil enriched with compost. Cover with a mixture of sand and compost. Water every 2 days. As soon as the seedlings are established, thin the plants out so that they are spaced 20 cm (8 in) apart.

— Mulch the soil with peat. As soon as the main crop of flowers is over, cut the plants back with scissors to encourage a second show. If this is long in coming, resow without waiting.

Height: 20 cm (8 in).
Spacing and planting distance: 20 cm (8 in).
Soil: ordinary.
Cultivation: sunny.
Propagation: from seed in spring or summer.
Flowering season: 2 months after sowing.
Type: annual.

Malope

MALOPE

Malvaceae

Taller than lavatera, *Malope trifida* provides excellent flowers for summer flowerbeds. Each clump forms a little shrub that flowers for more than 2 months. Their rose-purple colouring goes well with white or flesh-coloured old roses. Try them combined with large white antirrhinums, too, or simple marguerites.

Useful hints

— Sow in April cold in a cold frame, or one month later, directly in the flowering site. Thin out to a spacing of 30 cm (12 in). Water abundantly during the initial stages and until they flower. Do not over-fertilize, as this often causes excessive foliage development.

— When flowering is over, you can try extending the season by cutting back the dead flower stalks to prevent fruits from forming. Sadly *Malope* often dies suddenly from a disease caused by a fungus that attacks the stem.

Height: 1 m (40 in).
Spacing and planting distance: 30 cm (12 in).
Soil: ordinary, not too rich.
Cultivation: sunny.
Propagation: from seed in spring.
Flowering season: June–September.
Type: annual.

△ *Malva moschata*

Malva

MALLOW

Malvaceae

If you live in the country, you are bound to have found mallow (*Malva moschata*) flourishing in the wild. It often grows in sunny meadows with clay soil, and sometimes is even found in road gravel. It is an ideal companion to *Echium*, poppies, corn poppies, helianthemums—to all flowers, in fact, with a predilection for sunny soils.

Useful hints

— You can either sow the seeds (which are greyish-brown and are contained in pretty hexagonal plump pillows), plant divided clumps, or take cuttings.

— Seeds can be easily sown in a nursery bed in May, but the plants will not then flower until the next spring, so it is quicker to divide the roots.

Recommended

In addition to the mauve-pink type, there is also a white variety, 'Alba', which is extremely graceful but less robust.

Height: 40 cm (16 in).
Spacing and planting distance: 30 cm (12 in).
Soil: ordinary.
Cultivation: sunny.
Propagation: by division in spring.
Flowering season: June–September.
Type: perennial.

△ **Matteucia struthiopteris**

Matthiola incana △

Matthiola

STOCK

Cruciferae

Anyone who has not, at least once in his life, smelled a bunch of these stocks could never imagine their powerful, sweet and pleasant fragrance, with a touch of the carnation about it. In the garden, this rather upright plant merely serves to provide the home with cut flowers.

Useful hints

— Sow in April in a cold frame, or in May directly in rows in the kitchen garden. Cover the seeds with 1 cm (½ in) of sand. Water regularly to prevent attack by insects.

— Certain species may flower earlier, provided that they are sheltered in a greenhouse. They should be sown in July to flower in February or March.

Recommended

— Stocks in general grow to little more than 30 cm (12 in) but the variety 'Excelsior' will grow to more than 1.2 m (48 in). It often produces only one stem. The Nice stock flowers early in spring and can be forced in a greenhouse. The 'Dame' strain is bushy and is the best summer stock for flowerbeds.

Height: 30–120 cm (12–48 in).
Spacing and planting distance: 20 cm (8 in).
Soil: rather rich and well-drained, with a tendency towards chalkiness.
Cultivation: sunny.
Propagation: from seed in spring and summer.
Flowering season: February–October, depending on when sown.
Type: annual, biennial.

Matteucia

OSTRICH FEATHER FERN

Polypodaceae/Polypodiaceae

This could be confused with the male fern, but the fronds of *Matteucia struthiopteris* are of a more delicate texture that catches the light and makes the fronds take on a golden hue. Their tips are attractively curled, like ostrich feathers. They go well with *Lysimachias, Helxines* and aquilegias, wherever the garden soil is powdery and light, even if it sees little sun.

Useful hints

— Plant in spring, in well-dug soil, in a semi-shaded position. These ferns dislike full sun, which burns their fronds.

— Space the plants 1 m (40 in) apart They need space to develop.

Height: 70 cm (28 in).
Spacing and planting distance: 1 m (40 in).
Soil: fresh, rich in humus.
Cultivation: semi-shade.
Propagation: by division in spring.
Type: perennial.

207

△ *Maurandia scandens*
Maurandia erubescens △

Maurandia

MAURANDIA
Scrophulariaceae

It is surprising, sometimes, how little imagination the seed merchants show. How is it that so few of them have had the idea of offering maurandia seeds for sale when this is one of the most decorative climbing annuals of all? With their splayed, trumpet-shaped, velvet-coated flowers, they are well worth sowing early, in the warm, to be enjoyed all summer through. They are ideal for covering south-facing trellises, not to mention verandahs, which they will turn into a true paradise.

Useful hints

— Sow in the warm, like tomatoes, in April. Transfer the seedlings into pots, then plant out in their flowering site in May, as soon as all risk of frost is over. Water regularly and apply liquid fertilizer every month.

— Harvest the seeds at the end of the summer so that you always have some available. If you distribute them among your friends and acquaintances, you will make a number of people very happy.

Height: up to 3 m (120 in).
Spacing and planting distance: 1 m (40 in).
Soil: rich and cool in summer.
Cultivation: full sun.
Propagation: from seed in spring.
Flowering season: July–September.
Type: annual.

Meconopsis

HIMALAYAN POPPY/WELSH POPPY
Papaveraceae

These beautiful flowers are the darlings of those gardeners who have sufficiently green fingers to attempt growing them. To put it bluntly, apart from the delightful *Meconopsis cambrica*, getting them to grow successfully is no easy matter. But the effort is worthwhile when their sky blue petals begin to unfurl!

Useful hints

— Plant in early autumn to give time for their roots to become established before the cold weather. Cover with a cloche to protect from excessive moisture in winter. Treat with slug bait. In early May, fork pine bark or peat into the soil and water regularly.

— Most varieties will die after flowering if flowering has been abundant. As a precautionary measure, prevent one of the stalks from flowering by cutting off the flower stem. Collect the seeds from the others and sow them around the site generally and in a seed tray, which you should expose to the cold in winter. They will begin to sprout the next spring, and the plants will flower a year later.

Recommended

— While still the best known, *Meconopsis betonicifolia* is not the easiest to contain. *M. grandis* is preferable, its flowers being better arranged and of an even more exceptional blue. It is also less likely to die after a year.

— *M. cambrica* is more like a yellow celandine than its large azure brothers. It often reseeds itself spontaneously, and will rapidly colonize all shady areas. This pleasant little pest is in flower virtually all year. There are double and orange flowered varieties, but the type of the species is extremely pretty.

— The extremely rare *M. napaulensis*, a native of Nepal, is grown more for its foliage than for its curious plum-coloured flowers. It develops a rosette of leaves in the first year, then puts out its spike of flowers in spring. Its hairy leaves, retaining droplets of water like pearls of mercury, are exquisitely beautiful.

Height: 30–180 cm (12–72 in).
Spacing and planting distance: 30 cm (12 in).
Soil: acid (heath mould and sandy peat).
Cultivation: semi-shade.
Propagation: from seed in autumn.
Flowering season: June–September.
Type: biennial, perennial.

Meconopsis grandis △
Meconopsis betonicifolia ▷
Meconopsis napaulensis ▷
Meconopsis cambrica ▽

Mentzelia

BLAZING STEM

Loasaceae

Originally from America, this plant looks like a small bush, and its bright flowers make an attractive effect in borders, where they flower in midsummer. They have a delightful fragrance.

Useful hints

— Sow *Mentzelia lindleyi* in their flowering location in spring. Sow *M. hispida* at the same time, but in a greenhouse, to be transplanted the following spring.

— Remove dead flowers.

Recommended

M. lindleyi (syn. *Bartonia aurea*), an annual, has golden yellow flowers from June to August. *M. hispida*, a perennial, has yellow flowers from June to July.

Height: 40 cm (16 in).
Spacing and planting distance: 20 cm (8 in).
Soil: normal.
Cultivation: sunny.
Propagation: from seed in spring.
Flowering season: July–August.
Type: annual, perennial.

▽ *Mentzelia lindleyi*

△ *Mertensia virginica*

Mertensia

VIRGINIAN COWSLIP/VIRGINIA BLUEBELLS

Boraginaceae

This North American beauty charms us with both its glaucous luxuriant foliage and its flowers, of a heavenly blue, in gently curving clusters. The two colours, in perfect harmony, are evocative of the cool locations that are the plant's preferred habitat. Combine it with later-flowering plants such as asters as its foliage dies back from mid July onwards leaving nothing but a large, carrot-shaped root, which should under no circumstances be damaged by careless hoeing.

Useful hints

— Plant *Mertensia virginica* in early autumn or very early spring, in well prepared soil that has been dug over to a good depth and enriched with organic matter (leaf-mould and peat).

— Do not allow the plant to dry out prematurely in spring, and water in April or May if the soil is dry. In March, treat with 5 cm (2 in) broken pine bark.

Height: 30–50 cm (12–20 in).
Spacing and planting distance: 30 cm (12 in).
Soil: rich in humus.
Cultivation: semi-shade.
Propagation: by division in autumn or spring.
Flowering season: May.
Type: perennial.

209

Mesembryanthemum

MESEMBRYANTHEMUM

Aizoaceae

In the 1960s, *Mesembryanthemum crini-florum* was to be found in every flower bed, keeping the purslanes and busy lizzies company. Since then it has inexplicably gone out of fashion, even though, delightful and easy to grow, it tirelessly provides us with star-shaped corollas in the very brightest colours from June to September. The most dazzling pinks and oranges, dark reds and white, of course, are there, often surrounded with a halo of a paler colour.

Useful hints

— Sow at the end of March under cover in trays filled with compost, and transplant 1 month later into their flowering site, in full sun.

— Water well each evening in summer.

— You can also sow them directly *in situ* if the soil is good and the position sunny: these plants will often reseed themselves spontaneously.

Height: 15 cm (6 in).
Spacing and planting distance: 20 cm (8 in).
Soil: ordinary.
Cultivation: sunny.
Propagation: from seed in spring.
Flowering season: June–September.
Type: annual.

▽***Mesembryanthemum***

Mimulus cardinalis △ ▷

Mimulus

MONKEY FLOWER

Scrophulariaceae

Mimulus, which especially likes damp corners, is to be found in extremely bright colours, with particularly unusual spotted patterns. If the slugs in your garden spare them, they will provide you with some charming flower borders.

Useful hints

— Plant hardy mimulus in spring, in humus-rich soil that remains cool even in summer.

— Annual mimulus should be sown in April or May and thinned out one month later. They generally produce a spectacular show of flowers and then die. Combine them with marigolds or dwarf china asters to prolong their effect.

— Treat regularly with slug bait or surround with a ring of wood ash, which should be replaced from time to time.

Recommended

— Of the perennial mimulus, *Mimulus cardinalis* has an unusual fragrance and

flowers for almost three months in a purple-red shade. It will tolerate relatively dry soil.

— Of the annual varieties, the most remarkable is 'Calypso', with flowers in widely varying colours, and 'Malibu' in a velvety warm orange, almost unequalled in the plant world.

Height: 30 cm (12 in).
Spacing and planting distance: 20 cm (8 in).
Soil: cool in summer (enrich with peat).
Cultivation: not more than 6 hours sun per day.
Propagation: from seed in spring.
Flowering season: June–September.
Type: annual, perennial

Minuartia

MINUARTIA

Caryophyllaceae

If you are looking for a robust carpeting plant to cover the bare corners of your rockery, here you have a rare pearl: a single root of *Minuartia laricifolia* will produce a respectable-sized mat in a matter of a few months. It is covered in tiny white flowers that succeed one another in waves for 2 months at the end of the summer. Try combinations with spring bulbs, crocuses or botanical tulips to create some charming scenes.

Useful hints

— Plant early in autumn or spring, in a pocket of loose soil improved with sand.

— Divide clumps every 3 years and replant immediately. The best time for this is just after flowering, provided that you water regularly, but it can also be carried out in spring.

Height: 10 cm (4 in).
Spacing and planting distance: 30 cm (12 in).
Soil: ordinary, rather light.
Cultivation: sunny.
Propagation: by division in spring.
Flowering season: May–August.
Type: perennial.

Mirabilis

MARVEL OF PERU, FOUR O'CLOCK PLANT

Nyctaginaceae

The large black seeds of the marvel of Peru or four o'clock plant grow into vigorous plants giving bushes 1 m (40 in) in height that are soon covered in flared, trumpet-shaped flowers. You need to wait until the late afternoon to see them open—hence their common name. And what a sweet fragrance! Make a little space for them at the foot of

Minuartia stellata △
Mirabilis jalapa ▷

an east-facing wall and you will spend a large part of the summer season captivated by their charm.

Useful hints

— Soak the seeds of *Mirabilis jalapa* overnight before sowing. They will come up quickly if sown under glass. Otherwise wait for mid-May, and sow directly in the flowering site.

— Water regularly and treat with dilute fertilizer once every 3 weeks, as this is an extremely voracious plant.

— If you are particularly fond of a given colour, lift the tuberous roots in October, in the same way as dahlias, and store in the cellar in a little peat. You can then plant them out in their flowering sites in spring.

Height: 1 m (40 in).
Spacing and planting distance: 60 cm (24 in).
Soil: rich, remaining cool.
Cultivation: east and south-east facing.
Propagation: from seed in spring.
Flowering season: June–October.
Type: annual.

Miscanthus

EULALIA GRASS

Gramineae

This is a 'grass' that should please the lazy gardener: once it is planted, all you have to do is watch it grow taller and fill out, rustle in the wind and bend in the rain. A plant to accompany bamboo, another member of the *Gramineae* family, or ferns.

Useful hints

— Sow under cover at the end of March in trays of compost. Transplant in May in good garden soil, spacing 30 cm (12 in) in all directions.

— You can also buy plants in pots and plant them out either in autumn or in spring.

Recommended

Some varieties, such as 'Zebrinus' have cream-coloured stripes, while others, such as 'Gracillimus', have silvery grey foliage.

Height: 60–120 cm (24–48 in).
Spacing and planting distance: 40–60 cm (16–24 in).
Soil: ordinary.
Cultivation: sunny.
Propagation: by division in spring.
Type: perennial.

△ *Miscanthus* **'Zebrinus'**

△ *Molucella laevis*

Molucella

BELLS OF IRELAND

Labiatae

Bells of Ireland are often found in dried flower arrangements. The decorative part is the pale green calyx in the form of a shell that surrounds the flower. Grown in rows in the kitchen garden or close together in a separate bed, they can be quite impressive.

Useful hints

— Raising seeds of *Molucella laevis* can sometimes be a laborious task, particularly if the seeds are past their best. Sow in a cold frame in April and plant out 1 month later, spaced 20 cm (8 in) apart.

— Pick the stems after flowering, at the end of the summer, and dry them, heads down, for 3 months.

Height: 60 cm (24 in).
Spacing and planting distance: 20 cm (8 in).
Soil: ordinary.
Cultivation: sunny.
Propagation: from seed in spring.
Flowering season: July, August.
Type: annual.

△ *Monarda didyma* **'Cambridge Scarlet'**

Monarda

BERGAMOT, HORSEMINT/ BEE-BALM

Labiatae

Every part of *Monarda didyma* is aromatic, from its roots to its flowers and the leaves, which give off a strong smell of thyme when crushed. These are excellent plants for flowerbeds, provided the soil is good and moist in summer, as their leaves transpire a great deal.

Useful hints

— Plant in autumn or spring in well-prepared soil, dug to depth, and improved with peat and leaf-mould. From May, mulch with grass cuttings or semi-decomposed compost.

— To propagate, divide clumps in autumn. Monarda soon becomes invasive as it sends out rhizomes in all directions. Combine with polygonums and decorative dahlias with large purple flowers.

Recommended

— There is a whole range of colours to choose from in 'Alba', white; 'Blue Stocking', violet; 'Croftway Pink', pale pink and the most frequently grown; 'Mahogany', bright red, or 'Prairie Glow', a brighter colour than 'Croftway Pink'.

Height: 60–120 cm (24–48 in).
Spacing and planting distance: 40 cm (16 in).
Soil: rich, remaining cool in summer.
Cultivation: open, but not in fierce sun.
Propagation: by division in autumn.
Flowering season: June–September.
Type: perennial.

△ *Moraea tricuspidata*

Morina longifolia △

Montbretia

See *Crocosmia*

Moraea

MORAEA

Iridaceae

Still extremely rare, moraeas are among the jewels of the rich flora of Southern Africa. Although the flowers are only short-lived like the tiger flower, new flowers appear every day. If you look at them closely, you will be unable to resist the charm of their exceptionally fine colours, arranged in rings that appear to have been painted by the most inspired Japanese artist. While the bulbs are still very rare, it is possible to get hold of seeds if you are a member of one of the collectors' associations, or even to order them direct from South Africa, where certain nurseries specialize in these remarkable plants.

Useful hints

— Bury the bulbs at a depth of 5 cm (2 in) in soil that is both rich in humus and lightened by mixing with fine gravel. The species of *Moraea*, which will not withstand a normal winter in cool climates must be grown in a pot and put into a cold frame or greenhouse in winter.

— Stake stems discreetly to prevent the bulbs from being exposed. Stop watering when the foliage withers of its own accord and allow to rest for several months, until the next spring.

Height: 30–40 cm (12–16 in).
Spacing and planting distance: 10 cm (4 in).
Soil: rich in humus and very well-drained.
Cultivation: sunny.
Propagation: separate new bulbs after the foliage has withered.
Flowering season: early summer.
Type: bulb.

Morina

WHORLFLOWER

Dipsacaceae/Dipsaceae

'Is it a thistle?' your visitors will ask as they admire this plant in the mixed border. True, it could be mistaken for one, but when it comes into flower it will not fail to charm with its trumpet-shaped flowers, combining the white and pink of the *Morina longifolia*. As for the thorns on the leaves, they are not particularly vicious. An excellent plant for gardens with pebbly soil, with an extremely pleasing silhouette.

Useful hints

— Plant in autumn and cover with a cloche to avoid excessive damp in winter. It is perfectly hardy, but dislikes rot.

— Mulch the soil in June, and water generously. The foliage will generally dry out over the summer, partially regrowing again in autumn. You can hide it with marigolds, annual gypsophila or asters.

Height: 70–80 cm (28–32 in).
Spacing and planting distance: 30 cm (12 in).
Soil: rich and well-drained (improved with sand).
Cultivation: sunny.
Propagation: from seed or by division in spring.
Flowering season: July, August.
Type: perennial.

Muehlenbeckia

MUEHLENBECKIA/WIREVINE

Muehlenbeckiaceae/Polygonaceae

It is difficult to know how to classify this curious plant—as a climber, or as ground cover. It forms a network of fine stems bearing tiny leathery leaves. If given a trellis, it will act as a climber, otherwise it will trail along the ground, covering everything. Not truly hardy, *Muehlenbeckia complexa* should be grown only in milder climates.

Useful hints

— Plant in spring, in soil enriched with leaf-mould. Water regularly over the first summer, and remove weeds. In subsequent years, the matting will be so dense that weeding will not be necessary.

— Multiply by dividing clumps of rooted leaves at the ends of the mat in spring.

Height: 10–15 cm (4–6 in).
Spacing and planting distance: 30 cm (12 in).
Soil: rich in humus.
Cultivation: at least 3 hours sun per day.
Propagation: by division in spring.
Flowering season: June–August.
Type: perennial.

▽ *Muehlenbeckia complexa*

Muscari

GRAPE HYACINTH

Liliaceae

Grape hyacinths are rarely used very successfully. They are at their best in dense masses. Create a blue sea at the foot of bushes, and intersperse with daffodils and wood anemones, or with pink and white tulips, to produce an attractive effect in April.

Useful hints

— Plant in October or November, burying to a depth of 10 cm (4 in). Arrange in groups (of at least 20), planting clumps to be slightly more dense at the centre than at the edges.

— You can also plant them in pots combined with forget-me-nots, *Silene pendula* or wallflowers.

Recommended

— The best known of the blue grape hyacinths is *Muscari armeniacum* which naturalizes itself spontaneously, but *M. latifolium* and particularly *M. tubergenianum*, in a very bright blue, are worthy of attention too.

— The little-known yellow-flowering grape hyacinths offer opaline hues: *M. moschatum* 'Major' is the prototype, though its flowers are tipped with purple at the top of the spike.

— Quite different from those above, *M. comosum* 'Monstrosum' has highly ramified flowers of a violet blue. It is also nicknamed the 'feather hyacinth'.

Height: 10–30 cm (4–12 in).
Spacing and planting distance: 5–10 cm (2–4 in).
Soil: ordinary.
Cultivation: at least 3 hours sun per day.
Propagation: separate bulbils after the foliage has withered.
Flowering season: April, May.
Type: bulb.

△ *Muscari armeniacum*
▽ *Muscari tubergenianum*

△ *Myosotis alpestris* **'Ultramarine'**

Myosotis

FORGET-ME-NOT

Boraginaceae

Often, you need plant *Myosotis alpestris* in the garden only once to enjoy its flowers regularly afterwards, as it reseeds itself quite readily. And you will be thrilled when you see the lovely azure blue of its flowers. It colonizes cool areas, indicating its preference.

Useful hints

— Sow in June, and plant out into the flowering site in October. Keep some in a cold frame in reserve, as it is quite common for rot to kill off some of the plants.

— Combine your forget-me-nots with small-flowered botanical narcissi or lilies and in general with relatively tall plants that will have no difficulty in breaking through the carpet of myosotis.

Recommended

— Many people prefer the dark blue dwarf varieties such as 'Ultramarine' even though this colour tends to jar in spring. Instead, choose the classic myosotis of the Alps with its indigo blue that you will never tire of, or the variety 'Victoria' which forms very regular plant beds that flower for a number of weeks.

Height: 15–30 cm (6–12 in).
Spacing and planting distance: 15 cm (6 in).
Soil: ordinary, rather light and rich in humus.
Cultivation: at least 3 hours sun per day.
Propagation: from seed in summer.
Flowering season: April to the end of May.
Type: annual, biennial, perennial.

215

△ *Myrrhis odorata*

Myrrhis

MYRRH/SWEET CICELY

Ombelliferae

Everything about *Myrrhis odorata* is beautiful: its foliage, which is cut like that of ferns, its milky white flowers, similar to those of the wild carrot, and even its elongated fruits, which look like our grandmothers' combs. Add the aniseed fragrance of its foliage and an unbelievable ability to flourish in dark corners, and you have a picture of a highly useful plant. Myrrh goes well with ferns, digitalis and peonies.

Useful hints

— Plant in any season in soil that has been dug to depth, as it produces very powerful roots. Water until it flowers. The foliage often tends to dry out afterwards. Cut down to soil level and water from mid-August to obtain a further show of leaves.

— It will often reseed itself. Leave seedlings to become established, then transplant to their permanent position in autumn.

Height: 1 m (40 in).
Spacing and planting distance: 30 cm (12 in).
Soil: rich in humus.
Cultivation: shade.
Propagation: from seed in spring.
Flowering season: June, July.
Type: perennial.

Narcissus

NARCISSUS, DAFFODIL

Amaryllidaceae

There is such a wide range of varieties of narcissus that you can enjoy them for 3 months in spring without tiring of them for an instant. They become naturalized quite easily, yellow or white, and often give off a gentle perfume. Best grown in large clumps.

Useful hints

— Plant in autumn, from September to mid-December, but no later, as their roots should preferably have developed before the hard frosts.

— Do not cut back their leaves until they have dried out. To prevent your lawn from looking untidy while you wait for this to happen, plant narcissi in groups of 20, separated by paths that you can mow. In June, once the leaves have dried out, mow and treat with a little nitrogen fertilizer to restore the grass to an attractive colour.

— Also use dwarf narcissi in pots, which you should keep in a cold frame to speed up the production of their fragrant flowers. Combine them with forget-me-nots or other bulbs, such as scillas.

Recommended

— The best known are the **trumpet** narcissi. 'Golden Harvest', golden yellow; 'King Alfred', slightly later flowering; 'Mount Hood', white, and 'Mrs Backhouse', creamy white and apricot pink, are always effective.

— The **large cup** narcissi are easily recognizable, as they have darker centres. This applies to 'Carlton', yellow and primrose yellow; 'Flower Record', white and yellow edged with orange; 'Ice Follies', white and ivory; 'Professor Einstein', pale yellow and orange yellow; and 'Scarlet Elegance', golden yellow and scarlet red.

— The **double flower** narcissi are a little heavier and are suitable only for elaborate flower beds: 'Texas', an orange yellow, is the most famous, with 'Mary Copeland', pure white with an orange centre.

— The **small cup** narcissi are marvellous in lawns. The *Narcissus triandus* hybrids bear 2 to 6 pendant flowers on 20 cm (8 in) stems. They are delightful in rockeries: 'April Tears', yellow, and 'Liberty Bells', pale yellow, are our favourites. *N. cyclamineus* are little gems in pots. You will be enchanted by 'February Gold', 'Peeping Tom' and 'Tête à Tête', in slightly differing

Narcissus tazetta △
Narcissus **hybrids** ▷
Narcissus poeticus 'Actea' ▽

△ *Narcissus bulbocodium*

yellows. *N. jonquilla* give off a delicious fragrance: this also applies to the hybrid 'Trevithian', a pale lemon colour. Excellent cut flowers, *N. tazetta* hybrids and varieties tend to be later flowering. 'Geranium', 'Scarlet Gem' and 'Yellow Cheerfulness' will delight you in April and May. The poet's narcissi (*N. poeticus*) are the most fragrant of all. 'Actaea', white and orange edged with red, is delightful.

— We must not forget the **botanical species**, which have succeeded in retaining the charm of wild plants and are very easily naturalized in rockeries: *N. bulbocodium* (its flowers reduced to a single, widely flared trumpet), *N. canaliculatus*, *N. juncifolius* and *N. pseudonarcissus*, the very simple wild daffodil, are among the most attractive.

Height: 15–40 cm (6–16 in).
Spacing and planting distance: 5–15 cm (2–6 in).
Soil: ordinary, rather heavy.
Cultivation: at least 3 hours sun per day.
Propagation: separate new bulbs at the end of summer.
Flowering season: February–May.
Type: bulb.

217

△ *Nelumbo nucifera*

Nelumbo

LOTUS

Nymphaeaceae/Nymphaceae

If you want to add an exotic touch to an ordinary duck pond, this is the plant of your dreams: the sacred lotus of the Egyptians (*Nelumbo nucifera*). Much hardier than you might think, it produces sumptuous round leaves, quickly covering the entire area available. The flowers slip between them and open in the sun, in pink tinted white hues that should be contemplated from close at hand. The fruit, too, is quite amazing, punctured with large holes like the rose of a watering can.

Useful hints

— Plant in spring when the water has warmed up a little, in pots of soil enriched with well-rotted manure.

— In cooler climates in winter, remove the rhizomes and protect them in permanently damp sand, in a room that is unheated but above freezing point.

Height: 20–100 cm (8–40 in) depending on the depth of water.
Spacing and planting distance: 2 m (80 in).
Soil: rich and clay.
Cultivation: very sunny.
Propagation: by division in spring.
Flowering season: summer.
Type: perennial.

Nemesia

NEMESIA

Scrophulariaceae

The gaiety of their colours is a wonder to behold in the garden, yet they are rarely seen. Is it because of their relatively short flowering period—3 to 4 weeks? This is an injustice to be remedied since there are few flowers that offer such innocent freshness in summer. They are as happy in containers as in flowerbeds.

Useful hints

— Sow seeds of *Nemesia strumosa* in April, spacing them several centimetres apart, in an earthenware pot or the corner of a cold frame.

— Transplant the plants 1 month later, directly to their flowering site if the weather is fine. Pinch out at a height of 10 cm (4 in) to force them to branch out, increasing the mass of flowers.

— Water abundantly when in flower and cut the stems back afterwards, to the level of the leaves. You will then have a further show of flowers 3 weeks later.

Recommended

The seed stockists offer only a limited number of varieties. The most common is 'Carnival' which reaches a height of 40 cm (16 in) and provides all colours from the palest yellow to pink, through warm browns and velvety oranges.

Height: 20–40 cm (8–16 in).
Spacing and planting distance: 15–30 cm (6–12 in).
Soil: quite rich and light.
Cultivation: semi-shade, to prevent the colours from fading in the sun.
Propagation: from seed in spring.
Flowering season: 1 month, at any time between May and the first frost.
Type: annual.

▽ *Nemophila menziesii*

▽ *Nemesia strumosa*

Nemophila

BABY BLUE EYES

Hydrophyllaceae

This flower's nickname of 'baby blue eyes', derives from the delicate pale blue of *Nemophila menziesii*. While flowering rarely lasts for more than a month, the flowers are borne in abundance and provide magnificent borders for the end of spring. *N. maculata*, which is white, has mottled petals.

Useful hints

— Sow in March in a cold frame and transplant 1 month later, or sow directly in the flowering site in September. Young plants over-winter well. Thin out the seeds, leaving one plant every 20 cm (8 in).

— When flowering is over, pull up the plants and sow godetias or marigolds which will have time to flower in autumn. *Nemophila* is particularly attractive when combined with *Limnanthes*.

Height: 20 cm (8 in).
Spacing and planting distance: 20 cm (8 in).
Soil: ordinary.
Cultivation: sun and semi-shade.
Propagation: from seed in March or September.
Flowering season: May, June.
Type: annual.

▽ *Nemophila maculata*

△ *Nepeta (in the centre, Stachys macranta)*

Nepeta

CATMINT/PERSIAN GROUND-IVY

Labiatae

The gentle blue of *Nepeta × faassenii* reaches its peak in mid-summer, softening the mass of yellow and orange flowers blooming at the time. They are incomparable at the edge of rose beds, hiding the base of the rose, which is often quite ugly.

Useful hints

— Provide them with soil that is not too rich, and is well-drained in winter. Plant preferably in spring, so the plants are well-developed before the cold weather arrives.

— Cut back the clumps at the end of the winter to keep them compact. Cats will often sleep on them, as they love the smell of the foliage, hence the nickname of catmint.

Recommended

— The most common is the former *Nepeta mussinii*, nowadays known as *N. × fassenii*. The hybrid 'Six Hills Giant' is the most remarkable, as its blue is brighter and it is less likely to be beaten down by rain. 'Souvenir d'André Chaudron' is the tallest.

Height: 20–60 cm (8–24 in).
Spacing and planting distance: 30 cm (12 in).
Soil: slightly dry.
Cultivation: very sunny.
Propagation: by division in spring.
Flowering season: June–October.
Type: perennial.

△ *Nerine bowdenii*

Nerine

GUERNSEY LILY/CAPE COLONY NERINE
Amaryllidaceae

These relatively uncommon flowers, grown from bulbs, charm us with their delicacy: a bright pink colour, a chiselled form of flower, an elegance of shape and outline, and ribbon-like foliage. *Nerine bowdenii*'s only fault is that it is less than reliably hardy, requiring a particularly well-protected location, and a covering of dead leaves in winter.

Useful hints

— Plant in spring in soil enriched with sand at the foot of a south-facing wall. Foliage will appear during or just after flowering, in autumn. Allow clumps to fill out and do not divide too frequently, as they dislike being disturbed and will take several years to flower again.

— To increase the decorative effect, plant in groups (minimum of 10) and combine with artemisias, white asters and pink Japanese anemones.

Height: 60 cm (24 in).
Spacing and planting distance: 15 cm (6 in).
Soil: ordinary, slightly sandy.
Cultivation: sunny, at the base of a wall, sheltered from cold winds.
Propagation: separate new bulbs at the end of spring.
Flowering season: September–November.
Type: bulb.

Nicandra

NICANDRA/APPLE-OF-PERU
Solanaceae

Some plants are instantly evocative of other climes because of their form or their colours. Although *Nicandra physaloides* is by no means dazzling, it is immediately noticeable in flower beds. As the name of the species indicates, it is very similar to the physalis, commonly known as 'Chinese lantern'. Like this latter plant it forms a beautiful mass of leaves, but its flowers are more freely borne in a pale blue. It then produces plum-like fruits contained in a calyx of very thin parchment. It is grown as an annual for its fruits, which are used in dried flower arrangements.

Useful hints

— Sow under cover in April and prick out once before transplanting into the final flowering location, in May. Water regularly, and apply dilute fertilizer to encourage plump fruits.

— Cut the stems in September and dry, heads down. You can then lie them on the soil in a location that gets no rain. The fungi contained in the soil will attack the cellulose and remove part of the calyx, leaving only the veins.

— If you find any minute white flies hovering around the plants, treat once or twice with a decamethrine-based insecticide.

Height: 80 cm–1 m (32–40 in).
Spacing and planting distance: 40 cm (16 in).
Soil: rich, well-watered.
Cultivation: sunny.
Propagation: from seed in spring.
Flowering season: July, August.
Type: annual.

Nicotonia affinis 'Nicky' ▷
Nicandra physaloides ▽

Nicotiana

TOBACCO PLANT
Solanaceae

There are few flowers that can claim to be as fragrant as those of the white tobacco plant. Opening their flowers wide in the evening, tobacco plants give off a fragrance that is perceptible several yards away.

Useful hints

— Sow under cover in April and transplant once into pots before planting out into their flowering site in mid-May.

— Watch out for invasions of greenfly in June/July. Water regularly and apply soluble fertilizer every month, as these are voracious plants. In mild climates, they will often become perennial.

Recommended

— *Nicotiana alata* bears white flowers and will readily exceed 1 m (40 in) in height. The 'Lime Green' variety, with lime green flowers, and 'Sensation', in a variety of colours, are becoming increasingly rare in catalogues, even though these are magnificent plants for slightly informal flower beds. The 'Nicki' hybrids are very small, but have no fragrance whatsoever.

Height: 30 cm–2 m (12–80 in).
Spacing and planting distance: 20–50 cm (8–20 in).
Soil: rich in humus and always cool in summer.
Cultivation: partial shade or non-burning sun.
Propagation: from seed in spring.
Flowering season: June to first frosts.
Type: annual, biennial.

Nicotonia sylvestris ▽

Nicotonia affinis △
Nigella damascena ▷

Nigella

LOVE IN A MIST

Ranunculaceae

A familiar flower in country gardens, *Nigella* will readily reseed itself each year, spending winter in plantlet form. It is always delightful in the summer to see its fine parsley-like foliage and its flowers in the hues of old porcelain. Surrounded by a lacy collar, they well deserve their common name of 'Love in a mist'.

Combine with late flowering perennials such as hostas or *Sedum spectabile*. The dried fruits can be used in winter dried flower arrangements, as they are quite spectacular.

Useful hints

— Sow in March or April directly in the flowering site, or in a cold frame. Thin out 1 month later, to a spacing of 20 cm (8 in).

— Pinch back the main stems to half height after 2 months to encourage them to bush out.

Recommended

— The most common is the double-flowered *Nigella damascena*. This is available in blue, pink or white, the latter being truly magnificent.

Height: 45–60 cm (18–24 in).
Spacing and planting distance: 20 cm (8 in).
Soil: ordinary, even relatively poor.
Cultivation: sun and semi-shade.
Propagation: from seed in spring.
Flowering season: June–September.
Type: annual.

221

Nymphaea

WATER LILY

Nymphaeaceae/Nymphaeceae

Can there be anyone who is not familiar with the nymphea, which makes such a spectacular display on lakes and ponds? Fewer people however are aware that there are many different varieties, some of which will flourish in very small amounts of water. This puts them in everyone's range, since there is nothing to stop you creating a mini-pond in an ordinary barrel, cut in half.

Useful hints

— Plant in April or May, when the water has begun to warm up. Place the crown in a pot filled with heavy soil containing plenty of clay. The depth of planting under the water can be anywhere between 35 and 150 cm (14 and 60 in) or even more for the most vigorous varieties, which should be reserved for large pools.

— If the pond is sufficiently deep, the nympheas can be left in position over winter, with no protection. Otherwise keep in wet sand in a cold room.

Recommended

— There are several hundred! Some of the most readily available are: 'Candida', pure white; 'Colonel A. J. Welch', yellow; 'Ellisiana', red, with orange stamens; 'James Brydon', double crimson pink splashed with maroon; 'Madame Gonnère', pure pink; *N.* × *marliacea* 'Carnea', pink, and 'Chromatella', yellow; 'Paul Hariot', yellow and copper; 'Sioux', large-flowered copper.

Height: 20–120 cm (8–48 in) below the water level.
Spacing and planting distance: 30–137 cm (12–54 in).
Soil: heavy and rich.
Cultivation: sunny.
Propagation: by division in spring.
Flowering season: July–October.
Type: perennial.

◁ *Nymphaea* × *laydekeri* 'Fulgens'
Oenothera missouriensis ▷
▽ *Oenothera fructicosa*

Oenothera

EVENING PRIMROSE
Onagraceae

There are few perennials that offer such a sparkling yellow as the oenotheras. Their common name, evening primrose, comes from their customary habit of choosing the evening to open. Once their floral display is over, their foliage continues to delight with its interesting autumn tints. They are troubled by few diseases and even fewer insects and so are truly excellent plants for weekend gardeners.

Useful hints

— Plant preferably in spring in small groups of 5 or 6, scattered among other fuller plants. They will slip in between them with no need for staking.

— Divide clumps every 3 years, as they have a tendency to harden over a period of time and to flower less freely. Seeds are generally successful, but they will not come up until after the winter. Try sowing the dwarf varieties, which often die after flowering.

Recommended

— Dwarf oenotheras are wonderful in rockeries as they flower later than the other alpine plants. This applies to *Oenothera pumila* (syn. *O. perennis*) which does not exceed 30 cm (12 in) in height and flowers throughout the summer, *O. acaulis*, which has foliage similar to that of the dandelion and very large white flowers that smell delightful and, of course, the most spectacular of all, *O. missouriensis*, which forms a mat of foliage strewn with magnificent yellow flowers throughout the summer. It is extremely successful in tubs, where it can accom-

pany conifers, partially concealing the container itself.

— More suitable for flower beds than for rockeries, the medium-sized oenotheras brighten up our mixed borders at the beginning of summer. The most commonly found is *O. tetragona*, bright yellow, and its variety Fireworks, the buds of which are a surprising waxy red.

— The giant of the group is *O. biennis*. As its name indicates, this is a biennial. A native of North America, it is commonly seen in the company of *O. lamarckiana*. Its yellow flowers open only in the evening and are borne in succession over a number of weeks, on stems of more than 1 m (40 in) in height.

Height: 15–150 cm (6–60 in).
Spacing and planting distance: 20–50 cm (8–20 in).
Soil: ordinary.
Cultivation: at least 4 hours sun per day.
Propagation: from seed or by division in spring.
Flowering season: June–October.
Type: annual, biennial, perennial.

Omphalodes verna ▷

Omphalodes

NAVELWORT/CREEPING NAVELSEED, BLUE-EYED MARY
Boraginaceae

Although the leaves of *Omphalodes verna* are somewhat large, they make a perfect foil for the exquisite delicacy of the flowers, of an entrancing china blue. This very robust plant will thrive even in dry soil under trees. Combine with wood anemones, daffodils and snakes' heads, which will intermingle elegantly with its foliage.

Useful hints

— Plant preferably in autumn, in large groups. This plant will provide excellent ground cover that will compete with ivy and periwinkle. Improve the soil with peat or leaf-mould.

— In February, remove dead leaves from the crowns and dress with a little peat or pine bark. The clumps can be divided at the end of summer and replanted immediately.

Height: 15–20 cm (6–8 in).
Spacing and planting distance: 20 cm (8 in).
Soil: rich in humus.
Cultivation: shade and semi-shade.
Propagation: by division at the end of the summer.
Flowering season: February–May.
Type: perennial.

Onoclea

SENSITIVE FERN

Polypodiaceae

A medium-sized, hardy plant, this fern is wonderful at the water's edge, in damp corners and at the foot of a north- or west-facing wall. Its fronds, of a beautiful soft green, provide an attractive screen for peonies, lilies and Solomon's seals. Intersperse them among your shrubs to avoid patches of bare earth.

Useful hints

— Plant *Onoclea sensibilis* in spring after improving the soil with peat and leafmould. Plant in groups (of at least 10) to create a more natural mass effect.

— Leave the dried foliage on the plants in winter as it protects them from the cold. Cut back in April, but avoid pulling out roughly. Divide the clumps at around the same time.

— If as a result of frost, the plants turn brown, don't worry as they will grow up again in the spring.

Height: 50–60 cm (20–24 in).
Spacing and planting distance: 50 cm (20 in).
Soil: rich in humus.
Cultivation: shade and semi-shade.
Propagation: by division in spring.
Type: perennial.

Onopordum

SCOTCH THISTLE, COTTON THISTLE

Compositae

A masterly plant for the edge of a border. The distinction between the perennial and biennial plants is not always very clear. This is borne out by the thistle that appears to some people to last for only 2 years, while others regard it as a perennial. The explanation of this mystery is due in part to the prodigious ability of *Onopordum bracteatum* to reseed itself. The first year, it forms a rosette, close to the ground. It waits until the next spring to display its imposing foliage, so silvery that it looks almost artificial. Flowering continues for so long that the seeds will already have sprouted all around before it finishes.

Useful hints

— Plant 1 year-old rosette crowns in autumn. Do not disturb the rootball.

— If you are afraid of this plant becoming invasive, cut off the dead flower heads before the seeds form (wear gloves, as the leaves and stalks can be vicious).

— You can replant spontaneously sown seedlings to brighten up areas where nothing else will grow, e.g. at the foot of trees.

Recommended

— As well as *Onopordum bracteatum* why not try *O. acanthium*, the genuine donkey thistle? Its broad silver leaves have fine hairs but beware of the sting. The pale purple flowers come out in July and August.

— *O. arabicum* (also known as *O. nervosum*) is taller and bears reddish-purple flowers, 5 cm (2 in) in diameter, which bloom in July.

Height: 2 m (80 in).
Spacing and planting distance: 80 cm (32 in).
Soil: any, even poor.
Cultivation: sun and semi-shade.
Propagation: from seed at the end of summer.
Flowering season: July, August.
Type: biennial, perennial.

Ornithogalum

STAR OF BETHLEHEM

Liliaceae

This genus includes some relatively tender species and others that are extremely hardy. Ornithogalums generally have white flowers and are grown from bulbs.

Useful hints

— Plant in autumn and cover with a generous layer of dead leaves. Mark the site with a tag to remind you where you have planted them.

— Dig up clumps in July if you find them too dense after a number of years. Take advantage of doing this to split off the new bulbs, and keep in dry peat until planting.

— *Ornithogalum arabicum* must be kept in a cold frame over winter. Its relatively large flowers, marked with a black centre, are long-lasting as cut flowers. It needs a sunny, sheltered position, but does best as a pot plant.

— The largest is *O. magnum*, which grows to a height of more than 60 cm (24 in). Totally hardy, it bears green-striped flowers in June. It likes chalky or well-drained sandy soils.

— Extremely attractive in the company of ferns and wood tulips, *O. nutans* easily becomes naturalized in partial shade. It does not exceed a height of 30 cm (12 in).

△ *Onoclea sensibilis*
Onopordum arabicum ▷

— An exception among ornithogalums, *O. thyrsoides* is planted in spring. It flowers during the summer, and the cut flowers will last for a long time in water—up to 6 weeks.

— *O. umbellatum* flowers for more than a month at the end of spring. It will adapt to any soil.

Height: 20–80 cm (8–32 in).
Spacing and planting distance: 20 cm (8 in).
Soil: sandy.
Cultivation: sun or semi-shade.
Propagation: separate new bulbs after allowing the leaves to dry out.
Flowering season: May–September.
Type: bulb.

▽ *Ornithogalum arabicum*

△ *Ornithogalum umbellatum*

Osmunda

ROYAL FERN

Osmundaceae

The *Osmunda regalis*, which reigns majestically over damp sites, well deserves its name 'royal'. Sometimes growing to a height of 3 m (120 in), when it develops a kind of small trunk, it gives an impression of power and harmony unequalled among indigenous plants. In the wild, it is protected, and it would be particularly pointless to dig it up since it is generally difficult to transplant and is easily available from nurseries.

Combine with *florindae* primroses, astilbes and peltiphyllums to produce a luxuriant scene reminiscent of prehistoric times. At the end of the summer, fertile fronds bearing spores appear. Do not remove these, as they too are decorative.

Useful hints

— Plant in April in humus-rich soil and top dress with humus each spring.

— Tidy up each autumn by cutting back top growth.

Recommended

— *Osmunda regalis* 'Purpurascens' has unusually-coloured deep copper-pink fronds.

Height: 1–3 m (40–120 in).
Spacing and planting distance: 1 m (40 in).
Soil: rich, cool at all times.
Cultivation: sun and semi-shade.
Propagation: separate secondary crowns appearing around the mother plant in spring.
Flowering season: end of summer.
Type: perennial.

▽ *Onopordum bracteatum*

▽ *Osmunda regalis*

Osteospermum **'Las Vegas'** △
Osteospermum ecklonis ▽

Osteospermum

CAPE MARIGOLD

Compositae

Until recently known as *Dimorphotheca* and only lately renamed *Osteospermum*, these dwarf daisies, true sun-lovers, ought to be found more frequently in gardens, particularly in sun-trap sites. Worthy of their French common name 'souci pluvial' (rain marigolds), they open their flowers as soon as the sun appears and close them again at the slightest cloud.

Useful hints

— Sow seeds either under cover in March, transplanting them to their flowering site 1 month later, or directly at the edge of the flowerbed at the end of April. Thin out to 20 cm (8 in).

— For perennial varieties, take cuttings in March, as for pelargoniums, and harden them off before bringing them out in May to decorate your pots.

Recommended

— The best known is *Osteospermum auriantacum*, its flowers offering all possible orange hues. Note the beauty of the steel-blue circle around the heart. Its large seeds will germinate well only if at least a year old. Try the 'Pole Star' variety with white flowers and a blue heart. Your efforts will be rewarded.

— Almost hardy in warm and temperate climates, *O. ecklone* forms a bush, covered with flowers all summer long. It is marvellous in earthenware pots. Bring under cover in winter.

Height: 30–60 cm (12–24 in).
Spacing and planting distance: 20 cm (8 in).
Soil: light and fertile (pots should contain compost and sand).
Cultivation: very sunny.
Propagation: from seed or from cuttings in spring.
Flowering season: June to first frosts.
Type: annual, perennial.

Ourisia

OURISIA

Scrophulariaceae

An excellent little plant for damp corners, *Ourisia* will make itself at home in cool places and in some rockeries.

Useful hint

— Sow seeds in April and transplant the following spring, or divide clumps at the same time.

Recommended

— *Ourisia coccinea* forms dense mats with tubular red flowers. *O. macrophylla* has tubular white flowers.

Height: 20 cm (8 in).
Spacing and planting distance: 50 cm (20 in).
Soil: rich in humus, but well-drained.
Cultivation: semi-shade.
Propagation: from seed or by division in April.
Flowering season: May–September.
Type: perennial.

Oxalis

OXALIS

Oxalidaceae

This genus contains some real pests, and some interesting flowers. They are best used to produce mats in the rockery or on a dry stone wall. They can also be used in containers, together with aubretia or alyssums.

Useful hints

— Plant in autumn in light soil. *Oxalis deppei* can also be planted in spring.

— Lift the clumps 2 months after flowering to remove bulbils and replant immediately.

Recommended

— *Oxalis adenophylla* is decorative in terms both of its grey foliage, which is folded like a parachute, and its flowers of delicate pink with white hearts.

— Beware of *O. deppei*, also popularly known as the four leaf clover, as it can be extremely invasive. Restrict it to the edges of paths where few plants will grow.

Height: 20 cm (8 in).
Spacing and planting distance: 15 cm (6 in).
Soil: ordinary, preferably chalky.
Cultivation: at least 3 hours sun per day.
Propagation: separate bulbils after flowering.
Flowering season: May–September.
Type: annual, bulb, perennial.

Pachysandra

PACHYSANDRA/SPURGE

Buxaceae

If pachysandras are rather unpopular these days, it is perhaps because we have seen too many of them in public parks, where they are used solely for undergrowth decoration, giving them the reputation of being boring. By all means use *Pachysandra terminalis* in these dis-

△ **Oxalis adenophylla**
◁ **Ourisia macrophylla**
Oxalis deppei 'Iron Cross' ▷
▽ **Pachysandra terminalis**

advantaged locations, but put them with spring bulbs, hydrangeas and periwinkles to avoid the monotony of just a single type of plant.

Useful hints

— Plants raised in containers can be planted out in any season, while plants with bare roots should be planted out in spring. Cut back the foliage each spring to make the plants more dense. If the soil is of poor quality, apply a dressing of dried blood.

— Every 5 years, divide the clumps to renew them, preferably at the start of autumn.

Height: 40 cm (16 in).
Spacing and planting distance: 30 cm (12 in).
Soil: any, although growth will be faster in soil rich in humus.
Cultivation: shade and semi-shade.
Propagation: by division in spring.
Flowering season: April (insignificant).
Type: perennial.

227

Paeonia

PAEONY
Paeoniaceae

Peonies are central to a garden. Their rounded shape, their abundant foliage in a neutral green and their enormous flowers make them unbeatable in May and June. For the rest of the season, they serve as a backdrop.

Useful hints

— Plant in autumn, as soon as possible, i.e. from mid-September. Water abundantly to encourage rooting. Mark the location of the plants as growth starts late and has little volume the first year. Dress with dried blood to accelerate.

— Support each crown with hazel twigs from the beginning of May, to prevent the weight of the flowers from pulling down the stems. The plants can then be left to their own devices for decades.

Recommended

— **Japanese** peonies generally have single flowers: 'Bowl of Beauty', pink, with a pale yellow centre; 'Carara', totally white; 'Kimo-Kimo', carmine tinted with crimson and 'Watteau', pinkish white, are most attractive.

— **Chinese** peonies (*Paeonia lactiflora*) are the best known. Very large, and with an abundance of petals, they are available in every shade, from pure white to dark red, almost black. A selection of colours is given below:

— **White**: 'Candidissima'; 'Doris Cooper', with just a hint of pink; 'Madame Claude Tain', pinkish white developing to pure white; 'Vogue Praecox', tinged with pale pink.

— **Pink**: 'Albert Crousse', very much a double; 'Blush Queen', tinged with cream; 'Gilbert Barthelot', which produces an unbelievable quantity of flowers; 'Lady Orchid', bright pink; 'Madame Calot', brilliant pink; 'Mariette Vallée', 'Reine Hortense', 'Sarah Bernhardt'.

— **Red**: 'Chippewa', dark red; 'Felix Crouss', one of the best reds; 'Lord Kitchener', tending towards brown; 'Peter Brand', burgundy red.

Height: 1 m (40 in).
Spacing and planting distance: 1 m (40 in).
Soil: rich in humus and remaining cool in summer.
Cultivation: semi-shade or moderately sunny.
Propagation: by division in summer.
Flowering season: May, June.
Type: perennial.

△ *Paeonia mlokosewitschii*

△ *Paeonia officinalis*
▽ *Paeonia lactiflora* **hybrid**

Papaver

POPPY
Papaveraceae

This genus has both annual and perennial varieties, all of which bear sumptuously coloured flowers with a silky quality. Poppies are at home in both highly sophisticated and country gardens.

Useful hints

— Sow in March in the case of annuals and in May or June in the case of perennials. Plant out into small pots while still very young, or directly into their flowering site, as these plants dislike being transplanted once they are older.

— Water annual poppies regularly, and remove the first fruits to prevent them from dying prematurely. Cut back the foliage of perennial species in June when it is beginning to dry out.

— Plant by the side of asters or china asters to fill in spaces. New foliage will appear in September and October and remain throughout the winter.

Recommended

— The Iceland poppy (*Papaver nudicaule*) is grown as a biennial, i.e. it is sown in July to flower the next spring. Its flowers are excellent companions to tulips and forget-me-nots. The alpine poppy (*P. alpinum*) is smaller, and varies between yellow and orange.

— One of the annual poppies is the field poppy (*P. rhoeas*). The double varieties are delightful, e.g. 'Shirley Poppy'. Dot a few plants about your flowerbeds to give them a touch of gaiety. The opium poppy (*P somniferum*) bears just a few flowers, as large as peonies. Their flowering can be extended by removing the fruits as they form.

— The Oriental poppy (*P. orientale*), which is totally hardy, is originally red, but some enchanting selections have now appeared that combine all variations of pink and white with black centres: 'Allegro', dwarf red; 'Catharina', brilliant salmon pink; 'Corinna', luminous pink; 'Mary Finnen' with fringed red petals; 'Perry's White', white, with a brown centre; 'Rosenpokal', carmine pink.

Height: 15–80 cm (6–32 in).
Spacing and planting distance: 20 cm (8 in).
Soil: any, well-drained in winter.
Cultivation: sunny.
Propagation: from seed or by division in spring.
Flowering season: April–September.
Type: annual, biennial, perennial.

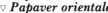

△ *Papaver somniferum*
◁ *Papaver orientale* **hybrid**
▽ *Papaver orientale*

229

△ *Paradisea liliastrum*

Paradisea

PARADISEA/ST BRUNO LILY

Liliaceae

A native of alpine meadows, the bulbous *Paradisea liliastrum* produces a gracious flower spike ending in flowers forming an immaculate white star. They are among the aristocrats of the rockery plants.

Useful hints

— Plant in autumn or spring, and mark their site carefully, as the vegetation is visible for only a short period and the plant is likely to be damaged by hoeing.

— Surround with slug bait not only in summer but also in autumn, as black slugs over-winter in the ground close to its tuberous roots.

Height: 60 cm (24 in).
Spacing and planting distance: 15 cm (6 in).
Soil: sandy.
Cultivation: sunny.
Propagation: by division in autumn.
Flowering season: June, July.
Type: bulb.

Pelargonium

GERANIUM

Geraniaceae

Everyone knows the garden geranium which is so frequently grown in pots on balconies, providing an incomparable display of colour for containers. They are so good-humoured that we simply could not do without them. Although the varieties are rarely named, a number of botanical species are offered, particularly in the major group of fragrant-leaved pelargoniums.

Useful hints

— Plant in April in warm climates, and in May in cool areas. Choose rich, porous soil, based on leaf mould, peat and sand. Make provision for drainage. Feed with soluble fertilizer every 2 weeks.

— Pinch out stalks mid-height at the end of May to force them to branch out. When the first show of flowers is over, remove dead flower heads and fertilize to encourage a further show.

— In October, cut the plants back and bring them under cover in a cool, light room. Cuttings can be taken in summer or in spring.

Recommended

— *Pelargonium zonale* (incorrectly known as geraniums) often have leaves marked by a darker, almost reddish area. These are the most common of all the pelargoniums. They come in all colours, from pure white, often damaged by the rain, to the darkest red.

— Ivy-leaved geraniums (*P. peltatum*) have smooth leaves and frequently a supple habit, climbing if provided with a trellis, otherwise trailing. The single-flowered 'Roi des Balcons' is the best known and the most free-flowering. It is available in pink and bright red.

— *P. regale* is extremely capricious. Even experienced gardeners are not always successful with it. Its large flowers, sumptuously washed with purple, show up well against its dentate yellowish green leaves. It requires a certain amount of warmth and regular feeding with fertilizer.

— Of the fragrant-leaved pelargoniums, the most noteworthy are: *P. tomentosum*, with velvety leaves that smell of peppermint, and *P. graveolens*, with highly aromatic, rough, denticulate leaves. If you keep an eye open, you will undoubtedly find others at random on the flower stalls.

Height: 30–120 cm (12–48 in).
Spacing and planting distance: 30 cm (12 in).
Soil: rich, well-drained.
Cultivation: very sunny.
Propagation: from cuttings in summer or spring.
Flowering season: all summer.
Type: annual and perennial in mild climates.

Pelargonium pelchellum △
Pelargonium tomentosum ▷
Pelargonium zonale ▷
Pelargonium pectatum ▽

△ *Peltiphyllum peltatum*

Peltiphyllum

UMBRELLA PLANT

Saxifragaceae

This is a plant that should never be used in small numbers. A well-established patch of *Peltiphyllum peltatum* is a rare spectacle, whether in spring when the pink flowers are in bloom, or in autumn when the leaves take on brilliant red hues.

Useful hints

— Plant in spring in well-prepared soil dug deep and enriched with peat to keep it moist in summer. Mulch the soil with pine bark, semi-decomposed compost or grass cuttings. Water regularly in hot weather.

— Leave the foliage in place until February. Then remove to show off the flowers, which follow shortly afterwards. Combine with lysichitons to create a highly exotic effect.

Height: 60–80 cm (24–32 in).
Spacing and planting distance: 60 cm (24 in).
Soil: permanently moist.
Cultivation: sun and semi-shade.
Propagation: division by clumps in autumn.
Flowering season: February, March.
Type: perennial.

Pennisetum

PENNISETUM/FOUNTAIN GRASS

Gramineae

This is the most elegant of the *Gramineae*. Ideal for livening up the most ordinary of gardens, these grasses marry perfectly with stone steps, heathers and conifers.

Combine pennisetums with wild tulips, *Dierama*, ground cover plants such as *Acaena*, or *Sedum spectabile*.

Useful hints

— Plant in any season but preferably in spring, in heavy soil. Improve with sand.

— Hoe carefully for the first year and dress with a little nitrogen fertilizer to encourage growth. Leave dried out leaves *in situ* until March, as they insulate the crown.

Recommended

— *Pennisetum alopecuroides* produces curious plumes that are particularly decorative in dried flower arrangements.

— *P. orientale* grows to little more than 60 cm (24 in) in height. Its leaves turn bronze in autumn.

— *P. japonicum*, which is extremely delicate, looks rather like a frightened cat's tail. Its dull pink colour is perfect for toning down excessively bright colour contrasts.

Height: 30–160 cm (12–64 in).
Spacing and planting distance: 30 cm (12 in).
Soil: ordinary.
Cultivation: sunny.
Propagation: by division in spring.
Flowering season: summer.
Type: perennial.

Pennisetum compressum ▽

231

△ *Penstemon heterophyllus* **'Blue Spring'**
Penstemon newberryi △

Penstemon

PENSTEMON

Scrophulariaceae

Lovers of dry soil, penstemons are valuable plants as they flower in midsummer. Their flowers are often of unusual colours, particularly in purples and pinks, but they are also available in very powerful reds.

Useful hints

— Plant in spring when the worst of the rains are over. Give a well-drained position, with a rich soil. Mulch in June with pine bark. Water plentifully during the flowering season to keep it in flower longer.

— In winter, protect the crown from excessive water with a sheet of plastic.

Recommended

— Of the **hybrid** penstemons: 'Andenken an Hahn', scarlet red; 'Le Phare' and 'Southgate Gem', bright red; 'Souvenir d'Adrien Régnier', gentle pink. 'Garnet' is one of the best red varieties and will withstand an average winter.

— Of the **botanical** varieties: *Penstemon heterophyllus* has blue flowers, those of 'Blue Spring' being particularly bright; *P. pinifolius* will form a little shrub in your rockery. Its flowers are an orangey red.

Height: 15–60 cm (6–24 in).
Spacing and planting distance: 20 cm (8 in).
Soil: rich and well-drained.
Cultivation: sunny.
Propagation: from cuttings in summer and by division in spring.
Flowering season: June–September.
Type: biennial, perennial.

△ *Penstemon* **'Heavenly Blue'**

△ *Petasites japonicus*
▽ *Petasites giganteus*

Petasites

COLTSFOOT

Compositae

When the flowers of coltsfoot appear suddenly like giant dandelions it is always surprising to remember that the somewhat ordinary-looking foliage they bloom amongst resembles that of a weed. It is in fact extremely invasive. Use only in poor sites such as the edges of ditches.

Combine with *Galanthus*, peonies, ferns and Solomon's seals.

Useful hints

— Plant *Petasites fragrans* in spring or autumn and ensure that they do not spread beyond the boundaries that you have set for them. They suffer from no particular parasites and need no particular care, but it is worth protecting the crowns with dead leaves as they can be damaged by extremely cold winters.

Height: 50 cm (20 in).
Spacing and planting distance: 30 cm (12 in).
Soil: ordinary, rather rich in humus.
Cultivation: semi-shade.
Propagation: by division, any season.
Flowering season: December, January.
Type: perennial.

Petunia

PETUNIA

Solanaceae

Great rivals of the pelargonium, petunias beat all records for length of flowering with little attention. Use them either in a mass or interspersed among borders of grey foliage plants such as *Cerastiums* or *Artemisia*.

Useful hints

— Sow *Petunia hybrida* under cover in March and transplant once before moving to their flowering site in mid-May. They like rich, well-drained soil. Feed with fertilizer every 2 weeks to encourage large flowers.

— Remove dead flowers regularly to prevent seeds from forming.

Recommended

— For balconies: all medium-sized flower varieties, which are more free-flowering than the large-flowered varieties. 'Resisto' is very tolerant of rain. 'Cascade' is often disappointing as the stems need to be curved by hand to make them trail.

△ *Phacelia campanularia*

△ *Petunia* **hybrids**

— For flower beds: the compact dwarf petunias 'Rose du Ciel' or 'Rose of Heaven' are the best as their flowers are produced in succession over a number of months.

Height: 20–35 cm (8–14 in).
Spacing and planting distance: 20 cm (8 in).
Soil: rich and well-drained (peaty compost).
Cultivation: sunny.
Propagation: from seed sown under cover in March.
Flowering season: June to first frosts.
Type: annual.

Phacelia

PHACELIA
Hydrophyllaceae

What a beautiful blue, and what lovely little upward-pointing bells. If you are looking for an original small annual flower, you should be delighted with *Phacelia campanularia*, although you may have difficulty in finding the seeds. Fortunately, just as pretty, just as blue and just as free-flowering, *P. tanacetifolia*, which flowers on plumed spikes, is very easy to obtain. Phacelias are fragrant and attract bees. Sow in the kitchen garden, in borders, or in the rockery.

Useful hints

— Like most annual flowers, they are easy to grow. Any good garden soil will suit them, but they need a sunny position to flower freely.

— An easy-going plant, they prefer to be sown directly in the flowering site. Thin the plants out to 15 cm (6 in) in all directions once they appear.

— To extend their flowering season, which is only just over a month, stagger sowing between April and June, and you will then have flowers through to September.

— In the kitchen garden, give yourself the pleasure of sowing little strips between rows of vegetables, and you will be rewarded with delightful mats of blue flowers that will be covered with bees and butterflies.

Height: 40 cm (16 in).
Spacing and planting distance: 15 cm (6 in).
Soil: ordinary.
Cultivation: sunny.
Propagation: from seed in spring.
Flowering season: June–October.
Type: annual.

Phalaris

PHALARIS/RIBBON GRASS

Gramineae

If you find your flower beds insufficiently filled in summer, make a little space for *Gramineae*, particularly *Phalaris arundinaceae*. With a marking of longitudinal white stripes, their foliage provides valuable assistance to poppies, tobacco plants or phlox by acting as an attractive space-filler.

Useful hints

— Plant in spring or autumn in relatively rich soil. Water regularly for the first year.

— Watch the clumps for spreading, as they can become invasive. Leave the foliage intact over winter and cut back only in March, leaving the new stems *in situ*. These are extremely attractive in fresh Japanese-style bouquets.

Height: 60–80 cm (24–32 in).
Spacing and planting distance: 40 cm (16 in).
Soil: ordinary.
Cultivation: sunny.
Propagation: by division in spring.
Flowering season: insignificant (June, July).
Type: perennial.

▽ *Phalaris arundinacea*

△ *Phlomis samia*

Phlomis

JERUSALEM SAGE

Labiatae

Though not always very hardy, *Phlomis* form attractive shrubby plants where they feel at home. If you combine them with *Cistus*, lavender and salvias you will create a border full of warm colours.

Useful hints

— Plant preferably in spring in the warmest corners of the garden. They are not afraid of the burning sun – indeed, it is precisely in these sites that their foliage is the most attractive.

— Mulch the soil with pine bark in June. When the first frosts arrive, allow vegetation to stop and cover the plant with a sheet of transparent plastic. As a precaution, place a few cuttings taken in summer under shelter.

Recommended

— The true Jerusalem sage is *Phlomis fruticosa*, its foliage covered with grey, slightly dirty-looking down. The yellow flowers are borne in succession throughout the summer. It is an excellent plant for containers on hot sunny balconies.

— *P. samia* is better suited than the previous variety to damp climates. Its flowers vary from pale yellow to orange, often ending in pink. They are produced in regular clusters along the length of the stems in May and June.

Height: 60–120 cm (24–48 in).
Spacing and planting distance: 50 cm (20 in).
Soil: very well drained.
Cultivation: very sunny.
Propagation: from cuttings in summer.
Flowering season: May–September.
Type: perennial.

Phlox

PHLOX

Polemoniaceae

It is difficult to imagine gardens before the phloxes were discovered, all having originated in North America. They are irreplaceable for adding colour and often fragrance to our flowerbeds, particularly since nature has provided them in all sizes and virtually all colours.

Useful hints

— Sow annual phloxes in March in a cold frame, or directly in the flowering site in April or May. To germinate well, seeds should be a year old. Thin out 1 month later, leaving a plant every 20 cm (8 in). Pinch out the main stalks of tall varieties to encourage them to branch out. *Phlox drummondii* are excellent cut flowers provided that the water is replaced regularly.

— Plant perennial hardy phlox varieties in autumn or spring. A rich soil that remains cool in summer will suit them best. If the foliage becomes wrinkled, this is a sign of attack by nematodes, tiny worms which invade the collar of the plant. Treat preventively by scattering disulphoton-based granules around the base of the plant. Extend the flowering season by watering regularly and feeding with dilute fertilizer every other watering.

Recommended

— Little gems of the rockery, the perennial *Phlox douglasii* explode with colour in spring. The red of 'Cracker Jack' is unbelievably strong. Tone it down with the white of *Thlaspis*.

— *P. drummondii* are annuals, and are available in dwarf and large varieties. The former are excellent in borders, e.g. 'Twinkle', its flowers marked with a deep eye. The latter provide enchanting cut flower arrangements.

— The most popular of the phloxes are without question the perennial varieties, including *P. paniculata*. Of the numerous hybrids, noteworthy reds are: 'Amos', 'August Fackel', 'Kirchenfurst' and 'Starfire'; the pinks 'Dodo Hanbury Forbes', 'Early Gem', 'Elisabeth Arden', 'Flamengo', 'Gnom', 'Tenor' The whites, 'Graf Zeppelin', 'Jacqueline Maille' and the most surprising of all the blues 'Blue Roy', 'Caroline van der Berg', 'Eventide' and 'Parma'.

— Less well-known than those above, and again perennial, *P. maculata* has spotted leaves and flowers arranged in elongated pyramids. 'Alpha', pink, and 'Omega', white, are the most common.

△ *Phlox drummondii*
◁ *Phlox subulata*
▽ *Phlox paniculata*

▽ *Phlox douglasii*

— *P. subulata*, which are very small in comparison with those above, resemble a mat of thorns for much of the year until hundreds of flowers cover them under a bright mantle in April and May. They are the friends of the botanical tulips. Our favourites: 'Betty', pale pink; 'Blue Eyes', mauvish blue; 'Daisy Hill', pink; 'Temiskaming', carmine red and 'White Delight', pure white.

Height: 15–20 cm (6–48 in).
Spacing and planting distance: 15–40 cm (6–16 in).
Soil: rich, remaining cool in summer.
Cultivation: at least 6 hours sun per day.
Propagation: by division in spring.
Flowering season: April–September.
Type: annual, biennial, perennial.

Phormium

NEW ZEALAND FLAX/FIBER-LILLY

Liliaceae

Phormium tenax requires a position in the warmest part of the garden, perhaps against a house wall, if it is to come through the winter in cooler climates. Its bold outline provides a focus of attention.

Useful hints

— Plant in spring in a corner which is sheltered from the cold winds and does not get too much water in winter. Lift the crown slightly so that it remains dry during the bad weather.

— Mulch the soil with pine bark from June onwards and feed regularly with soluble fertilizer as this plant is extremely voracious.

— From October onwards, cover the crown with straw or old cardboard and plastic sheeting to protect it against excess water and cold.

Height: 1–3 m (40–120 in).
Spacing and planting distance: 1.5 m (60 in).
Soil: rich and well-drained in winter.
Cultivation: very sunny.
Propagation: by division in April.
Flowering season: summer.
Type: perennial.

Phormium tenax ▽

235

Phygelius

PHYGELIUS/CAPE FUCHSIA

Scrophulariaceae

Much hardier than is generally realized, *Phygelius* will simply shed the part of the plant above ground if the winter is bad. It will then grow all the more vigorously from April onwards, and rapidly forms a good-sized clump. You will have to wait until August to admire its trumpet-shaped red or yellow flowers, but they are worth waiting for.

Useful hints

— Plant in April in soil that has been dug deep and enriched with leaf-mould. Water regularly and mulch the soil in June.

— Leave stems intact in winter, covering only the crown with straw or a good matting of dry leaves.

Recommended

— *Phygelius aequalis* adds a touch of gracefulness to slightly cool corners. Its greenish-yellow flowers go well with the shades of ferns and the 'Tri-color' fuchsia.

— Its cousin, *P. capensis*, which is a real sun-worshipper, occupies the centre stage for a good 3 months at the end of summer. It precedes the asters, and goes extremely well with blue agapanthus.

Height: 60–100 cm (24–40 in).
Spacing and planting distance: 40 cm (16 in).
Soil: rich in humus.
Cultivation: sun and semi-shade.
Propagation: from cuttings in summer.
Flowering season: August–October.
Type: perennial.

Phyllitis

HART'S TONGUE/HARTS-TONGUE FERN

Polypodiaceae

Hart's tongues are ferns with elongated, pleated leaves. They often adorn cool, shady locations like the approaches to caves or the insides of wells. They can be used very successfully to edge a path under the trees, where the soil is cool, or north-facing stone steps. The leaves of *Phyllitis scolopendrium* will then serve as a backdrop for bleeding hearts, arum lilies and Solomon's seals.

Useful hints

— Plant any season if grown in containers, otherwise in spring. Plant in rich soil, even slightly heavy. Water fre-

quently and mulch the soil with light peat in May.

— Divide the clumps every 3 years, in spring.

Height: 50 cm (20 in).
Spacing and planting distance: 30 cm (12 in).
Soil: rich in humus, enriched with peat.
Cultivation: shade.
Propagation: by division in spring.
Type: perennial.

Physalis

CHINESE LANTERN

Solanaceae

When we see the pretty white star-shaped flowers of *Physalis franchetii*, we might guess it to be a little cousin of the tomato and potato – although much more graceful! At home in any soil as long as it is in the sun, it will flower freely in July or August before revealing its aerial calyces, which change from a tender green to the most beautiful orange in the autumn months. Extremely hardy, it sometimes becomes invasive. Plant in the company of robust plants such as tansy, *Stachys olympica* or *Cerastium*, which set it off beautifully.

Useful hints

— Plant pieces of fleshy roots (they look rather like a fat bindweed) in autumn or spring, in any good, loose soil, cleared of weeds.

— Position preferably at the edge of a path, to restrict its spread.

— Every 3 years, dig out your planting and rearrange, to tidy up.

Height: 40 cm (16 in).
Spacing and planting distance: 20 cm (8 in).
Soil: ordinary.
Cultivation: sunny.
Propagation: by division in spring.
Flowering season: July, August.
Type: perennial.

Physostegia

OBEDIENT PLANT/VIRGINIA LION'S-HEART

Scrophulariaceae

An attractive clump of *Physostegia virginiana* in flower always creates a kind of event in the garden. Not only because it is attractive, but also because the flowers have a curious feature: they sit on a type of ball-joint and can be moved into any position, where they will remain. Colours include white and pink.

△ *Physalis franchetii*
◁ *Phygelius capensis*
◁ *Phytolacca americana*
Physostegia virginiana ▷
▽ *Phyllitis scolopendrium*

Useful hints

— Plant in autumn or spring, providing them with soil rich in humus that remains cool in summer. In spite of their vigorous development, these plants do not like competition from weeds. Mulch the soil in with grass cuttings.

— Divide clumps as late as possible, no more than every 5 years. The large white roots are similar to those of bindweed.

Recommended

— *Physostegia virginiana* is found in pink in the type of the species, in 'Rose Bouquet' and 'Vivid', a little smaller, and in white in 'Alba', which is also slightly earlier flowering (it flowers in July rather than August).

Height: 50–70 cm (20–28 in).
Spacing and planting distance: 30 cm (12 in).
Soil: rich in humus.
Cultivation: full sun and semi-shade.
Propagation: by division in spring.
Flowering season: July–September.
Type: perennial.

Phytolacca

PHYTOLACCA/POKEBERRY, POKEWEED

Phytolaccaceae

Known mainly in the tropics where this genus grows as a tree, *Phytolacca americana* is quietly beginning to invade us. It is an amazing plant capable of competing with castor oil plants for its rate of growth and exotic appearance. If the soil and climate suit it, you will have an extremely vigorous plant reaching more than 2 m (80 in) in height. The white flowers are followed by violet red berries which are highly decorative but also stain.

Useful hints

— Plant preferably in spring after breaking up the soil to depth and enriching it with manure.

— Shortly before the cold weather, cover the crown with straw and plastic sheeting. It is not unusual for this plant to reseed itself spontaneously.

Height: 1.5–2.5 m (60–100 in).
Spacing and planting distance: 50 cm (12 in).
Soil: very rich and cool in summer.
Cultivation: full sun.
Propagation: by division in spring or from ripe seeds in autumn.
Flowering season: July, August.
Type: perennial.

237

△ *Pinguicula grandiflora*

Pinguicula

BUTTERWORT

Lentibulariaceae

Pinguicula grandiflora resembles a violet but is not a violet: it is in fact a strange little carnivorous plant that likes nothing better than the moist atmosphere of damp gardens, as it is a native of the marshes. A hardy plant in regions where winters are relatively mild, it should only be grown by careful gardeners who know the attention that it requires. Beware: like *Platycodon*, it disappears completely in winter. Combine with helxines and maidenhair ferns.

Useful hints

— Plant preferably in spring, in damp soil in partial shade.

— Mark the site with a twig, e.g. a stem of holly, to locate your plants.

— It is most effective in a border, or planted in little groups of 5 or 6 plants.

Height: 15 cm (6 in).
Spacing and planting distance: 15 cm (6 in).
Soil: rich in humus, damp.
Cultivation: semi-shade.
Propagation: from seed in autumn or by division in spring.
Flowering season: June.
Type: perennial.

238

△ *Platycodon grandiflorum*

Platycodon

BALLOON FLOWER

Campanulaceae

A delicate blue, due to the diaphanous texture of its corollas, or porcelain white, sometimes pink, *Platycodon* is in fact an attractive campanula that is delightful in carefully tended flowerbeds exposed to partial shade. Grow in the company of decorative foliage plants such as ferns and hostas.

Useful hints

— Plant preferably in spring, and remember to mark its location with a stick. It disappears completely in winter and often falls victim to the spade.

— Give it good soil, rich and well-drained. In heavy soils it will disappear quite rapidly, suffering from winter damp.

Recommended

— Although there are some double species such as 'Plenum', the single varieties with blue flowers are the prettiest, such as *Platycodon grandiflorum mariesii*, the best known, or 'Apoyama' which has dark blue flowers.

Height: 30 cm (12 in).
Spacing and planting distance: 20 cm (8 in).
Soil: ordinary, well-drained.
Cultivation: sunny.
Propagation: by division or from seed in spring.
Flowering season: June–August.
Type: perennial.

▽ *Plumbago capensis*

Plumbago

PLUMBAGO

Plumbaginaceae

There can be no more attractive decoration for earthenware pots in a warm climate than a *Plumbago capensis* in flower. The almost unreal blue of its corollas seems to compete with that of the sky. And how robust it is, even in the worst heat. It has just one drawback: its rather unremarkable foliage is slightly sticky where the minute tendrils surround the base of the flowers. Don't forget to bring it inside, to protect it from the cold, in winter. Do not confuse plumbagos, particularly *Plumbago larpentae*, the botanical name of which is now *Cerastostigma plumbaginoides*.

Useful hints

— Sow seeds in March under cover and continue growing under cover until May. The plants will flower abundantly from the first summer. You can also keep cuttings or plants on the verandah, growing them in spring. Pinch out at least twice in spring to encourage them to send out side shoots.

— They like a light but substantial mix best. Where frosts are relatively infrequent, you could try overwintering them protected under a plastic sheet.

— You can train them against a south-facing wall on your terrace. They will then climb to a height of more than 2 m (80 in).

Height: 50 cm–2 m (20–80 in).
Spacing and planting distance: 30 cm (12 in).
Soil: rich and well-drained in winter.
Cultivation: full sun.
Propagation: from seed or from cuttings.
Flowering season: June–November.
Type: annual and perennial in mild climates.

Podophyllum

PODOPHYLLUM/MAY APPLE

Podophyllaceae/Berberidaceae

This plant, which is difficult to find in the catalogues, has a relatively short period of growth, from March to July, providing us with a curious spectacle: it begins with elegant denticulate leaves tinged with purple when they first appear. Then the flowers open: they are often large and pale pink, like apple blossom, followed by fruits as large as hens' eggs of a redcurrant colour, which are edible but not particularly tasty. This plant has its place in informal corners of the garden with a cool, acid soil, as under trees.

△ *Podophyllum emodi*

Useful hints

— Plant in autumn or spring in deep soil rich in humus. Combine with ferns and *Meconopsis* which grow in the same conditions.

— Collect the ripe fruits to remove the seeds. Sow in autumn. They will generally come up the following spring, and the young plants can be established the next year.

— Mulch the soil with pine bark at the beginning of spring to show off the beauty of the young foliage at its best.

Height: 50 cm (20 in).
Spacing and planting distance: 30 cm (12 in).
Soil: rich in humus, permanently cool.
Cultivation: semi-shade.
Propagation: from seed or by division at the beginning of spring, before vegetation appears.
Flowering season: April.
Type: perennial.

Polemonium caeruleum △

Polemonium

JACOB'S LADDER, GREEK VALERIAN

Polemoniaceae

Far more common in the past than it is today, *Polemonium caeruleum* has some of the most handsome foliage to be found in any plant: divided and attractively arched, it makes dense mounds from which the flower spikes protrude upwards. It produces flowers continuously for almost 2 months at the end of spring, at the same time as the late tulips, oriental poppies and peonies with which it can be combined.

Useful hints

— Plant preferably in autumn or in spring. Mark the site because the foliage disappears in winter. The best position is partial shade. Polemoniums will therefore flourish at the base of bush roses, particularly old roses.

— The best method of propagation is to sow seeds at the end of spring. Protect young plants in a cold frame and transplant to their flowering locations the following spring.

Recommended

— The type of the species is a soft blue, but it also comes in 'Sapphire', an intense blue, and 'Album', a very pure white. Lovers of unusual plants should look out for *P. foliosissimum* which is a little larger, its foliage being more denticulate. It is found in dark blue and white forms.

Height: 30–60 cm (12–24 in).
Spacing and planting distance: 30 cm (12 in).
Soil: ordinary soil, rather well-drained.
Cultivation: sun and semi-shade.
Propagation: from seed or by division in spring.
Flowering season: May–July.
Type: perennial.

△ *Polygonatum officinale*
▽ *Polygonatum × hybridum*

△ *Polygonum affine*

△ *Polygonum campanulatum*
▽ *Polygonum orientale*

▽ *Polygonum amplexicaule*

Polygonatum

SOLOMON'S SEAL

Liliaceae

Towards mid-May, the undergrowth is brightened up by the fresh floral spikes of Solomon's seal, a restful sight that takes over from scillas with their intense blue flowers. Perfect for a shady garden or for under trees, they are very popular with English gardeners. Combine them with magnolias, flowering cherry trees and apple trees. Plant them in the company of Caucasian *Heracleums* and *Macleayas* in an informal corner of the garden. They will give you no trouble, and will flower again reliably.

Useful hints

— Plant wild species from July to September in fresh soil rich in humus, preferably in partial shade.

— Plant cultivars from September onwards. For the plants to flower well, they must be established early in the season.

Recommended

— For preference, choose *Polygonatum multiflorum* or *P. commutatum*, the giant Solomon's seal with spectacular flowers, easily growing to a height of 1.2 m (48 in).

Height: 30–120 cm (12–48 in).
Spacing and planting distance: 30 cm (12 in).
Soil: ordinary, cool.
Cultivation: semi-shade.
Propagation: by division and from seed in spring.
Flowering season: May, June.
Type: perennial.

Polygonum

KNOTWEED/FLEECE-FLOWER

Polygonaceae

Knotweeds have an unmistakable family likeness: a certain propensity to spread, leathery green foliage, and spiked flowers, which are often red. In fact there is a certain diversity in flowering season, from June to November, and in the height of the plants, which is extremely variable.

Useful hints

— Plant in spring or autumn in groups (at least 6) to create a mass effect.

— Check growth to prevent harm to neighbouring plants. Mulch the soil in June to keep it cool for longer. Divide plants in October every 3 years and replant elsewhere, as they will tend to exhaust the soil.

Recommended

— *Polygonum affine* are excellent at the edges of flowerbeds, as they form compact mounds. Their straight leaves turn bronze in autumn and remain for much of the winter. The flowers are dark red in 'Darjeeling Red', salmon pink in 'Donald Lowndes' and bright pink in 'Superbum'.

— Larger than the previous variety, *P. amplexicaule* grows to a height of 1.5 m (60 in). 'Atrosanguineum' is an intense carmine pink, while 'Firetail' is a bright scarlet red.

— An improved cousin of the snakeweed, *P. bistorta* 'Superbum' forms vast colonies producing groups of flowers in the form of luminous pink brushes.

— One of the most attractive knotweeds is without doubt *P. campanulatum*, with deeply-veined leaves and pale pink bell flower heads produced in succession throughout late summer and much of autumn.

— Beware of *P. cuspidatum compactum* (or *P. compactum* 'Roseum' in catalogues) as this is a real pest. Its branches, reminiscent of bamboo, are propagated at a stupendous rate. Leave them for the roadside and unmanageable slopes.

— Not, unfortunately, reliably hardy, *P. vaccinifolium* is wonderful in rockeries, as its pink flowers are produced late, shortly before the change in colour of the foliage. Suitable for sunny positions only: protect in winter.

Height: 15–120 cm (6–48 in).
Spacing and planting distance: 20–50 cm (8–20 in).
Soil: ordinary.
Cultivation: sun and semi-shade.
Propagation: by division in autumn or spring.
Flowering season: June–November.
Type: perennial.

△ *Polypodium vulgare*

Polypodium

POLYPODY
Polypodiaceae

Its name is unfailingly evocative of natural science lessons, as this delightful little fern found at the edges of cool, clay areas under trees comes into every schoolchild's curriculum. *Polypodium vulgare* has its place in the garden, in a flowerbed exposed to partial shade, or to liven up a rather shady corner with a carpeting of dentate fronds. As it is very much at home on slopes, beneath large trees, use as a border for an informal hedge. It will look highly sophisticated,

and needs no other work than that of initial planting.

Try setting up a miniature Japanese garden by planting with all sorts of wood mosses.

Useful hints

— Plant in any garden soil, preferably in spring. It is equally happy in dry or moist soil, and can cope with both sand and clay.

Height: 15 cm (6 in).
Spacing and planting distance: 20 cm (8 in).
Soil: ordinary.
Cultivation: semi-shade.
Propagation: by division or from seed in spring.
Type: perennial.

Polystichum setiferum △
Pontederia cordata ▷

Polystichum

POLYSTICHUM/CHRISTMAS FERN, HOLLY FERN

Polypodiaceae

A delicate fern for well-tended gardens, this is at its most effective in flowerbeds that already contain fuchsias, *Lysimachias* and bicolour *Eucomis*. You can also grow them under trees, but the area must be well-tended. Beware! Certain ferns in this family are only moderately hardy – as in the case of *Polystichum falcatum*, for example.

Useful hints

— Plant in spring, in soil that is very rich in humus. Allow one spadeful of well-rotted compost per plant and mulch the soil as necessary with semi-decomposed compost to lighten and enrich it if at all compacted.

— Grow away from draughts and sun, which would damage its foliage.

Recommended

— *Polystichum falcatum* (or *Cyrtomium falcatum*) is the best known. It will readily grow in pots, but dislikes frost. It is also worth mentioning the evergreen *P. aculeatum* for growing at the water's edge, and *P. setiferum*, which is semi-evergreen, with delicately denticulate fronds. *P. achrostichioides* with its wonderful strong green – which remains throughout the winter – is a good garden plant; it goes well with groups of fuchsias.

Height: 60 cm–1 m (24–40 in).
Spacing and planting distance: 30 cm (12 in).
Soil: rich in humus, cool.
Cultivation: semi-shade.
Propagation: from seed or by division in autumn or spring.
Type: perennial.

Pontederia

PONTEDERIA/PICKERELWEED

Pontederiaceae

A native of Virginia, *Pontederia cordata* is an attractive aquatic plant with heart-shaped leaves borne on long, sheath-like stalks. It flowers in summer with attractive spikes of blue, brightened up by a yellow eye. Totally hardy, it quickly takes over pools and ponds, giving them an almost tropical appearance. Its cousin the water hyacinth (*Eichhornia crassipes*) has to be brought in each winter, for protection.

Useful hints

— Plant in spring when the water has begun to warm up. Set in pots filled with clay soil and arrange at a depth of 30 cm (12 in). If you plant them at the edge of a pond, choose a somewhat peaty soil.

— When the individual crowns begin to impinge upon one another, divide, in spring.

Height: 50 cm (20 in).
Spacing and planting distance: 30 cm (12 in)
Soil: heavy.
Cultivation: sunny.
Propagation: by division in April.
Flowering season: June–September.
Type: perennial.

Portulaca

SUN PLANT/PORTULACA

Portulaceae/Portulacaceae

You will sometimes see these sun plants with silken flowers flourish in the most unbelievably dry sites. They are succulent plants, and their leaves reveal the fact that they belong to a genus that loves the sun. Indeed, *Portulaca grandiflora* needs the sun for its flowers to open: they close at the first sight of a cloud. Choose double varieties in preference, as these give a more attractive effect when massed.

Useful hints

— As the seeds are as fine as dust, mix them with sand before sowing directly in the flowering site in May. You can also sow them in a cold frame 2 weeks earlier and plant them out into containers or directly into the ground in mid-May.

— In spite of their ability to withstand drought, they should be watered from time to time to achieve the best flowers.

Height: 15 cm (6 in).
Spacing and planting distance: 15 cm (6 in).
Soil: ordinary, even dry.
Cultivation: full sun only.
Propagation: from seed in spring.
Flowering season: July–September.
Type: annual.

▽ *Portulaca grandiflora*

Potentilla 'Gloire de Nancy' △

Potentilla

CINQUEFOIL

Rosaceae

This is a family with many species including bushes, such as *Potentilla fruticosa*, woody plants, hybrid cinquefoils and tiny alpine plants like *Potentilla nitida*. Yet they all share a preference for dry and sunny gardens and all have sprawling growth. Show off their serrated leaves, veined like a strawberry plant's, by planting them amidst full foliage like perennial pinks, thlaspis, yarrows, *Stachys olympica*, senecios and artemisia.

Useful hints

— Plant, preferably in spring, in soil which has been dried out well, choosing a sunny spot.

— In heavy soil, dig the planting holes quite deep and let them drain by pouring over 5 cm (2 in) of gravel before filling them with porous soil.

Recommended

— Herbaceous cinquefoils like *Potentilla atrosanguinea* are our favourites because of their highly coloured, double flowers. The most popular are: 'Gloire de Nancy', russet, 'M. Rouillard', tan, 'Yellow Queen' sunshine yellow.

Height: 10–50 cm (4–20 in).
Spacing and planting distance: 15–30 cm (6–12 in).
Soil: ordinary, well-drained.
Cultivation: sunny.
Propagation: from seed or by division in spring.
Flowering season: July–September.
Type: perennial.

△ *Primula palinuri*
▽ *Primula vialii*

△ *Primula bulleyana*
Primula sieboldii 'Alba' ▷
▽ *Primula nutans*

△ *Primula juliae*

▽ *Primula auricula* 'Irish Blue'

Primula

PRIMROSE

Primulaceae

The primrose family is a vast one running from the tiniest rockery plants to plants which are almost giant-sized, growing to nearly 1 m (40 in) in height. There is a similar diversity of habitats and colours, with a definite preference for pastel shades. Both very well-known plants and rarities for collectors are to be found here.

Useful hints

— Plant in spring, preferably, or in early autumn for the early flowering varieties which must establish themselves well before winter sets in if they are to flower correctly in the first days of spring.

— Mulch with pine bark or peat and water regularly throughout the first summer as primroses enjoy coolness.

— Divide clumps which have become too large at the beginning of autumn and replant them immediately.

Recommended

— *Primula acaulis* is the name given to many of the hybrids which flower early, some even from autumn onwards. They are ideal companions for tulips and forget-me-nots. Flowering continues for 2 months.

— Of the candelabra primroses, with flowers arranged in little clusters around

244

△ *Primula florindae*
▽ *Primula waltoni*

△ *Primula denticulata*
Primula japonica ▷
▽ *Primula japonica*

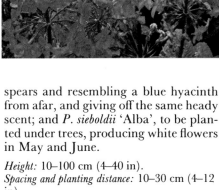

the tall stems, *P. beesiana* is lilac-pink while *P. bulleyana* is yellow-orange, colourings which are rare among primroses. Mention should also be made of the Japanese primroses (*P. japonica*), which are similar in appearance and love damp corners.

— *P. florindae* (giant yellow cowslip) can grow to a height of 1 m (40 in) and has enchanting pale lemon flowers which are delightfully perfumed.

— There are delights for our rockeries, too; *P. juliae*, pale pink, is a real gem.

'Verveana' is violet and 'Wanda' purple. *P. viali* has unusual flowers similar to those of the red hot poker and needs a great deal of care to thrive.

— Other beauties, in brief: *P. denticulara* (drumstick primrose) with its pink, white or lilac flowers clustered in pompoms; *P. auricula* and *P. pulverulenta* with fleshy leaves covered in a floury substance; *P. rosea*, which is very compact but with quite large flowers; *P. capitata*, not very hardy, which dazzles with the beauty of its flowers clustered into

spears and resembling a blue hyacinth from afar, and giving off the same heady scent; and *P. sieboldii* 'Alba', to be planted under trees, producing white flowers in May and June.

Height: 10–100 cm (4–40 in).
Spacing and planting distance: 10–30 cm (4–12 in).
Soil: cool and rich in humus.
Cultivation: semi-shade.
Propagation: from seed or by division in spring.
Flowering season: February–July.
Type: biennial, perennial.

245

Close to water and set in rocks,
Primula japonica *and* **P.
denticulata, Meconopsis** *and ferns
flourish in moist, acid soil.*

246

△ *Prunella webbiana*

Prunella

SELF-HEAL

Labiatae

Common self-heal often happens to take root in the shady corners of our gardens. There is nothing to stop you leaving it there permanently as very few plants can rival it for forming dense ground cover, carpeted with flowers in summer.

Useful hints

— Plant in autumn and mulch from

spring. Water regularly to promote rooting. Cut the clumps down at the end of the summer to make them even prettier next year.

— Divide the clumps in spring when they become hollow in the centre.

Recommended

— *Prunella grandiflora* has given birth to two varieties, lilac pink and white, along with the classic pale purple.

— *P. webbiana* is in fact a hybrid of the above and the Pyrenean self-heal. Its flowers are pale violet, pink or white depending upon the variety. These are prettily named 'Loveliness'.

Height: 15–20 cm (6–8 in).
Spacing and planting distance: 20 cm (8 in).
Soil: ordinary, preferably rich in humus.
Culiiavion: shade.
Propagation: by division in April.
Flowering season: June–September.
Type: perennial.

Pulmonaria

LUNGWORT

Boraginaceae

Why is it that lungworts are not more widely used as ground cover? Their evergreen foliage, spotted with silver, is certainly the equal of supposedly decorative plants like dead nettles or ornamental bramble, for example. When they flower, at the end of March, they herald the return of spring, even outstripping the primroses and violets.

Useful hints

— Plant, in spring or autumn, under shrubs or as ground cover, in half-shade in good ordinary soil, spacing the plants every 20 cm (8 in).

— Although they do prefer well-drained soils, lungworts will grow quite easily in damp soils.

Recommended

As well as *Pulmonaria officinalis* with its red and blue flowers, you can try *P. angustifolia* 'Azurea' with its sky blue flowers and vivid green foliage, and, best of all, *P. saccharata* (Bethlehem sage) with its eye-catching flowers of pink through to blue.

Height: 20 cm (8 in).
Spacing and planting distance: 20 cm (8 in).
Soil: ordinary.
Cultivation: semi-shade.
Propagation: by division in autumn, or early in spring.
Flowering season: March, April.
Type: perennial.

△ *Pulmonaria saccharata* 'Mrs Moon'
▽ *Pulmonaria saccharata*

△ **Pulsatilla vulgaris**

Pulsatilla

ANEMONE/PASQUE FLOWER
Ranunculaceae

A real pearl for the rockery, every spring *Pulsatilla vulgaris* opens out its little bell-shaped flowers of violet-blue, whose petals form perfect stars. The hairy leaves develop as the flowers fade. With foliage as pretty as their flowers, these little plants will be shown off to best advantage set against a miniature landscape to serve as a backdrop for them: a rockery, of course, but also steps of sunny stones, ferns in the half-shade. The only requirement is well-drained soil to make them flourish.

Useful hints

— Any good, well-drained soil is suitable for it to fill out quickly. Take care when planting by incorporating half a shovelful of ripe compost.

— Plant in autumn or at the beginning of spring.

— Avoid damp soil in winter. If your garden is chalky and quite dry, on the other hand, you will have nothing to fear.

Recommended

— As well as the typical violet blue, there is a white variety, *Pulsatilla vulgaris* 'Alba' and a red one, *P. vulgaris* 'Rubra'.

Height: 20 cm (8 in).
Spacing and planting distance: 15 cm (6 in).
Soil: well-drained.
Cultivation: sunny.
Propagation: from seed or by division in autumn.
Flowering season: April, May.
Type: perennial.

Puschkiana scilloides △

Puschkinia

STRIPED SQUILL
Liliaceae

When spring comes *Puschkinia scilloides* form, along with glory of the snow, grape hyacinths, squills and hyacinths, the prettiest borders of all. They thrive quite happily in any position as long as the soil is rich. They can be planted alongside hardy perennials like coral flower or tellima whose foliage, reddened by the cold, blends well with their china blue flowers. To stop your window-boxes looking sad once the crocuses lose their blooms mix striped squill with the crocus bulbs when you plant them; they will then grow in sequence. *Puschkinia scilloides* is often known as *Puschkinia libanotica*.

Useful hints

— Plant in September or October, at a depth of 10 cm (4 in) and with 10 cm (4 in) spacing, in all directions, in good soil, rich in humus.

— Plant, preferably, in borders or well-drained, sunny beds; the plants will flourish.

Recommended

— As well as the typical variety with blue flowers, you will love a pretty white variety, 'Alba'.

Height: 15 cm (6 in).
Spacing and planting distance: 20 cm (8 in).
Soil: rich in humus.
Cultivation: sunny to semi-shade.
Propagation: by separating bulbs, after leaves have died off completely.
Flowering season: February, March.
Type: bulb.

△ *Ramonda pyrenaica*

△ *Ranunculus* 'Turban'

Ranunculus

BUTTERCUP

Ranunculaceae

Do not hesitate to plant these buttercups with their shimmering colours. They will provide the material for any number of posies, as they last well in water. Some species are invasive and therefore unsuitable.

Useful hints

— *Ranunculus asiaticus* is planted in autumn in warm climates and in spring elsewhere.

— Plant at a depth of 5 cm (2 in) with the shoot uppermost, spacing the tubers every 20 cm (8 in) as each clump grows very large.

— Water little in winter and more and more in spring, adding, from time to time, some liquid manure.

— Lift the tubers when the foliage turns yellow.

— Keep the dry tubers in sand or peat, protected against the frost, during winter.

Recommended

— Often called the 'Geante d'Anjou' in catalogues, the florists' buttercup is sold only in mixed colourings. That is, in fact, how it is most attractive. The rarer 'Turban' buttercup has rounder, pretty flowers.

Height: 20–40 cm (8–16 in).
Spacing and planting distance: 20 cm (8 in).
Soil: cool and very rich in humus.
Cultivation: sun and semi-shade in hot climates.
Propagation: by division in autumn.
Flowering season: May, June.
Type: perennial.

Pyrethrum

See *Chrysanthemum*.

Ramonda

RAMONDA/ROSETTE-MULLEIN

Gesneriaceae

Although burdened with the reputation of being a difficult plant to grow, the *Ramonda pyrenaica* in fact will thrive if given a northerly aspect and will endure the most extreme winters. We know of some which have thrived in pots for several years and are now as large as plates. And the flowers bring to mind the shades of some cyclamens. This plant has the feature of being able to dry itself out and then return to life, rather like some mosses. Do not despair if they look a bit dry when you come back from your holidays! Some catalogues list *Ramonda pyrenaica* under the name *R. myconi*.

Useful hints

— Plant in a crack between two rocks in a pocket of sandy soil.

— If you want to enjoy them from closer to hand, plant them in pots which are wider than they are deep, filled with a mixture of peat and sand. Shelter them from the sun by placing them at the foot of a north-facing wall and in winter bring them in under a cold frame.

— Seeds are possible in spring but they take at least a year to give any results.

Height: 20 cm (8 in).
Spacing and planting distance: 20 cm (8 in).
Soil: sandy.
Cultivation: north-facing.
Propagation: from seed or by division, and by leaf propagation in spring.
Flowering season: May, June.
Type: perennial.

250

Raoulia

RAOULIA

Compositae

What fascinating plants these *Raoulia australis* are. Originally from New Zealand, they provide carpeting at ground level, following the contours of any slight unevenness in the ground. Their cultivation is no picnic, however, as they dislike excessive dampness in winter.

Useful hints

— Plant them, in spring, in a well-drained pocket of earth among paving stones. Water regularly during the first summer. As the frosts approach, cover with crushed bark and a plastic film to avoid excessive water.

— At the end of winter, take a small handful of sand and shake it gently over the clump. You can divide them at the same time, too, and let the portions root in sand.

Height: 2 cm (¾ in).
Spacing and planting distance: 20 cm (8 in).
Soil: very sandy.
Cultivation: sunny.
Propagation: by division in spring.
Flowering season: barely visible, in April.
Type: perennial.

▽ *Raoulia australis*

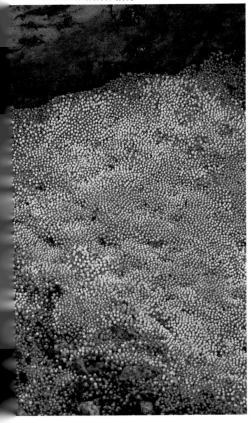

△ *Reseda alba*

Reseda

MIGNONETTE

Resedaceae

The fragrant mignonette (*Reseda odorata*), with its golden spears, is well known in our gardens. Less known, the *R. alba* deserves greater attention as it is much more spectacular. With its long thick spears of a milky white, it has its place in beds where, in the company of bell flowers, old roses and delphiniums, it can give a breathtaking display which needs hardly any attention. Although cultivated as an annual it can survive in warmer climates for 2 or 3 years. However, like the snapdragon, it unfortunately tends to lose some of its charm with age.

Useful hints

— Any good ordinary soil, even quite heavy, suits it.

— Loving the light, it enjoys growing in sunny, well-aerated beds.

— As it cannot stand being transplanted, sow it *in situ*, in April.

Recommended

— As well as the *Reseda alba* you can buy fragrant mignonettes in improved varieties such as the 'Goliath'.

Height: 30 cm (12 in).
Spacing and planting distance: 15 cm (6 in).
Soil: ordinary.
Cultivation: sunny.
Propagation: from seed, at beginning of spring.
Flowering season: June, July.
Type: perennial.

Rheum

ORNAMENTAL RHUBARB

Polygonaceae

The sight of *Rheum palmatum* occupying the place of honour in many of the grandest gardens is an inspiring one. It is a truly imposing plant which needs, like its cousin the edible rhubarb, plenty of room to develop. As it is very greedy, give it a good bed and, as bedfellows, sturdy and economical plants such as *Gaura*, tansy, hogweed and loosestrife, which will keep it company while allowing it its pride of place.

Useful hints

— Before planting, in March or April, carefully enrich the soil with half a barrowload of very ripe manure per square metre.

— Always plant it in rich soil which is cool and deep. It is not averse to clay.

— Plant in full sunlight, but do not stint on watering in summer.

— As soon as flowering is over, cut off the dead heads. To maintain the beauty of the plants, one can even prevent them from flowering by cutting off the flower stems as soon as they appear.

Height: 1.5 m (60 in).
Spacing and planting distance: 1 m (40 in).
Soil: cool and deep.
Cultivation: sunny.
Propagation: by division in autumn.
Flowering season: June, July.
Type: perennial.

Rheum palmatum ▽

Rhodante Manglesii

See *Helipterum Manglesii*

△ *Rhodohypoxis baurii*
◁ *Ricinus communis*

Rhodohypoxis

RHODOHYPOXIS

Hypoxidaceae

This plant is really an investment; you pay a fortune for a tiny bulb, you cosset it for a few years, and you find yourself the owner of something magnificent, and priceless. For it is hard to resist the beauty of these rather waxy flowers, with a purity of colour ranging from white to magenta. The most amazing feature is the length of the flowering season: almost 5 months, from May to October. A real pearl for your collection.

Useful hints

— Plant in spring in a well-drained pot filled with a mixture of compost and sand. Bury the bulb 5 cm (2 in) under and sprinkle gravel over the soil to prevent it settling.

— Water regularly in summer. Shelter under a cold frame in winter.

Height: 5–10 cm (2–4 in).
Spacing and planting distance: 5 cm (2 in).
Soil: light and rich in humus.
Cultivation: sunny.
Propagation: by separation of new bulbs at beginning of spring.
Flowering season: May–September.
Type: bulb.

Ricinus

CASTOR OIL PLANT

Euphorbiaceae

Effortless and spectacular. If you have a corner in your garden which could benefit from the speedy instalment of an imposing and decorative plant, then the castor oil plant could be the answer. With its big palmate leaves, as shiny as

252

an oil-cloth, and its crimson fruits, which look like cane apples, it is full of charm. Thanks to its remarkable vitality, *Ricinus communis*, in the space of a few months, presents you with a bush as tall as you are . . . from a few large mottled seeds (which are *very poisonous*), which you sowed, in the warm, in the first days of spring. *Ricinus communis* 'Impala' produces scarlet fruits which stand out against the red-brown leaves.

Useful hints

— Sow at 20°C (68°F) after soaking the seeds for 24 hours to soften them. Then keep the young plants warm until planted, in May, in a hot position.

— Give it a very rich soil if you want it to grow to full size. At the time of planting, give it 2 handfuls of Triple 17 fertilizer, in granule form.

— On the coast, beware of winds. Provide supports.

Height: 1.5 m (60 in).
Spacing and planting distance: 1.5 m (60 in).
Soil: very rich.
Cultivation: full sunlight.
Propagation: from seed in spring.
Flowering season: July.
Type: annual.

Rodgersia

RODGERSIA/ROGER'S-FLOWER

Saxifragaceae

Along with *Gunnera* and ornamental rhubarb, *Rodgersia* is one of the most majestic of our garden plants. Planted in cool soils, which they love, they develop imposing foliage, similar to, depending on the particular variety, that of the chestnut, the elder or the lotus. Give them a damp corner alongside false goat's beard, ferns and Japanese primroses and you will have a stunning effect.

Useful hints

— Plant in spring or in September. Break up the soil at depth and improve it with peat so that it stays cool in summer. Mulch the soil with pine bark or peat, in June.

— Slugs can devour part of the young shoots; dissuade them from doing so with bait. In winter, let the frozen foliage protect the clumps from the cold.

Recommended

— *Rodgersia aesculifolia* can really be mistaken for a dwarf horsechestnut except when the flowers, creamy white spears, appear, reaching more than 1 m (40 in).

△ *Rodgersia aesculifolia*

— *R. pinnata* has divided leaves but they are arranged on either side of a central spine. Often the leaves have a bronze sheen.

— The most spectacular of the *Rodgersias* is undoubtedly *R. tabularis*, the leaves of which are almost circular and grow to 90 cm (36 in) in diameter. Their edge is folded down, giving them the appearance of certain Chinese ceremonial parasols.

Height: 80–120 cm (32–48 in).
Spacing and planting distance: 60 cm (24 in).
Soil: rich and always cool.
Cultivation: semi-shade.
Propagation: by division in spring.
Flowering season: June, July.
Type: perennial.

▽ *Rodgersia aesculifolia*

Romneya coulteri △

Romneya

TREE POPPY

Papaveraceae

This looks like a crêpe-paper flower. Imagine a huge armful of silvery stems, a host of big white flowers, ruffled and crowned with a pompom of golden yellow stamens, and there you have the almost unreal picture of the beauty of *Romneya coulteri*. These plants reach their full splendour in the height of the summer, in wide, rather disorderly strips in the sandy gardens of seaside areas. This fragile beauty is in fact reserved only for the most protected southern gardens. Further north only the most careful gardeners are lucky. But if you are successful, you may get hooked – it is worth taking a risk.

Useful hints

— Like most of the poppy family, the tree poppy does not like to be transplanted. Nurserymen sell it in pots, which means it can be planted without disturbing the rootball.

— Loving light soil, it must have lavished upon it 2 shovels of leaf-mould or peat, to be incorporated into the soil at the time of planting.

— At the onset of winter, cut it back to 15 cm (6 in) from the ground and cover its clump with 20 cm (8 in) of dried-out dead leaves or ferns.

Height: 1.5–2 m (60–80 in).
Spacing and planting distance: 1.5–2 m (60–80 in).
Soil: light.
Cultivation: sheltered and sunny.
Propagation: from seed in spring.
Flowering season: July, August.
Type: perennial.

ROSE TREES AND ROSES

CLIMBING ROSES NEEDING LITTLE ATTENTION

Intrepid climbers, knowing no fear! They mount their assaults on trees, houses and pergolas. They do not require much upkeep and for a good reason: their cascading bouquets are often out of reach. They sometimes flower only briefly, but in such profusion that one cannot hold it against them.

White flowers

— *Rosa filipes* '**Kiftsgate**', I call this the 'rose tree express' as it grows about 1 m (40 in) a year. Thousands of small, single, fragrant flowers conceal the delicate foliage. In autumn the little red hips are a bonus. Flowering in June. Height: 10 m (33 ft). Spread: 4 m (13½ ft).

— '**Wedding Day**' bears some resemblance to the previous rose tree but has larger blooms which give off a scent of banana. Flowering: beginning of July. Height: 9 m (30 ft). Spread: 4.5 m (15 ft).

Pink flowers

— '**Kew Rambler**' has pretty grey-green foliage which shows off its pale pink flowers very well. In autumn, the little orange hips adorn this large climber which loves rambling over trees. Flowering in summer. Height: 5.5 m (19 ft). Spread: 3.5 m (12 ft).

SHRUB ROSES FOR GROUND COVER

These small shrubs adapt very well to all situations: tubs, rockeries, slopes, borders. But beware, their thorns are nasty. At the end of the season don a pair of gardening gloves, remove the dead wood, thin the branches, and cut back the healthy branches at least halfway. These rose bushes are not at all fussy as long as they are not left to stand in damp areas and they have a place in the sun which allows them to spread out comfortably.

White flowers

— '**Snow Carpet**', with full double flowers, blooms throughout the summer. Height: 90 cm (36 in). Spread: 90 cm (36 in).

— '**Swan**' flowers all summer with many small double flowers. It provides excellent ground cover for slopes. Cut off

the dead heads. Height: 50 cm (20 in). Spread: 1.5 m (60 in).

Pink flowers

— *Rosa* '**Raubritter**' has semi-double flowers of a pretty silvery pink, with a spicy scent. Flowering: mid-June, July. Height: 50 cm (20 in) Spread: 1.8 m (72 in).

— '**The Fairy**', with its mass of little single flowers, is breathtaking in the front of a border. Flowering: most of the summer. Height: 60 cm (24 in). Spread: 1 m (40 in).

— '**Frau Dagmar Hastrup**' has single flowers which should not be deadheaded as they will bear beautiful fruit in the autumn. Flowering: summer. Height: 90 cm (36 in). Spread 1.2 m (48 in).

— '**Max Graf**' has single pink flowers like the wild rose and a pretty pale foliage. It provides excellent ground cover for slopes and large areas. Flowering: mid-June, July. Height: 60 cm (24 in). Spread: 2.5 m (100 in).

'**Wedding Day**' △
◁ '**Kiftsgate**'
'**Zéphirine Drouhin**' ▷
▽ '**Swany**'

— '**Nozomi**', with the long spiny stems covered in tiny delicate flowers which are single and pale pink, has a short flowering season: end of June or July. Height: 40 cm (16 in). Spread: 1.5 m (60 in). It is especially charming when planted at the foot of a tree, for example, *Prunus* 'Amanogawa'.

Red flowers

— '**Fiona**' makes a pretty picture with its semi-double flowers. It is excellent for covering the tops of walls. Flowering: all summer. Height: 1 m (40 in). Spread: 80 cm (32 in).

CLIMBERS AND RAMBLERS

With a little patience you can have beautiful plants which flower prolifically. Do not allow your rose tree to flower in the first year; but remove the buds to encourage the plant to put down strong roots and establish a good framework instead. Roses do not climb alone but must be trained, not with metal wire but with raffia or plastic tapes. Some small climbing roses (2 m–2.5 m) (80–100 in) can be treated as shrubs, in which case they must be pruned. Cut back about a third of the length of the branches in March or April to produce big and beautiful shrubs.

White flowers

— '**Alberic Barbier**' is a hardy rose bush, and very vigorous, with a beautiful perfume. Its delicate, glossy foliage reddens in autumn and stays on the plant during the early winter months. Flowering: June. Height: 5 m (16½ ft).

— '*Félicité et Perpétue*' offers creamy white semi-double flowers which are fringed with pink. Flowering: all summer. Height: 4.5 m (15 ft).

— '**Handel**' is ravishing with its cream flowers edged in pale pink and its shiny olive green foliage. It is as well to treat it against black spot in damp years. Flowering: all season. Height: 2.5 m (100 in).

— '**Mme Alfred Carrière**', with its double, scented blooms, flowers all summer. Height: 3.5 m (12 ft).

Pink flowers

— '**Albertine**' will adorn a pergola beautifully with its clusters of salmon pink double flowers. Its perfume is exquisite but beware its thorns. Flowering: mid-June or July. Height: 4.5 m (15 ft).

— '**American Pillar**', hardy, is very vigorous. Its charm lies in its pink flowers with their white hearts, grouped in trusses, and in its glossy dark foliage. Flowering: from mid-June to mid-July. Height: 4.5 m (15 ft).

'**Max Graf**' △

'**Handel**' △
◁ '**Fiona**'
◁ '**Albéric Barbier**'
'**American Pillar**' ▽

△ 'Mermaid'
'Paul's Scarlet Climber' ▷
'New Dawn' ▷
▽ 'Veilchenblau'

— '**Mme Grégoire Staechelin**' (Spanish Beauty) has pink flowers with a coral underside, which are semi-double and beautifully perfumed. It grows well on a north-facing wall and keeps its foliage even in winter. Flowering: from May to July. Height: 4.5 m (15 ft).

— '**New Dawn**' produces many semi-double, fragrant flowers on a solid stem. It climbs merrily over trees. Flowering: in June and again in September. Height: 4.5 m (15 ft).

Red flowers

— '**Lilli Marlene**' will enchant you with its dark red velvety flowers in little clusters, rather like peonies. And they have a delicate fragrance, too. Flowering: all summer. Height: 3 m (10 ft).

— '**Paul's Scarlet Climber**' has brilliant scarlet flowers. Each year cut back at least half of the branches which have flowered. Flowering: in June or July. Height: 3 m (10 ft).

Yellow, apricot or orange flowers

— '**Alister Stella Gray**' has apricot buds which open into bouquets of fragrant flowers. Flowering: intermittent, but all summer. Height: 4 m (13½ ft).

— '**Gloire de Dijon**', a rose with big buff flowers with orange tints, beautifully perfumed. Its long supple boughs are easy to train as they have few thorns. Flowering: beginning of the season. Height: 3.5 m (12 ft).

— '**Golden Showers**' is perfect for pergolas with its pale golden yellow, sweetly scented flowers. It should be treated like the *Marssoenina rosae* against black spot. Flowering: all summer. Height: 3m (10 ft).

— '**Mermaid**' can be trained to climb against a sunny wall, well protected from draughts. Its big single flowers are very pale yellow and its foliage almost evergreen. Flowering: intermittent, all summer until frosts. Height: 7.5–9 m (25–30 ft)

Violet, mauve flowers

— '**Veilchenblau**' (violet blue) should be more popular. Its little mauve fragrant flowers are very attractive on an arched trellis. The rose buds are mauve then turn to violet and become lighter as they wither. What a romantic rose tree! Flowering: in summer. Height: 2.5 m (100 in).

MODERN FLORIBUNDA HYBRID PERPETUAL ROSES

These are the masterpieces of our rose growers, the fruits of long, patient research, of marriages between varieties trying to reproduce the best qualities of each: the colour from one, resistance to disease from another, but the main aim being longer flowering. To take full advantage of this, it is essential to remove flowers as they fade. After a harsh winter, prune the roses twice: in October, by taking about 20 cm (8 in) off the branches, and then the final trim in April by removing those which are spindly or crossing and those which have been hit by frost. Cut back the remaining stems.

White flowers

— 'Iceberg' (syn. 'Fée des Neiges') gives semi-double flowers, not very large but perfectly formed, pure white with dazzling green leaves. Its light scent is a plus, but it often comes down with mildew. Flowers all summer. Height: 1.2 m (60 in). Spread: 80 cm (32 in).

— 'Virgo' has large, pure white flowers 12 cm (5 in) in diameter, but not very many. You can also admire its handsome foliage. Flowers all summer. Height: 80 cm (32 in). Spread: 80 cm (32 in).

Pink flowers

— 'Centenaire de Lourdes' is a beautiful, profusely-flowering hardy variety. Its pretty semi-double flowers, lightly scented, cover the plant non-stop. Flowers all summer. Height: 1.2 m (50 in). Spread: 90 cm (36 in).

— 'Queen Elizabeth' is a popular rosebush, with its well-formed flowers giving off a sweet scent. Providing you don't prune it too short, it will grow into a handsome bush some 2 m (80 in) tall without training. Flowers all summer. Height: 1.2 m (50 in). Spread: 90 cm (36 in).

— 'Sylvie Vartan' gives semi-double peony-shaped scented flowers. They are a strong pink and surrounded by lush foliage. Flowers all summer, and abundantly in autumn. Height: 80 cm (32 in). Spread: 80 cm (32 in).

Red flowers

— 'Papa Meilland', with purple/crimson iris-shaped flowers with bluish black highlights and strongly scented, flowers all summer. Height: 60 cm (24 in). Spread: 80 cm (32 in).

— 'Rose Gaujard' has semi-double, elegant, scented flowers, vermilion with copper striations, silvery-white on the back. Flowers all summer. Height: 1 m (40 in). Spread: 1 m (40 in).

'Iceberg' △
'Centenaire de Lourdes' ▷
◁ 'Sylvie Vartan'
'Queen Elizabeth' ▽

Yellow flowers

— '**Joseph's Coat**', with semi-double yellow flowers with a hint of red, lightly scented, is a rosebush whose petals change colour with age. Flowers throughout June. Height: 1.2 m (48 in). Spread: 1 m (40 in).

— '**Mme A. Meilland**' (syn. '**Peace**'): what a marvellous apricot yellow with pink highlights! Large, full, scented flowers. Flowers all summer. Height: 1.2 m (48 in). Spread: 90 cm (36 in).

— '**All Gold**', golden flowers which don't like the sun, and are prone to disease. Flowers all summer. Height: 80 cm (32 in). Spread: 80 cm (32 in).

— '**Nevada**', a superb bush, pink-white flowers with yellow stamens, long lithe branches which I don't trim. Lots of single flowers. You *must* remove faded flowers in June. Flowers: mainly in June, then another flowering in July–August. Height: 2.2 m (88 in). Spread: 1 m (40 in).

OLD ROSES

I love old roses, and I'm not alone. In the sixth century, King Childebert of France created a rose garden at his palace near the abbey of Saint-Germain-des-Prés. In the eighth century, Charlemagne issued a decree ordering that roses should be grown in gardens. In the eleventh century, abbess Sainte-Phildegarde recommended growing roses as a therapeutic plant. And the ancestors of our old roses took root and blossomed out to come down to us today. These old roses are not only the forbears of our modern ones, but also still the glory of our gardens.

Alba rosebushes. These are very hardy bushes, often with silvery-green foliage. They are marvellous when trained against a low trellis.

— '**Cuisse de Nymphe Emue**' with pink-white flowers has an enchanting perfume. Flowers in summer. The only drawback is that the flowering season is short – 15 to 20 days at the maximum. Height: 1.8 m (72 in).

— '**Céleste**' is seductive, with its delicate pink semi-double flowers. Flowers: June–July. Height: 1.5 m (60 in) Spread: 1.2 m (48 in).

Bourbon roses. Very hardy bushes which can be trained or cut short and used for spectacular effect. Their foliage is a handsome, slightly dark green.

— '**Fantin-Latour**' is pleasing, with its warm pink flowers with their wealth of

crumpled petals. Flowers briefly in summer. Height: 1.8 m (72 in). Spread: 1.5 m (60 in).

— '**Mme Isaac Pereire**' (my ancestor's rose) produces deep pink flowers with an unsurpassable scent, the most perfumed of all. It is still beautiful if used as a climbing rose or bush. Remove flowers as they fade. Flowers virtually all summer. Height: 2 m (80 in). Spread: 1.2m (48 in).

Damask roses. These roses (*Rosa damascena*) have dense, recurved, slightly crumpled petals. Their slightly velvety foliage has a hint of silver. Most damask roses produce long, slightly hairy fruit in autumn. Watch out for the thorns on the long flexible stems.

— '**Celsiana**' is a vigorous plant with sparkling pink flowers and yellow stamens. Flowers in summer, with a delicious scent. Height: 1.5 m (60 in). Spread: 1.2m (48 in).

— '**Mme Hardy**' is a creeper which reaches 2 m (80 in) with a spread of 1.7m (68 in) if used as a shrub. Its perfectly-formed flowers are pure white with a greenish eye, which is startling when you see the pink highlights on the buds. Flowers in June–July.

Gallica. Grown in France since the sixteenth century, these roses were used mainly for perfumes and potpourris. Easy to grow and look after, they have the pleasant ability to put up with poor soil easily and have few thorns. Marvellously scented, the flowers are double. They flower in summer.

— '**Belle de Crécy**' is a supple rose-bush which needs a stake. The highly-scented flowers are purple to violet with a green 'bud' in the centre of the crumpled petals. Height: about 1.2 m (50 in). Spread: 80 cm (32 in).

— '**Cardinal Richelieu**' is a good rose-bush for making hedges. The pale pink flowers turn violet or purple when they unfurl. Flowers: June–July. Height and spread: 80 cm (32 in).

— '**Complicata**' can be used as a climber or 'specimen', on its own in a corner of a lawn or a large-scale border. The single, brilliant pink flowers with slightly recurved petals are reminiscent of tousled dog roses. Flowers: June–July. Height: 1.5 m (60 in). Spread: an unbelievable 2.5 (100 in).

Hybrid perpetuals flower continuously, sometimes sporadically, all summer until the frosts.

— '**Frau Karl Druschki**', a very pretty rose, has double, pure-white, but unscented flowers. You will find that if you

△ '**Mme Isaac Pereire**'
'**Nevada**' ▷
◁ '**Joseph's Coat**'
◁ '**Mme Hardy**'
▽ '**Cuisse de Nymphe émue**'

261

only prune the plant lightly, and bend the branches towards the ground, you will get a wealth of flowers all along the stems. Flowers: June–July. Height: 1.5 m (60 in). Spread: 1.2 m (48 in).

— '**Général Jacqueminot**' is a little rosebush with very full, dark red, sumptuous, heavily scented flowers. Height and spread: 1 m (40 in).

— '**Reine des Violettes**' ('queen of the violets') is well-named: in fact, its purple-mauve flowers contrast delightfully with its greyish foliage. To give lots of flowers in summer, prune the branches very short, 15 to 20 cm (6–8 in) from the ground in February. Flowers: June–July. Height; 1.8 m (72 in). Spread: 1.5 m (60 in).

Rugosa. These are vigorous rosebushes with thorny branches and generally well-scented flowers and fruit in autumn, which means you mustn't remove the flowers when they fade.

— '**Agnes**' has an abundance of double yellow flowers in sparkling yellow, highly-scented pompoms. Flowers: all summer. Height: 2 m (80 in) Spread: 1 m (40 in).

— '**Blanc Double de Coubert**' is a slightly formal shrub with pretty white flowers and slightly toothed leaves. It goes well as a hedge shrub and can reach 2 m (80 in) in height. Spread: 1 m (40 in). Flowers: sporadically all summer.

Moss roses. There is a wide variety of rosebushes in this category, from little border roses to large climbing shrubs, but all have stems and petioles covered in little hairs which give an impression of 'moss'. Perfumed and hardy, they are full, sumptuous roses.

— '**Gloire de Mousseux**' has spindly branches with little dark leaves. Also known as 'Old Black', because of its dark purple flowers and golden stamens. Flowers: June–July. Height: 1.5 m (60 in). Spread 1 m (40 in).

— '**Salet**' is a very flowery, scented shrub. Its double flowers are bright pink. Flowers: nearly all summer. Height: 1.5 m (60 in). Spread: 1 m (40 in).

— '**Mousseline**' is a compact shrub which goes well in a border with hardy perennials. Its pretty globular white flowers are a delicate flesh colour. Flowers: in summer. Height: 80 cm (32 in). Spread: 80 cm (32 in).

Portland. Flowers early in summer then rests until September, when new, fairly sparse flowers appear. Flowers singly or in bunches.

'**Blanc Double de Coubert**' △
◁ '**Jacques Cartier**'
'**Mme Meilland**' ▽

'Comte de Chambord' △

△ 'Papa Meilland'
▽ 'Stanwell Perpetual'

— 'Comte de Chambord' is a slightly stiff shrub with pink, full, sumptuous flowers with dense petals. Highly scented. Flowers: all summer. Height: 1.2 m (48 in). Spread: 1 m (40 in).

— 'Jacques Cartier', vigorous, has semi-double flowers of deep pink with a green centre. Flowers: intermittently throughout the summer. Height: 1.2 m (48 in). Spread: 1 m (40 in).

— 'Yolande d'Aragon' has an upright appearance, generous foliage and nice double flowers of a deep pink, all of which make it one of the most sumptuous jewels of the garden. And it keeps on flowering to boot! Height: 1.2 m (48 in). Spread: 1.5 m (60 in).

And one which does not fall into any of these categories, a botanical rose hybrid, *Rosa spinosissima*, which I couldn't bear to leave out:

— 'Stanwell Perpetual' is a dense shrub with little light green leaves. Remove some old branches from the centre of the bush each year to let air in. Its scent is soft but enchanting and the tender pink flowers appear from June until . . . in fact, I have picked the last ones for Christmas. Height: 1.8 m (72 in). Spread: 1.5 m (60 in).

263

Rudbeckia bicolor △
Rudbeckia laciniata ▽

▽ **Ruta graveolens**
Ruscus aculeatus ▽

Rudbeckia

CONEFLOWER

Compositae

With its strange corollas with a prominent heart, in either black or green, its petals folded back like the ears of a suspicious cat, the coneflower has a look that is all its own. Flowering at the end of summer, at the same time as the golden beauty, coneflowers make a beautiful end to the season grown with ornamental tobaccos, and will keep the Chinese lanterns company until the first frosts. The warm tones of their corollas are a joy to the eye in autumn, when misty days abound.

Useful hints

— Sow annual coneflowers in March and April in seed trays, under shelter, then plant out in May in groups of about ten.

— Plant perennial varieties early, in the spring.

— Any good garden soil suits them well, provided that they are given a sunny position.

Recommended

— From among the annuals choose *Rudbeckia bicolor* 'Marmalade', with its warm gold colour. From the perennials, opt for *R. fulgida* 'Deamii' for its orange flowers ringed with yellow, *R. laciniata* for its foliage and *R. nitida* for its huge yellow flowers topped with a little green crown.

Height: 60–80 cm (24–32 in).
Spacing and planting distance: 30 cm (12 in).
Soil: ordinary.
Cultivation: sunny.
Propagation: by division in autumn or in spring.
Flowering season: July–October.
Type: annual, perennial.

Ruscus

BUTCHER'S BROOM

Liliaceae

It is hard to imagine that this little evergreen is a distant relative of the ornamental asparagus. And just like the asparagus, its leaves are in fact flattened stems. It is only at the time of fertilization, which occurs when male and female plants are planted side by side, that the resemblance becomes more striking as the red berries are almost identical to those of the asparagus, and are also similar to the holly's from a distance. Plant them next to fuchsias, busy-lizzies, bleeding hearts, and lilies to create informal or formal arrangements.

Useful hints

— Plant *Ruscus aculeatus* in spring, in a shady corner. Water regularly throughout the first year. Growth is very slow during the first years and the plants only really establish themselves at the end of 3 years.

— Divide the clumps every 5 years or else their hearts tend to lose their leaves. The same might also occur after exceptionally hard frosts. The normally evergreen foliage can even disappear quite suddenly. A dose of fertilizer in spring will aid regrowth.

Height: 40–60 cm (16–24 in).
Spacing and planting distance: 30 cm (12 in).
Soil: ordinary, preferably slightly heavy.
Cultivation: at least 3 hours sun per day.
Propagation: in autumn, by taking cuttings or from seeds.
Flowering season: June, July.
Type: perennial.

Ruta

RUE

Rutaceae

In former times *Ruta graveolens* was cultivated for its medicinal powers but it is now largely enjoyed for its sea-green foliage and acid yellow flowers. It is an excellent border plant and a good bedfellow for old roses and the yellow flowers so prevalent in summer. There is a slightly more compact variety, 'Jackman's Blue', and another with variegated leaves.

Useful hints

— Plant in spring, preferably. Water regularly during the first summer and mulch the soil. In later years rue can survive quite harsh droughts.

— Take cuttings from the ends of the stems in summer and root in a very sandy mixture or sow in spring. These usually take well and produce great quantities of young plants which flourish from the second year.

— Create good quality borders by planting them 30 cm (12 in) apart and pruning them back every spring to half their height to make them bushier.

Height: 1 m (40 in).
Spacing and planting distance: 60 cm (24 in).
Soil: rich in humus.
Cultivation: shade.
Propagation: by division in spring.
Flowering season: almost unnoticeable, in March and April.
Type: perennial.

Sagina

SAGINE

Caryophyllaceae

Sagina subulata is one of the favourite plants of those who are interested in Japanese-style gardens because, like *Helxine*, it gives the impression of a newly mown lawn. Moreover, in summer it is covered in tiny white flowers. Sometimes its greenery is used for filling in spaces between the flagstones of a path, and at other times it is used for marking out large geometrical shapes on top of a flagstone base. Unfortunately it is not always as hardy as one would wish. Like other small perennial plants it is more attractive when grown among other foliage plants, such as hostas or ferns, or when it serves as a foil to a clump of fuchsias. It is also suitable for town gardens where grass doesn't do so well.

Useful hints

— Plant rooted cuttings or divided clumps in spring in a well-dug soil completely cleared of weeds in a good location.

— Water copiously and regularly during the summer, adding some liquid nitrogen fertilizer to the water once a month.

Height: 5 cm (2 in).
Spacing and planting distance: 10 cm (4 in).
Soil: ordinary.
Cultivation: sunny.
Propagation: by division all year round.
Flowering season: summer.
Type: perennial.

Sagittaria

ARROWHEAD

Alismataceae

Arrowhead is easily recognizable by its leaves shaped just like the tips of arrows children draw. It is an aquatic plant native to the edge of rivers and streams. The flowers, white with purple at the centre, grow above the water on strong stems. An excellent plant for small ponds, *Sagittaria sagittifolia* never actually hides the water but rather lends elegance to the setting.

Useful hints

— Plant out in May or June in a rich soil covered by at least 30 cm (12 in) of water. Divide the clumps in April by separating basal shoots.

— Any leaves growing underwater should be left in place even if they do

△ **Salpiglossis sinuata**
◁ **Sagittaria sagittifolia**
▽ **Sagina subulata**

look more like grass than adult leaves, as they will aid the plant's growth.

Height: 30–80 cm (12–32 in) underwater, 30–60 cm (12–24 in) above.
Spacing and planting distance: 50 cm (20 in).
Soil: rich.
Cultivation: sunny.
Propagation: by division in spring.
Flowering season: July, August.
Type: perennial.

Salpiglossis

SALPIGLOSSIS

Solanaceae

Few plants have such a visual impact as these. With their trumpet-shaped blooms, striped or veined in the brightest colours, *Salpiglossis sinuata* create a really lovely effect. Although the individual flowers are short-lived they are constantly renewed throughout the summer. You can grow them in clumps or alternatively place them in small groups here and there in terraces. Since they have only a modest foliage, all you will see are the magnificent blooms. You could also try placing them among grey-leaved plants, such as *Artemisia*.

Useful hints

— Sow in April in a cold frame. Plant out 20 cm (8 in) apart once they are a few centimetres high. They can also be sown direct into their final position, but for this you should wait until mid-May.

— Keep well watered and remove withered flowers to prolong the flowering period. Pruning the branches in August will encourage new growth.

Height: 60 cm (24 in).
Spread and planting distance: 20 cm (8 in).
Soil: ordinary, preferably light.
Cultivation: sunny.
Propagation: from seed in spring.
Flowering season: July–September.
Type: annual.

265

△ *Salvia guaranatica*
▽ *Salvia involucrata* **Bethellii**

△ *Salvia microphylla grahamii*

Salvia

SAGE

Labiatae

Without salvias, summertime would seem quite dull. Not only is there the popular red salvia, sometimes a little too commonplace, but also a whole host of relatives, more or less perennial, which can put on a splendid show of blues and purples. They reign supreme over sunny, slightly dry places.

Useful hints

— Sow annual salvias in March or April in warm conditions. Harden them off before finally planting them out in May in soil enriched with leaf-mould. Cut back the main stems by half to encourage bushiness. Mulch the soil with peat or semi-decomposed compost. Water every week adding plant food once a month. Trim withered flowers regularly.

— Plant perennial salvias in early autumn or in spring. Lighten the soil with sand and be careful not to over-feed otherwise the plant will become too leafy. Trim withered stems and cut back growth in late summer once the leaves have dried out. New leaves will begin to appear right up until the first frosts.

Recommended

— **Annual salvias**: Above its leaves, *Salvia horminum* produces stems sporting visible bracts which surround the real, rather small flowers. Available in several colours, from pink to deep purple, they also make good dried flowers.

— *S. splendens* is the famous red salvia seen in so many gardens. Each supplier has his own particular varieties on offer, but they are all in fact very similar. Rather than choosing the super dwarfs, which are really not at all elegant, try going for the medium-tall varieties like 'Bonfire', which although they appear later are more decorative.

— Best for dampening the blaze of colour caused by the red salvia is *S. farinacea* which is available in blue, 'Victoria', and white, 'Ivory'—a mixture of rare delicacy. They will remain in flower for several weeks.

— **Perennial salvias**: Without doubt the loveliest of all is *S. argentea* with its fabulous silvery leaves. To keep it at its best protect the clump with sheets of glass throughout the winter months as this plant cannot tolerate the combination of cold and humidity.

— *S. officinalis* is well known for its leaves used in herbal teas. The flowers together with the violet-tinted silver foliage are a particularly successful combination and they provide a good foil for a range of plants including roses and carnations.

— *S. patens* isn't really hardy but the extravagant blue of its flowers (one of the brightest in nature) makes it well

△ *Salvia patens*

△ *Salvia buchananii*
▽ *Salvia horminum*

worth the trouble of protecting it in winter with a layer of pine bark. If you plant it next to a white tobacco plant, its rather uncertain green leaves will be less in evidence.

— The meadow salvia is an attractive weed found in ditches. Its natural variety, *haematodes*, will astonish you by the amazing mass of flowers it produces.

— The striking *S. sclarea* is another beautiful salvia with a very natural look. Whether the scent of its leaves is pleasant or disagreeable is debatable but everyone loves the pale blue flowers, which provide some of the best associations for traditional roses. It does very well as a biennial and will quite happily seed itself.

— The most widespread of all the perennial salvias is *S. superba*, noted for its compact shape. There are many varieties to choose from, among which 'Lubecca' is violet and 'Ostfriesland' is even darker.

— I could go on to mention several more types, such as *S. grahamii*, *S. uliginosa* or *S. coccinea*, but their hardiness is not always reliable.

Height: 20 cm–1.5 m (8–60 in).
Spacing and planting distance: 15–50 cm (6–20 in).
Soil: ordinary, but well-drained.
Cultivation: sunny.
Propagation: from seed or by division in spring.
Flowering season: June–October.
Type: annual, biennial, perennial.

△ *Salvia sclarea*
◁ *Salvia splendens*
▽ *Salvia sclarea tukerstanica*

Salvia superba *massed at the edge of a field, gives a profusion of blue-violet spikes in summer.*

Sanguinaria

BLOODROOT

Papaveraceae

Don't go looking for any red in the flowers of *Sanguinaria canadensis*, a relative of the celandine, as it is in fact the root which 'bleeds' when you pull it out. The flowers are as white as snow. The double-flowered variety 'Flore Pleno' lasts longer and is considered to boast some of the most beautiful double flowers in existence. They are almost as round and full-bodied as some old-fashioned roses.

Useful hints

— Plant in autumn in a shady corner with a soil rich in peat. Growth is rapid and the plants will burst into flower only a few weeks after the leaves have begun to appear in the spring. You can encourage leaf growth by mulching the soil with pine bark or peat. It may also be necessary to continue watering right through the summer.

— The rhizomes should be carefully dug up every 5 years and replanted some distance away with a handful of sand scattered into the soil.

Height: 20 cm (8 in).
Spacing and planting distance: 20 cm (8 in).
Soil: rich in peat.
Cultivation: shade.
Propagation: by separating new rhizomes once the leaves have died back.
Flowering season: May.
Type: bulb.

△ *Sanguinaria canadensis*
Sanguisorba obtusa △
◁ *Sanguinaria canadensis*
◁ *Santolina virens*
▽ *Santolina chamaecyparissus*

Sanguisorba

BURNET

Rosaceae

Our good old burnet, with its edible leaves similar in taste to cucumber, has a number of decorative Canadian and Japanese relatives, such as *Sanguisorba obtusa* which grows to a height of 20 cm (8 in) with pale purple flowers. All the sanguisorbas have in common a pretty green, pinnate foliage and flowers borne on long and slender stems. They are ideal for the wild garden and grow well with hellebores and ferns. They can be grown together with spring bulbs which easily acclimatize, such as tulips, the small-flowered narcissus, and *Fritillaria meleagris* (snake's head).

Useful hints

— Plant in autumn or spring in well-dug soil. Water regularly for the first summer. Thereafter they can be left to their own devices.

— Divide clumps every 3 years and replant immediately.

Height: 60–120 cm (24–48 in).
Spacing and planting distance: 60 cm (24 in).
Soil: rich in humus.
Cultivation: sun or semi-shade.
Propagation: by division in spring.
Flowering season: June, July.
Type: perennial.

Santolina

COTTON LAVENDER
Compositae

If you are looking for a foliage that stands out, is silver-coloured and has an attractive scent, what could be better than *Santolina*? It is a very graceful plant with its grey leaves which are both dense and finely delineated. Bushy, but easy to keep in shape, and with prolific flowers, santolina will fill out gaps in sunny paving and low walls.

Useful hints
— Good garden soil will be sufficient for this plant, but it has a Mediterranean temperament and does best in the sunniest positions. It will be happiest in nooks and crannies of dry stone walls, along with valerian, stonecrop and wallflowers.

— As soon as flowering is over in July, trim it lightly to restore its beauty.

— Avoid planting it in moist or waterlogged soil as this is its worst enemy.

Recommended
— The most popular is *Santolina chamaecyparissus*, but *S. virens* is a very pretty, delicate green and bears the same yellow pompom-shaped flowers as its relative.

Height: 30 cm (12 in).
Spacing and planting distance: 30 cm (12 in).
Soil: ordinary, well-drained.
Cultivation: sunny.
Propagation: by division in spring.
Flowering season: June, July.
Type: perennial.

Sanvitalia

CREEPING ZINNIA
Compositae

If you are looking for a small plant for a neat border, look no further than *Sanvitalia procumbens*. Sowing in spring will provide you with beautiful neat 'cushions', covered in little yellow flowers with black centres, throughout the summer.

Useful hints
— Sow in the final position in mid-May and water every other day until the plant is well established. Thin out the seedlings one month later to one plant every 20 cm (8 in). At the same time, mulch the soil with grass cuttings.

— Remove all faded flowers once a fortnight and use garden shears to tidy up the border as necessary.

Height: 15 cm (6 in).
Spacing and planting distance: 20 cm (8 in).
Soil: ordinary.
Cultivation: sunny.
Propagation: from seed in spring.
Flowering season: from July until the first frosts.
Type: annual.

Saponaria

SOAPWORT
Caryophyllaceae

The little pink soapwort (*Saponaria ocymoides*) grows on dry stone walls, rockeries and sunny terraces. The pink soapwort will soon make a carpet of flowers as it seems to have only one aim in life: to spread out as much as possible. Be careful therefore not to cramp it but allow it as much room as possible, for it will happily cover your whole terrace. If you mix it with *Cerastium tomentosum* you will obtain a marvellous pastel-coloured carpet.

Useful hints
— It is best to plant in spring, in an ordinary well-drained soil, in a sunny site.

— Water once a week to begin with, to ensure the roots take, and then gradually more sparingly until the plants are well established when watering will no longer be necessary.

— Divide the clumps every 3 years.

Recommended
— The bright pink flowers of *Saponaria* × 'Bressingham' bloom earlier (May to July) than those of *S. ocymoides*.

Height: 15 cm (6 in).
Spacing and planting distance: 15 cm (6 in).
Soil: ordinary, well-drained.
Cultivation: sunny.
Propagation: by division in autumn or in spring.
Flowering season: June, July.
Type: annual, perennial.

△ *Sanvitalia procumbens*
▽ *Saponaria ocymoides*

Sarracenia

SARRACENIA/PITCHER-PLANT

Sarraceniaceae

It's hard to say what is the most striking feature of *Sarracenia*; its brilliantly coloured rolled-up leaves, reminiscent of old-fashioned gentleman's breeches which serve as a trap for insects, or for its flowers which are unique in the plant world. It is well worth allowing them a small space, if you can provide the humid spot they need, unless you prefer to grow them in pots, where it is easier to appreciate their strange shape.

Useful hints

— Plant them in spring in pockets of peaty soil around a pond or pool. Spread march moss (sphagnum) around the clumps to create a natural environment and combine them with Venus fly-trap or sundew. *Sarracenia* will do well in a mild winter, but it's a good idea to cover the crown with peat and plastic film so that the birds cannot disturb them.

— When planting in pots, see that these are wider than their height, and fill with light peat, which should be kept moist. In winter, place the pots under a cold frame or shelter in a very slightly heated greenhouse. In the summer they can be put in a sunny position and should be watered twice weekly.

Height: 30–60 cm (12–24 in).
Spacing and planting distance: 30 cm (12 in).
Soil: peat.
Cultivation: sunny.
Propagation: by division in spring.
Flowering season: April, May.
Type: perennial.

△ **Sarracenia flava maxima**
▽ **Sarracenia rubra**

Saxifraga

SAXIFRAGE

Saxifragaceae

Saxifrages are very well known to rock-garden lovers, particularly for their ability to break up rocks. It's certainly true that they do well in crevices. Many of them are sought by collectors who go to great pains to grow them on flat ground, and others are a boon to the gardener as they will grow in even the densest shade.

Useful hints

— Plant in spring in light and well-drained pockets of soil. Add sand if necessary; they are best suited to a semi-sunny position.

— Before the winter sets in, sprinkle gravel around the neck of the plant so that water won't collect there.

Recommended

— Among the **rosette** saxifrages, *Saxifraga paniculata* forms large silvery rosettes with leaves encrusted with lime secretions. The light, delicate flowers are usually white, but are pink in *S. p. rosea*. *S. cochlearis* and *S. caespitosa* are barely taller than 15 cm (6 in) and are both white, as is *S. linguaeformis* or *S. umbrosa*, the well-known 'painter's despair', thus named because of its very delicate flowers which will move in the slightest breeze. There is also a pink variety and a yellow variety with variegated leaves.

— Among **clump** saxifrages, the finest have to be *S. cortusifolia* or (*S. fortunei*) and *S. stolonifera* (or *S. sarmentosa*). Both flower late, in October or November, and look delightful in the shade and in window-boxes. Their flowers have two petals longer than the others, making them look like little comets.

— The **moss** saxifrages have two miniature types which strangely resemble moss: *S. oppositifolia*, a gem in a well-kept rockery which is covered in pink flowers in March and April. *S. hypnoides* or 'Turkish lawn' will grow up to 10 cm (4 in) and has pink flowers. Along with *S. decipiens* this is one of the best plants to choose to fill in the spaces between paving stones.

Height: 10–30 cm (4–12 in).
Spacing and planting distance: 15 cm (6 in).
Soil: rich in humus and well drained.
Cultivation: sun or semi-shade.
Propagation: by separating non-flowering rosettes in spring.
Flowering season: March–November, depending on variety.
Type: perennial.

△ *Saxifraga goodsefiana*
Saxifraga 'Rosea' △
Saxifraga 'Tumbling Waters' ▷
▽ *Saxifraga hypnoides*

Saxifraga cortusifolia △
Saxifraga crustata ▷
Saxifraga × *irvingii* ▽

273

△ *Scabiosa caucasia*
Scabiosa atropurpurea ▷

Scabiosa

SCABIOUS, PINCUSHION FLOWER
Dipsacaceae

Once very fashionable, scabious has fallen out of favour, possibly because of its sad-looking flowers. Their violet and almost black purple colouring is certainly very sombre, but they are as delicate and elegant as many other flowers. Don't hesitate to use them, especially the Caucasian variety which look so pretty with pink carnations.

Useful hints

— Sow annual scabious in March or April, under a cold-frame, or plant out directly in May, in a row in the kitchen garden, for example. Prick them out a month later and nip the stems in the middle to make them branch out. Remove withered flowers so that seeds do not form.

— Plant perennial scabious in spring or autumn. Mulch the soil in June with grass cuttings and divide up clumps every 3 years to rejuvenate them.

Recommended

— Annual scabious (*S. atropurpurea*), a large, double, varied type is the best for

bouquets and clumps. Support them discreetly, because they can grow up to 90 cm (36 in). *Scabiosa caucasica* is perennial and produces lavender-blue flowers, and also bright blue ones in the 'Nachtfalter' (moth) variety. The perennial *S. ochroleuca* produces pale-yellow flowers.

Height: 60–90 cm (24–36 in).
Spacing and planting distance: 30 cm (12 in).
Soil: normal, preferably chalky and well-drained.
Cultivation: sunny.
Propagation: in spring, from seeds and by division.
Flowering season: June–October.
Type: annual; perennial.

Schizanthus

BUTTERFLY FLOWER
Solanaceae

Schizanthus flowers are often compared with butterfly wings. They come in a whole range of colours from the purest white to the darkest violet and contain yellow markings in their curly flowers. It is a delicate flower which can fill a pot beautifully and could even be used as a border plant in the garden, although its flowering season is sadly limited.

Useful hints

— Sow in October and keep under a cold frame for the winter or wait until April. Harden off before the final planting. Water regularly and add a little nitrogen fertilizer if the leaves are yellow. This often means that it is too cold for the plant.

— Plant outside in May alongside stiffer species, which will serve to prop them up, like *Cistus*, *Godetia*, or even stock.

Recommended

— *S. pinnatus* 'Dwarf Bouquet' is an attractive variety with deep rose-pink flowers with yellow centres.

Height: 30–40 cm (12–16 in).
Spacing and planting distance: 20 cm (8 in).
Soil: fresh and rich in humus.
Cultivation: at least 3 hours sun a day.
Propagation: from seed, in October or April.
Flowering season: June–September.
Type: biennial.

▽ *Schizanthus pinnatus*

Schizostylis

KAFFIR LILY/CRIMSON FLAG

Iridaceae

A smaller relative of *Croscosmia* (or *Mont-bretia*), *Schizostylis coccinea* shares a preference for well-drained soil near the sea. Its flowers, which range from pink to vermilion, look striking by the seaside. In the right place—next to the shining leaves of *Pittosporum*—the flowers will be shown off to full effect, and if planted near rough calceolaria will look particularly effective.

Useful hints

— Plant in September or October in pockets of rich compost, spacing the bulbs out 10 cm (4 in) in all directions and covering with 5 cm (2 in) of soil.

— Protect from frost with a good bedding of leaves.

— Let the clumps fill out for 3 or 4 years so that the plants remain in flower.

— In regions where the climate is mild, they can be grown in pots (use 5 bulbs per 30 cm (12 in) pot); they will provide a lovely show in your window boxes throughout the autumn.

Height: 30–50 cm (12–20 in).
Spacing and planting distance: 10 cm (4 in).
Soil: rich in humus.
Cultivation: Sunny.
Propagation: by separating bulbs in spring.
Flowering season: September–November.
Type: bulb.

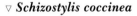

▽ **Schizostylis coccinea**

△ **Scilla sibirica**
Scilla peruviana ▷
▽ **Scilla campanulata**

Scilla

SQUILL, BLUEBELL

Liliaceae

From very early spring scillas begin to unfold their corollas; first the Persian scillas (*Scilla tubergeniana*) as early as January, then Siberian scillas (*S. sibirica*) and, finally, S. campanulata in March or April. These pretty pastel-coloured little flowers make a fine decoration for a wild garden with moist soil.

Useful hints

— Plant scillas in October in large groupings by scattering a handful of about 10 bulbs under your spring-flowering shrubs and planting them where they fall.

— Don't mix all the colours together; go for single colour splashes in quite wide areas.

— They will thrive in any kind of good garden soil.

— They can be grown successfully in bowls or pots indoors.

Recommended

— Among *Scilla campanulata* the loveliest varieties are 'Blue Queen', a bright blue; 'Alba', white; 'Rose Queen', pink. Among *S. sibirica* the variety 'Spring Beauty' is a Prussian blue. *S. tubergeniana* is a milky-blue colour and one of the first to flower, often on ground level.

Height: 10–30 cm (4–12 in).
Spacing and planting distance: 15 cm (6 in).
Soil: ordinary, well-drained.
Cultivation: sun or semi-shade.
Propagation: by separating bulbs, when foliage is dry.
Flowering season: January–April.
Type: bulb.

Scutellaria

SKULLCAP

Labiatae

Scutellarias are widely used to decorate rock gardens. Their relatively late flowering season and mauve colouring provide useful cover for a bare, summer rockery.

Useful hints

— Sow in spring in pockets of earth lightened with sand. Water regularly until they flower. Each spring add a little leaf compost around clumps to encourage lateral roots which may otherwise detach themselves.

— Watch out for *Scutellaria alpina*; it's very pretty but it tends to take over.

Recommended

— *Scutellaria alpina* grows no higher than 20 cm (8 in) but creates a carpet of almost 60 cm (24 in) in diameter. Light-grey leaves encase purplish-blue flowers.

— *S. baicalensis* is a perennial species, originating from Siberia, around Lake Baikal. It forms clumps nearly 60 cm (24 in) high and looks a little like some nepetas.

Height: 20–60 cm (8–24 in).
Spacing and planting distance: 30 cm (12 in).
Soil: ordinary, well-drained in winter.
Cultivation: sunny.
Propagation: by division in spring.
Flowering season: July, August.
Type: perennial.

▽ **Scutellaria baicalensis**

Sedum

STONECROP

Crassulaceae

These plants are a boon to gardens where the soil is thin. Their fleshy leaves, showing their relationship to the large family of succulent plants, are a proof of their durability where water is lacking. The genus is so varied that it contains types which thrive in full sunshine as well as those which will flourish in semi-shade; the latter could even also be grown in the sun if the soil is moist. Use them liberally to fill up all the spaces in your rockery or the cracks between the stones of a low wall. Pair them with *Graminaceae* and grey-leaved plants, which are just as well suited to poor conditions.

Useful hints

— Plant tall stonecrop in containers in September or October, or even in spring if you are worried about heavy rainfall. Cuttings planted directly in the earth at the same time often do very well.

— Once the flowering season is over, cut off withered stalks to encourage new, more abundant ones in the following season. If cobwebs appear on the ends of stems of *Sedum spectabile*, this is an indication of an invasion by tiny caterpillars. Treat the plants with a trichlorphon-based insecticide.

— Each spring bank up the crowns a little by adding a few handfuls of compost in the centre.

Recommended

— **Dwarf** stonecrop which look good in rockeries or as a border plant:

— *Sedum aizoon* is a deep yellow and flowers in high summer; it is reminiscent of the well-known fiery stonecrop or wall pepper (*S. acre*) which is used to highlight the tops of walls.

— *S. lydium* are an even smaller species with a delightful sea-green or golden foliage, depending on their type, 'Glaucum' or 'Aureum'.

— Two other well-known series of rampant stonecrop are *S. spathulifolium* and *S. spurium*. The former create cushions of rosettes, giving rise to stems bearing bright yellow flowers, while the latter favour white ('Album Superbum'), purple ('Atropurpureum'), bright pink ('Coccineum') or have yellow and pink variegated leaves ('Variegata Tricolor').

— **Medium and tall** species which look best in clumps:

— The best known is *S. spectabile*, whose pink, bright scarlet ('Brilliant') or deep red ('Meteor') blooms come out in autumn. They make an unforgettable sight when married with fuchsias and asters. Crossed with *Sedum telephium* which grows on embankments, this Chinese species has given birth to the hybrid 'Autumn Joy', which is a lighter plant and whose flowers change colour as they bloom.

Height: 15–50 cm (6–20 in).
Spacing and planting distance: 25 cm (10 in).
Soil: ordinary, well-drained.
Cultivation: sun or semi-shade.
Propagation: by division in March.
Flowering season: June–November.
Type: perennial.

△ **Sedum spathulifolium**
◁ **Sedum spectabile**
Sedum spurium ▷
▽ **Sedum acre**

Sempervivum

HOUSELEEK

Crassulaceae

This is another family of small, sparse plants. There is no need to lavish attention on them; you can just pop them in the ground, forget them and the house-leek will take root! If you have an old, thatched roof, or a spare corner in a gloomy low wall, try the houseleek. They are used traditionally to decorate timbers on thatched roofs, just as the iris can be used, and to such an extent that *Sempervivum tectorum* has won the name 'roof houseleek'.

Useful hints

— Plant in any ordinary soil, well-drained and in full sunshine, or between stones in a wall.

— Use in borders, but also in clumps; *Sempervivum arachnoideum* is particularly decorative, especially when it shows its pink flowers.

Recommended

— There are in fact many species, but I am recommending two—*Sempervivum arachnoideum*, called 'bride's veil', because of its fleecy veil covering, is decked with pretty pink flowers in summer, and *S. tectorum*, which has bronze-coloured rosettes and garnet flowers, but is unfortunately quite rare.

Height: 5–10 cm (2–4 in).
Spacing and planting distance: 10 cm (4 in).
Soil: ordinary.
Cultivation: sunny.
Propagation: by division in autumn or spring.
Flowering season: June–August.
Type: perennial.

Sempervivum tectorum ▽

277

△ *Senecio maritima*

Senecio

GROUNDSEL

Compositae

The only kinds of *Senecio* we can discuss here are *S. greyii*, which could also be classified as a small shrub, and maritime cineraria (*S. cineraria*). The first is widely used to break up monotony and add interest or to provide screens for other plants. Its foliage is such a beautiful silver-grey colour that it blends with just about everything, except perhaps for the yellowish flowers it produces and which you can remove quickly. The latter species fulfils the same functions on a lower level. Put it with red sage for a brilliant contrast.

Useful hints

— Plant *Senecio greyii* only in spring because it does very badly in winter. Add sand and even a few pebbles to lighten the earth. Plant slightly raised to protect the plant's neck from too much moisture. As winter draws on, put a handful of rock wool around the base of the plant. If the leaves freeze, the plant will die.

— Sow maritime cineraria in March, in the warm, and harden off before its final planting in May. Pinch the stems so that a good clump will form. Water regularly during the dry days of summer and cut the flowers off as soon as they appear.

Height: 15–150 cm (6–70 in).
Spacing and planting distance: 15–60 cm (6–24 in).
Soil: dry and well-drained.
Cultivation: sunny.
Propagation: from seed in spring or from cuttings in summer.
Flowering season: end of summer.
Type: annual, perennial.

Shortia

SHORTIA

Diapensiaceae

Shortia is a perennial plant for the rockery. Its leaves have a reddish tint in winter, making a pretty ground covering which could be more widely used.

Useful hints

— Divide the plants in June and replant immediately with peat.

— Alternatively take cuttings in June or July and plant in one-third peat, one-third sand and one-third leaf compost. Grow under glass in winter and plant out in spring.

— Remove dead flowers to prolong flowering.

Recommended

— *Shortia uniflora* has pale pink, waxy flowers with frilled edges which grow in spring. *S. galacifolia* has pale green leaves tinted with red around the edges. Its flowers are white and funnel-shaped.

Height: 10 cm (4 in).
Spacing and planting distance: 30 cm (12 in).
Soil: peat or ordinary earth.
Cultivation: semi-shade.
Propagation: by division in June or from cuttings in June, July.
Flowering season: spring.
Type: perennial.

Sidalcea

SIDALCEA/CHECKER-MALLOW

Malvaceae

Sidalcea malvaeflora is much like *Lavatera*. Its slightly stiff carriage and doubtful flowering ability left it somewhat in the shade until good-quality cultivars appeared on the scene. Use large splashes of it with grey-leaved plants – *Artemisia* or *Stachys*, thistles or even lilac scabious.

Useful hints

— Plant in compost and well decomposed, manure-rich soil. Mulch the soil in June with pine bark and water regularly to maintain blooms; add soluble fertilizer with every other watering.

— Divide clumps every 5 years. You could also try sowing fresh seeds which generally appear the following spring. But the colours may not be the same as that of the parents.

— Stake at the beginning of May with hazel twigs and put down some slug bait, as the young shoots tend to attract them.

Recommended

— 'Interlaken' is carmine and 'Rosy Gem' is a bright pink. There is also a white species which is extremely beautiful and flowers late.

Height: 70–120 cm (28–48 in).
Spacing and planting distance: 30–40 cm (12–16 in).
Soil: rich in humus.
Cultivation: sun or semi-shade.
Propagation: by division in spring.
Flowering season: June–September.
Type: perennial.

Silene

CAMPION/CATCHFLY

Caryophyllaceae

Carmine pink is the favourite colour of the *Silene* genus which includes annuals, biennials and even some perennial species. There are few sunny positions where they will not be happy, from window-boxes to the rockery and dry-stone walls.

Useful hints

— Sow *Silene pendula* in July and move to a nursery bed before final planting in October. It will survive the winter without mishap and flower in April. Marry with multi-flowered pink tulips and the poet's narcissus.

— Perennial catchfly should be planted in spring in pockets of light, slightly chalky earth. Divide when the blooms become sparse.

Recommended

— *Silene pendula* comes from Crete, where it tumbles from window-boxes in the springtime in decorative pink or red blocks of colour.

— *S. acaulis* is a very sought-after gem for the rock garden. Rarely taller than just over 2.5 cm (1 in), it provides a thick cushion dotted with flowers. The mountain air is best if you want to see it flower most colourfully.

— *S. schafta* is less capricious, but not everyone likes its very bright pink colour. Its flowers from July until the frosts set in.

— Bouquet silene (*S. armeria*) forms dense pink or purple clusters in summer. This is an excellent bouquet flower, if somewhat sticky to touch. Sow directly in place in April.

Height: 3–60 cm (1–24 in).
Spacing and planting distance: 20 cm (8 in).
Soil: ordinary, preferably light.
Cultivation: sunny.
Propagation: in spring, from seed or by division.
Flowering season: April–October, according to species.
Type: annual, biennial, perennial.

△ **Shortia uniflora**
Sidalcea malvaeflora ▷
▽ **Silene pendula**

Silybum

SILYBUM/MILK-THISTLE

Compositae

This is a striking plant for a wild garden. Annual or biennial, it has pretty leaves, mottled with white veins, in the shape of large, decorative rosettes. Deep violet, lightly-perfumed flowers bloom at the end of the summer, on *Silybum marianum* (Our Lady's milk thistle) at the end of long stalks. Perfect companions would be delphiniums or old roses.

Useful hints

— Sow annuals in place in spring or in autumn and biennials in May or June. Thin out as soon as the young plants are quite tall.

— Don't spoil them too much. They are quite happy in a poor soil, as long as they can grow in a dry sunny spot.

Height: 1 m (40 in).
Spacing and planting distance: 50 cm (20 in).
Soil: ordinary.
Cultivation: sunny.
Propagation: from seed, in spring or autumn for annuals and in May or June for biennials.
Flowering season: July–September.
Type: annual, biennial.

▷ *Sisyrinchium macroearpum*
▽ *Silybum marianum*

Sisyrinchium

SISYRINCHIUM

Iridaceae

With similar foliage to the iris, this plant looks very elegant in a rock garden or a border. It has numerous flowers along the stalk, like pale blue or yellow stars.

Useful hints

— Plant in well-drained soil, enriched with leaf compost or peat.

— Remove the seeds and plant in seed trays; transplant into pots the following year. Wait 3 years before the final planting.

— Do not disturb established clumps, except to divide them.

Recommended

— *Sisyrinchium angustifolium* has violet flowers from May to October. *S. bermudianum*, a hardy species, has light blue, star-shaped flowers with a yellow base in May and June. *S. striatum* produces

△ *Smilacina racemosa*

Smilacina

FALSE SOLOMON'S SEAL

Liliaceae

Smilacina racemosa is happiest in the light shade provided by shrubs. The light green, lanceolate, erect leaves protect a delicate branch of white, scented flowers.

Useful hints

— In November cut down to ground level and mulch with leaves. Don't disturb for 3 years, as the plants grow slowly but surely.

— Plant from October to March in rich, preferably slightly moist soil.

— Divide clumps every 3 or 4 years and replant immediately.

Height: 50 cm (20 in).
Spacing and planting distance: 25 cm (10 in).
Soil: rich, slightly moist.
Cultivation: semi-shade.
Propagation: by division in October.
Flowering season: May, June.
Type: perennial.

◁ *Sisyrinchium striatum*
Sisyrinchium bermudianum △

abundant creamy-yellow flowers from June onwards.

Height: 40 cm (16 in).
Spacing and planting distance: 20 cm (8 in).
Soil: ordinary, well-drained.
Cultivation: sunny.
Propagation: from seed in autumn or by division in autumn or spring.
Flowering season: summer.
Type: perennial.

Solanum

ORNAMENTAL PIMENTO/FALSE JERUSALEM-CHERRY

Solanaceae

Solanum is a sub-shrub and parent of the aubergine plant. Some are evergreen, climbing varieties and these are the most decorative, in spite of their being not very hardy.

Useful hints

— Sow seeds in February or March or take 10 cm (4 in) cuttings, in August, and plant in a mixture of sand and peat. When the cuttings have rooted, transplant to pots containing one-third compost, one-third peat and one-third sand. Don't let the soil dry out and see that the temperature does not fall below 13–14°C (57–59°F). Plant out in May.

— In colder regions grow the pimento in pots under cover in winter; in any case, protect the plants from frost.

— To obtain really fine specimens, prick out the young plants when they grow to 10 cm (4 in).

Recommended

— *Solanum capsicastrum* is usually grown in containers. It is popular for its red fruit and evergreen appearance; not very hardy, it should be treated as an annual. Misting will encourage it to bear fruit.

— *S. crispum* is practically evergreen and can grow to 2.5 m (100 in). Its blue, star-shaped flowers appear from June to September.

— *S. jasminoides* is more hardy than the preceding variety and grows even taller. Its flowers are light blue and bloom from July to October.

Height: 50 cm–2.5 m (20–100 in).
Soil: ordinary.
Cultivation: sunny, but sheltered.
Propagation: from seed, in spring or cuttings in August.
Flowering season: summer.
Type: annual, perennial.

Solanum crispum ▽

Soldanella minima △
Solidago canadensis ▷
Soldanella montana ▽

Soldanella

SOLDANELLA/ALPENCLOCK

Primulaceae

Soldanellas provide a pretty mauve carpet between stones or rocks, which echo their natural habitat as they come from mountain regions. Part of their attraction lies in their fringed petals.

Useful hints

— Plant in September or October in peat-enriched soil. Put a handful of coarse sand or gravel around each plant to help it resist rainfall; for the same reason it is a good idea to cover the plants with a 'roof' of glass or transparent plastic film over their heads during the rainy season, which they find hard to survive.

Recommended

— *Soldanella alpina*, with its lavender flowers, does well in rock gardens at the beginning of spring. *S. montana*, is a taller and more robust species, a little like the preceding one, with bell-shaped, mauve flowers.

Height: 5–15 cm (2–6 in).
Spacing and planting distance: 30 cm (12 in).
Soil: ordinary, well-drained.
Cultivation: sun or semi-shade.
Propagation: by division in June.
Flowering season: March, April.
Type: perennial.

Solidago

GOLDENROD

Compositae

This genus is really easy to grow. The goldenrod has narrow leaves and tiny flowers, which look like golden feathers. Plant on its own or in beds alongside asters and veronica. An excellent flower for bouquets, the blooms are also lovely when dried.

Useful hints

— Plant from October to March in any soil, even a chalky one.

— Watch out for mildew on the leaves; as soon as you notice a white powdery substance, treat the whole plant.

— Cut back all the flower stems in October or November.

Recommended

— *Solidago canadensis* will grow to 1.8 m (72 in) and flowers in September or October. It forms the origin of many hybrids. Some grow no taller than 50 cm

on the same stem; the foliage is narrow and pointed as in the iris. *Sparaxis tricolor* flowers in May and June and there are varieties in red, yellow, violet and even white.

Useful hints

— If you want to grow them for cut flowers, plant bulbs in November 10 cm (4 in) deep. Be sure to keep the ground around them weed-free.

— When the leaves have withered in July, dig up the bulbs and allow to dry, away from frost and humidity, until November, when they can be replanted in rich, well-drained soil.

— Be careful: *Sparaxis* is a small plant which will suffer from frost so grow in a sheltered position.

Height: 40 cm (16 in).
Spacing and planting distance: 10 cm (4 in).
Soil: rich and well-drained.
Cultivation: facing south, sheltered from the wind.
Propagation: by separating bulbs when leaves have withered.
Flowering season: May, June.
Type: bulb.

Sprekelia

SPREKELIA/AZTEC-LILY, JACOBEAN-LILY
Amaryllidaceae

Grown in either tubs or pots, each stem of *Sprekelia formosissima* bears a scarlet-red, spectacular, funnel-shaped flower. The genus is of Mexican origin, so the bulbs prefer warmth and are not very hardy in cooler climates. The few long leaves grow as the flowers finish.

Useful hints

— Plant bulbs in summer in pots or tubs of fresh earth or compost, sheltered from the cold; they will flower 3 or 4 years later.

— Do not water before May, keep soil moist thereafter until the leaves have withered.

— Repot every 3 years in September.

Height: 50 cm (20 in).
Spacing and planting distance: 15 cm (6 in).
Soil: mixture of earth, compost and sand.
Cultivation: sunny.
Propagation: by separating bulbs after foliage has withered in summer.
Flowering season: June, July.
Type: bulb.

△ *Sparaxis* hybrid
▽ *Sprekelia formosissima*

(20 in) and have a small spread, such as 'Golden Dwarf' and 'Goldenmosa'.

Height: 20–180 cm (8–72 in).
Spacing and planting distance: 75 cm (30 in).
Soil: ordinary.
Cultivation: sun or semi-shade; does well by the sea.
Propagation: by division at the beginning of winter or in spring.
Flowering season: August–September.
Type: perennial.

Sparaxis

AFRICAN HARLEQUIN FLOWER/ WANDFLOWER
Iridaceae

The harlequin flower's six petals come in many different colours. Several bloom

Stachys

LAMB'S EARS/BETONY

Labiatae

The silvery-white leaves (like a lamb's ears) look woolly. The rather ordinary violet or pale pink flowers nestle along a thick, short stalk. When they form a border with roses or perennial plants, *Stachys* look like a velvety carpet.

Useful hints

— Plant in autumn or spring.

— Cut back the leaves in November and place a layer of sand at the foot of the plant to protect it from moisture.

Recommended

— *Stachys olympica* (syn. *S. lanata*), most frequently known as lamb's ears, is an excellent ground cover for a poor, dry soil. You will find it in many catalogues under the name *S. bizantina*.

— The foliage of *S. macrantha* is greener than the preceding species and it has whorl-shaped violet flowers.

— Known under the common name, betony, *S. officinalis* sports purple flowers, which are tubular-shaped. 'Grandiflora' variety is one of the most decorative *Stachys*, with pink flowers; it grows to over 60 cm (24 in).

Height: 30–60 cm (12–24 in).
Spacing and planting distance: 20–40 cm (7–15 in).
Soil: ordinary or poor, well-drained.
Cultivation: sun or semi-shade.
Propagation: by division in September or April.
Flowering season: summer.
Type: perennial.

▽ **Stachys lanata**

Sternbergia

LILY OF THE FIELD

Amaryllidaceae

The brilliant yellow small flowers of *Sternbergia* look a little like the crocus, but they are clever enough to bloom in autumn. It's a good idea to put them with poppies, as their flowering seasons are complementary. As legend would have it, this little plant is one of the Biblical lilies which grew in the wild on Mediterranean hills.

Useful hints

— Plant in August or September, 10 cm (4 in) deep, in well-drained soil.

— The bulbs should be left undisturbed until they become swollen, then separate them and replant straight away; they will flower either the following year or in 2 years' time.

Recommended

— The golden yellow flowers of *Sternbergia clusiana* appear at the beginning of September and last until the end of October.

— The brilliant yellow flowers of *S. lutea* open at the same time.

— Unlike its two cousins, *S. fischeriana* flowers in March, and is a bright yellow colour.

Height: 10 cm (4 in).
Spacing and planting distance: 10 cm (4 in).
Soil: ordinary, well-drained.
Cultivation: full sun and semi-shade.
Propagation: by separating bulbs in summer.
Flowering season: autumn, spring for *S. fischeriana*.
Type: bulb.

Stipa

FEATHER GRASS

Gramineae

The leaves of *Stipa* are so feathery light that they look like waves when the wind blows over them. They lend a feeling of space and lightness to plants around them. But don't put them with anything which makes too much of a contrast. A carpet of *Bergenia* or *Sedum* with some clumps of feather grass on top would not work at all well. They go much better with meadow daisies, red poppies and Caucasian scabious.

Useful hints

— Plant in spring and fork the soil during the season. Mulch the soil in

Sternbergia lutea △

Stipa gigantea △
Stipa tennifolia ▷

June and July and water regularly during the first summer.

— Divide clumps in spring every 3 years when they get too thick.

Recommended

— Only size differentiates *Stipa gigantea*, over 2 m (80 in) tall, and *S. calamagrostis*, 120 cm (48 in). Their feathery quills can be used in bouquets of dried flowers, where their violet shades make a lovely complement to copper-coloured perennials.

Height: 1.2–2 m (48–80 in).
Spacing and planting distance: 50 cm (20 in).
Soil: ordinary.
Cultivation: sunny.
Propagation: by division in spring.
Flowering season: June–September.
Type: perennial.

*△ **Stokesia laevis***

Stokesia

STOKES' ASTER/STOKESIA

Compositae

The plant is often mistaken for the China aster (*Callistephus*), which has similar flowers. It is quite a rare event to catch a sight of the lovely *Stokesia laevis* in a garden, but this is a hardy border plant, none the less, with the fine lines and harmony found among wild flowers. The flowers, which are perfectly set off by its blue-green foliage, range from all shades of white to purple, with a particular predilection for mauve. One word of advice: let the clumps fill out. They are at their most spectacular after 3 or 4 years.

Useful hints

— Plant out in pots preferably in autumn, or in spring if the soil is heavy and sticky in winter.

— Mulch the earth in April and water properly during the first summer.

— Seeds will give you a variety of colours, often with very interesting results.

Height: 30–50 cm (12–20 in).
Spacing and planting distance: 40 cm (16 in).
Soil: quite rich, moist in summer.
Cultivation: sunny.
Propagation: by division in autumn, or from seeds in March.
Flowering season: July–October.
Type: perennial.

Symphytum

COMFREY

Boraginaceae

This is a most undemanding plant! It is happy in shade or sunshine and will even thrive in moist environments or undergrowth. Its flowers are shaped like little hanging bells. *Symphytum caucasicum* is quite unusual in that the flowers start out pink and then turn a beautiful blue.

Useful hints

— Plant out in October or at the beginning of spring, in ordinary garden soil.

— To set off the blooms, use hazel twigs to stake the plants.

Recommended

— *Symphytum* × *uplandicum*, often sold under the name *S. peregrinum*, is a hardy hybrid with tubular flowers of reddish blue.

— *S. orientale* is good ground cover under trees; its white flowers blossom in May or June.

— *S. rubrum* also flowers at this time, but has a deep red colour and flowers for a longer period.

Height: 60 cm (24 in).
Spacing and planting distance: 40 cm (16 in).
Soil: normal.
Cultivation: anywhere.
Flowering season: May, June.
Type: perennial.

Symphytum caucasicum ▽

△ *Tagetes erecta*

Tagetes

MARIGOLD, INDIA ROSE
Compositae

These two plants take the centre stage in a summer garden, although they can be faulted for a slightly unpleasant smell and very strident colouring, somewhere between a lemony yellow and deep orange. They are extremely easy to grow; the seeds simply flourish on their own and the young plants are very vigorous. You can buy them as young plants, which are not costly and will flower after just a few weeks. Whatever you do, don't marry them with red, pink or blue flowers, but use them in small groups surrounded by masses of greenery (rows of *Kochia*, for example, or even nasturtiums), or opt for grey colours like *Artemisia* and *Stachys*.

Useful hints
— Sow under glass at the end of March, in a protected spot in April or directly in place in May. Plant out 1 month after shoots appear or thin out the seeds, leaving 1 plant every 20 cm (8 in).

— Water until the first flowers appear, then continue to water the base of the plant without touching the blooms, as too much water will kill them.

— Remove withered flowers regularly and you will be rewarded by new ones right until the frosts arrive.

Recommended
— Among the French marigolds (*Tagetes patula*) choose scabious-like flowers such as 'Boy-O-Boy' or 'Bonanza', dwarf forms with large tubular flowers, such as 'Honeycomb' or 'Yellow Jacket' and the more compact dwarf varieties 'Lemon Drop', 'Bonita', 'Carmen' and the simple 'Legion d'Honneur' and 'Dainty Marietta'. *T. sinuata* make very dense clumps covered with smaller flowers, golden yellow in 'Gnom' and lemony yellow for 'Lulu'.

— Don't choose the very small dwarf varieties among the African Marigolds (*Tagetes erecta*), because they don't last very long and do not create good bushes. Preferred varieties are 'Jubilee' which grow up to 60 cm (24 in) and 'Sunset' 100 cm (40 in).

Height: 20–100 cm (8–40 in).
Spacing and planting distance: 20–40 cm (8–16 in).
Soil: ordinary.
Cultivation: full sun.
Propagation: from seed in spring.
Flowering season: from June to frosts.
Type: annual.

Tanacetum
See *Chrysanthemum*

Tellima

TELLIMA/ALASKA FRINGECUP
Saxifragaceae

Tellima grandiflora is grown more for its perennial foliage than its rather ordinary, lightly perfumed yellowish flowers, which bloom in May. This is an excellent ground cover which is easy to establish but is not intrusive. *Tellima grandiflora* 'Purpurea' is very similar in appearance, but boasts very attractive, bronzed green leaves. You can create a very pretty spring tableau by putting *Tellima* with jonquils or tulips.

Useful hints
— Plant in autumn or spring, in any kind of soil.

— Remove withered flowers, unless you want to collect seeds.

Height: 40 cm (16 in).
Spacing and planting distance: 40 cm (16 in).
Soil: any.
Cultivation: sun or shade.
Propagation: by division in September or March, or from seed when ripe.
Flowering season: spring.
Type: perennial.

▽ *Tagetes patula*
Tellima grandiflora ▽

▽ *Teucrium scordonia crispa*
Teucrium polium ▽

Teucrium

GERMANDER

Labiatae/Gentianaceae

These plants look quite sober until their flowers appear. They have a long lower lip and sport pastel colours. As the foliage is perennial, they can be used in small borders in place of *Santolina* in colder climates.

Useful hints

— Plant in spring, preferably in soil lightened with sand. Germander loves sunshine but will also do well in slightly shady areas.

— Cut down twice a year, first in April to shape the border and again in August to clear clumps of withered flowers.

— Plant spring bulbs between them; ornamental garlic or botanical gladioli are perfect for this.

Recommended

— The best border variety is the small oak germander (*Teucrium chamaedrys*), so called because of the shape of its leaves. There is also *T. crispum* with creamy yellow flowers and waxy leaves, a purplish colour in autumn, and *T. polium*, which has nearly white leaves. They are all perennial species and will form small, hardwooded shrubs.

Height: 20–50 cm (8–20 in).
Spacing and planting distance: 30 cm (12 in).
Soil: ordinary, well-drained.
Cultivation: sunny.
Propagation: from cuttings at the end of summer.
Flowering season: June–October.
Type: perennial.

▽ *Thermopsis montana*

Thalictrum

MEADOW-RUE

Ranunculaceae

Meadow-rue is grown for its lovely, delicate flowers and slightly blue-grey foliage. The flowers grow as small pink, yellow or mauve tufts at the end of long slender stalks, but unfortunately they are short-lived.

Useful hints

— Plant out in March or April in a humus-rich soil.

— Sow seeds in boxes in spring in a compost made up of equal parts of soil, sand and peat, and plant out the following spring.

— Stake before plants reach their maximum height.

— In March topdress with a layer of peat and well-rotted manure.

Recommended

— *Thalictrum adiantifolium*, 1.2 m (48 in) tall, is grown for its silver foliage, as the greenish flowers which appear in July are not very impressive.

— *T. aquilegifolium* has pretty silver leaves and mauve flowers which come out in July or August.

— *T. dipterocarpum*, which originates from China, also has mauve flowers, but with prominent bright yellow anthers, in July and August. The rare 'Album' variety is white, as its name suggests.

— *T. kiusianum* comes from Japan and has silver-green foliage. Its light violet flowers blossom in May.

— *T. speciosissimum* bears blue-grey leaves and its bright yellow flowers appear on 20 cm (8 in) long spikes, in July or August.

Height: 1–1.5 m (40–60 in).
Spacing and planting distance: 50 cm (20 in).
Soil: normal, preferably rich in humus.
Cultivation: sun or semi-shade.
Propagation: by division in March or April.
Flowering season: summer.
Type: perennial.

Thermopsis

THERMOPSIS

Leguminosae (family unconfirmed)

Stout and tough-rooted, *Thermopsis* looks a little like a lupin with a somewhat

△ *Thalictrum aquilegifolium*

△ *Thalictrum dipterocarpum*

glaucous foliage. Although easy to grow, its roots spread like wildfire.

Useful hints

— Plant in autumn or at the beginning of spring in any well-drained soil.

— Cut withered flowers down to 5 cm (2 in) from the ground and you will get a second show.

— It is easy to divide clumps and replant, but the plant only really starts to thrive after 2 or 3 years.

Recommended

— *Thermopsis lanceolata* has pretty light yellow flowers along its stalk. *T. montana* forms lovely yellow clumps, but its roots need to be carefully controlled.

Height: 80 cm (32 in).
Spacing and planting distance: 50–100 cm (20–40 in) for *T. montana*; 45 cm (18 in) for *T. lanceolata*.
Soil: well-drained.
Cultivation: sunny.
Propagation: by division in March or April.
Flowering season: May–June.
Type: perennial.

287

Thunbergia

THUNBERGIA/CLOCKVINE

Acanthaceae

Climbing *Thunbergia* is an annual, vigorous plant, which will be happy only in a sheltered garden with a mild climate. Flowers grow from a purple tube, expanding into five bright yellow petals, which have a dark, almost black middle. It can grow up to 3 metres (9 ft) which makes it ideal for pergolas, where it will climb without needing any support.

Useful hints

— Sow seeds in March in a fairly warm location (16–18°C) (61–64°F). Harden off before final planting in mid May.

— Water generously and regularly during the growing period with a liquid fertilizer, twice monthly from June to August.

Recommended

— *Thunbergia alata* grows to a medium height, roughly 2 m (6 ft). *T. grandiflora* can grow as tall as 7 m (21 ft) and over and bears mauve flowers 6 cm (3 in) across.

Height: 2–7 m (6–21 ft).
Spacing and planting distance: 50 cm (20 in).
Soil: normal.
Cultivation: sunny, sheltered.
Propagation: from seeds in pots, in March.
Flowering season: June–September.
Type: annual.

Thymus

THYME

Labiatae

This is a native of sun-drenched hills and can look very attractive in a rockery or paving area. Cut back regularly and then allow it to flower to best appreciate its scent and small flowers.

Useful hints

— Plant in autumn or spring in well-drained soil.

— Grow in pots 20 cm (8 in) in diameter and water once a week. Cut back regularly to keep it dense.

— For the rockery, plant in spring in a well-drained pocket of earth.

Recommended

— *Thymus cilicicus* forms a compact clump with pink tubular flowers.

— *T.* × *citriodorus* (lemon-scented thyme) has pale lilac flowers with a light, lemony smell.

— *T. hirsutus doerfleri* is a mat-forming plant with grey-green leaves and lilac flowers.

— *T. membranaceus* is the most fragrant species with pale lilac tubular flowers with whitish bracts in July.

— The grey-green leaves of *T. serpyllum* (wild thyme) are a perfect complement to its pink flowers.

Height: 15 cm (6 in).
Spacing and planting distance: 30 cm (12 in).
Soil: ordinary, well-drained.
Cultivation: sunny.
Propagation: by division in March or in August/September.
Flowering season: summer.
Type: perennial.

△ *Thunbergia alata*

Tiarella

FOAM FLOWER

Saxifragaceae

An excellent ground cover with perennial foliage, *Tiarella* is not a difficult plant to grow. The large leaves provide rapid ground cover, even under trees and shrubs. The plant bears feathery white flowers which grow straight and erect.

Useful hints

— Plant in spring or in November with a generous handful of peat around the roots.

— Don't let the soil dry out if you want to achieve a dense, very green ground cover.

Recommended

— *Tiarella cordifolia* is an extremely good ground cover with white or pink flowers on 15 cm (6 in) high stalks, which contrast well with its bright or light green foliage.

— *T. wherryi* is a more compact species with smaller leaves which turn russet brown in autumn. Its flowers appear in abundance from June to September.

— *T. trifoliata* has foliage like the ivy and it produces many pinkish-white flowers throughout the summer.

Height: 15–50 cm (6–20 in).
Spacing and planting distance: 30 cm (12 in).
Soil: all, except for dry.
Cultivation: shade or semi-shade.
Propagation: by division in October or April.
Flowering season: summer.
Type: perennial.

△ *Tiarella wherryi*
▽ *Thymus serpyllum*

Useful hints

— Plant corms in April, about 10 cm (4 in) deep, in a rich soil.

— Do not allow them to dry out but they appreciate gentle warmth.

— Remove corms before the frosts set in and leave to dry in a heated room. Keep in well-dried sand or peat boxes for the winter.

— Each year you can replant cormlets and they will flower 2 years later.

— Corms can be left in the soil for the winter in well-protected borders. Remove them and divide them up every 2 or 3 years, when the leaves are withered.

Height: 50 cm (20 in).
Spacing and planting distance: 10 cm (4 in).
Soil: normal, well-drained.
Cultivation: sunny.
Propagation: by separating corms in spring.
Flowering season: August, September.
Type: corm.

Tigridia

TIGER FLOWER

Iridaceae

Each shimmering flower lasts only a day! Our only consolation is that each stalk bears six or seven flowers. The leaves are puckered and the flowers have six petals, three large ones separated by three tiny, spotted ones. Some gardeners find it resembles the iris, others believe it to be like the tulip. *Tigridia pavonia* has numerous, brightly coloured varieties, except for blue. It flowers between July and September.

Tolmiea

TOLMIEA/PIGGY-BACK PLANT

Saxifragaceae

Because of its peculiar habit of producing young plants directly on the perennial leaves, it has been given a variety of nicknames, such as 'thousand mothers', 'youth-on-age' or 'piggy-back plant'. The tubular flowers appear in June on long, slender stalks. *Tolmiea menziesii* produces downy leaves and tiny white flowers. An excellent ground cover, this plant can also be grown indoors, but in cool rooms only.

Useful hints

— In autumn or March remove only leaves which have smaller, well-formed plants on them and plant in pots. Water regularly from March and April onwards.

— You can plant leaves containing small, new plants directly in a nursery bed and as soon as they have taken root transfer them to their permanent spot.

Height: 15 cm (6 in).
Spacing and planting distance: 40 cm (16 in).
Soil: rich in humus, well-drained.
Cultivation: sun or semi-shade.
Propagation: from leaves with plantlets in spring or autumn.
Flowering season: June.
Type: perennial.

289

△ *Torenia fournieri*

Torenia

TORENIA

Scrophulariaceae

This Asiatic plant is grown as an annual in our climate. The long, serrated foliage is covered in summer with a profusion of flowers. *Torenia fournieri* (wishbone flower) will simply charm you with its tubular, violet, yellow-speckled flowers. The 'Alba' variety, naturally, has white flowers.

Useful hints

— Sow seeds in March at a temperature of 18°C (64°F) with just a very light covering of soil. Transplant young plants under glass before final positioning in May at the earliest.

— Pinch the top of stalks 8 to 10 cm (3–4 in) tall, to encourage branching growth.

— Hazel twigs make good supports for the plant.

Height: 30 cm (12 in).
Spacing and planting distance: 15 cm (6 in).
Soil: moist.
Cultivation: semi-shade and protected.
Propagation: from seed in spring, in the warm.
Flowering season: all summer.
Type: annual.

Tradescantia

POVERTY/VIRGINIA SPIDERWORT

Commelinaceae

The three-petalled flowers are accompanied by long, pointed, sad-looking foliage. The flowers only last for a day but are replaced rapidly. Poverty is well known as a houseplant, but doesn't belong to the same species that you will find in the garden. These are hardy hybrids, such as *Tradescantia × andersoniana* (also known as *T. virginiana*) with pink, white, violet or red flowers.

Useful hints

— Sow in March and transplant when the plants are large enough to handle. Plant out in October.

— Don't let soil dry out in summer.

— Cut back foliage to ground level in November.

Height: 50 cm (20 in).
Spacing and planting distance: 40 cm (16 in).
Soil: normal, drained, moist.
Cultivation: sun or semi-shade.
Propagation: by division in April.
Flowering season: June–September.
Type: perennial.

▽ *Tradescantia × andersoniana*

Tricyrtis

TRICYRTIS/TOAD-LILY

Liliaceae (family unconfirmed)

These unusual plants, which come from Holland, have inhabited our gardens for only a few years. You can guarantee that their spectacular, orchid-like blooms will prompt much admiration from visitors to your garden. Groups of stalks grow from one stem and are topped in the autumn by pretty speckled flowers. Plant these Japanese beauties next to *Sedum spectabile*, hostas and ferns to cheer up a shady corner.

Useful hints

— Plant in spring in a humus-rich soil, acidified if necessary with the addition of light peat. Don't put them in a spot that is too windy, as their stalks are liable to collapse at the first sign of a storm.

— Put down slug pellets in spring. Divide up clumps after a period of 3 years, either in autumn or the beginning of spring.

Recommended

— *Tricyrtis hirta*, 75 cm (30 in) tall, has white flowers with a smattering of brown and spreads very well, while *T. macroposa* can grow over 90 cm (36 in) and its creamy white and mauve flowers make it the more decorative of the two.

Height: 40–90 cm (16–36 in).
Spacing and planting distance: 30 cm (12 in).
Soil: rich in humus and moist.
Cultivation: semi-shade.
Propagation: by division in autumn or spring.
Flowering season: August–October.
Type: perennial.

Trillium

TRILLIUM

Trilliaceae

The foliage, petals and sepals of *Trillium* all come in groups of three and the feature is common to all varieties. They are most effective when grown in large clumps in a rockery or border. The marbled, dark-green and silvery leaves are punctuated with pointed, twisted, stemless flowers.

Useful hints

— Plant 10 cm (4 in) deep in groups in a wooded location during August.

— Dig up rhizomes and divide them as

soon as leaves start to wither, from July through to March. Replant straight-away in a well-drained soil, without letting them dry out.

— Don't divide up the clumps too often, as the plant takes a long time to establish itself.

— You can also grow them from seeds, but they take up to 18 months to germin-ate and it will be several years before you see any flowers.

Recommended

— *Trillium erectum* has purple flowers with groups of three petals reflexed at the tips.

— *T. grandiflorum* is one of the prettiest varieties, sporting white flowers which become flushed with rose-pink, nestling in a group of three leaves.

— The flowers of *T. ovatum* also change colour, but from a pale to a fiery deep pink.

— The leaves of *T. sessile* are marbled grey and green and the stemless flowers appear to be screwed into its cluster of three leaves.

— *T. undulatum* has white flowers with a deep red zone at the base. The petals are more spread out than in other varieties.

Height: 30 cm (12 in).
Spacing and planting distance: 30 cm (12 in).
Soil: moist with plenty of humus.
Cultivation: semi-shade or shade.
Propagation: by division when leaves are dry.
Flowering season: April–June.
Type: perennial.

▽ *Tricyrtis hira*

Trollius

GLOBE FLOWER

Ranunculaceae

The common feature of *Trollius* is its globe-shaped flower, ranging from yel-low to orange. The bud is slow to open, but they are easy plants to grow pro-vided the roots are kept moist, so it's a good idea to plant them at the margins of streams and ponds.

Useful hints

— Plant preferably in the sun or semi-shade in October or spring.

— Cut back flower stems after flower-ing to achieve a second show.

— Water regularly during high sum-mer, so that the leaves do not dry out prematurely.

Recommended

— *Trollius cultorum*, with double flowers, and *T. europaeus*, with single ones, flower a lemony yellow, orange or golden colour in May or June. *T. chinensis* has orange flowers which appear in June or July.

Height: 30 cm (12 in).
Spacing and planting distance: 40 cm (16 in).
Soil: moist.
Cultivation: sun or semi-shade.
Propagation: by division in autumn or early spring.
Flowering season: May–July.
Type: perennial.

△ *Trillium ovatum*
▽ *Trillium sessile*

▽ *Trollius europaeus* '**Canary Bird**'

Tropaeolum

NASTURTIUM

Tropaeolaceae

Both the annual and perennial varieties of nasturtium can climb up to 3 m (9 ft). They enliven pergolas and embankments with their warm red, yellow and orange hues, but some people find their scent unpleasant.

Useful hints

— Sow annuals direct in April. Thin out as soon as the plants appear overcrowded, so that only the most vigorous are left.

— The bulbs of perennial species can be planted in spring but it's preferable to buy them already started in pots.

— Nasturtiums will flower best if the soil is not too rich; fertilizers will encourage leaves to the detriment of flowers.

Recommended

— **Annuals**: *Tropaeolum majus* is used as a climbing and trailing plant, and has red, yellow or orange flowers. Some hybrids have variegated leaves, while others are dwarves (30 cm–2.5 m) (12–100 in).

— *T. peregrinum* (Canary creeper) can grow up to 4 m (12 ft) in a year and has blue-green leaves and irregular, yellow flowers from July to October. It grows in shade but prefers sun.

— **Perennials**: *T. polyphyllum* has a good spread (1.5 m for 15 cm height) (60 in for 6 in). With its silver-green leaves and yellow flowers which appear in June or July, it's a good species for trailing over a stone wall.

— Climbing *T. speciosum* easily reaches 3 m (9 ft) and dies down in winter. From July to September it produces scarlet flowers and is at home in a moist soil.

— *T. tuberosum* grows up to 3 m (9 ft) with a spread of 1 m (3 ft). Its yellow and red flowers appear from June to October, but it is often cut down by frost and will need protecting in winter.

Height: 30 cm–4 m (1–12 ft).
Spacing and planting distance: 30 cm–1 m (1–3ft).
Soil: poor, no fertilizer.
Cultivation: sunny.
Propagation: from seed or by division in spring.
Flowering season: summer.
Type: annual, perennial.

△ ***Tropaeolum speciosum***
▽ ***Tropaeolum majus***

△ *Tropaeolum tuberosum*
◁ *Tropaeolum polyphyllum*
Tropaeolum tricolorum ▷
▽ *Tropaeolum minus*

Tulipa

TULIP

Liliaceae

Everyone knows the tulip, or at least thinks they do, yet it's surprising just how small a number of the numerous varieties are grown in gardens. I have classified them in order of flowering time, leaving aside botanical types which are rarely used in beds and tend to appear in rockeries or window-boxes. Most tulips last about three weeks, so it's a good idea to put them with biennials, such as forget-me-not or stock, so that you are not confronted with an empty space. Plant the biennials first and then fill in the gaps with tulips.

Useful hints

— Plant from September through to December in soil twice as deep as their diameter: any well-dug soil will do. Never add fresh compost or manure as the bulbs could well rot on contact. Don't worry if leaves appear as early as February, as they will withstand frosts, but put down slug pellets if slugs start to look hungry!

— After flowering, dead-head them so as not to exhaust the bulbs. Water once a week, adding a soluble fertilizer so that new bulbs will increase in size. Cut back the leaves when they have almost died. Allow bulbs to mature in a dry and dark spot until planting.

Recommended

— **Kaufmanniana hybrid** tulips will flower almost at ground level in March and have brilliant colours. They are suitable for the rockery, border or window-box.

— 'Heart's Delight', pale pink with red on the outside, has leaves marbled with violet; 'Johann Strauss' is a pure white with external red and yellow; 'Stresa' is a brilliant yellow with red interior, marbled leaves and is one of the finest; 'The First' is a very early variety, ivory on a yellow base with a carmine-washed exterior, a very natural-looking flower despite its large size.

— **Fosteriana hybrids** do tend to stand out because of their extremely large flowers. They are usually grown for one year only, as their powerful colouring can be somewhat overpowering. Rather than opting for perennials like bright-red 'Madame Lefeber', or pure yellow 'Candela' or 'Golden Emperor', choose lighter colours, such as white 'Purissima' or 'Sweetheart', a lemon yellow with ivory edges.

— **Single early** tulips grow in March or April to a height of 40 cm (16 in). The finest are: 'Bellona', pure yellow, often fragrant; 'General de Wet', orange and also fragrant; 'Pink Beauty', deep pink and white'; 'Van der Neer', a purplish violet colour which looks magnificent with pale yellow stock; 'White Virgin', a pure white. Also appearing at this time are the multi-flowered tulips, producing several flowers per bulb. They look delightful in window-boxes where they outlast other tulips: choose 'Georgette', a yellow bordered with red, or 'Orange Bouquet', a scarlet-orange.

— **Double early** tulips are the amateur's favourite for an even display, as they all grow to the same height (an average of 30 cm (12 in); among them you will find 'William of Orange', an orange variety; 'Mr Van der Hoef', golden yellow; 'Peach Blossom', pink and white with a delicate fragrance; 'Triumphator', deep pink. They are often sold in a mixture of colours as Murillo tulips.

— **Mendel** tulips are a kind of cross between simple early tulips and the Darwin variety. They grow in April on 40 to 50 cm (16–20 in) long stalks. 'Apricot Beauty' is one of the best with its salmon-pink colour and strong fragrance. 'Pink Trophy', a bright pink, and 'Bestseller', a coppery red, are two excellent varieties.

— **Greigii** hybrids are the last of the large-flowered dwarf species. Their brown marbled foliage screens warm-coloured flowers. Instead of the very popular 'Red Hat', a brilliant red, try 'Easter Surprise', a bright yellow edged with orange; 'Yellow Dawn', yellow with a pink exterior, or even 'Donna Bella', a creamy-white with red exterior.

— **Triumph** tulips have sturdy stems, making excellent flowers for bouquets. There are hundreds of varieties including: 'Spring Charm', white edged with deep pink; 'Peerless Pink', smooth pink; 'Pax', pure white with a deep pink base; 'Merry Widow', red edged with white; 'Orange Wonder', brilliant scarlet and 'Dutch Princess', an apricot tinged with mahogany.

— **Darwin** tulips are the best-known. Their often long stems, 70 cm (28 in), bear enormous brightly-coloured corollas from their *fosteriana* heritage. Go for something unusual. Instead of the variety 'Apeldoorn', a bright red, and 'Golden Apeldoorn', a hard yellow, opt for 'Big Chief', an antique rose tinged with a hint of orange; 'Elizabeth Arden',

△ *Tulipa* **'Red Riding Hood'**
▽ *Tulipa* **'Electra'**

△ *Tulipa* 'General de Wet'
Tulipa 'Attila' ▷
▽ *Tulipa* Darwin
Tulipa 'Texas Flame' ▽

◁ *Tulipa clusiana*
Tulipa 'West Point' ▷
▽ *Tulipa* 'Eros'

△ *Tulipa* 'Groenland'
◁ *Tulipa* Triomphe
▽ *Tulipa* Fosteriana

▽ *Tulipa* Greigii

▽ *Tulipa* 'Flaming Parrot'
Tulipa Kaufmanniana ▽

a salmon-pink, or even 'Vivex', carmine-pink bordered with yellow and orange.

— **Single late** tulips, also known as Cottage tulips, beat all height records, up to 80 cm (32 in)! Their height lends them elegance and they add an old-fashioned charm to the garden. Match them with peonies and pale stock. My favourites include: 'Aristocrat', a pinkish lilac; 'Dillenburg', deep orange, one of the later varieties; 'Queen of Night', a deep brown; 'Temple of Beauty', light salmon-pink shaded with lilac; 'Queen of Bartigons', light salmon-pink with white markings on the base, or even 'Maya', yellow with strangely fringed petals.

— **Lily-flowered** varieties also flower from April to May. Their very slender petals give them an extremely elegant look. 'China Pink', a pure pink; 'Queen of Sheba', red with orange edges; 'Red Shine', a deep red; 'West Point', acidulous yellow and the remarkable 'White Triumphator', a sparkling white, are among my choices. Put them together with euphorbia and Corsican hellebore for a splendid flowerbed.

— **Parrot** tulips are always very successful, as their irregularly fringed edges to the large petals are quite stunning. 'Black Parrot', a black purple; 'Texas Gold', yellow, and 'White Parrot', a pure white, are the most popular varieties.

— Finally, there are the **double late** tulips, which flower with azaleas and peonies, thereby creating flowerbeds of true beauty. The loveliest include 'Angelique', a porcelain pink, 'Mount Tacoma', sporting large white corollas, and 'Rosalia', a pink and slightly earlier variety.

— There are numerous varieties of **botanical** tulips, which root easily and make natural clumps, for example: *Tulipa acuminata* (also known as *T. cornuta*) which has straight petals (it gave birth to the lily-flowered tulip); *T. clusiana*, pure white and crimson, nicknamed 'straight tulip' (also known as lady tulip); *T. marjoletti*, yellow with red on the exterior, very elegant and flowering only in May; the latest of all, *T. sprengeri*, an expensive but magnificent variety having retained the natural grace of a wild flower – its powerful red colour is the perfect complement for white flowers like the musky chervil or rockets; *T. sylvestris*, a yellow and almost round flower which spreads quickly in undergrowth; *T. tarda* blooms in May and bears white star-shaped flowers with a yellow eye.

Height: 15–80 cm (6–32 in).
Spacing and planting distance: 15 cm (6 in).
Soil: ordinary, preferably deep.
Cultivation: at least 6 hours of sun per day.
Propagation: by separating new bulbs when leaves have withered.
Flowering season: February–June.
Type: bulb.

Tunica/Petrorhagia

TUNICA/TUNICFLOWER
Saxifragaceae (family unconfirmed)

If you are desperately looking for a small plant to put in your rose beds, this is it! *Tunica saxifraga* will create a magnificent carpet in very few years; it is covered in hundreds of minute flowers which are grouped into rose shapes. It has its origins in mountain paths and will do best in an average rather than rich soil. Recommended for the rockery or for stone walls. Its new name is *Petrohagia*.

Useful hints

— Plant in spring, preferably in specially adapted pots, as the young plants do not often survive wet winters in small pots.

— At the beginning of each spring, cut clumps down to ground level to make them more dense and add a few handfuls of sandy mixture so that new stalks will root.

— Propagate by cuttings in summer or just from seeds which will do well in spring.

Height: 15–20 cm (6–8 in).
Spacing and planting distance: 20 cm (8 in).
Soil: ordinary, pebbly.

▽ *Tunica saxifraga*

△ *Typha latifolia*

Cultivation: sunny.
Propagation: from cuttings in summer or by division, or from seed in spring.
Flowering season: summer.
Type: perennial.

Typha

REEDMACE, CAT'S TAIL/CAT TAIL
Typhaceae

Like the bulrush, these dark-looking aquatics are found near ponds and spread wildly on the edges of marshy copses, where they harbour migrating wild birds. Excellent for a small garden pool, but be careful they do not invade too much. Like many aquatic or semi-aquatic plants, once they are planted they are extremely difficult to control.

Useful hints

— Plant in spring or autumn in the mud-bank bordering pond or pool.

— Every 3 years cut stalks back where they are spreading beyond the limit you have marked out.

— They will make lovely, long-lasting dried bouquets.

Recommended

— The most common, *Typha angustifolia*, easily measures 1.5 m tall (48 in), whereas *Typha minima*, a smaller variety, grows no taller than 50 cm (20 in).

Height: 50 cm–1.5 m (20–48 in).
Spacing and planting distance: 30 cm (12 in).
Soil: ordinary, moist.
Cultivation: any.
Propagation: by division in spring.
Type: perennial.

Veratrum

VERATRUM/AMERICAN FALSE HELLEBORE
Liliaceae

This plant has poisonous, black rhizomes and pleated foliage; numerous, tiny, star-shaped flowers are borne at the end of erect stems.

Useful hints

— Divide rhizomes and replant in spring or autumn.

— Alternatively, sow ripe seeds at the beginning of autumn under glass. Prick out seedlings when large enough to handle and grow on in a nursery bed before planting in permanent sites in spring.

— Don't let the soil dry out; it is important to water in spring and summer.

— Cut back stalks in October or November and in spring mulch with peat.

— Don't worry if you don't see flowers for some time, as it can be 3 or 4 years before they appear.

Recommended

— *Veratrum nigrum* bears purple flowers in August on long, narrow stems. *V. viride* will grow up to 2 m (6 ft); sprays of yellow-green flowers open in July on slender branches.

Height: 1–2 m (3–6 ft).
Spacing and planting distance: 40–60 cm (16–24 in).
Soil: light, normal.
Cultivation: semi-shade.
Propagation: from seed or by dividing rhizomes.
Flowering season: summer.
Type: perennial.

△ *Veratrum album*
◁ *Veratrum viride*
▽ *Verbascum* **'Gainsborough'**

Verbascum

MULLEIN
Scrophulariaceae

You will be surprised by the graceful appearance of the mullein when it spreads its large, oval, silvered leaves atop your compost heap or in the corners of your flowerbeds. They grow at an amazing rate, both tall and wide. Stems are peppered with lemony yellow flowers, which look tiny in comparison with this great giant of a plant. It is a real godsend for those awkward slopes, especially when planted alongside stone-crop and valerian.

△ **Verbascum phoenicum**
▽ **Verbascum bombyciferum 'Polar Bear'**

Useful hints

— Plant in any soil with a favourable situation, preferably in spring if the soil is heavy, so that plants will not suffer in a damp winter.

Recommended

— *Verbascum bombyciferum*, a biennial, looks proud in flowerbeds with its clusters of yellow flowers, borne like spears. *V. chaixii*, a hardy variety, has yellow flowers with a mauve eye, and looks equally good. *V. thapsus*, commonly known as 'White Bubble', is a biennial and has yellow flowers from June to August.

Height: 1.5 m (50 in).
Spacing and planting distance: 50 cm (20 in).
Soil: ordinary.
Cultivation: sunny.
Propagation: from seed in April.
Flowering season: June–September.
Type: hardy and biennial.

Verbena

VERBENA

Verbenaceae

You may well be amazed by the sight of a rich carpet of verbena in a cottage garden in summer. Most have no fragrance, unlike the lemon-scented verbena, which is not a hardy species, nor the medical properties of the true verbena, which is in fact an unsightly weed. But some varieties will make an attractive display.

Useful hints

— Buy them as young plants as they are quite difficult to grow from seeds. Plant in May in rich soil. Water regularly and add liquid fertilizer once a month. Remove dead flowers in July, so that plants are not exhausted and will form new blooms.

— Cover the base of hardy varieties with pine bark in November and cover with glass to protect from rain.

Recommended

— Among annuals: everyone has a favourite. 'Sparkles' has a decorative light centre, whilst pure red 'Tropic' is a little taller and forms magnificent beds. *Verbena venosa* is often grown as an annual; its best colour is mauve and it will grow to 40 cm (16 in).

— Hardy varieties include: *V. hastata* which can grow to 1 m (40 in) and is decked with candelabras of small purple flowers. *V. bonariensis* will survive a mild winter. It will cheerfully grow over 1 m

△ **Verbena venosa**
▽ **Verbena hybrid**

high (40 in) and bears rose-lavender flowers for most of the summer.

Height: 15 cm–1.5 m (6–60 in).
Spacing and planting distance: 20–40 cm (8–16 in).
Soil: rich and well drained.
Cultivation: sunny.
Propagation: from seed planted in spring (but difficult).
Flowering season: from June to the arrival of frosts.
Type: annual and hardy.

Veronica

SPEEDWELL

Scrophulariaceae

In moist soil, speedwell quickly grows into beautiful clumps with blue spikes. The blues vary from the very pale sky blue of *Veronica gentianoides* to the deep indigo blue of certain *V. longifolia*. Put them together with mauve phlox, bergamot, China asters or scabious for a rich display.

Useful hints

— Plant in October or spring, into soil improved with peat or leaf-mould. If the speedwell's leaves wilt on hot afternoons, it is a sign that the earth is not cool enough and you should mulch the soil with peat and soak the plants before transplanting them during the following season.

— Divide the clumps once they have begun to produce fewer flowers. If white marks appear, vine-mildew is probably to blame and should be treated with a solution of triforine.

Recommended

— *Veronica gentianoides* offers a smooth and thick foliage with fairly bright blue-violet spears. It has been crossed with *V. spicata* to produce the deep pink 'Barcarolle'. Using these varieties combined with auricula, you can create some very subtle borders.

— *V. incana* is elegant with its silver leaves and pale blue erect flowers.

— *V. longifolia* has very dark blue flowers and quickly forms into beautiful clumps. It looks at its best beside some of the old roses such as 'Cornelia' or 'Felicia'.

— *V. orientalis* is most suited to sunny rockeries. Its flowers are pink or blue.

— The commonest type of speedwell is *V. spicata*, which exists in several varieties: 'Alba', pure white; 'Rosea', pink; 'Erika' and 'Heidekind', deep pink; 'Exaltata', sky blue.

— *V. virginica* grows vigorously and can attain a height of approximately 2 m (6 ft). Its flower spears, however, are relatively short, being only 25 cm (10 in) long. There are blue, light pink and white varieties.

Height: 20–180 cm (8–72 in).
Spacing and planting distance: 20–40 cm (8–16 in).
Soil: rich and humid.
Cultivation: sun or semi-shade.
Propagation: by division in spring.
Flowering season: May–September.
Type: perennial.

Veronica longifolia △
△ *Veronica gentianoides*
◁ *Veronica incana*
Veronica orientalis ▽

△ *Vinca minor*

Vinca

PERIWINKLE

Apocynaceae

This is an ideal plant for ground cover in the most difficult conditions, whether for a sunny bank or a dry meadow, or anywhere where trees or hedges are consuming all available moisture. Thanks to periwinkles, however, it is possible to transform these tricky places into carpets of flowers. The greater periwinkle, *Vinca major*, readily grows between the stones of old buildings, apparently quite happily sustaining itself on the mortar in the walls. If you are growing periwinkles in good soil, try planting a few squill, tulip or narcissus bulbs among them, and you will have some pleasant surprises as the year progresses.

Useful hints

— Plant young stems with roots 15 cm (6 in) long in well-dug soil.

— For ground cover thick enough to walk on, choose the blue- or white-flowered lesser periwinkle, *Vinca minor*, 15 cm (6 in) high.

— *V. rosea* is not very hardy and requires a sheltered spot.

Height: 15–40 cm (6–16 in).
Spacing and planting distance: 15 cm (6 in).
Soil: ordinary.
Cultivation: any aspect.
Propagation: by division in spring.
Flowering season: March–January.
Type: perennial.

Viola

PANSY, VIOLET

Violaceae

Once popular, the pansy and violet seem to have fallen from favour, which is strange as they are very easy to grow. Once they are planted they will spread and flower tirelessly for months without needing any further attention. Do as gardeners used to and put them in your borders and window-boxes to decorate your windows in spring, you won't regret it!

Useful hints

— Sow pansies and violets between mid July and mid August, so that they will flower the following spring.

— If you plant them in a humus-rich soil, in a good situation, they will behave like perennials and last for several years. But do note that hybrid pansies with large flowers (*Viola wittrockiana*) are at the prettiest in their first year and will then tend to wither, especially if allowed to go to seed.

△ *Viola* **hybrid**
▽ *Viola papilionacea* **'Immaculata'**

△ *Viola* × *wittrockiana* **'Jacknapes'**

Recommended

— Hybrid pansies are far too numerous to be listed here, but I would note 'Trimardeau', a very hardy, and always pretty, old variety with average flowers. There are also the many pansies from Switzerland.

— Horned violets (*Viola cornuta*) include the well-loved, small-flowered varieties, like 'Prince Henry', dark violet with a small yellow eye, and 'Bambini', a pretty hybrid.

— Lovers of the violet will certainly appreciate 'Purpurea', *Viola labradorica*, a 'doggy' shape, violet with purple leaves, and the pretty *V. papilionacea* 'Immaculata', white and flowering like meadow violets; *V. odorata* flowers later in May and June.

Height: 10–20 cm (4–8 in).
Spacing and planting distance: 15 cm (6 in).
Soil: rich in humus.
Cultivation: sunny.
Propagation: from seed in July, August, by division in spring.
Flowering season: February–October.
Type: annual and perennial.

△ *Zantedeschia elliottiana*
▽ *Zantedeschia rehmannii*

Viscaria alpina

See *Lychnis alpina*

Vittadenia triloba

See *Erigeron karvinskianus*

Zantedeschia

ARUM LILY/CALLA LILY

Araceae (family unconfirmed)

About twenty years ago the arum lily was the queen of orangery plants, but it seems to have fallen out of favour for this use. It has reappeared, however, to decorate the margins of pools or lend emphasis to a border in a fresh and slightly wild garden. The white variety, *Zantedeschia aethiopica*, is the most popular, no doubt deservedly so, as this is the most elegant variety and marries well with Solomon's seal and royal lilies, not to mention ground plants like periwinkle or *Cerastium*. Use them to create a bed which will give you a very fine show.

Useful hints

— Plant in spring or in September in good garden soil enriched with compost, say one spadeful for every plant.

— Plant deeply in a sunny position, but avoid too much sun.

— If you decide to grow them in pots, water each evening during the summer.

Recommended

— You will be delighted by the yellow variety, *Zantedeschia elliottiana*, and a pink one, *Z. rehmannii*, which has white-flecked leaves.

Height: 1 m (40 in).
Spacing and planting distance: 30 cm (12 in).
Soil: rich and moist.
Cultivation: semi-shade.
Propagation: by division in April.
Flowering season: April–July.
Type: bulb.

Zauschneria

CALIFORNIAN FUCHSIA

Onagraceae

Zauschneria californica, with its unpronounceable name, is not exactly a hardy plant. It is one of the last in our alphabetical list, and is one of the last in the garden to flower. It waits until September before delighting us with the quite spectacular red of its tubular flowers. The sprays appear on grey-green foliage and, even when dried, still prompt exclamations of admiration. Grow them in sunny window-boxes.

Useful hints

— Plant in spring in a very light mixture (half leaf compost, half sand). Water regularly until they come into flower so that the leaves do not dry out prematurely.

— Pinch out stalk ends in summer and place in a sheltered spot.

— Complement them with grey-leaved plants, particularly *Artemisia* or *Chrysanthemum haradjanii*.

Height: 50 cm (20 in).
Spacing and planting distance: 30 cm (12 in).
Soil: light.
Cultivation: sunny.
Propagation: from cuttings at the beginning of summer.
Flowering season: September, October.
Type: perennial.

△ *Zinnia elegans*
◁ *Zauschneria californica*

Zinnia

ZINNIA

Compositae

It is no longer fashionable to deck out the July garden with *Zinnia elegans*, although it hardly deserves a reputation for being difficult to grow. Its huge flowers with finely arrayed petals and warm colours, ranging from reds, yellows and an unusual cream, make the Zinnia appeal to all gardeners. It flowers from July until frosts set in. It is a delightful cut flower and smells of beeswax.

Useful hints

— Sow in April in uncovered seed trays.

— Plant out in beds in a sunny position. Any good garden soil will do, so long as it is well-drained.

— Dead-head plants regularly to obtain further blooms.

Recommended

— Large varieties include 'Californian Giant' with amazingly tall flowers. The 'Giant Double Mixed' is more delicate in appearance, but sadly not very common. Well worth growing for cut flowers, even if you have to take a lot of care over staking them.

Height: 60–90 cm (24–36 in).
Spacing and planting distance: 20 cm (8 in).
Soil: ordinary, well-drained.
Cultivation: sunny.
Propagation: from seed in April.
Flowering season: July–October.
Type: annual, perennial.

303

THE ESSENTIALS
from
ABELIA to YUCCA

Not long ago, purists were claiming that only hardy perennials and annuals belonged in beds and borders.

I, on the other hand, would go as far as to state that shrubs play an essential part in creating a satisfying overall effect.

Abelia

ABELIA

Caprifoliaceae

Abelias combine a wealth of flowers with a graceful silhouette, thanks to their delicately-drawn foliage which is sometimes semi-evergreen. Their only drawback is that they cannot stand up to the very worst winters, but they start afresh the following spring.

Useful hints

— Plant in spring or early summer in a sunny spot. Water generously until September, then cover the stump with a thin layer of dead leaves.

— No real pruning required; all you need do is to remove excessively tangled branches from the centre in March.

Recommended

— *Abelia* × *grandiflora*, semi-evergreen, in flower in late summer, or *A. chinensis*, less tall, whose delicate lilac-pink flowers remain until October.

Height: 1.5–1.8 m (5–6 ft).
Spacing and planting distance: 1 m (3 ft).
Soil: ordinary, not too heavy.
Cultivation: sunny, sheltered from cold winds.
Propagation: from cuttings in winter.
Flowering season: June–October.
Type: deciduous or semi-evergreen shrub.

▽ *Abelia* × *grandiflora*

△ *Abutilon vitifolium* 'Veronica Tennant'
◁ *Abutilon megapotamicum*

Abutilon

ABUTILON/FLOWERING-MAPLE

Malvaceae

While most abutilons are greenhouse or verandah plants which can't take our average winters, some are hardy enough to decorate our beds, especially if given a sheltered position at the base of a south-facing wall.

Useful hints

— Plant in spring, adding sand to lighten the soil if need be. Put down anti-slug pellets and water regularly in summer. When the frosts draw near, shelter the neck of the stem with some handfuls of rock wool.

— Each spring, prune down to ground level to let the young branches develop.

In July/August, take cuttings and root them in an equal mixture of peat and sand, and shelter under a well-draughtproofed frame.

Recommended

— *Abutilon megapotamicum* is hardy if well-mulched against a south-facing wall. Plant in company with *Ceanothus* and *Clematis tangutica*. *A. vitifolium* is hardier still. It has mauve flowers, whereas 'Album' has white and 'Veronica Tennant' a brighter violet.

Height: 1–2 m (3–7 ft).
Spacing and planting distance: 1 m (3 ft).
Soil: light, well-drained.
Cultivation: sunny.
Propagation: from cuttings in summer.
Flowering season: all summer.
Type: deciduous shrub.

△ *Actinidia kolomikta*

Actinidia

ACTINIDIA/KIWI, SILVERVINE
Actinidaceae (family not confirmed)

While *Actinidia* is often grown for its fruit, so rich in vitamin C, let's not forget that it is also a very decorative climbing plant, with leaves both full and delicate and creamy white flowers. Let it loose on a pergola or trellis along with large-flowered clematis.

Useful hints

— Plant in spring once the frosts have gone. Mulch generously and water regularly, because this plant is very thirsty. Put some mesh around the base to stop cats getting their claws into the branches, which seem to attract them.

— If you want fruit (kiwi fruit), plant two *Actinidia* of different sexes next to one another. Prune in spring, cutting branches on long creepers back by a third.

— Since the roots are formed at the end of the summer for the following year, don't forget to water at this critical period and add special rose fertilizer.

Recommended

— As well as the fruiting varieties, leave room for the superb *Actinidia kolomikta*, more hardy and stunning in summer when the leaves turn pink and white.

Height: 3–6 m (10–20 ft).
Spacing and planting distance: 2 m (7 ft).
Soil: rich, well-drained.
Cultivation: sunny, but not scorched.
Propagation: from cuttings in autumn.
Flowering season: June, July.
Type: deciduous climber.

Althaea frutex
See *Hibiscus syriacus*

Amelanchier

SNOWY MESPILUS, JUNE BERRY/
SHADBLOW, SERVICEBERRY
Rosaceae

If there is any shrub set to become the fashion in the next few years, it must be *Amelanchier canadiensis*, and for good reason. Adapting well to all soils and climates, it shoots gently, flowers like a white cloud in early spring, produces pink leaves at first which then turn a flame colour in autumn before delighting birds with its red berries. There is nothing like it to give a bed some height, and it goes very well with old roses, peonies and the wilder hardy perennials.

Useful hints

— Often sold cheap with bare roots in winter, it has to be planted quickly in well-turned-over soil. It doesn't do much for the first few years, then starts growing at some speed.

— No pruning: all you need do is remove dead branches.

— Mulch in May with lawn trimmings or household compost.

Recommended

— You never quite know what nursery-men will be offering in terms of *Amelanchier*, but they're all pretty. The most common are *A. laevis* and *A. lamarckii*. There is also a 'Ballerina', but this does not have any obvious advantages.

Height: 2–5 m (7–17 ft).
Spacing and planting distance: 2 m (7 ft).
Soil: ordinary.
Cultivation: sun or semi-shade.
Propagation: from cuttings in winter.
Flowering season: April.
Type: deciduous shrub.

△ **Amelanchier canadensis**
▽ **Amelanchier canadensis**

Amelopsis

See *Parthenocissus*

Artemisia

ARTEMISIA/WORMWOOD

Compositae

We have already come across artemisia in the section on flowers, but we couldn't resist mentioning the shrub species which have a very woody stump. Hardier than you might think, they can be used to brighten up difficult corners where the sun beats down in summer and the soil is really pebbly: it's under these conditions that they give their best.

Useful hints

— Plant in spring, adding 2 handfuls of sand around the base of each plant. Water a little to help them take. As winter draws near, surround the stump with a few handfuls of rock wool. Even if the top freezes, shoots will appear next spring.

— Prune in July/August to remove the flowers which are not very interesting and to keep the shrub dense. Use this opportunity to take cuttings, which you should then root in sand under a shady frame before sheltering them from the cold over winter. Planted in March, they will give shrubs over 1 m (1 ft) wide in a single season.

Recommended

— *Artemisia arborescens* has magnificent feathery silvery-grey leaves. The variety 'Powis Castle' is hardier than the true species but all other varieties are slightly tender and should be protected by a cold frame during their first winter. *A. absinthium* 'Lambrook Silver' (semi-evergreen) smells of absinthe when you rub its silvery leaves; its long branches are covered in yellow leaves like those of mimosa. If you want to grow a dwarf artemisia try *A. schmidtiana* 'Nana', which is only 7.5 cm (3 in) tall. It will spread to form a tough and compact shrub 30 cm (12 in) wide with pretty silvery-grey leaves'

Height: 60 cm–1 m (2–3 ft).
Spacing and planting distance: 1 m (3 ft).
Soil: pebbly, well-drained.
Cultivation: full sun.
Propagation: from cuttings in summer.
Flowering season: late summer.
Type: evergreen shrub.

△ *Artemisia absinthium* **'Lambrook Silver'**   △ *Aucuba picturata*

Aucuba

AUCUBA

Cornaceae

Aucuba is one of those plants whose reputation has suffered because it was used so extensively in public gardens at the turn of the century. Inevitably, the wheel of fashion swings full circle, and people are now beginning to rediscover its good points, its hardiness, its ability to withstand pollution and the sober beauty of its fruit emerging from between pleasantly variegated evergreen leaves.

Useful hints

— Plant in spring or early autumn. Add fertilizer in March. It prefers a semi-shady spot, although it will also grow in the shade.

— If you want a lot of fruit, mix a variety of shrubs, since the sexes are separate.

Recommended

— There are at least ten known varieties of *Aucuba japonica*, recognizable by the shape of their leaves, their variegations and the colour of their fruit. One of the best known is 'Variegata', a variegated yellow variety which came over from Japan last century. There is also the willow-leaved 'Salicifolia', which is very elegant and makes an excellent show with its fragile flowers (female variety).

Height: 1.2–2 m (4–7 ft).
Spacing and planting distance: 1.5 m (5 ft).
Soil: any, but well turned over.
Cultivation: sun or semi-shade.
Propagation: from cuttings in spring.
Flowering season: negligible
Type: evergreen shrub.

Berberis

BARBERRY
Berberidaceae

In this survey of shrubs which can be used in gardens along with hardy perennials and bulbs, it would be unfair not to mention *Berberis*. We have restricted ourselves here to the more decorative varieties.

Useful hints

— Once planted in good conditions, *Berberis* needs no care at all: just add a little fertilizer once a year if it is still under-developed. A generous mulch of dead leaves or half-rotted compost will also help the plant's growth. Once the leaves have dropped take care to avoid the nasty spines on the stems.

— To propagate, all you have to do is take cuttings at the end of summer and let them take root at their own pace under glass in a mixture of equal parts of sand and peat. Prick out once into pots in spring, then plant out the following autumn

Recommended

— Very widespread, *Berberis thunbergii* has many varieties, including 'Atropurpurea Nana' which never grows over 60 cm (24 in) high and 'Rosy Glow' with delicate pink young leaves. You can also intersperse your hardy flowers with *B. darwinii*: this is an evergreen with tough dark green leaves and bright yellow flowers in April/May; or *B. linearifolia* 'Orange King', more upright, with rich orange flowers. Nor should we forget *B. × stenophylla* which forms an impenetrable screen of yellow flowers in April/May that smell deliciously of honey. *B. darwinii* is also recommended for making superb defensive hedges.

Height: 60 cm–2 m (2–7 ft).
Spacing and planting distance: 50 cm–1.5 m (1½–5 ft).
Soil: any.
Cultivation: at least 6 hours of sun a day for the purple varieties.
Propagation: from cuttings in late summer.
Flowering season: April, May.
Type: deciduous or evergreen shrub.

▽ ***Berberis linearifolia* 'Apricot Queen'**

▽ ***Berberis thunbergii* 'Atropurpurea'**

Buddleia alternifolia △

Buddleia lochinch △
Buddleia davidii **'Black Knight'** ▷
Buddleia globosa ▽

Buddleia

BUDDLEIA/BUTTERFLYBUSH

Loganiaceae

Buddleias have made a remarkable breakthrough in gardens in recent decades: today, everyone knows their clusters of highly-scented blue or violet flowers. Few shrubs are as simple to keep, since pruning once every 3 years is enough to give it a good density. Use it to make hedges or screens behind rosebushes or hardy beds with *Syringa* and *Althea*.

Useful hints

— Plant in autumn or spring. Water regularly for the first year. Mulch the soil in June with pine bark or lawn trimmings.

— Every 3 years, in March, prune the stump back to ground level to make it produce short, flowering branches. If your buddleia hasn't been pruned for years, cut the biggest branches first and cut back one-third of the plant each year for a three-year cycle.

Recommended

— *Buddleia davidii* has given rise to numerous varieties, such as 'Black Knight' (dark purple), 'Harlequin' (red with variegated leaves), and 'Nanho Blue', a little shrub with silvery leaves and mauve-blue flowers. *B. alternifolia* flowers earlier in purple. *B. globosa* is stunning, with its round, yellow-orange flowers in bunches. *B. lochinch* gives mauve flowers in August if pruned back.

Height: 1.2–4 m (4–14 ft).
Spacing and planting distance: 2 m (7 ft).
Soil: ordinary.
Cultivation: sunny.
Propagation: from cuttings in summer.
Flowering season: June–September.
Type: deciduous or evergreen shrub.

△ *Buxus sempervirens* **'Suffruticosa'**

Buxus

BOX

Buxaceae

Who has never heard of box, the queen of little trimmed borders and formal gardens? It's coming back into fashion, and people value its hardiness and its modest growth rate which means it doesn't have to be trimmed regularly.

Useful hints

— Plant in spring. Add peat to lighten the soil. Adding a few handfuls of hoof and horn each spring will keep its vigour. If the leaves suddenly turn yellow, this is a sign of an attack by tiny insects which live amongst its leaves. Treat with systemic insecticide in March/April.

— For successful cuttings, take them in September/October and let them root in a mixture of equal parts of peat and sand. They will take slowly but surely. Prick them out in late spring in a corner of your kitchen garden and plant out the following spring.

Recommended

— It is *Buxus sempervirens* which has given us the border box 'Suffruticosa' with deep green oval leaves, and also the large-leaved box which is so useful for round or cone-shaped bushes.

Height: 15 cm–2 m (½–7ft).
Spacing and planting distance: 10 cm–1 m (4–40 in), depending on ultimate width.
Soil: any, even slightly chalky.
Cultivation: anywhere.
Propagation: from cuttings in autumn.
Flowering season: negligible.
Type: evergreen shrub.

Callicarpa

CALLICARPA/BEAUTYBERRY
Verbenaceae

One of the weirdest colours visible in the garden is probably that of the fruits of *Callicarpa*, a delicate violet tinged with lilac glowing softly in autumn. The chance of admiring this fruit in a slightly gloomy season is reason enough to want this shrub, even if it lacks a pedigree.

Useful hints

— Plant in autumn or spring. If you want a lot of fruit, it is a good idea to plant a number side by side to increase fertilization.

— To show off the colour of the fruit, plant them among *Lysimachia clethroides* or hostas which turn golden in autumn. *Weigela*, largely variegated in yellow, also go well with them.

Recommended

— *Callicarpa bodinieri giraldii* is the one most often found in catalogues; its variety 'Profusion' has slightly less fruit. *C. japonica*, with purple-lilac berries, is more compact.

Height: 2.5 m (8 ft).
Spacing and planting distance: 1.5 m (5 ft).
Soil: any soil, well turned over.
Cultivation: sunny.
Propagation: from cuttings in summer.
Flowering season: summer.
Type: deciduous shrub.

▽ *Callicarpa bodinieri giraldii*

Camellia

CAMELLIA
Theaceae

While camellias are mainly grown on their own for the beauty of their leaves and flowers, we tend to forget that where the climate is suitable (by the sea) they can also be used as hedges and as a background for other flowers. This is particularly true of the hybrids *Camellia* × *williamsii* we will look at here.

Useful hints

— Buy them in flower, choosing the short, dense plants. Shelter them on a verandah until planted in April once the danger of frost is past. They like an acid, humus-rich soil and a position sheltered from the midday sun.

— Each autumn, gather a 20 cm (8 in) thick mulch of dead leaves and let them decompose around the plants to give them nourishment. A little bonemeal or hoof and horn completes their diet each spring.

— In winter, protect them from snow, which they cannot stand.

Recommended

— The camellias best at home with other plants are undoubtedly the hybrids *C.* × *williamsii* with their longer leaves and less formal silhouette than *Camellia japonica*. 'Donation' (orchid pink), 'J. C. Williams' (blush pink),

△ *Camellia* 'Donckelarii'
Camellia japonica 'Hearn's' △
▽ *Camellia* 'Adolph Audusson'
Camellia japonica 'Bella romana' ▽

'November Pink' or 'Saint Ewe' (bright pink) are particularly pretty. *Camellia sasanqua* is very interesting since it flowers early (from October onwards) and has a soft, exotic scent, but it is less hardy and is confined to the warm climates and the seaside.

Height: 1–3 m (3–10 ft).
Spacing and planting distance: 1 m (3 ft).
Soil: acid, humus-rich.
Cultivation: semi-shade.
Propagation: difficult.
Flowering season: October–April.
Type: evergreen shrub.

△ *Caryopteris incana*
▽ *Campsis radicans*

▽ *Ceanothus impressus*

Campsis

BIGNONIA, TRUMPET CREEPER, TRUMPET VINE

Bignoniaceae

Bignonia, trumpet creeper, trumpet vine, etc. are common names for *Campsis* which is found in so many pretty gardens in mild climates. These exotic climbing plants are easily recognized by their orange or yellow trumpets. Climbing on tendrils, they can reach an impressive size but take pruning well.

Useful hints

— Plant in spring or summer in well-turned-over soil, keeping the base at least 60 cm (24 in) from a wall since the powerful roots are capable of unseating the most solid foundations.

— Train the first stems, then just prune the branches back to the trunk in March. The flowers will appear in bunches on the end of that year's branches.

— Plant violet blue agapanthus at the foot of *Campsis* to give a beautiful contrast.

Recommended

— *Campsis grandiflora* has almost-closed bright orange flowers, while the well-known hybrid, 'Mme Galen' is much prized for its wide-open salmon-pink trumpets. *C. radicans* can reach 10 m (33 ft) and flowers in August/September.

Height: up to 10 m (33 ft).
Spacing and planting distance: 3 m (10 ft).
Soil: rich and cool in summer.
Cultivation: sunny.
Propagation: from cuttings in summer.
Flowering season: summer.
Type: deciduous climber.

Caryopteris

CARYOPTERIS/BLUEBEARD

Verbenaceae

You only have to see the delicate violet flowers of *Caryopteris* once to succumb to their charms. They are the ideal companions for roses, since they flower in late summer and coincide with the second flowering of remontant roses, showing them off to best advantage.

Useful hints

— Plant in spring, since winter often kills them if they are not well-rooted. A shoot no size at all will give a shrub over 60 cm (24 in) wide in the first year. Don't forget this when planting.

— Prune back to ground level each spring to give dense, round shrubs.

Recommended

— The commonest is *Caryopteris* × *clandonensis* 'Heavenly Blue', with slightly silvery leaves and dark blue flowers, but the fashion will undoubtedly swing towards the new hybrids of *C. incana*, more creeping and a brighter blue, even though they haven't the silvery leaves to which the true species owe their charms.

Height: 60 cm–1.2 m (2–4 ft).
Spacing and planting distance: 60 cm (2 ft).
Soil: ordinary, on the pebbly side.
Cultivation: sunny.
Propagation: from cuttings in spring or summer.
Flowering season: August–October.
Type: deciduous shrub.

Ceanothus

CEANOTHUS/NEW JERSEY-TEA, SISIYOU-MAT

Rhamnaceae

While many *Ceanothus* are more at home trained against a wall than planted on their own, some are perfect for use with your hardy perennials.

Useful hints

— Plant in spring in soil lightened with a little sand and peat. Prune back short each spring to give squat plants.

— Their subtle colours are set off in company with *Perovskia*, polyanthus roses and *Gaura*. *Ceanothus* does well by the sea.

Recommended

— *C.* × 'Gloire de Versailles', sky blue, is still one of the most-planted varieties. 'Trewithen Blue' is deliciously scented, with large bunches of deep blue flowers. You could also try 'Topaz' (bright blue), more compact or 'Henri Desfosse' (violet-blue). As for *Ceanothus thyrsiflorus* 'Repens', its leaves are evergreen while those above are deciduous, and it is literally covered with mid-blue flowers in May. It does not need any pruning. If you are looking for a pink, *C.* × 'Marie Simon' will enchant you all summer. *C. burkwoodii* has a long flowering season from summer to autumn. *C. impressus* (evergreen) has solid blue flowers.

Height: 1–2 m (3–7 ft).
Spacing and planting distance: 1 m (3 ft).
Soil: rich and light.
Cultivation: sunny.
Propagation: from cuttings in summer.
Flowering season: June–September.
Type: deciduous or evergreen shrub.

Chaenomeles

JAPANESE QUINCE/FLOWERING QUINCE

Rosaceae

From the end of February onwards, the Japanese quince brings us flowers which are delightful in their simplicity in all shades of red and pink. Very spiny, it particularly likes growing along walls, where it grows to 3 m (10 ft) and so can be used as a support for a little flowering clematis of the *montana* species, since its branches are relatively airy. Quinces are also excellent in defensive hardy hedges. Only one problem: they either refuse to take at all or invade everywhere. Watch out!

Useful hints

— Plant at any time in humus enriched, carefully turned-over soil. Weed and water for the first summer. To encourage flowering, which happens on the old wood, cut the long straight branches in September/October.

— Propagating? Nothing could be simpler: use the shoots which inevitably appear at the base.

Recommended

— The true Japanese quince (*Chaenomeles japonica*) is relatively small, and produces red flowers and then large numbers of little quinces.

— *C. speciosa* has given rise to many fairly tall varieties which are useful as a background to beds: 'Moerloesii', with delicate pink apple-blossom; 'Nivalis' (pure white), 'Simonii' (smaller, crimson red) are some of the best.

— The hybrids *C.* × *superba* are smaller and denser, giving little round bushes which are easily spread over beds of any size: 'Crimson and Gold', crimson with golden stamens, 'Fire Dance', more spread out and brighter, and 'Knap Hill Scarlet', brilliant red, are some of the prettiest.

Height: 1–3 m (3–10 ft).
Spacing and planting distance: 1–2 m (3–7 ft).
Soil: ordinary.
Cultivation: sun or semi-shade.
Propagation: by taking off shoots in summer.
Flowering season: February–May.
Type: deciduous shrub.

Chimonanthus

CHIMONANTHUS/WINTERSWEET

Calycanthaceae

It's impossible to go near a *Chimonanthus* in bloom without noticing it. Not for the beauty or size of its flowers (they are a slightly dull yellow and no bigger than a golden button), but because of their heady scent, a mixture of narcissi and hyacinths, which can be smelt from several metres away. When you realize that it flowers in winter, from February to March, you will understand why this shrub is interesting, since it heralds the arrival of good weather.

Useful hints

— Hardy and unfussy, *Chimonanthus* can be planted in any soil. Give it a sunny position sheltered from cold winds and gusts to keep the flowers intact. Place it above all by a gateway or passage to make the most of its delightful scent.

Recommended

— Only *Chimonanthus praecox* with flowers ranging between ivory and ochre is available from nurseries. There are two varieties: 'Grandiflorus', a darker yellow striated with red and 'Luteus', a waxy yellow.

Height: 2.5–4 m (8–14 ft).
Spacing and planting distance: 2 m (7 ft).
Soil: ordinary, well-drained.
Cultivation: sunny, along a south-facing wall.
Propagation: by layering in summer.
Flowering season: February–March.
Type: deciduous shrub.

Choisya

MEXICAN ORANGE

Rutaceae

Its membership of the same family as orange and lemon trees explains some of the characteristics of *Choisya*: its varnished leaves smelling of orange peel when rubbed, its divinely scented white flowers and its sometimes doubtful hardiness. It is an excellent patio shrub, since it likes a certain amount of shade. It takes on a pleasant, naturally round shape; you can also grow it in tubs to decorate a terrace, but take it inside on your verandah each winter, since the plants in tubs freeze more easily than in the garden.

Useful hints

— Plant in spring after the worst of the frosts, giving it a south- or west-facing spot. Water regularly. Protect the stump with straw or rock wool since it may come away from the roots after a severe frost. Planted against a house, *Choisya* can reach 2 m (7 ft) and is wonderful.

— Mix them with opulent hardy perennials such as *Hosta plantaginea* with flow-

△ *Chimonanthus praecox*
▽ *Chaenomeles japonica* **'Crimson and Gold'**

▽ *Choisya ternata*

ers as scented as its own, or delphinium or phlox.

Recommended

— As if *Choisya ternata* were not pretty enough, a golden-leaved variety, 'Sundance', has been produced, stunning but even less hardy.

Height: 1–2 m (3–7 ft).
Spacing and planting distance: 1 m (3 ft).
Soil: rich in humus, well-drained.
Cultivation: sun or semi-shade.
Propagation: from cuttings in summer.
Flowering season: May, June and slightly into summer.
Type: evergreen shrub.

Cistus

ROCK ROSE, SUN ROSE

Cistaceae

Few shrubs are as useful as *Cistus* when it comes to decorating a pebbly sun-scorched corner of a garden, or by the seaside where salt spray causes such damage. But using them for that alone would be to forget the decorative quality of their evergreen downy grey leaves, and especially their flowers which open each morning like slightly rumpled silky poppies.

Useful hints

— Plant in spring, in pebbly, well-drained soil where they will last longer.

— Surround the neck with bracken each winter. Do not prune.

Recommended

— The hardiest species are *Cistus corbariensis* with pink flowers and *C. laurifolius* with largish white flowers. *C. × purpurens* (purple cistus) has pink flowers with a purple spot in the centre and is over a 1 m (3 ft) tall, but is only for gardens in warm climates. Give a welcome to your garden also to *C. salvifolius* which has white flowers and is useful for ground cover. Blend them with sclerous sages, lavender and caryopteris. Protect *C. ladanifer* from cold; this species has very large flowers.

Height: 60 cm–1 m (2–3 ft).
Spacing and planting distance: 1 m (3 ft).
Soil: very poor and pebbly.
Cultivation: full sun.
Propagation: from cuttings or by layering in summer.
Flowering season: June–August.
Type: deciduous or evergreen shrub.

Cistus purpureus ▷
▽ *Cistus ladaniferus*

Clematis

**CLEMATIS/VIRGIN'S BOWER,
TRAVELLER'S JOY**

Ranunculaceae

We could hardly leave clematis out, but to keep within the scope of this book we will limit ourselves to the ground cover and small-flowered varieties which go best with other flowers and shrubs.

Useful hints

— Plant from October to May in thoroughly worked soil with leaf-mould and sand added. The secret of growing beautiful clematis is to add a thin mulch of fresh compost. These very greedy plants will then have all the humus and nutrients they need at their disposal.

— Prune as little as possible, simply removing dead branches. You can prune it back to ground level every 3 years to make it form strong new branches. Herbaceous clematis species used as ground cover start from scratch each spring.

Recommended

— **Herbaceous clematis**: *Clematis durandii* creeps between other plants and then produces very visible violet blue flowers. *C. heracleifolia* flowers in late summer with purple blue bells, while *C. integrifolia* is a few weeks ahead of it, with indigo-violet blooms. These clematis produce very decorative fruit in autumn.

— **Climbing, small-flowered clematis**: the earliest is *C. alpina*, often no more than 2.5 m (8 ft) but charming with its white and blue corollas. It is followed by *C. montana*, more vigorous and flowery. 'Tetra-rose' is very dense, 'Rubens' a bright pink. There are also a large number of small-flowered clematis which bloom in summer: *C. spooneri* and *C. flammula*, white and highly scented, *C. rehderana*, spring yellow and delicately scented, *C. tangutica*, bright yellow in falling bells and *C. texensis*, with scarlet-red flowers. *C. viticella* do not grow more than 3 m (10 ft) and flower well into summer in mauves and purples.

— **Hybrid large-flowered clematis**: 'Ville de Lyon', carmine-red with golden stamens; 'Marie Boisselot' with enormous white flowers all summer; 'The President', the best known blue clematis; the stunning 'Nellie Moser', rose and mauve striated, excellent on a north-facing wall where its ravishing colours won't fade; the vigorous 'Comtesse de Bouchaud' has delicate pink flowers all summer; 'Vyvyan Pennell'

△ *Clematis* 'Marie Boissolot'

offers double blue-violet flowers in June–July and autumn.

Height: 60 cm–10 m (2–33 ft) (*C. montana*).
Spacing and planting distance: 2 m (7 ft).
Soil: fairly light, rich in humus.
Cultivation: sun or semi-shade. The base must be sheltered from the direct rays of the sun by netting or another plant.
Propagation: from cuttings, but especially by layering in summer.
Flowering season: April–September.
Type: deciduous climber.

△ **Clematis 'Marcel Moser'**
◁ **Clematis**
Clematis montana ▷
▽ **Clematis 'Nelly Moser'**

Clematis spooneri ▽

Clethra alnifolia △

Clethra

CLETHRA/SUMMERSWEET

Clethraceae

Clethras will be stars in a few years' time! All it needs is for their qualities to become better known: a pretty silhouette once their upright youth has passed, white, highly-scented flowers at the height of summer and autumn colours reminiscent of the golds of Watteau. Mix them with maples from Japan or *Callicarpa*, whose indigo blue fruits go well with the golden screen of their leaves.

Useful hints

— Plant in winter in groups of 3, preferably in acid soil. Add peat and heath soil to lighten. Mulch with dead leaves each spring. Water regularly in July/August if the shrubs are in full sunlight.

— Trim only to remove desiccated branches. The branches are very straight at first, but then droop prettily.

Recommended

— The commonest is *Clethra alnifolia*, with scented white flowers turning to orange-yellow in autumn. *C. fargesii* is slightly bigger and flowers longer.

Height: 2–3 m (7–10 ft).
Spacing and planting distance: 2 m (7 ft).
Soil: rich in humus, acid, not soaked in winter.
Cultivation: sunny.
Propagation: from cuttings in summer.
Flowering season: August, September.
Type: deciduous shrub.

315

△ *Cornus nuttallii*
◁ *Cornus florida* 'Rubra'
▽ *Cornus kousa chinensis*

Cornus

CORNEL/DOGWOOD

Cornaceae

Leaving aside the large cornels like *Cornus kousa* and *C. controversa*, let's look at the shrub varieties which go so well with other plants to brighten up our beds and give them both volume and liveliness in winter thanks to their colourful bark.

Useful hints

— Plant at any time of year if raised in containers, or in November–March if bare-rooted.

— Prune short in spring in March to force them to develop vigorous branches whose bark is more colourful.

— Mix them with hellebores against a screen of dark leaves to show them at their best. Cornels also like being beside water, even if they are sometimes submerged. Their wood becomes very hard as it gets old and can be used for making tool handles.

Recommended

— The *Cornus alba* quickly form real copses. The variegated varieties are the most decorative. The male cornel (*C. mas*) has very early yellow flowers, and also has variegated varieties such as 'Aurea Elegantissima'; it ends up as a little tree. Very widespread in our forests, the blood cornel (*C. sanguinea*) has bright red bark and dark red leaves in autumn. Contrasting with its yellow bark, *C. stolonifera* 'Flaviramea' rapidly grows in width. *C. nuttallii* (virtually a tree!) has lots of creamy white flowers which then turn pink.

Height: 1.8–3 m (6–10 ft).
Spacing and planting distance: 1 m (3 ft).
Soil: ordinary, even drenched in winter.
Cultivation: sun or semi-shade.
Propagation: from cuttings of dry wood in winter.
Flowering season: March.
Type: deciduous shrub.

Coronilla

CORONILLA/CROWN VETCH

Leguminosae

These charming 'tree' coronillas—in fact, they never grow to more than 2 m (7 ft)—are very common in the mountainous central regions of the south of France. They are perfectly at home in rockeries and pebbly spots providing they have sun. Once in place, their evergreen, finely divided leaves and bright yellow flowers make them first class for decorative purposes.

Useful hints

— Plant in spring, throwing a handful of sand into each hole. Water slightly for the first year.

— Prune each spring to remove dead branches and make the shape better proportioned.

— Plant them along with asphodelines and *Cistus* to rejuvenate a scree-covered corner.

Recommended

— The glaucous *Coronilla glauca* is the less hardy of the two, with bluish-green leaves. Plant it at the foot of a south-facing wall and protect the roots each winter with bracken. *C. emerus* is stunning, with its fruit shaped like a scorpion's tail. Its yellow flowers are often veined with red.

Height: 1.5–2 m (5–7 ft).
Spacing and planting distance: 1 m (3 ft).
Soil: pebbly.
Cultivation: sunny.
Propagation: from cuttings in summer.
Flowering season: May–September.
Type: deciduous shrub.

▽ *Coronilla glauca*

△ *Corylopsis sinensis*

Corylopsis

CORYLOPSIS

Hamamelidaceae

Few shrubs have inherited such grace as *Corylopsis*. Its very unusual stance, first erect and then horizontal, its incredibly diaphanous leaves, so moving when they first appear, its little falling clusters of flowers, make it one of the prettiest of little shrubs. All the more reason to give it the shady spot and frequent watering it needs. As it is slow-growing, you can also grow it in tubs on the terrace. Take it inside in the warm when it flowers to enjoy it to the full, and then place it back outside again.

Useful hints

— Plant *Corylopsis* in winter in light, acid soil enriched with peat and sand.

— Give it a spot sheltered from the burning sun in summer. Mulch each autumn with a generous layer of dead leaves.

— It does not need pruning, and suffers no diseases, provided you water regularly; otherwise the leaves will spoil in summer.

Recommended

— *Corylopsis pauciflora* is the most common, with its little 2 cm (¾ in) long clusters. It is less spectacular than *C. spicata*, with inflorescences four times as long, or *C. willmottiae* with leaves which emerge in an incredible purple red. *C. sinensis* has highly-scented yellow flowers in April.

Height: 1.5–3 m (5–10 ft).
Spacing and planting distance: 2 m (7 ft).
Soil: acid, well-drained.
Cultivation: semi-shade.
Propagation: by layering in summer (difficult).
Flowering season: February, March.
Type: deciduous shrub.

△ *Cotinus obovatus*

Cotinus

SMOKE TREE

Anacardiaceae

Cotinus is well known for its flowery inflorescences which have given it its name. Add an incredible resistance to pollution and beautifully coloured leaves, and you have the makings of an essential shrub. Its only drawbacks are its tendency to disappear suddenly for no apparent reason, and especially the fact that nurserymen insist on offering just the purple-leaved variety while the true species, much rarer, is much less artificial.

Useful hints

— Plant from October to March. Water regularly for the first two summers, after which no pruning or special care is required.

— Mix with *Sedum spectabile* (purple) and *Ceratostigma* to give autumn scenes rich in colour. The purple-leaved varieties contrast highly with white or yellow flowers: but don't overdo it, since they make the garden look artificial.

Recommended

— *Cotinus coggygria* (syn. *Rhus cotinus*) is most frequently marketed as 'Royal Purple'. *C. obovatus* is more vigorous and takes on sublime autumnal colours.

Height: 2–6 m (7–20 ft).
Spacing and planting distance: 2 m (7 ft).
Soil: any, not too rich.
Cultivation: sunny.
Propagation: by layering shoots in summer.
Flowering season: June, July.
Type: deciduous shrub.

317

△ **Cotoneaster lacteus**
▽ **Cotoneaster splendens**

▽ **Cotoneaster × watereri 'Pendula'**

Cotoneaster

COTONEASTER
Rosaceae

Badly hit by fireblight (a notifiable disease) and the threat it represents, cotoneasters are increasingly difficult to find in nurseries, which have to abide by the draconian rules designed to prevent the disease spreading: so we will limit ourselves to the most resistant species.

Useful hints

— Plant from September to April. Mulch the soil in May and water regularly in hot weather.

— If branches dry out mysteriously in summer, prune them back mercilessly to the joint and burn them. Disinfect your secateurs with alcohol and treat the pruning wound. Watch the plant carefully and destroy it if the symptoms recur: this is the sign of an attack of fireblight, for which there is no cure and which will spread to your neighbouring pear trees.

Recommended

— **Creeping varieties**: *Cotoneaster dammeri* takes the lion's share, since few creeping shrubs are so well attached to the soil or so dense, so much so that you can ride over them without doing any harm. There are several cultivars such as 'Eisholz' with scarlet red fruit, 'Radicans' with smallish leaves, 'Skogholmen', very vigorous, one of the best ground covers. *C. splendens* and *C. horizontalis* 'Dart's Splendid' and 'Variegatus' (variegated leaves) are also worth planting. *C. microphyllus* has very decorative fruit and also enchants by its round, gleaming leaves. The form 'Thymaefolia' is evergreen. *C. salicifolius* 'Parkteppich' has long leaves and is often used as a ground cover in Germany. *C. × watereri*, a weeping variety with evergreen leaves, has white flowers and red berries in autumn.

— **Upright varieties**: *C. franchetii* is interesting in hedges, as is *C. lacteus* with crimson red flowers in winter, or *C. salicifolius*, one of the most vigorous of all. It can even be trained on a pergola where its branches will tumble prettily and full of festoons.

Height: 10 cm–3 m (4 in–10 ft).
Spacing and planting distance: 30 cm to 1 m (1–3 ft).
Soil: ordinary.
Cultivation: any except fully northwards.
Propagation: from cuttings in summer.
Flowering season: late spring.
Type: deciduous, semi-evergreen or evergreen shrub.

△ **Daphne mezereum**

Daphne

DAPHNE
Thymaealaceae

Daphne's scent makes up for the roughness of the wood and some very monotonous colours. Flowering very early, sometimes in mid-winter, it gives off an incredible scent of stocks mixed with hyacinth.

Useful hints

— Buy them in flower in mid-winter and admire them before planting when any risk of severe frost is past, or wait until autumn to get the evergreen species which take better then.

— Don't prune daphne except to remove branches which suddenly die off due to attacks by a virus for which there is no cure.

Recommended

— The best known is *Daphne mezereum* (nicknamed 'pretty wood'), shaped like a large chandelier covered with bright pink flowers in January. *D. odora* is evergreen and better resistant to cold in its very elegant variegated form 'Aureomarginata'. Note: these shrubs are poisonous, particularly the berries of *D. mezereum* which are so attractive to children. *D. cneorum* and *D. collina* are hardy and are scented in May/June.

Height: 1.2–1.8 m (4–6 ft).
Spacing and planting distance: 1 m (3 ft).
Soil: ordinary, lightened with sand.
Cultivation: sunny.
Propagation: from cuttings in summer (difficult).
Flowering season: January–March.
Type: deciduous, semi-evergreen or evergreen shrub.

△ *Daphne odora* 'Variegata'
▽ *Daphne odora* 'Marginata'

△ *Daphne cneorum* 'Eximia'
▽ *Daphne collina*

Deutzia

DEUTZIA

Philadelphaceae

Deutzias are going out of fashion, which is a shame because of their graceful silhouette, their bowed branches, their white flowers, like a springtime snowstorm, and above all their hardiness.

Useful hints

— Plant *Deutzia* at any time of year if raised in containers, or between November and March if bare-rooted. They will take easily provided you remember to water them in very hot weather.

— To propagate, take cuttings in July and plant in a mixture of equal parts of sand and peat. Shelter the young plants under glass in winter, prick them out in the kitchen garden then plant in their permanent position the following autumn.

— Prune after flowering to remove the central branches whose bark comes off in tatters.

Recommended

— As well as *Deutzia gracilis*, with low vegetation, the most commonly planted are hybrids such as 'Magnifica' with large bouquets of white flowers, 'Atropurpurea', almost red-pink, 'Mont Rose' with purple highlights and 'Pride of Rochester' with double flowers.

Height: 80 cm–1.8 m (3–6 ft).
Spacing and planting distance: 1 m (3 ft).
Soil: ordinary.
Cultivation: sun or semi-shade.
Propagation: from cuttings in summer.
Flowering season: May, June.
Type: deciduous shrub.

▽ *Deutzia* × *rosea*

△ *Elaeagnus pungens* 'Maculata'

Elaeagnus

ELAEAGNUS/RUSSIAN-OLIVE, SILVERBERRY

Eleagnaceae

All seaside gardeners know and love these shrubs which grow very well beneath the sea spray. The other *Elaeagnus* are also the preserve of milder climates, since they are not very hardy in their youth. Note that they flower very late, in November, and are highly scented.

Useful hints

— Plant in March or September in soil lightened with sand. Mulch with pine bark in spring.

— Protect the young plants against their first winter with a windbreak to the west and by covering the base with bracken or a thick mulch of dead leaves.

Recommended

— *Elaeagnus angustifolia* ('Bohemian olive tree') has pretty grey leaves. *E. pungens* has a large number of cultivars with a variety of variegations, such as 'Argentea' (white variegations), 'Maculata Aurea' (yellow markings) and 'Silver Lining', superb as a hedge because of its olive-green leaves with silvery backs. But the best is *E.* × *ebbingei*, a large shrub with evergreen, silvery-backed leaves. This is one of the hardiest and has a truly delicious scent: trained against the wall of a house, it is a permanent, unusual ornament.

Height: 2–3 m (7–10 ft).
Spacing and planting distance: 1.50 m (5 ft).
Soil: ordinary, perhaps a little on the dry side.
Cultivation: sun or semi-shade.
Propagation: from cuttings in summer.
Flowering season: November.
Type: deciduous or evergreen shrub.

△ **Enkianthus campanulatus 'Albi florus'**

Enkianthus

ENKIANTHUS
Ericaceae

Totally unlike other heathland shrubs, *Enkianthus* combines grace and power when it takes on the flamboyant colours of autumn on its finely-drawn outline. Its white bell flowers fringe its slightly weeping branches, making an enchanting sight in spring. A very resourceful shrub.

Useful hints
— Plant in autumn or March/April in a cool, shady spot, in an acid soil lightened with leaf-mould or peat. Light, woodland conditions suit this plant best.

— Mulch each spring with pine bark, and water regularly and generously throughout the summer (the leaves must not be allowed to wilt).

— Plant in company with tree peonies, royal lilies and chervil to give a magic, scented corner of the undergrowth.

Recommended
— *E. campanulatus* is well-known, with its hanging white flowers and red and yellow leaves in November, but the most famous of all is *E. perulatus* which turns bright red at that time; it grows very slowly.
Height: 1–1.8 m (3–6 ft).
Spacing and planting distance: 1 m (3 ft).
Soil: acid, not waterlogged in winter.
Cultivation: semi-shade.
Propagation: by layering or from cuttings in summer (difficult).
Flowering season: May.
Type: deciduous shrub.

Escallonia

ESCALLONIA
Escalloniaceae

Fast-growing and capable of forming little evergreen hedges in a very short period, *Escallonia macrantha* are stars anywhere the mild climate enables them to withstand the winter. They are covered in thousands of tubular flowers in summer and are easily trimmed to make low hedges.

Useful hints
— Plant in spring. Mulch and water generously in summer. Don't hesitate to prune from the first year onwards to give dense shrubs down to the ground.

— To propagate, take cuttings from the ends of shoots in summer as you would with fuchsias. Put them under glass for the first winter.

— Inland, escallonias can be planted at the foot of well-exposed walls.

Recommended
— There are available over 20 hybrids, such as 'Apple Blossom' (pink and white), 'Crimson Spire' (brilliant red), 'Donard Star', with large pink flowers and big leaves, and 'Exoniensis' with trailing branches and pink-white flowers.
Height: 2–3 m (7–10 ft).
Spacing and planting distance: 1.50 m (5 ft).
Soil: ordinary, even slightly chalky, dry in summer.
Cultivation: sunny.
Propagation: from cuttings in summer.
Flowering season: July–September.
Type: evergreen shrub.

▽ **Escallonia macrantha**

△ **Euonymus japonicus 'Manophyllus alb**

Euonymus

SPINDLE TREE/EUONYMUS, STRAWBERRYBUSH, WAHOO, WINTERCREEPER
Celastraceae

Often only seen in the shape of its Japanese versions with evergreen leaves making them mainly usable as hedges, *Euonymus* is much more versatile than that. It may be deciduous, with flamboyant colours in autumn and pink and orange fruit.

Useful hints
— Plant in autumn. Prune as soon as it is planted to give denser shrubs.

— Mulch with pine bark in spring and water *E. alatus* generously in summer.

— Watch out for possible aphids attacks on evergreen varieties.

Recommended
— **Deciduous**: *E. alatus* is stunning, with its open, highly geometrical bearing and its branches bearing corky wings. Its large leaves turn a bright red in autumn. The cultivar 'Compactus' never grows over 1.5 m (5 ft) high. The European spindle tree (*E. europaeus*) puts colour into our country hedges. Its variety 'Red Cascade' literally sags under the weight of fruit.

— **Evergreens**: the large Japanese spindle tree was the basis of many hedges at the turn of the century, because it likes the shade. It has variegated varieties and manages well by the sea, but is vulnerable to aphids and oidium, not forgetting that it freezes down to ground level in very cold winters. *E. fortunei* exists in numerous variegated versions and is at present used as a ground cover since it is barely 80 cm (2½ ft) high: 'Emerald 'n Gold', yellow-variegated but turning pink in winter, and 'Dart's Gold', a carpet of gold, are amongst the best known.

Height: 60 cm–3 m (2–10 ft).
Spacing and planting distance: 50 cm–1 m (2–3 ft).
Soil: ordinary but well turned over.
Cultivation: any.
Propagation: from cuttings in summer.
Flowering season: scarcely visible, in late spring.
Type: deciduous or evergreen shrub.

Exochorda

EXOCHORDA/PEARLBUSH

Rosaceae

Why have the exochordas been consigned to semi-obscurity? They have a part to play in May with their outbursts of flowers. White is their favourite colour, and they use it profusely, turning in a few weeks into a little, incredibly delicate cloud.

Useful hints

— Plant in autumn or spring in soil which is not too chalky, otherwise the leaves tend to turn yellow.

— No particular pruning is required—these shrubs flower abundantly enough as they are. Just remove diseased or unsightly branches.

Recommended

— The most common *Exochorda* is the hybrid *E. macrantha* 'The Bride'. It works wonders in the sun or in semi-shaded spots where it lasts slightly longer.

Height: 3 m (10 ft).
Spacing and planting distance: 2.5–3 m (8–10 ft).
Soil: ordinary, not too chalky.
Cultivation: sun or semi-shade.
Propagation: from cuttings or by layering under glass in summer.
Flowering season: May, June.
Type: deciduous shrub.

▽ *Exochorda* **'The Bride'**

△ *Forsythia suspensa*

Forsythia

FORSYTHIA

Oleaceae

Originating mostly from the Far East, *Forsythia* was practically unknown last century. Plant in mixed hedges or train up sunny walls to give curtains of gold.

Useful hints

— Plant at any time of year, even when in bloom, providing you don't forget to water regularly. Water abundantly in the first summer. Plant near white narcissi and hostas for summer and train a small-flowered clematis amongst its branches.

— Prune just after flowering, cutting secondary branches back to a few centimetres from their joints. The weeping forsythias flourish very well without any special pruning, while the stiff-wooded varieties must also be left to themselves to lose some of their artificial appearance.

Recommended

— The *Forsythia* × *intermedia* varieties are vigorous and flowery: 'Beatrix Farrand', upright stance and canary-yellow flowers, 'Karl Sax' (Paris mimosa), with big, dark yellow flowers, 'Lynwood Gold', flowering all along the stems, 'Spectabilis', one of the most popular because of its truly intense flowers, 'Spring Glory', earlier than the others. A new variety, 'Minigold', is interesting for its big, light yellow

△ *Forsythia* × *intermedia*

flowers veined with green which stand out well against dark green leaves.

— *F. suspensa* is very supple, which makes it suitable for training along trellis-work. It flowers in March and throughout April. After flowering, prune back old wood and shorten lateral growths to within two buds of the old wood.

— Finally, if you want something to go with your early shrubs, such as *Rhododendron praecox,* with which it goes so well use *F. ovata,* which flowers from the beginning of March.

Height: 1.5–3 m (5–10 ft).
Spacing and planting distance: 1.5 m (5 ft).
Soil: any.
Cultivation: at least 6 hours sun per day.
Propagation: from cuttings in summer.
Flowering season: March, April.
Type: deciduous shrub.

△ *Hamamelis mollis*
▽ *Forthegilla gardenii*

▽ *Genista lydia*

Fothergilla

FOTHERGILLA

Hamamelidaceae

One of the most sublime shrubs of all when it takes on its autumn colours: an incredible mixture of gold and flamboyant red which flutters at the least breath of wind. For its dreamlike appearance and spikes of highly-scented white flowers, you owe it to yourself to welcome this classic shrub.

Useful hints

— Plant where it is sunny but not scorched in summer. It likes acid soil improved with equal parts of sand and peat.

— No pruning, no diseases.

Recommended

— There aren't many different species: apart from *Fothergilla major*, which flowers in April, the only ones you will find are *F. monticola*, which also grows very slowly and flowers in spring, and *F. gardenii*.

Height: 1–1.8 m (3–6 ft).
Spacing and planting distance: 1.5 m (5 ft).
Soil: light, acid.
Cultivation: sun or semi-shade.
Propagation: difficult and slow: by layering in autumn.
Flowering season: April.
Type: deciduous shrub.

Genista

**BROOM/DYER'S GREENWEED,
SPANISH GORSE, WOODWAXEN**

Leguminosae

Broom, always pure yellow, generally flowers in spring, bringing a little light to rockeries or beds near the house. It is quite slender generally and its small leaves allow other plants to be planted around the base.

Useful hints

— Plant in autumn or spring if you live in an area where the winters are very cold. Lighten the soil with sand.

— Prune after flowering, so as to bring air to the inside of the shrubs. Gather some seeds and sow them immediately, scratching them a little first, since their seed-coats are tough.

Recommended

— Mt Etna broom (*Genista aetnensis*) is virtually a small tree, with very sparse flowers. Spanish gorse (*G. hispanica*) is dwarf, very compact, spiny and produces masses of yellow flowers in May–

June. Lydian broom (*G. lydia*) is a creeper and very useful for decorating a rockery or pond. Dyers' greenweed (*G. tinctoria*) flowers in mid-summer.

Height: 60 cm–3 m (2–10 ft).
Spacing and planting distance: 50 cm–1 m (2–3 ft).
Soil: light, not too chalky.
Cultivation: sunny.
Propagation: from cuttings, but preferably from seed in summer.
Flowering season: May–September.
Type: deciduous shrub.

Hamamelis

WITCH HAZEL

Hamamelidaceae

With witch hazel, we come to an almost perfect species, one of the most beautiful plants in winter. Imagine a shrub with branches at first at an angle and then virtually horizontal, giving it an appearance both languid and majestic. Winter is not yet past when the flowers, streaked with bright yellow, give off a delightful scent of hyacinth and narcissus, slightly preceding the oblong, delicate green leaves. It may seem to be sleeping when October arrives, with its cool nights; but then, as if by magic, its leaves turn red, orange or pure yellow in a symphony of warm shades. A shrub worth watching.

Useful hints

— A native of cold regions, witch hazel is hardy. Give it a position sheltered from cold winds to take advantage of its scent and prevent the leaves being swept away by autumn squalls.

— Don't prune, since the flowers appear the whole length of the branches.

— Plant in autumn in acid soil lightened with leaf-mould and sand. Mulch and water regularly in summer.

Recommended

— *Hamamelis mollis* is quite big and is superb; its two varieties 'Goldcrest', with golden yellow flowers with red highlights at their base, and 'Pallida', sulphur yellow, are the best known. *H. × intermedia* and its varieties have relatively large leaves: 'Diane', whose flowers are almost red, and 'Jelena', coppery red, are the most stunning.

Height: 1.8–2 m (6–7 ft).
Spacing and planting distance: 2 m (7 ft).
Soil: light, acid.
Cultivation: sun or semi-shade.
Propagation: long and difficult: by layering in summer.
Flowering season: January–March.
Type: deciduous shrub.

Hebe

HEBE

Scrophulariaceae

Even though severe winters will ravage *Hebes*, there are still some people who like these somewhat stiff plants. It has to be said that there are few other shrubs capable of showing so much colour late in the season. If you are lucky enough to live in a mild region, use it widely to make evergreen hedges and punctuate your beds.

Useful hints

— It is best planted in spring in soil which is not too heavy. Water regularly for the first summer and add fertilizer, for this is a greedy plant.

— Mix with gold-leaved shrubs, since its purple and violet colours are a bit gloomy.

Recommended

— Most nurserymen will have dozens available. Some varieties are most decorative for their foliage: this is so with *Hebe armstrongii*, with copper-yellow branches like those of a cypress, *H. buxifolia*, very compact, ideal for low hedges, and 'Pagei' (or *H. pageana*) with glaucous leaves which make a good background for other plants, a' little plant for your rockery. The other hybrid *Hebes* are grown for their tapering spikes of flowers, and vary in size from 30 cm (12 in) to nearly 2 m (7 ft). The hardiest is 'Miss Fithall', lavender blue, from June to October. *H. × franciscana* withstands the wind very well, even very salty winds, and also has variegated varieties. *H. elliptica*, average height, has large white scented flowers.

Height: 30 cm–2 m (1–7 ft).
Spacing and planting distance: 30 cm–2 m (1–7 ft).
Soil: ordinary, preferably light.
Cultivation: sunny.
Propagation: from cuttings in summer.
Flowering season: June–October.
Type: evergreen shrub.

Hedera

IVY

Araliaceae

Clinging anywhere it can get a hold, ivy extends slowly but surely until it covers an entire tree trunk – or front of a house, which can be a worry. But do all those old oaks it is supposed to have killed really exist, and would not some castles now be in ruins if ivy had not acted as scaffolding down the centuries? Don't be over-afraid of this determined invader which is so good at hiding unsightly toolsheds.

Useful hints

— Plant at any time of year. Tie the branches in place as they grow for the first 2 years.

— Water regularly, and mulch the soil with dead leaves in autumn.

— Ivy can also be used as a very thin hedge trained along a trellis: in 3 years, it will form a very thin, opaque screen which will save you a lot of space compared with the thuyas.

— To propagate, all you have to do is to bind branches to the earth and let them take root before lifting them at the end of summer and transplanting carefully.

Recommended

— There is an incredible range of shapes and colours of leaves. The Canary Island ivy, for example (*Hedera canariensis*) has very big leaves, often variegated in cream like 'Gloire de Marengo'. Persian ivy (*H. colchica*) has even bigger leaves, more oval than triangular, with yellow variegations like 'Aurea' or with bronze veins like 'Monty' (an excellent ground cover). The common ivy (*H. helix*) has numerous variegated or yellow varieties: the most famous are 'Glacier', with silvery-grey and white edges and 'Silver Gem', with white edges. Irish ivy (*H. hibernica*) is vigorous and dark green.

Height: 30 cm–4 m (1–14 ft).
Spacing and planting distance: 50 cm–1 m (2–3 ft).
Soil: any.
Cultivation: semi-shade or shade.
Propagation: by layering or from cuttings in summer.
Flowering season: October.
Type: evergreen climber.

△ *Hebe* 'Midsummer Beauty'
▽ *Hedera helix*

▽ *Hedera colchica dentata* 'Variegata'

▽ *Hedera helix* 'Sagittaefolia'

△ *Hibiscus syriacus*
▽ *Hibiscus rosa-sinensis*

△ *Hibiscus syriacus* 'Red Heart'

Hibiscus

HIBISCUS/KENAF, ROSEMALLOW
Malvaceae

Hibiscus is enchanting when opening into hundreds of flowers like those of hollyhocks, generally in pale colours against a neutral green background. Only one problem: its upright stance makes it look slightly military. There is nothing like it for making a medium-sized hedge which flowers well in summer.

Useful hints

— Plant in spring, but don't be surprised if the leaves do not appear until May.

— Prune just after flowering to prevent too much fruit forming, which would exhaust it unnecessarily. On the other hand, do not prune systematically in spring, since this will simply make it even more upright without actually producing more flowers: just remove any tangled branches.

Recommended

— You can choose between the numerous hybrids of *Hibiscus syriacus* (syn. *Althaea frutex*): 'Duc de Brabant', double purple; 'Hamabo', delicate pink with splashes of carmine red; 'Lady Stanley', white with purple spots at the base; 'Oiseau Bleu', blue with red centres and 'Woodbridge', dark red.

Height: 1.5–2.5 m (5–8 ft).
Spacing and planting distance: 1 m (3 ft).
Soil: any, even slightly chalky.
Cultivation: sunny.
Propagation: from cuttings in winter.
Flowering season: July–September.
Type: deciduous shrub.

Hydrangea

HYDRANGEA/TEA-OF-HEAVEN
Saxifragaceae

While garden hydrangeas are the best known, we should not forget the other members of this famous family. Resembling viburnum in many ways, *Hydrangea* combines fertile flowers, generally small, and sterile ones, more developed and colourful. White is the most common colour of the botanical species, but everyone knows and loves the blue and violet purples of the hybrids, the flowers very often changing to a delicate red-washed green in late autumn, superb when used in floral arrangements.

Useful hints

— Rather than a really acid soil, hydrangeas need soil which is rich in organic matter; so add a lot of leaf-mould to the soil and use a mulch of dead leaves and peat each spring.

— Don't prune very much; just remove dead or sickly branches. In cold areas, cover the trunk with dead leaves covered with plastic foil. Protect the large terminal shoots which contain the future flowers.

— Hydrangeas are voracious shrubs. Each spring, add some handfuls of wood ash soaked by rain, bonemeal and a little hoof and horn. They are only really blue in very acid soils: you can heighten this colour by adding aluminium salts now available in the shops.

— To propagate, cut the ends of the stems in late summer and autumn. Shelter under a cold frame for the first winter.

Recommended

— *Hydrangea macrophylla* is the most widely available, usually in the form of its varieties. In pink, you can choose between 'Altona' and 'Eldorado' (darker), 'Floralia' (very early), 'Marechal Foch' (dark pink often turning to gentian blue) and 'Merveille Rose' with very large flowers. In blue, 'Iris' and 'Enziandom', dark blue, are the most stable. The best white is 'Soeur Therese'.

— 'Lacecap' hydrangeas have fertile flowers in the centre, giving them a particularly delicate lace bonnet appearance. The most celebrated are 'Blue Wave', pink or blue depending on the type of soil, 'White Wave', white and blue, and 'Mariesii' with very large flat bunches in rich pink or a variety of blues.

△ *Hydrangea macrophylla*
Hydrangea xanthoneura ▽
▽ *Hydrangea arborescens* 'Annabella'

▽ *Hydrangea macrophylla* hybrid

△ *Hydrangea paniculata* 'Unique'

— Amongst *H. paniculata*, recognizable by their long pyramid-shaped bunches, 'Grandiflora', white mixed with pale pink, 'Kyushu', more compact, and 'Praecox', flowering from July onwards, are the best known. 'Tardiva' is slightly less interesting since it does not flower until mid-October.

— Among the botanical hydrangeas, the most beautiful are *H. quercifolia*, with oak leaves and magnificent white flowers, *H. petiolaris*, the climbing hydrangea, which climbs walls using its tendrils like those of ivy, and *H. M. serrata*, round shrubs with large, very decorative leaves and white flowers edged in blue or pink. Of the garden forms, 'Preziosa' is one of the most superb, with its red stems and pink flowers turning a warm red in autumn.

Height: 1–3 m (3–10 ft).
Spacing and planting distance: 1 m (3 ft).
Soil: acid, rich in organic matter.
Cultivation: semi-shade: they withstand a north-facing position.
Propagation: from cuttings in late summer.
Flowering season: July–November.
Type: deciduous shrub.

▽ *Hydrangea serrata*

▽ *Hydrangea petiolaris*

325

Ilex

HOLLY/INKBERRY, WINTERBERRY

Aquifoliaceae

Hollies are the basic shrubs which are indispensable for designing a garden for winter; and don't forget the numerous variegated varieties or its fruit, so cheerful in the dark months.

Useful hints

— Plant in September–October or March–April. In either case, protect it from the wind with a cloth windbreak fixed on a framework of stakes.

— Each spring, add 2 or 3 handfuls of hoof and horn at the base.

— If you are shaping holly, use secateurs and not hedge-trimmers to avoid damaging the lovely varnished leaves.

— Plant holly in random hedges along with deciduous shrubs such as amelanchiers, rowans, elders and medlars.

Recommended

— There are many different varieties of holly. *Ilex aquifolium* has given rise to dozens of hybrids with varying variegations and even different-coloured fruit, such as 'Fructu-luteo', brilliant yellow, or 'J.C. van Tol', orange. To get a lot of fruit, mix the shrubs since some are male and some female. *I. crenata* has no spines and goes well in beds along with hardy perennials or in low hedges which won't scratch your legs. *I. ×️ altaclarensis* withstands urban pollution well and grows quite vigorously; among the numerous variegated varieties, 'Golden King', with yellow-edged leaves, which has won much praise for its beauty, and 'Camellifolia', with large non-prickly leaves and a very elegant pyramid shape which makes it a natural choice for large, regular hedges.

Height: 80 cm–3 m (2–10 ft).
Spacing and planting distance: 1 m (3 ft).
Soil: any, not too chalky.
Cultivation: any, even deep shade.
Propagation: from cuttings in winter.
Flowering season: negligible.
Type: evergreen shrub.

Jasminium

JASMINE

Oleaceae

While most jasmines aren't hardy enough to be used in many areas, some are robust enough to decorate well-exposed façades for many years, giving colour and scent. Don't hesitate to prune

regularly, otherwise you'll find yourself with an untidy tangle.

Useful hints

— Best planted in spring at the foot of a trellis to enable the stems to twine around a base.

— Water regularly and use the opportunity to add soluble fertilizer on two or three occasions in summer, since jasmines have big appetites.

— To propagate, take cuttings in summer and root in equal parts of sand and peat – or layering in autumn.

Recommended

— *Jasminum nudiflorum* is completely hardy; it flowers in March, but has no scent at all, unlike *J. officinale*, which flowers in summer and smells divine. Plant this in a sunny spot and protect it from the cold winds in winter.

Height: 2–4 m (7–14 ft).
Spacing and planting distance: 2 m (7 ft).
Soil: rich and light.
Cultivation: sunny (not morning sunlight for *J. nudiflorum*, otherwise the flowers will be roasted).
Propagation: by cuttings in summer.
Flowering season: March–August.
Type: deciduous creeper.

Kalmia

KALMIA/LAMBKILL, SHEEP-LAUREL, MOUNTAIN-LAUREL

Ericaceae

If you're looking for something other than rhododendrons (with which it goes well) to decorate an acid piece of ground, *Kalmia* is made for you. With its long, attractive leaves and pretty pink flowers, it adds a touch of originality. In moist areas, it grows vigorously, often becoming quite bushy.

Useful hints

— Plant in October–November or March–April in acid soil enriched with peat and leaf-mould to help it retain more water. Mulch each spring with pine bark or peat.

— Do not prune: the flowers appear in large numbers on the ends of stems. To make these shrubs more attractive, just remove faded flowers and budding fruit.

Recommended

— Perhaps it's not really a pity that nurserymen have done so little with this family. For this has meant the decorative qualities of *Kalmia latifolia* (brilliant

△ *Ilex crenata* 'Mariesii'
▽ *Ilex aquifolium* 'Handsworth New Silver'

▽ *Jasminum nudiflorum*

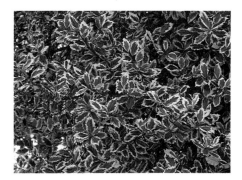

△ **Kerria japonica**
◁ **Ilex aquifolium 'Aureo-marginata'**
▽ **Kalmia latifolia 'Clementine Churchill'**

▽ **Kalmia latifolia**

pink) and those of *K. angustifolia* (smaller, with cherry-red flowers) have been left untouched.

Height: 1–3 m (3–10 ft).
Spacing and planting distance: 1 m (3 ft).
Soil: acid.
Cultivation: sunny.
Propagation: by layering in summer.
Flowering season: June.
Type: evergreen shrub.

Kerria

JEW'S MALLOW/KERRIA
Rosaceae

A vigorous shooter, *Kerria* puts out stems just about everywhere. They end almost horizontally and bend under the weight of bright yellow pompoms of flowers: a very comforting sight at the end of a hard winter.

Useful hints

— Plant in autumn. All you need to do is to get a cutting with a few roots from a neighbour to get a fine shrub in just a few years. But watch out: *Kerria* is an invasive neighbour as far as other plants are concerned: this should be taken into account when planting and its growth restricted by a pathway or wall.

— Prune after flowering, removing the branches from the centre to let the light in better.

Recommended

— While it may be more chic to have a true *Kerria japonica* on show in your garden, with its single, scarcely-visible flowers, don't forego the pleasure of the double-flowered version, which is much prettier. Devotees of variegated leaves will have a field day with *K. japonica* 'Variegata', which has a very graceful appearance.

Height: 1.8–2 m (6–7 ft).
Spacing and planting distance: 2 m (7 ft).
Soil: any, even chalky.
Cultivation: sunny, semi-shade.
Propagation: from cuttings in summer.
Flowering season: April, May.
Type: deciduous shrub.

Kolkwitzia

KOLKWITZIA/BEAUTYBUSH
Caprifoliaceae

Growing steadily without being invasive, *Kolkwitzia* will in a few years form an attractive shrub covered in pink trumpets of flowers in spring. Equally at

△ **Kolkwitzia amabilis 'Pink Cloud'**

home in a low hedge or in among hardy perennials or roses, this shrub retains its elegance in summer thanks to its velvety leaves and feathery fruit. It is certainly well worth having.

Useful hints

— Plant at any time of year if grown in containers; but it is better to buy it in full bloom, since there are some varieties which have very few flowers. Water regularly in the first year.

— To propagate, cut the tender shoots in June or July and leave them under a cold frame for the first winter.

— Plant in company with Chinese peonies, marigolds and iris.

Recommended

— 'Pink Cloud' is an improved true variety, with slightly more flowers and a deeper pink colour.

Height: 1.5–1.8 m (5–6 ft).
Spacing and planting distance: 1.5 m (5 ft).
Soil: ordinary, even slightly chalky.
Cultivation: sunny, semi-shade.
Propagation: from cuttings in summer.
Flowering season: late May, early June.
Type: deciduous shrub.

327

△ *Lavatera* **bicolor**
▽ *Lagerstroemia* **indica**

▽ *Laurus* **nobilis**

▽ *Lespedeza* **thunbergii**

Lagerstroemia

INDIAN LILAC/GRAPE-MYRTLE

Lythraceae

Grown as a shrub, *Lagerstroemia* can withstand temperatures as low as −15°C (5°F): below that, it will regrow from the stump and flower in summer in spite of everything. Planted on a sunny terrace, it will bring you compliments from everyone.

Useful hints

— It is best planted in spring. Mulch and water generously in summer. When the frosts approach, cover the stump with a mulch of straw or dead leaves covered by plastic sheeting. Remove this protection in March to take advantage of the milder weather and prune the branches back to ground level: it will then grow more vigorously.

— Mix with *Campanula pyramidalis* and *Salvia sclarea* in a bed against a south-facing wall: this will give an effect of vibrant colour.

Recommended

— There are a number of hybrids selected by colour, pure white to dark pink, which flower abundantly in ample clusters.

Height: 1–2 m (3–7 ft).
Spacing and planting distance: 2 m (7 ft).
Soil: rich and light.
Cultivation: full sun.
Propagation: from cuttings in summer.
Flowering season: July–September.
Type: deciduous shrub.

Laurus

**BAY LAUREL, SWEET LAUREL/
LAUREL, SWEET BAY**

Lauraceae

Although badly hit by severe winters, the sweet laurel, which should not be confused with *Nerium oleander* or *Viburnum tinus*, is still much appreciated by gardeners. It combines elegant foliage with ease of cultivation and aromatic leaves. Trained against sunny walls, it can bring a touch of grandeur to the space. The species *Laurus nobilis* 'Agustifolia' has narrower leaves.

Useful hints

— Choose a spot well-sheltered from the wind when planting.

— The sweet laurel does very well in tubs, providing it is overwintered in a sheltered place. It thrives on being pruned.

— In a freezing winter, cut it back to ground level. Shoots will soon reappear, and the bush will recover in just a few years.

Height: 2–4 m (7–14 ft).
Spacing and planting distance: 2 m (7 ft).
Soil: rich, well-drained.
Cultivation: full sun.
Propagation: from cuttings in summer.
Flowering season: March, April.
Type: evergreen shrub.

Lavatera

TREE MALLOW

Malvaceae

In just a few months, this mallow will grow from nothing at all into a sturdy shrub. With pink flowers throughout the summer, it goes perfectly with *Perovskia*, *Caryopteris* and hybrid perpetual roses. It grows very well beside the sea.

Useful hints

— Plant *Lavatera arborea* in spring: water regularly, adding liquid fertilizer to encourage it to flower. In November, put a mulch of dead leaves around the base to protect it from the cold. In March, prune to 10 cm (4 in) from the ground to encourage the growth of new, healthy stems.

— In September, take cuttings from the ends of branches and bury them horizontally in a mixture of sand and peat (in equal parts), when roots will appear without fail. Keep cuttings out of the cold to replace roots hit by frost.

Height: 1.5–2 m (4–7 ft).
Spacing and planting distance: 1 m (3 ft).
Soil: light and rich, thoroughly turned over.
Cultivation: full sun.
Propagation: from cuttings in summer.
Flowering season: July–September.
Type: deciduous shrub.

Lespedeza

LESPEDEZA/BUSH-CLOVER

Leguminosae

Lespedeza is a strange but attractive shrub: its large, vigorous branches grow each spring, slow down in summer and flower in autumn in a ravishing purple pink. Its flowers are like those of sweet peas. With its cascading shape, it is decorative for slopes, but can also be used as ground cover at the bottom of the garden. Just one root will end up covering an impressive area. The divided leaves, very elegant in summer, can be used as a background for other flowering plants.

Useful hints

— Plant in autumn or spring. Prune all stems to ground level in March, since new branches have the most flowers.

— Mix with white Japanese anemones, small-flowered asters and *Saxifraga fortunei* to give colour and charm to an otherwise autumnal scene.

Recommended

— Still often sold under its synonym, *Desmodium penduliflorum*, *Lespedeza thunbergii* has purple flowers in September. *L. bicolor*, more upright, has pink and purple flowers.

Height: 1.2–2 m (4–7 ft).
Spacing and planting distance: 3 m (10 ft).
Soil: fertile, thoroughly turned over.
Cultivation: sunny.
Propagation: from cuttings in summer.
Flowering season: late August–October.
Type: deciduous shrub.

Leycesteria

LEYCESTERIA /FORMOSA-HONEYSUCKLE

Caprifoliaceae

Still largely unknown, *Leycesteria formosa* is nonetheless one of the best shrubs for decorating a slightly wilder corner of a garden. Its long supple stems end in summer in clusters of white flowers, followed by deep-purple berries, which are a great favourite with birds, especially pheasants.

Useful hints

— Plant in spring, digging a trench several centimetres deep.

— Mulch each autumn with a thick layer of dead leaves. Severe frosts may destroy the exposed section, but new canes will shoot from the soil. In any event, you can get prettier shrubs by pruning stems down to ground level each spring.

— Mix with *Helleborous corsicus*, ferns and hostas.

Height: 1.5–1.8 m (5–6 ft).
Spacing and planting distance: 1 m (3 ft).
Soil: rich in humus.
Cultivation: sun or semi-shade.
Propagation: by division in autumn or from seed in spring.
Flowering season: August.
Type: deciduous shrub.

△ *Leycesteria formosa*
▽ *Ligustrum japonicum*

Ligustrum

PRIVET

Oleaceae

Privet was in its heyday at the turn of the century, before thuya arrived. Few shrubs are as easy and economical, with the result that it has undoubtedly been misused to create unimaginative hedges. It is worth rediscovering its qualities, which deserve to be better known.

Useful hints

— Plant from October to March. Turn the soil over thoroughly and enrich with humus if necessary. Add a compost mulch each spring, since the roots are very shallow.

— Prune at least three times a year (April/June/September) to give a dense hedge. If you don't like the flowers, with their faint smell of vinegar, prune in June only. When trimmed to shape they are not hardy, so they must be kept in a sheltered position in winter. Privet has a voracious appetite: don't plant flowers or other shrubs nearby.

△ *Ligustrum japonicum*

Recommended

— Japanese privet (*Ligustrum japonicum*) is very compact, with evergreen leaves reminiscent of camellias. Its flowers are among the largest in the genus. Its Chinese cousin, *L. lucidum*, is more upright and its branches grow in very geometric fashion. It has a number of variegated varieties such as 'Aureovariegatum' or 'Tricolor', which combine green, white and pink. The most common privet is *L. ovalifolium*, widely used in hedges. Left to itself, it will grow very tall, reaching nearly 4 m (14 ft). Nor should we forget *L. vulgare*, found in country hedges and fond of chalky soils; its black fruit are quite decorative in autumn.

Height: 1–4 m (3–14 ft).
Spacing and planting distance: 1 m (3 ft).
Soil: any.
Cultivation: sun or semi-shade.
Propagation: from cuttings in autumn (outside) or summer (under glass).
Flowering season: June, July.
Type: deciduous or evergreen shrub.

329

△ *Lonicera sempervirens* '**Dropmore Scarlet**'
Lonicera caprifolium △
▽ *Lonicera periclymemum* '**Serotina**'

Lonicera

HONEYSUCKLE

Caprifoliaceae

Who could resist the scent of honeysuckle? This genus, which includes as many creepers as shrubs, belongs in all gardens in that it couldn't care less about the quality of the soil and tolerates shade and pollution well.

Useful hints

— Plant honeysuckle at any time of year if grown in a container, which is the best way. Don't damage the rootball, and bury it so as to protect the base of the stem from the cold. Mulch in spring

and water regularly in summer to help it take.

— Pruning is generally pointless, except for *L. nitida* which must be pruned three times a year at least to stay properly dense. If this freezes, cut the branches back to ground level: they will regrow directly from the stump.

Recommended

— **Shrubs**: *Lonicera nitida* is widely used to make low hedges or even decorative shapes, since it is fast-growing and stays dense providing it is pruned regularly. There are green and yellow-variegated versions ('Baggesen's Gold'). *L. tatarica* has sparser vegetation and pretty glaucous leaves showing up the pink flowers in 'Arnold Red' and cherry red in 'Hack's Red'. Flowering 2 months earlier than these, *L. fragrantissima* is a shrub whose rather unattractive appearance is made up for by its extraordinary scent. Train it against a trellis and give it a small-flowered clematis or a summer jasmine for company to hide its awkward skeleton a little.

— **Creepers**: the most highly scented are those that lose their leaves in winter, such as *L. periclymenum* (woodbine) a little invasive but so enchanting in June to August. This has given rise to 'Belgica', more compact and flowering in June, and to 'Serotina', which flowers slightly later. *L. caprifolium* flowers a month earlier than the latter, from the beginning of June. It can also be distinguished by its leaves which seem to be perforated by the stems. Asiatic honeysuckles are often evergreen: this is the case with *L. japonica*, with white flowers turning to yellow. 'Halliana' is a typical highly-scented variety, while 'Aureoreticulata' has curiously yellow-veined leaves. Twine it between hardy perennials with opulent leaves like peonies or hellebores. *L. sempervirens* has brought a rich orange colour to many hybrids, but has lost its scent; the famous 'Dropmore Scarlet' is also totally unscented. The most impressive honeysuckle is *L. hildebrandiana* with large, scented flowers 9–15 cm (3–6 in) long, and creamy white; but this is not truly hardy and is confined to gardens in warm climates.

Height: 1–9 m (3–30 ft).
Spacing and planting distance: 1 m (3 ft).
Soil: ordinary, fairly rich in humus.
Cultivation: sun or semi-shade.
Propagation: from cuttings or by layering in autumn.
Flowering season: February–September.
Type: deciduous/evergreen creeper or shrub.

Lupinus

TREE LUPIN/TREE LUPINE

Leguminosae

In sandy, well-exposed soil, this lupin will give you such a mass of flowers that it runs the risk of dying of exhaustion. To be on the safe side collect seeds or cuttings to propagate at leisure. Mix with iris: the leaves, although very different, go together well.

Useful hints

— Plant in spring without damaging the twisting root. Lighten the soil with half a bucketful of sand. To avoid exhausting the plant in its first summer, remove most of the seedpods. Collect the seeds when they mature, scrape them with a knife to weaken the very tough husk and sow immediately in sand. The young plants can spend the winter under a cold frame and can be planted out in spring. You can also take cuttings in summer and plant them in sand.

— Protect the stump from cold with dead leaves and remove any frost-bitten sections in February. The vegetation will generally re-emerge more vigorously a few weeks later.

Recommended

— *Lupinus arboreus* 'Snow Queen' is white, 'Mauve Queen' mauve and 'Golden Spire' yellow.

Height: 1 m (3 ft).
Spacing and planting distance: 1 m (3 ft).
Soil: sandy.
Cultivation: full sun.
Propagation: from seed in spring or cuttings in summer.
Flowering season: June, July.
Type: deciduous shrub.

▽ *Lupinus arboreus*

Mahonia

MAHONIA

Berberidaceae

Mahonias used to be confused with berberis, but can be distinguished by their leaves, which are usually quite large and very reminiscent of holly. All evergreen and with yellow flowers in spring, they have no equal when it comes to filling a garden in winter, since their varnished leaves are enhanced by a stunningly stylized silhouette. Use them widely in wild hedges mixed with amelanchiers, elders and viburnums, or with bamboo and ferns to create an Asiatic atmosphere.

Useful hints

— Plant in September–October or March–April. Mulch the soil and water generously in the first summer. Do not prune unless some branches are awkward in shape, in which case cut them back by half in June.

— *Mahonia* × 'Charity' and *M. lomariifolia* are not quite as hardy as *M. aquifolium*: give them a position sheltered from cold winds.

— In winter, mahonia leaves can be used to make very pretty flower arrangements, but try not to pick when there is sharp frost.

Recommended

— The holly-leaved mahonia (*Mahonia aquifolium*) is the best known. It bears yellow flowers in March or April, with a scent of honey; its dark blue berries are very decorative and can even be used to make very original jellies. It grows in the worst places, in the shade and in poor soil, but then only very slowly. The 'Apollo' variety turns bronze in winter. The Japanese mahonias, such as *M. japonica* and in particular *M.* × 'Charity', flower from Christmas to February. Their Chinese cousins, *M. bealii* and *lomariifolia*, are very decorative, with their yellow lily-scented flowers in February or March and their somewhat hieratic appearance. Plant them by your gateway to enjoy such perfumed flowers all winter. *M.* × 'Media', a hybrid of *M. japonica* and *M. lomariifolia*, is an evergreen: it is highly scented and flowers in winter.

Height: 1–3 m (3–10 ft).
Spacing and planting distance: 1.5 m (5 ft).
Soil: any.
Cultivation: shade, semi-shade or sun.
Propagation: from cuttings in summer.
Flowering season: January–May.
Type: evergreen shrub.

△ *Mahonia* 'Media'
▽ *Nandina domestica*

△ *Mahonia bealii* 'Buckland'
▽ *Mahonia aquifolium*

Nandina

NANDINA

Berberidaceae

Nandina domestica has certainly been in fashion in the last few years. Few low shrubs have such presence as this native of China. Imagine a kind of bamboo, upright at first then veering to horizontal. The tough dark green leaves whose backs turn red in winter then serve as a background for the red berries which follow the large summery bouquets of white flowers. Hardy down to −15°C, (5°F) this shrub is particularly attractive in large numbers. Mixed with tree peonies, *Rudbeckia* or *Spiraea japonica* 'Little Princess', these Japanese shrubs take on divine colours in winter.

Useful hints

— *Nandina* is best planted in spring. Water frequently in summer.

— Protect the stump from the cold with a thick mulch of dead leaves or rock wool. If the exposed section freezes, prune it back to ground level in February.

Height: 1–1.6 m (3–5 ft).
Spacing and planting distance: 1.2 m (4 ft).
Soil: rich in humus.
Cultivation: sun or semi-shade.
Propagation: from cuttings in summer or seed in spring.
Flowering season: June, July.
Type: evergreen shrub.

△ *Olearia macrodonta*

Olearia

DAISY BUSH

Compositae

Olearia is used in medium-height hedges, especially by the sea: it is very much at home in that difficult environment, and its tough, evergreen foliage shows off its little, white, often scented 'marigolds'. Growing it inland is much riskier since it is not of the hardiest.

Useful hints

— Plant in spring. Mix with *Phormium*, *Pittosporum* and *Osmanthus* to give very exotic-looking medium-height hedges.

— Protect the neck with a few handfuls of dead leaves each autumn. Remove branches killed by the cold at the end of winter; no other pruning is necessary.

Recommended

— Most flower in May or June, except for *Olearia paniculata*, with olive-green leaves, which flowers in November – December.

— *O. traversii* is considered the best shrub for making windbreaks by the sea, its round, fleshy leaves tolerating sea spray well. This is also true of *O. waikarensis* with divided leaves, white on the back, and with bells of white flowers.

— The hardiest is *O. × haastii*, which forms a round shrub 1.2 m (4 ft) in diameter with scented stars of white flowers in July.

— *O. macrodonta* is more vigorous, gives off a powerful odour of musk, and has leaves like those of holly.

Height: 90 cm–3 m (3–10 ft).
Spacing and planting distance: 1 m (3 ft).
Soil: fairly light, even chalky.
Cultivation: full sun.
Propagation: from cuttings in summer.
Flowering season: May–November.
Type: evergreen shrub.

Osmanthus

OSMANTHUS

Oleaceae

Osmanthus has more than one card up its sleeve with which to charm us: a fine, always elegant outline, intense green varnished leaves and deliciously-scented white flowers. It is hardy enough to withstand quite severe winters.

Useful hints

— Plant from November to March, adding humus in the form of compost if necessary.

— Prune after flowering to give a pretty shape or simply make it more compact.

Recommended

— The hybrid *Osmanthus × burkwoodii*, impeccable in medium-height hedges, flowers in April–May. *O. delavayi*, lower, with tough leaves and highly-scented flowers, gives its best in well-sheltered positions. *O. heterophyllus*, with prickly holly leaves, flowers in autumn: it is widely used in hedge-making.

Height: 80 cm–2 m (3–7 ft).
Spacing and planting distance: 1 m (3 ft).
Soil: light and rich in humus, not too chalky.
Cultivation: sun or semi-shade.
Propagation: from cuttings in summer.
Flowering season: April–September.
Type: evergreen shrub.

▽ *Osmanthus delavayi*

△ *Paeonia suffruticosa*
▽ *Paeonia suffruticosa*

Paeonia

SHRUB PEONY/TREE PEONY

Paeoniaceae

Very different from herbaceous peonies, 'tree' peonies (they are barely 1.8 m [6 ft] tall) have an undeniable charm. Their ample, glaucous foliage and the tortuous shape of their branches give them a rare presence. Mix with *Dicentra spectabilis* (bleeding hearts) and primulas.

Useful hints

— Plant in spring, placing the union of stock and scion 7.5 cm (3 in) below the surface.

— If an exceptionally hard frost hits them, prune back to ground level in April. The branches will be back in one year and you will have magnificent plants once more.

△ *Paeoniu* **'Souvenir de Maxime Cornu'**
▽ *Paeonia suffruticosa*

Recommended

— Very often imports from Japan, tree peonies are most often sold by colour. *Paeonia* × *lemoine* 'Chromstella' (sulphur yellow) and 'Souvenir de Maxime Cornu' (yellow speckled with carmine pink) are still without equal. Among *P. suffruticosa* (syn. *P. moutan*), the Japanese varieties have a sublime beauty, such as 'Renkaku' (pure white), 'Hanakishoi' (cherry red), 'Higurashi' (crimson) or 'Godaishu' (white and golden), not to mention dozens of others.

Height: 1–1.6 m (3–5 ft).
Spacing and planting distance: 1 m (3 ft).
Soil: humus-rich.
Cultivation: semi-shade or sun, especially for *P. suffruticosa*.
Propagation: from seed or cuttings in early spring.
Flowering season: May, June.
Type: deciduous shrub.

Parthenocissus

VIRGINIA CREEPER

Vitaceae

Do not confuse Virginia creepers: *Ampelopsis* has tendrils and smooth bark (unlike the true creeper, which has rough bark), while *Parthenocissus* has suckers. The latter has decorative leaves and fruit, especially in hot autumns.

Useful hints

— Plant in autumn or spring; guide the first shoots on a trellis or grid.

— To propagate, cut a branch and bury it two-thirds down in a mixture of equal parts of sand and peat. In a few months, it will have rooted and you can plant it out.

Recommended

— Leaving aside *Parthenocissus tricuspidata*, which is fairly common, *P. henryana*, more colourful and *P. tricuspidata* 'Veitchii' (syn. *Ampelopsis veitchii*) with big leaves, are marvellous.

Height: 1.5–6 m (5–20 ft).
Spacing and planting distance: 3 m (10 ft).
Soil: any.
Cultivation: sun or semi-shade.
Propagation: by layering in summer.
Flowering season: negligible.
Type: deciduous creeper.

△ *Parthenocissus quinquefolia*
▽ *Parthenocissus tricuspidata* **'Veitchii'**

△ *Pernettya mucronata*

Pernettya

PERNETTYA

Ericaceae

Now fairly common, *Pernettya* should be called the 'pearl shrubs': their bells of white flowers open in June and are followed by round berries in colours varying from white to dark red via a wide variety of pinks. Grow it in the foreground of rhododendron beds.

Useful hints

— Plant from November to March. Add peat if necessary. Plant several shrubs, one male, to give more fruit.

— To avoid the monotony of mass beds, mix *Pieris* and *Enkianthus* amongst your *Pernettya*. They all have the same requirements and will give a decorative effect all year round.

Recommended

— *Pernettya* is worth having, but you will need to visit several nurseries to find it. 'Bell's Seedling' (dark red) is one of the most common, since it is hermaphrodite and hence capable of bearing fruit even if on its own. Other hybrids of *P. mucronata* have berries in a variety of colours, such as 'Crimsoniana' (red), 'Mother of Pearl' (pink) or 'Winter Times' (white).

Height: 60 cm–1 m (2–3 ft).
Spacing and planting distance: 50 cm (2 ft).
Soil: staying cool in summer.
Cultivation: sun or semi-shade.
Propagation: from cuttings in late summer.
Flowering season: June.
Type: evergreen shrub.

△ *Perovskia atriplicifolia*
Philadelphus 'Silver Shower' △

Perovskia

PEROVSKIA

Labiateae

This is undoubtedly one of the most beautiful and useful little shrubs of all. With very aromatic, delicate grey foliage, *Perovskia* flowers in mid-summer in ravishing shades of blue which match the season perfectly. Mix with shrub lavateras and remontant rosebushes to give very colourful beds which need no maintenance. *Perovskia* goes equally well with white-flowered shrubs and hardy perennial blues such as *Aconitum* or against a background of grey leaves such as the shrub *Artemisia* or lavender.

Useful hints

— Wait until spring before planting *Perovskia*, since it is somewhat sensitive to cold in the first year. They don't mind pebbly soil as long as it is sunny.

— Taking cuttings in the late summer is child's play, and you will have lots of shoots the following spring if you have kept them under a cold frame over winter.

Recommended

— *Perovskia abrotanoides* has grey leaves, and flowers in August and September, not long after *P. atriplicifolia* with its lavender-blue tubular flowers. 'Blue Spire', with larger flowers, is an improved variety.

Height: 1.5 m (5 ft).
Spacing and planting distance: 1 m (3 ft).
Soil: any, not too moist in winter.
Cultivation: full sun.
Propagation: from cuttings in summer.
Flowering season: August, September.
Type: deciduous shrub.

Philadelphus

MOCK ORANGE

Philadelphaceae

Our fine June evenings would not be the same without mock oranges, those inseparable companions of rosebushes, giving off their ravishing scent. So plant at least one mock orange in your garden or on your balcony. Its hardiness should ensure a long life.

Useful hints

— The young shrubs are best planted in containers. Growth is often slow in the first year: if there is no sign of life by May, prune the clump down to ground level – the shoots will then appear direct from the neck. Then water regularly in the first summer.

— Prune after flowering, removing the old wood with cracked bark but leaving the green, often very straight, branches intact: these will then bear flowers the following spring.

— Mix mock oranges with old roses, lilies, irises and peonies and have a small late-flowering clematis trailing amongst their foliage, such as *C. flammula*, while a few *Sternbergia* will brighten up the scene in September. Mock oranges are completely at home in country hedges.

Recommended

— There are a great many, largely with French names, since the person who produced the most early this century was Victor Lemoine, a nurseryman of genius from Lorraine. 'Enchantement', 'Coupe d'Argent' (very compact) and 'Bouquet Blanc' are all white with single flowers; 'Beauclerk', 'Belle Etoile' and 'Sybille', have a powerful scent of orange blossom and a touch of red; 'Virginal', 'Girandole' and 'Glacier' have double pompom flowers. All are scented. There is also a golden variety of *Philadelphus coronarius*, called 'Aureus': this is very much at home in dry, chalky soils, and prefers the shade. 'Manteau d'Hermine' does not grow very tall, and has fairly small double flowers. The most resistant to cold is 'Snowflake' with very large flowers but unfortunately very little scent.

Height: 1–3 m (3–10 ft).
Spacing and planting distance: 1 m (3 ft).
Soil: ordinary, even slightly chalky.
Cultivation: sun or semi-shade.
Propagation: from softwoood cuttings in summer or hardwood cuttings in winter.
Flowering season: June, July.
Type: deciduous shrub.

△ *Photinia fraseri*

Photinia

PHOTINIA

Rosaceae

Photinia created a stir some years ago when it burst on the market, since there at last seemed to be a hedge shrub somewhat out of the ordinary. Mostly evergreens, they have young bright red shoots in spring, then white flowers like those of hawthorn. As pretty as *Pieris*, they are much less fussy about soil: but the attraction has faded somewhat, since photinias are vulnerable to fireblight and hence increasingly avoided by nurserymen, who don't fancy the risk. In an average-sized garden, however, it is easy to get round this problem by pruning all suspect shoots immediately in May–June, i.e. any which suddenly dry out. It would be a great pity not to have such a shrub.

Useful hints

— Plant in spring beside white-flowering shrubs such as amelanchiers or *Spiraea*.

— *Photinia* can be pruned to good effect (generally at the end of summer to avoid harming future flowers).

Recommended

— *Photinia glabra* has leaves which are bronze at first (or bright red in the variety 'Rubens'), then dark green, and white flowers in May-June, followed by red fruit. *P. × fraseri* 'Red Robin' is the commonest, and its undeniable vigour makes it one of the best for evergreen hedges: its young shoots are a brilliant red, while those of 'Birmingham' are more copper-coloured.

Height: 2–3 m (7–10 ft).
Spacing and planting distance: 1 m (3 ft).
Soil: ordinary, rich in humus, domestic compost or leaf-mould.
Cultivation: sunny, sheltered from cold winds.
Propagation: from cuttings in summer.
Flowering season: May, June.
Type: evergreen shrub.

Pieris

ANDROMEDA

Ericaceae

Even if it can sometimes be accused of looking somewhat artificial, particularly in recent variegated versions, *Pieris* has a part to play in the garden, and even in tubs on a semi-shaded terrace. Mixed with rhododendrons, it brings a touch of colour in early spring with its leaves often opening bright red and its clusters of white flowers.

Useful hints

— Plant in autumn or spring.

— Each spring, add 3 handfuls of dried blood and a generous mulch of bracken fronds or rotted dead leaves.

Recommended

— *Pieris formosa forrestii* 'Wakehurst', with marvellous foliage starting out as an incredible red, has long been a 'must'. It has now been joined by *P. floribunda* 'Forest Flame', less sensitive to spring frosts, while lovers of variegated leaves will rush to take advantage of the new Dutch plants.

Height: 2–3.5 m (7–12 ft).
Spacing and planting distance: 2 m (7 ft).
Soil: acid, not drenched in winter.
Cultivation: semi-shade.
Propagation: by layering in early summer (difficult).
Flowering season: April.
Type: evergreen shrub.

▽ *Pieris glaucophylla*

△ *Polygonum aubertii*

△ *Polygonum baldschuanicum*

Polygonum

POLYGONUM, RUSSIAN VINE/ BINDWEED, FLEECE-FLOWER, KNOTWEED, SMARTWEED, PRINCE'S-FEATHER

Polygonaceae

This is one of the most invasive creepers there is: use only where you can keep an eye on it and restrict its spread. On the other hand, it has no equal when it comes to hiding an unsightly building in a hurry.

Useful hints

— Plant at any time of year in well-turned-over soil enriched with compost.

If you want it to develop fast, feed it each spring with 3 handfuls of complete fertilizer and a good covering of half-rotted compost.

— To propagate, all you have to do is cut off a section of stem at ground level: this will quickly root in summer.

Height: up to 12 m (40 ft) and over.
Spacing and planting distance: 3 m (10 ft).
Soil: ordinary, rather rich.
Cultivation: anywhere.
Propagation: from cuttings in summer.
Flowering season: July–September.
Type: deciduous creeper.

Prunus

PRUNUS/ALMOND, APRICOT, CHERRY, PEACH, PLUM

Rosaceae

Prunus is one of the most important tree genera, not only in terms of numbers but also because of the ornamental qualities of its members. In the scope of this book, they will be limited to the shrub varieties, leaving out trees.

Useful hints

— *Prunus* is generally planted from October to March in carefully turned soil enriched with humus by adding leaf-mould or peat.

— If you want natural shapes, prune the vegetation down to ground level at the end of the second winter: this will give you a mushroom shape with many branches near the ground.

— Avoid regular pruning of *Prunus*, which have a tendency to produce gum. Only cherry plums take repeated pruning well, providing this is done with secateurs or well-sharpened scissors.

— Most of these little trees or shrubs find their place quite naturally in beds of hardy perennials, to which they give substance. Mix with amelanchiers, *Spiraea*, viburnums and mock oranges, either to give hardy flowering hedges able to give shelter and nourishment to birds in the area or to brighten up a corner of a lawn.

Recommended

— Amongst the little **cherry trees** not over 3 m (10 ft) tall, *Prunus cerasus* 'Semperflorens' has flowers intermittently right through the good weather on very supple branches. *P. serrula* is valued mainly for its trunk with polished mahogany bark. The hybrid 'Amanogawa' sometimes grows over 6 m (20 ft) tall, but is so narrow that it can be used in even the smallest gardens; its masses of flowers turn it into a pink candle in April. *P. glandulosa* reaches about 1.5 m (5 ft) in all directions, and flowers in white or pink at the end of spring.

Prunus × *cistena* △
Prunus padus 'Coloratus' ▷
Prunus laurocerasus ▽

— **Ornamental almond trees** (*Prunus amygdalus*), 'Roseaplena', for example, a pretty pink, develop a twisted shape. They are one of the earliest to flower, from late February or March, and are ahead of the **ornamental peach trees** (*P. persica*), the prettiest of which is 'Clara Meyer', with double, bright pink flowers. Nor should we forget 'Foliis Rubris' with purple leaves which stand out in a bed of silver-leaved plants. In this category of early-flowering *Prunus* are *P. tenella*, a little shooting shrub with pink flowers in mid-spring, and *P. triloba*, taller and very graceful with its bright pink pompoms in March: it is particularly striking trained against a wall. Prune right back after flowering to keep it well into the wall.

— The **Japanese apricot** (*P. mume*) is a little tree with zigzag branches, flowering early in spring. Its variety 'Alphandii' has reddish-yellow leaves which turn green in summer. The **plum tree** or blackthorn (*P. spinosa*) is an essential in hardy defensive hedges. It turns into a little white cloud when it flowers but watch out for its sharp spines!

— The **cherry plums** are the evergreens of this large family. The most common, the famous Caucasian laurel (*P. laurocerasus*) has large varieties as well as smaller ones such as 'Otto Luyken'. It is thought to be not quite as hardy as the Portuguese laurel (*P. lusitanica*), which has longer leaves. While the former flowers in April, the latter waits until June to bring forth spikes of little white flowers with a very pleasant hawthorn scent. Rather than use these shrubs in classic style by pruning them into geometric shapes, let them assume a more natural ball shape.

Height: 1.5–5 m (5–17 ft).
Spacing and planting distance: 2–3 m (7–10 ft).
Soil: ordinary, preferably cool in summer.
Cultivation: sunny.
Propagation: by grafting in spring or from cuttings in early autumn.
Flowering season: spring.
Type: deciduous or evergreen shrub.

△ *Prunus glandulosa* **'Alba'**
◁ *Prunus triloba*

Prunus serrulata ▷

▽ *Prunus glandulosa*

Planted in clumps or singly, viewed from near or far, azaleas and rhododendrons bring incomparable elegance and gaiety to any garden.

Pyracantha

FIRETHORN

Rosaceae

This plant's formidable spines have no doubt contributed to its success; but rather than use it to make impenetrable hedges, it is better to train it against a wall. Here, carefully pruned a few times, it will cover a vast expanse of wall, transforming it into an incredible backcloth of colour for much of the winter thanks to its innumerable berries.

Useful hints

— Plant in autumn or spring. Mulch each winter with pine bark to prevent weeds, which would be difficult to dig out from amongst its spines. Prune before flowering at the end of winter.

— Be careful: use of weedkillers containing dichlobenyl causes the leaves to turn yellow very suddenly. Try to avoid using too near the base.

Recommended

— *Pyracantha angustifolia* is distinguished by its narrow grey-backed leaves and orange fruit which stays all winter.

— *P. atalantioides* (syn. *p. gibbsii*) looks like a little tree, and has orange ('Berlioz') or red ('Mozart') fruits.

— The commonest firethorns are the hybrids of *P. rogersiana* or *P. coccinea*. Among the most spectacular: 'Golden Glow' (golden yellow); 'Lalandei Monrovia' (upright, with luminous orange fruit); 'Mohave' (very vigorous, also orange); 'Navaho', which is said to be the most disease-resistant; 'Orange Glow', orange; 'Rosedale' (brilliant red, excellent when trained against a wall); 'Shawnee', with a natural pyramid shape.

Height: 2–5 m (7–17 ft).
Spacing and planting distance: 1.5 m (5 ft).
Soil: ordinary, enriched with humus.
Cultivation: at least 6 hours of sun per day.
Propagation: from cuttings in autumn.
Flowering season: June.
Type: evergreen shrub.

▽ *Pyracantha coccinea*

Rhododendron

RHODODENDRON, AZALEA

Ericaceae

Azaleas and rhododendrons now form a single genus since specialists discovered that they are similar in botanical terms. This makes them an enormous group covering several hundreds of species and varieties. They all like heathland soil. Very hardy, they go marvellously in woodland flowerbeds or even rockeries. They can also be grown in tubs on a terrace providing they are not allowed to dry out.

Useful hints

— Plant in heathland soil (acid), moist but well-drained. Exposure to wind is not recommended, especially for the large-leaved varieties. In the first few years, add a leaf mulch. Don't forget to water in summer.

— No need to prune, except to remove dead branches in winter.

— Dead flowers can be removed by hand, using the thumb and index finger (not secateurs).

Recommended: rhododendrons

— **Reds**: 'Blood Red', 'Britannia', 'Carmen', with bells of dark waxy red flowers, 'Fire-ball', 'Gigha' with silvery green foliage and huge funnel-shaped flowers, 'Grenadier', compact and with bunches of blood-red flowers and 'Lord Roberts'.

— **Pinks**: *R. fulvum* can be made into a tree by pruning the lower branches. *R. williamsianum* has spread-out branches, bells of flowers and heart-shaped leaves. 'Pink Pearl', very popular and flowery, grows very large with age; 'Bow Bells'; 'Roseum Elegans' flowers in May, and is very vigorous.

— **Yellows**: *R. flavidium* has dark green, aromatic leaves and is a very upright shape. *R. lutescens* 'Exbury' has reddish bronze leaves, while 'Crest', with bronze leaves, produces huge bunches of flowers in the shape of a primrose-yellow bell.

— **Blues and mauves**: *R. ponticum*, which has become naturalized in our forests, excellent for making large compact hedges, is known to all; 'Blue Diamond' grows slowly to 1 m (3 ft). 'Blue Tit' is ravishing in a rockery with its blue flowers.

Recommended: azaleas

— **Evergreens**: *R. nudiflora* has brilliant leaves and scented pink flowers. *R. tosaense* 'Barbara' has pink flowers and

△ *Rhododendron indicum*
▽ **Azalea Knap Hill**

'Orange Beauty' orange ones. 'Blue Danube' has blue flowers, 'Paestra' white ones and 'Rosebud' pink. *R. nakahari* is useful for ground cover as it has a creeping habit. It carries terracotta red flowers in late June and July.

— **Deciduous**: the Ghent hybrids are amongst the most highly scented, and flower from May onwards: 'Narcissiflorum', with double, pale yellow flowers and 'Corneille' with pink ones. The mollis azaleas are very colourful, the flowers often appearing before the leaves in May. They easily reach 2 m (7 ft). 'Koster's Brilliant Red' is a brilliant red and 'Spek's Orange' is very pretty. The Knap Hill hybrids have trumpet-shaped flowers, and can grow up to 2.5 m (8 ft) tall. 'Hotspur' is a real flame red, and 'Klondyke' a golden flame. 'Silver Slipper' blooms in white and pink.

Height: 20 cm–3 m (8 in–10 ft).
Spacing and planting distance: 1½ times height of adult shrub (ask your nurseryman).
Soil: acid, well-drained but moist.
Cultivation: sunny.
Propagation: by layering or from cuttings in August.
Type: deciduous or evergreen shrub.

△ *Rhododendron* 'Val d'Aulnay'
▽ *Rhododendron williamsianum*

▽ *Rhododendron* 'Fire Ball'

△ **Azalea Knap Hill 'Klondyke'**
▽ *Rhododendron fulvum*

△ *Rhododendron* 'Mrs G. W. Leak'
▽ *Rhododendron* 'Molle'

341

△ *Rhus typhina*

Rhus

SUMACH/SUMAC

Anacardiaceae

Sumach is a little tree which can be used as a shrub, particularly interesting for its autumnal colours and its fruit covered in crimson velvet. Its relatively light shade allows hardy perennials to be planted at its base, such as peonies, ancolias, brunneras or primroses, to which you can add scillas, snowdrops and narcissi in spring and cyclamens in autumn.

Useful hints

— Plant in spring. Water generously for the first summer. Avoid damaging the roots when hoeing, otherwise shoots will appear and threaten to invade everywhere.

— Every 3 years, remove dead wood in autumn; but be careful, the sap is an irritant, so wear gloves.

Recommended

— While *Rhus coriara* is fairly common in scrubland, it is less common in nurseries than *R. typhina* with cut-out leaves and purple cones of flowers. The 'Laciniata' variety has magnificent feathery leaves which are breathtaking in autumn.

Height: 3 m (10 ft).
Spacing and planting distance: 3 m (10 ft).
Soil: ordinary, enriched with humus.
Cultivation: sunny.
Propagation: from cuttings in summer or by suckers or layering in autumn.
Flowering season: summer.
Type: deciduous shrub.

Ribes

FLOWERING CURRANT

Grossulariaceae

The flowering currant really deserves to be rescued from its semi-obscurity, since it is one of the most charming shrubs in spring: not only are its colours sweet, but its flowers and young leaves give off delicious scents ranging from carnation to blackcurrant. Discover them quickly for your hardy hedges and at the back of beds of hardy perennials.

Useful hints

— Plant from October to March: the vegetation often grows slowly, only appearing the next spring. Don't hesitate to bury part of the stem when planting, since new branches can then root directly.

— Prune very slightly after flowering, removing half the new branches.

Recommended

— The alpine currant (*Ribes alpinum*) has yellow flowers followed by red berries. It withstands shade very well, and also has a golden-leaved version ('Aureum'). *R. odoratum* is also yellow in April, but gives off a smell of carnations apparent some metres away. The best-known flowering currants, however, are still varieties of *R. sanguineum*: 'Atrorubens', crimson red, 'King Edward VII', brighter and 'Pulborough Scarlet' in exactly the same red as a *Spiraea* 'Anthony Waterer'.

Height: 2.5 m (8 ft).
Spacing and planting distance: 1 m (3 ft).
Soil: ordinary.
Cultivation: anywhere.
Propagation: from cuttings in winter.
Flowering season: April.
Type: deciduous shrub.

△ *Ribes speciosum*
▽ *Ribes sanguineum*

Rosmarinus

ROSEMARY

Labiatae

Known mainly for its medicinal and aromatic qualities, rosemary would benefit from being used more often for its beauty in company with rosebushes or to decorate corners of dry, pebbly earth. Here it is hardier and flowers magnificently in May in very soft colours. An excellent source of nectar for butterflies and bees.

Useful hints

— Wait until spring before planting, in well-drained soil, even if poor. Cover the base with some handfuls of straw before winter.

— Don't prune: just remove any branches affected by frost. Take cuttings from the ends of stems in late spring if

△ **Rubus calycinoides**
Rubus × tridel △

△ **Rosmarinus lavandulaceus** 'Repens'

you want a medium-sized hedge at low cost.

Recommended

— Medicinal rosemary is available in a variety of colours, intense blue in 'Corsican Blue', pink in 'Roseus' and even white ('Albus'). It may be very upright, like 'Fastigiatus', ideal for decorating the corner of a lawn. The climbing rosemary (*R. lavandulaceus* syn. *officinalis prostratus*) is superb for decorating slopes or pots, but is less hardy than its cousins.

Height: 30 cm–1.75 m (1–6 ft).
Spacing and planting distance: 50 cm (2 ft).
Soil: light, well-drained in winter.
Cultivation: full sun.
Propagation: from cuttings in summer.
Flowering season: May.
Type: semi-evergreen shrub.

Rubus

RUBUS/BLACKBERRY, DEWBERRY, RASPBERRY, THIMBLEBERRY
Rosaceae

Few people suspect that there are such things as elegant brambles. They are generally very graceful due to their thin branches with often highly-coloured bark. The flowers, white or pink, then give rise to berries loved by birds. These are dual-purpose shrubs: their flowers and the graphic beauty of their wood in winter standing out against a background of bare earth or snow.

Useful hints

— Plant from November to March amongst other flowers or in front of beds of shrubs. Their branches should show against a neutral background, such as a brick wall or hedge of evergreen shrubs (*Photinia* or holly).

— Prune old branches right back to ground level each spring (identifiable by their crackly bark). Leave strong branches alone.

Recommended

— *Rubus calcynoids* is an excellent ground cover with evergreen leaves, whose branches end up rooting themselves as they go. It has white flowers in summer, followed by scarlet berries, whether in sun or shade. *R. cockburnianus* also has white flowers, but is mainly known for the waxy, very white bark of its year-old branches: so prune each autumn to remove older wood. *R. tricolor* is vigorous and invasive: its white flowers are followed by edible red fruit. But the best *Rubus* are undoubtedly the hybrid *R. × tridel* and the elm-leaved bramble (*R. ulmifolius* 'Bellidiflorus'): the former grows very fast, producing stakes over 3 m (10 ft) long, covered with large white flowers in May: it would go very well amongst your rosebushes, accompanied by blue and pink irises. The latter is almost a creeper, and has big bunches of pink flowers in July–August: its strength allows it to be used in the wild corners of the garden. *R. spectabilis* is one of the most colourful brambles, with magenta pink flowers in April: it grows very well in the shade of tall trees.

Height: 50 cm–4 m (2–14 ft).
Spacing and planting distance: 1–3 m (3–10 ft).
Soil: ordinary, preferably rich in humus.
Cultivation: sun or semi-shade.
Propagation: by layering in summer.
Flowering season: April–August.
Type: evergreen shrub.

△ **Sambucus racemosa** 'Plumora Aurea'

Sambucus

ELDER
Caprifoliaceae

Completely at home in the wilder corners of a garden, elder is always spectacular when in flower, when its flat creamy-white bunches open up to almost 50 cm (20 in) across. Mix with vigorous plants like *Gunnera*, *Ligularia*, large ferns and *Macleaya* to give an impressive view, providing the soil is rich enough to feed them all.

Useful hints

— Plant from November to March and prune in early spring to give it a vigorous start.

— Cut short the secondary offshoots each March: in this way, you will concentrate the sap on terminal bunches which will be magnificent.

Recommended

— The black elder, *S. nigra*, has given rise to many variegated varieties, even divided like ferns ('Laciniata') or totally golden ('Aurea'). The American elder (*S. canadensis*) is particularly spectacular in the shape of 'Maxima', with magnificent bunches of flowers followed by dark red fruit which the birds love. The red elder, *S. racemosa*, has very divided leaves, almost reminiscent of Japanese maples.

Height: 2–4 m (7–14 ft).
Spacing and planting distance: 2 m (7 ft).
Soil: ordinary.
Cultivation: sun or semi-shade.
Propagation: from cuttings in autumn.
Flowering season: June.
Type: deciduous shrub.

Skimmia

SKIMMIA
Rutaceae

△ *Skimmia japonica*

△ *Spiraea* × *bumalda* 'Anthony Waterer'
▽ *Stephanandra tanakae*

Still largely unknown, *Skimmia* is a genus of low evergreen shrubs with white flowers in April, quickly followed by brilliant red berries. It does very well in most soils, even slightly chalky ones.

Useful hints

— Plant from October to March. Mulch with pine bark each spring.

— Plant male and female *Skimmia* side by side. Mix with decorative garlic, seas of primroses, *Asperula* and *Anemone japonica* for an autumn scene.

Recommended

— *Skimmia japonica* has given rise to varieties with a wide range of coloured fruit, such as 'Foremanii', a female-only clone with bright red fruit; 'Rubella', a male clone valued mainly for its buttons of red flowers throughout the winter; 'Rogersii', a female ground cover clone.

— *S. laureola* gives off a pronounced aromatic scent when its leaves are rubbed; its scented flowers are followed by red fruit on the female stems. Those of *S. reevesiana* are decorative right through winter.

— *Skimmia reevesiana* 'Rubella' is a male form valued mainly for its buttons of red flowers throughout the winter.

— *S.* × 'Foremanii' is a female form with attractive bright red fruit, preceded by sweet-scented creamy white flowers. The berries will last all through the winter season.

Height: 60 cm–1.5 m (2–5 ft).
Spacing and planting distance: 1 m (3 ft).
Soil: rich in humus.
Cultivation: sun or semi-shade.
Propagation: from cuttings in late summer.
Flowering season: April, May.
Type: evergreen shrub.

Spiraea

SPIRAEA
Rosaceae

Spiraea is at the peak of its reputation: easy to grow, undemanding, very flowery. They flower in spring, generally in white but numerous varieties which flower virtually all summer have recently come on to the market. Those which bloom in summer are more pink, sometimes even red. Some varieties have white, pink and even red flowers on the same plant, such as *Spiraea japonica* 'Little Princess', a very useful dwarf variety.

Useful hints

— Plant *Spiraea* at any time of year: they are very hardy, but when planting, bear in mind that *Spiraea* × *arguta*, *S. vanhouttei* and *S.* × *billiardii* can reach 2 m (7 ft) from the ground.

Recommended

— *Spiraea arguta* ('bride's veil') has a drooping appearance. *S.* × *bumalda* 'Anthony Waterer' is decorative and very flowery. *S.* × *billiardii* has bright pink flowers in summer and slightly pinkish leaves. *S.* × *bumalda* 'Gold-flame', with golden leaves, compact and with little deep pink flowers, goes well where there is not much room.

Height: 50 cm–2 m (2–7 ft).
Spacing and planting distance: 80 cm (32 in) (40 cm [16 in] for 'Little Princess').
Soil: deep and fertile.
Cultivation: sun or semi-shade.
Propagation: from cuttings in autumn.
Flowering season: spring or summer.
Type: deciduous shrub.

Stephanandra

STEPHANANDRA
Rosaceae

Closely related to *Spiraea*, *Stephanandra* is a very subtle shrub: not for its stunning flowers or spectacular fruit – its beauty lies mainly in its very supple bearing. The long, asymmetric leaves are spread along elegantly bowed branches. A shrub for beginners, who can mix it with hostas, *Hydrangea paniculata* and white cornflowers to give a refined picture. It also acts as excellent ground cover in large beds, when mixed with *Nandina* and Japanese mahonias: a sight guaranteed all year round.

Useful hints

— Plant in early spring and divide in autumn.

— Prune every third year, in March, to remove the branches from the centre and those that are out of balance.

Recommended

— *Stephanandra incisa* has cut-away leaves and white flowers in June: its variety 'Crispa' forms a very decorative dome. *S. tanakae* looks like a fountain: its leaves, larger than the last variety, turn to gold in autumn and its wood takes on a very pleasant warm brown colour in winter.

Height: 1.5–2.5 m (5–8 ft).
Spacing and planting distance: 2 m (7 ft).
Soil: ordinary, fairly cool.
Cultivation: sun or semi-shade.
Propagation: by layering or from cuttings in summer.
Flowering season: June, July.
Type: deciduous shrub.

Symphoricarpos

SNOWBERRY/CORALBERRY

Caprifoliaceae

Snowberry will quickly take up all the space it can find thanks to its incredibly sturdy shoots: so use these shrubs as low hedges, or place a few in an out-of-the-way corner where they can grow to their heart's content, along with other sturdy shrubs like brambles and mahonias. They can even prosper in the shade of large conifers and beeches.

Useful hints

— Plant from November to March. Mulch the soil and water in the first summer; after that, just remove untidy suckers.

— Prune in March if you want to keep it a definite shape, but respect its natural tendency to roundness.

Recommended

— *Symphoricarpos orbiculatus*, the small-flowered snowberry, has a yellow variegated variety ('Variegatus'). The commonest snowberries are hybrids like 'Mme Lemoine' (pure white), 'Mother of Pearl' with large pink fruit and 'Magic Berry', more compact, pink so dark as to be almost red. *S. × chenaultii* 'Hancock' makes excellent ground cover, growing scarcely 1 m (3 ft) high, with pink and white fruit. *S. albus* (the pearl tree) 'Laevigatus' has snow-white berries, bigger than those of the more common variety 'White Hedger'.

Height: 60 cm–2 m (2–7 ft).
Spacing and planting distance: 1 m (3 ft).
Soil: any.
Cultivation: anywhere.
Propagation: by separating suckers in winter.
Flowering season: negligible.
Type: deciduous shrub.

Syringa

LILAC

Oleaceae

Everyone loves lilacs for their magnificent flowers and distinctive scent. Use them abundantly in flowering hedges, mixed with dog roses, mock oranges, mahonias, deutzias and amelanchiers. Plant *Campanula persicifolia* at the base.

Useful hints

— Plant from November to March, avoiding times of severe frost. Growth will be very slow the first year. Mulch and water regularly until September. The colour of flowers may vary the first time; so don't complain to the nursery if they seem paler than you expected.

— Prune in the week after they flower, removing faded bunches without harming the young shoots. Prune back further every 3 years to assist the branches nearer the ground. Carefully remove shoots growing from the ground since they will quickly exhaust the base.

Recommended

— **Single flowers**: here, the best-known are varieties of *Syringa vulgaris*: 'Blue Hyacinth,' a lavender blue; 'Congo', more squat and tending to red; 'Firmament', sky blue; 'Marechal Foch', carmine-pink, astounding in its fullness; 'Primrose', one of the first yellow lilacs and still one of the best; 'Souvenir de Louis Späth', wine-red or 'Vestale' pure white and very flowery.

— **Double flowers**: 'Charles Joly' a dark purple red, very late; 'General Pershing', violet purple; 'Katherine Havemeyer', highly scented violet-blue; 'Mme Lemoine', white and slightly later; 'Paul Thirion', one of my favourites since it stays denser and flowers in pure wine-colour. We should also mention 'Belle de Nancy', satin pink, 'Joly' wine-red; 'Duc de Masse', lilac pink, 'Mme Edouard Harding', bright red with pink spots and 'President Poincare', with largish light-mauve flowers.

— Some **botanical lilacs** and their varieties are not without interest, such as *S. velutina*, never over 1.5 m (5 ft) high, with beautiful grey-backed leaves and bunches of flowers 10–15 cm (4–6 in) long and pale lilac in May–June. Or again, *S. microphylla* 'Superba', a little wonder which not only flowers in mauve pink in May but again in late summer, with an incredible scent. Lastly, there are hybrids worth a look, such as *S. × josiflexa* 'Bellicent', with enormous light pink bunches, or *S. × prestoniae*, very vigorous but rather late, since it flowers in June. *S. vulgaris* (common lilac) is one of the most highly scented in May–June.

Height: 1.5–4 m (5–14 ft).
Spacing and planting distance: 50 cm–2 m (2–7 ft).
Soil: ordinary, even chalky.
Cultivation: sunny.
Propagation: from cuttings in summer.
Flowering season: May, June, sometimes September.
Type: deciduous shrub.

△ **Symphoricarpos albus**

△ **Syringa hybrid**
▽ **Syringa 'Mme Lemoine'**

Viburnum carlesii △
△ *Viburnum opulus* 'Sterile'

Viburnum opulus △

Viburnum tomentosum 'Mariesii' △
Weigela florida 'Variegata' ▷
▽ *Vitus coignetiae*

Viburnum

VIBURNUM

Caprifoliaceae

Viburnums are available in a number of species and varieties. They are very easy to grow, and most have superb autumnal colours and a delightful scent. Some have evergreen leaves and pretty fruit.

Useful hints

— Plant in autumn; a handful of hoof and horn will help the young plants grow.

— No need to prune: simply remove any branches which spoil the shape.

Recommended

— **Deciduous**: *Viburnum* × *bodnantense* has pink, highly-scented flowers in autumn, and vertically-growing branches. *V. opulus* 'Sterile' (snowball bush) blooms in spectacular globes of white flowers. *V. tomentosum* has leaves a pretty wine colour in autumn, and white flowers and red fruit which then turns black in autumn. 'Mariesii' has branches which grow horizontally in stages.

— **Evergreens**: *V.* × *burkwoodii*, with brilliant green leaves, has pink buttons which open out into white flowers from January–February. *V. carlesii*, semi-evergreen, has white flowers which are some of the most scented of all. *V. rhytidophyllum* has the advantage of growing fast, which makes up for its slightly gloomy appearance with its leaves of leathery appearance on top and grey felt underneath. *V. tinus* has pink-white flowers in winter and black fruit from February: a good seaside shrub.

Height: 2 m (7 ft).
Spacing and planting distance: 1 m (3 ft).
Soil: good, with humus.
Cultivation: sun or semi-shade.
Propagation: by layering in autumn or from cuttings in summer.
Flowering season: May, June.
Type: deciduous or evergreen.

Vitis

VINE/GRAPE

Vitaceae

Everyone knows the vine, but not many know that there are dozens of species and even more varieties: all share tendrils devoid of suckers and often take on superb autumn colours.

Useful hints

— Plant from November to March in well-turned-over, not too acid soil. Fix the first climbing stems to stakes. Vines love trellis-work and trellis-covered arches (they cannot get a hold on smooth walls).

— Treat once with Bordeaux mixture in August to prevent massive attacks of mildew which can wreck a vine completely in 2 weeks. Likewise, treat with a benomyl-based mixture if white leaves appear.

Recommended

— The grape vine (*Vitis vinifera*) has numerous decorative varieties, such as 'Purpurea' (dyer's vine) with leaves at first red then green then turning to purple red, or 'Brandt', very vigorous, with delicious dark red fruit and intensely-coloured leaves in autumn. *V. coignetiae* has very large leaves in spectacular crimson colours just before the frosts.

Height: up to 8 m (27 ft).
Spacing and planting distance: 3 m (7 ft).
Soil: pebbly.
Cultivation: sunny.
Propagation: by layering in summer.
Flowering season: negligible.
Type: deciduous creeper.

Weigela

WEIGELA

Caprifoliaceae

Although *Weigela* is in fashion at the moment, its habit of putting out gloomy red flowers in summer makes one think twice about using it. Give it more graceful companions, such as *Stephanandra* or variegated cornflowers, to disguise its military bearing. It also goes well with light coloured iris, white rockets and slender flowers in general.

Useful hints

— They can be planted at virtually any time of year (they are almost always sold in containers). Mulch in spring with half-rotted compost and water generously in the first summer.

— Prune after flowering, removing any wood over 2 years old to leave room for new branches in full growth. Leave the latter intact to let them weep gracefully.

Recommended

— The botanical *Weigela* are hardly grown now, except for *W. middendorffiana*, fairly compact, with sulphur-yellow flowers in April or May. *W. florida* 'Foliis Purpureis' (purple) gives a strong contrast with silver- or gold-leaved shrubs. *W. florida* 'Variegata' is popular but looks artificial unless surrounded by more flexible plants (*Armeria*, *Dianthus*, *Erinus*). There are numerous hybrids flowering in early summer: 'Ballet', dark red, 'Bristol Ruby', very upright, ruby red, 'Eva Rathke', crimson red, slow-growing, 'Fiesta', rich in flowers, bright red, 'Newport Red', light red and 'Styriaca', carmine red.

Height: 80 cm–2 m (3–7 ft).
Spacing and planting distance: 1 m (3 ft).
Soil: ordinary.
Cultivation: sunny.
Propagation: from cuttings after flowering.
Flowering season: April–September.
Type: deciduous shrub.

Wisteria syn. Wistaria

WISTERIA, WISTARIA
Leguminosae

Undoubtedly one of the prettiest climbers and one of the easiest to grow. Who could resist its beauty in full flower, cascading down a pergola, adorning a building or trained to form a little tree? You can achieve a refined effect by mixing a pale blue Chinese wisteria and an early yellow rosebush such as 'Maigold' or *Clematis montana*, white. You can also bring their colour to earth by planting lavender-coloured iris or dog's tooth violets.

Useful hints

— Plant at any time, turning the soil over thoroughly and adding sand if it seems too dense. Mulch in spring and water regularly in the first summer. If wisteria grows too fast, it may forget to flower. Add phosphorus-rich fertilizer and wait patiently for a few years.

— To propagate, cut off a stem and bury it about 20 cm (8 in) deep. Roots will appear after a few months; all you then have to do is to replant in the chosen position.

Recommended

— Chinese wisteria (*Wisteria sinensis*) has mauve and white varieties, and even one with double flowers. All are scented. Japanese wisteria (*W. floribunda*) has longer racemes, lighter but unscented. The most stunning is 'Macrobotrys', whose racemes are sometimes over 1 m (3 ft) long! Its flowers are the largest in the genus and come in intense violet.

Height: up to 10 m (33 ft).
Spacing and planting distance: 3 m (10 ft).
Soil: not chalky.
Cultivation: sunny.
Propagation: by layering in summer.
Flowering season: May (occasionally in September).
Type: deciduous climber.

Yucca

YUCCA
Liliaceae

This is one of the most architectural plants there is. It goes marvellously in large rockeries and Mediterranean-type beds: *Yucca* prefers a sunny and dry spot. Its flowers are impressive, generally appearing 2 to 3 years after planting.

Useful hints

— Plant in spring. The soil must be well-drained.

— Do not prune. Remove the dried leaves at the base and faded flowers. Watch the spikes!

Recommended

— *Yucca filamentosa* is the most impressive, sometimes reaching 2 m (7 ft) and forming dense clumps. *Y. flaccida* easily reaches 1 m (3 ft) high. *Y. glauca* has a short trunk with sword-shaped leaves.

Height: 60 cm–2 m (2–7 ft).
Spacing and planting distance: 1 m (3 ft).
Soil: poor, dry.
Cultivation: full sun or semi-shade.
Propagation: by transplanting suckers in spring.
Flowering season: August.
Type: evergreen shrub.

△ *Wisteria floribunda* 'Macrobotrys'
Wisteria venusta △

△ *Wisteria sinensis*
▽ *Yucca flaccida*

At Giverny, ornamental cabbages make an attractive autumn
decoration, beside a small path.

BEDS AND BORDERS

The landscaping of a garden is subject to the constraints of its environment and requires creative use of shapes and colours. In the first chapter I offer guidance which will guarantee you success, taking into account the limitations of each individual garden, its soil and the sort of plants that you might want to establish there. However, I am well aware that beds and borders are always a particular problem for amateur gardeners. I offer some ideas here to get over this which, with a bit of imagination, will be sure to help you.

BEDS

A bed is usually found next to a lawn and is designed to be viewed from all sides. It tends to be planted with species which have similar requirements. Its shape will depend on where you want it to be, your taste, and if there are already any trees. It is only in parks that you find beds raised higher than the grass or the pathway (this is probably so that they can be admired from a distance by people going for a stroll). In private gardens they tend to be dug lower than ground level so that watering is easier and also so that winter mulching with leaves or peat does not show as much.

—When planting always start from the middle of the bed, using plants that are the most important and the tallest. Then view your planting from all angles. Next plant the border edges, then fill in the in-between space. Here are some examples to start you off.

Beds in a sunny spot

—In the centre plant *Eremurus* and foxgloves together with some *Delphinium* and if the bed is to be seen from a distance and is a fair size try *Heracleum*. On the outside try several groups of dahlias and scattered cleomes and several *Guara*. In one third sow *Lavatera* and *Eryngium*.

—In the foreground the plants should be fairly small and longer lasting, such as *Anaphalis*, *Geranium cinereum*, *Potentilla* and bunches of white and pale yellow daffodils for the beginning of spring.

Beds in the shade

—The arrangement I suggest, fortunately, needs very little upkeep and will look quite spectacular, especially if you can make the bed long and narrow.

—At one end plant *Helleborus lividus corsicus* with mahonias and narcissi for the spring. Keep the other end for columbines, hostas, ferns and *Fritillaria* with the quite unusual bulbs (which you leave in the ground). In the centre plant *Digitalis purpurea*, *Astrantia* and large clumps of *Rodgersia*.

—The border edges could be packed with crosuses, and *Pulmonaria* used as a ground cover.

In classical style, this bed offers a mixture of yellow flowers **(Achillea, Coreopsis, Santolina)** *red* **(Geum),** *pink* **(Geranium endressii)** *and mauve* **(Salvia).**

Beds with damp soil

—These beds can be really outstanding. Make sure you arrange yours so that you can look at it from all angles.

—In the middle, *Rodgersia* and *Ligularia*, surrounded by *Astilbe* and *Anemone japonica*, will be really attractive towards the end of the year.

—At one end the large mauve spikes of the *Lythrum* can really stand out from the vivid yellow of a group of *Lysimachia*.

—At the other end bunches of iris, especially *Iris siberica*, look much more attractive blended in with ferns, while a group of *Zantedeschia* in a tapestry of *Symphytum* or of *Myosotis palustris* make a pretty blue and white display.

—To minimize upkeep, plant *Polygonum* generously round the edges.

Beds by the water's edge

—The crowning glory here will be a sumptuous *Gunnera* or two if you leave enough space for them. Plant *Zantedeschia* in the foreground.

—Right at the edge of the water, plant separate groups of *Lysichiton* and *Iris kaempferi*.

—The foreground is perfect for *Primula japonica* and *Hosta fortunei*. To get a lovely mass of feathery flowers try *Aruncus*, which grows up to 1 m (40 in) in height, next to *Filipendula*.

—Contrary to popular belief, *Aster novi-belgii* flower even more profusely in slightly damp positions. Don't forget to use them here for the autumn display.

351

BORDERS

Borders are generally situated in front of a hedge, a wall or house. Here are some planting ideas. If you have got enough room you can include shrubs, although a purist would never have any shrub or tree in their herbaceous borders. But times have changed. Nowadays, when time is at a premium, it is important to have as many plants as possible which can look after themselves. Shrubs fall into this category and it is worth considering both flowering species and evergreens. I tend from time to time to put the odd tree in my borders, especially flowering cherry, magnolias and dogwood, which also have the benefit of providing shelter to flowers like *Trillium*, primula, *Brunnera*, hosta, *Pulmonaria* and *Helleborus*. It is not necessary to follow any strict rules; just be guided by your own personal taste and the availability of species and varieties that you prefer.

—I would advise separating plants with very similar foliage, such as iris and *Hemerocallis*, and in the same way flowers of the same colour and height.

—Vary the shape of each group of plants and leave a space between them.

—If the border is in front of a hedge, leave a 30 to 40 cm (12–16 in) gap to give yourself space to work in.

Planting

—Always leave plenty of room between different plants. As soon as they become established, they fill out and look much better if they are not all crowded together.

—Create a shallow basin around shrubs so that they get the maximum benefit from watering.

—Instead of using stakes, try branches or a wide mesh-net strung between posts that are concealed by shrubs. The flowers will blossom through the mesh and hide the net.

—If you are late in planting out, do so in the evening when the sun has gone down. Before planting, water the area thoroughly, leave to drain, put the plant in and then water again.

Upkeep

—Watering and weeding are essential, particularly from May until the end of September.

—Extend the flowering period by removing dead flowers.

—Before the winter arrives, put down mulch to protect the plants from the cold and frost.

—Roughly every three years, lift perennials in autumn or March/April. Divide them and replant wherever there are gaps.

Pink borders

This border is, without doubt, the easiest to arrange and so is ideal for the weekend gardener. It is based on the rose 'Centenaire de Lourdes' which has exceptionally lovely flowers and can be planted in groups of two or three. I prefer to sow *Lavatera* and *Cosmos* directly into the ground. Their long flowering season can be extended even further if they are dead-headed regularly. I would then include antirrhinums in a choice of several shades of pink, and dahlias and chrysanthemums which flower almost till the frost arrives.

—Large clusters of astilbes give solidity to a border but they need regular watering to keep them looking attractive.

—Gilly-flower will fill the garden with perfume and blossom at the beginning of spring, and pink lupins look nice in clusters. A few groups of tulips will provide a pretty springtime border. Plant *Chelone obliqua* in a shady corner. Whenever I try to include this arrangement it is always a big success. If you are a petunias fan then plant them out for summer at the end of the gilly-flower and tulip season.

—I have a weakness for cleomes which have an unusual blossom and look so beautiful underneath roses. If you have a semi-shaded spot put in *Anemone japonica* for autumn flowering.

—It takes three years to establish a cluster of peonies but it is well worth waiting for. Look out particularly for *Paeonia* 'Bowl of Beauty' with its crinkled petals and golden colour and you won't be disappointed.

—The dark pink of *Sedum spectabile* looks lovely with several clusters of *Sidalcea*. Remember to include phlox which can add several different tones of pink. Choose two or three different tones and separate them with *Galega*.

In a southern garden, **Begonia semperflorens** *bring gaiety throughout the summer.*

353

—It is worth making a special effort to get hold of *Diascia* to use in the front together with dwarf asters. Just behind them the spears of *Dierama* add a touch of elegance to a carpet of *Androsace* or *Aubrieta*.

—A plant that can be relied on to perform every year is *Alstroemeria*, whose profusion of flowers gives the garden a sort of untidy charm. It can be a bit dull so I would suggest using *Macleaya* behind it. The pale pink flowers of this plant hang from stems that grow to 2.5 m (100 in) without staking. In autumn it should be cut back flush with the ground and the root covered with a thick layer of leaves. Another way of displaying *Macleaya* is behind the dense foliage of *Geranium sanguineum* or *macrorrhizum*.

—Plant *Dianthus* at the front of the border for early summer together with masses of *Helianthemum* for its silvery evergreen foliage and its soft, tiny pink flowers.

—There are many shrubs suitable for pink borders. One of the best is *Lavatera trimestris* which grows to 80 cm (32 in) in one season and flowers continually from June to September. Do not hesitate to use it but be warned that it needs plenty of space. It takes up more than a square metre. *Chaenomeles* are particularly leggy, but the colour is lovely. Plant *Cistus* in front to hide the bare branches.

—*Deutzia* and *Escallonia* are both very easy to maintain. *Viburnum carlesii* with its fragrant clusters of flowers is a most elegant shrub. The flowering cherry is also very charming and *Weigela* has the advantage of flowering in summer like the shade-loving hortensias.

—Be careful: if you put too many shrubs in a border it will make it look cluttered; five for every 20 sq m (24 sq yd) is plenty.

Blue borders

Blue borders should be established in the brightest part of the garden so that the mauves and violets do not seem too dark when the sky is overcast.

—Backgrounds and corners can be filled very effectively with 'metallic' foliage plants like *Acanthus*. They provide a setting for the intense colour of *Geranium* 'Johnson's Blue' which stands out all the more against its dark green foliage.

—Pride of place must go to groups of delphinium in different blues next to bunches of late-flowering asters. The compact clumps of *Brunnera* with its tiny blue flowers reminiscent of myosotis are indispensable, not only as a foreground to conceal the bare stems of the delphiniums, but also to accompany sizeable bunches of scabious which tend to have thin foliage. The picture is complete with waves of *Gentiana asclepiadea*, a few branches being set among them to give support. *Echinops* sits well in the centre of the border alongside the more luminous blue of the catananches. For mid-summer flowering, an essential ingredient is provided by violet phloxes and pale blue *Phlox paniculata* in the company of *Veronica teucrium* and *Veronica gentianoides*.

—There could be no blue border without campanulas and all varieties are of interest from the majestic *Campanula pyramidalis* to the charming ground-cover plant, the unpronounceable *Campanula portenschlagiana*. *C. persicifolia* should also be planted in large patches together with *Salvia* at the front of the border.

—For spring flowering, grow plenty of *Scilla* and *Allium* or a number of other blue bulbs that can be left in the ground.

—For summer flowering, choose *Camassia*, a lovely blue in the centre and at the front of the border.

—One of the most striking blues of all comes from the agapanthus and, although it is a demanding plant, it is worth laying in a dozen bulbs which must be protected in winter by a mound of peat. To set off the elegant spikes of the agapanthus, provide surrounding ground cover with *Vinca minor* and bunches of *Polemonium* with its light blue flowers.

—Lavender blends easily with different shades of blue, as does nepeta which can easily be pruned to form a hedge.

—The scene would not be complete without a group of irises, many of which are a delicate blue. To conceal their dead leaves after the flowering season, plant them among later-flowering *Perovskia* which are powdery blue with a touch of silver.

—Shrubs that can be used to set off the blue flowers include *Ceanothus* (if the region is not too cold), *Perovskia* and *Cariopteris*, all of which are easy to come by, to site and to maintain. They can be planted on their own or, if the border is a large one,

This beautiful flower bed is largely composed of white flowering plants. You can pick out **Anaphalis, Campanula latifolia, Centranthus, Cosmos, Physostegia** *and the silvery-leaved* **Stachys lanata.** *The* **Ageratum** *in the foreground adds a touch of pink.*

in threes. Another much-admired shrub with pale blue flowers is *Clematis heracleifolia davidiana*.

—Silver foliage shrubs, especially *Artemesia*, heighten the effect of blue borders. Buddleia has superb shades of violet and long, perfumed spikes that attract butterflies.

White borders

It was in the famous gardens at Sissinghurst, in Kent, that Vita Sackville-West created her White Garden in 1930. It remains an inspiration for gardeners and landscapers everywhere. The great spikes of delphinium, in the background, the delicacy of *Gypsophila* and the masses of *Phlox paniculata* all combine to give an impression of grace and solidarity. If you want to create a white border it is best to set it against a green hedge (holly or yew for example) to bring out the different tones of white.

—If the border is quite wide, then plant a *Crambe* whose high stems and abundance of fine flowers lend presence to the composition. The robust single flowers of the *Leucanthemum* will provide summer flowers in plenty if withered ones are removed as they fade. Dahlias too, especially the cactus type of dahlia, are very useful for filling the odd corner.

—Silver foliage plants make a welcome addition, for example *Anaphalis* has a long flowering season and santolinas are also attractive when trimmed and the yellow flowers removed.

355

—For the least sunny part of the garden I would suggest putting in *Tradescantia*, *Campanula glomerata* 'Alba' and *Campanula carpatica* which are good for ground cover. The unusual spikes of *Physostegia* lend elegance to the composition especially when arranged in a sinuous wave from background to foreground.

—*Lysimachia clethroides* is somewhat invasive but forms a compact arrangement that takes care of itself. Lilies can be difficult to integrate but their whites blend well with *Eryngium*; the two also provide each other with physical support.

—For the foreground, there is quite a choice: *Dianthus* with its delicate perfume, *Iberis* with its dense evergreen foliage and *Geranium pratense* 'Album' with its equally pretty leaves. Use *Lynchnis coronaria* with its fine flowers above rosettes of silvery leaves for splashes of white, and *Stachys lanata*, *Aubrieta* and *Phlox subulata* to fill the spaces.

—There is also a good choice among the white-flowering shrubs. I would suggest *Choisya ternata* for three reasons: the flowers are perfumed, its evergreen foliage is attractive and it can be pruned if growth is excessive. *Hydrangea paniculata* and *Spiraea* are good for the summer and I am particularly fond of *Olearia* with its daisy-like flowers. The 'Sterile' variety of *Viburnum opulus*, popularly known as the snowball tree, is spectacular.

—For smaller shrubs choose *Potentilla fruticosa* 'Mandschurica' or 'Vilmoriniana'. For early flowering it is worth thinking about *Prunus* and *Viburnum × bodnantense*, whose flowers appear from December to February before the foliage.

—It is not very traditional, but there really is nothing to stop you using a spectacular plant like a yucca in a white border and this really can look quite stunning.

—To complete the list, don't forget that the rosebush 'Swany' provides excellent ground cover and that the inimitable 'Iceberg' should be included.

Red borders

The only thing to remember with red borders is to take care where you put them.

—If the garden is small the number of different species needs to be restricted. For areas up to 20 sq m (24 sq ft), red roses look marvellous flowering over *Geum* planted under the bushes. Try sowing *Nicotiana* to enliven the border. For spring flowers, red tulips should be planted amongst a carpet of daisies. Line the edges with iris and bergenia. You will find these seven species enough to complete your border.

—For a larger area offering some perspective, a dazzling scene can be created with the differently textured foliage and varied flower forms of *Althaea*, *Aster*, *Lythrum* and *Rheum*. In the centre, a cluster of *Phygelius* is very effective with its light bell-shaped flowers. For those who like gladioli, this is the place for them. One corner should be filled with large clumps of peonies and *Hemerocallis*. *Kniphofia* and *Amaranthus caudatus*, provided that they are kept well apart, add a novel touch. A mixture of dahlias and phlox will be attractive in the centre. Sages are useful, especially *Salvia officinalis* whose dark red foliage lends a sort of stability to more ephemeral neighbours. The same applies to *Sedum spectabile* when it is put next to *Chrysanthemum rubellum*. Lupin spikes make a pleasing contrast to the denticulate petals of cornflowers. *Phygelius* flowers are elegant next to the thicker mass of *Canna*, which should be placed in the background as the leaves do not look attractive when they wither.

—A long narrow border could be a quarter filled with bunches of *Crocosmia* scattered among the heathers. The remainder can be given over to *Polygonum*, *Bergenia* and *Impatiens*, provided the latter can have semi-shade available.

—In a border of this kind purple and red foliages are more effective than flowering shrubs. *Photinia* or *Cotinus coggygria* are both good, and the sword-like foliage of *Phormium* can be used to great advantage.

—The red berries of *Cotoneaster* are very decorative and space should also be found for *Weigela* 'Newport Red' and the delightful *Spiraea* 'Antony Waterer'.

—The clematis 'Ville de Lyon' provides good cover, clambering over *Cotoneaster* during its long summer-flowering season.

Yellow and orange borders

For many years I was against putting orange in my borders. Then one day I found that orange and yellow used together look good. Moreover it brings a touch of sunshine to the garden, even when the weather is overcast.

—Dahlias should be in the centre against a background of *Althaea, Hellanthus, Ligularia* and *Solidago*. Use *Anthemis tinctoria* to separate such strongly-coloured flowers as *Achillea, Crocosmia, Gaillardia* and *Rudbeckia*. Introduce *Euphorbia* and *Heliopsis* into the centre.

—An indispensable plant, but one that must be protected from too much sun, is *Hemerocallis*. Another favourite for the front is *Alchemilla mollis*, which has astonishing foliage that always seems to be covered with droplets of water, even in dry weather. If the dead flowers are not removed, the seeds will disperse and take root all over the garden. I don't usually bother to pull them out as they look nice almost anywhere. *Asphodeline* and *Aquilegia* should be placed among the *Alchemilla* and given plenty of room. They should be planted in long clumps rather than in small circles. For an original note, plant one or two groups of *Fritillaria imperialis* among the *Alchemilla*: their flowers are reminiscent of pineapples on stalks.

—For a border flowering in April, *Inula, Iris pumila* and narcissi are lovely.

—*Lysimachia* is a marvellous asset once established and will thrive and flower anywhere every year. *Oenothera*, with its remarkable though rather garish flowers, can be placed in front of *Lysimachia*. Plant these next to santolinas and keep the latter's button-like yellow heads (rather than cutting them off as you would for a white border).

—In this kind of border there is an excuse for introducing conifers, such as a small *Chamaecyparis lawsoniana* 'Minima Aurea' with its golden spirals of foliage or a ground-cover plant such as *Juniperus* 'Depressa aurea'. The scene can be completed with a *Mahonia* or a variegated *Ilex*.

—Further possibilities include *Genista* and *Phlomis fruticosa* with its downy evergreen foliage. *Euonymous fortunei* is a good ground-cover plant which has the merit of keeping its foliage in winter like *Hypericum*, another that is easy to plant and quick to become established.

—Among the flowering shrubs to consider are *Kerria japonica* and forsythia, the latter being one of the earliest to bloom in spring. Some people swear by forsythia and could not even imagine their garden without it; personally I am not very fond of it. I prefer the charm and fragrance of *Philadelphus coronarius* 'Aureus' in a golden border.

Pastel borders

As the variety of flowers available is almost infinite, pastel borders are easy to arrange for any size and type of garden. For those, I love any simple plants that flower in spring and summer. Plant them in front of a hedge and the green background will bring out the harmony of colours from soft pink to pale yellow, sky-blue and all the different shades of white.

—To avoid an impression of muddle, it is better to plan for a crescendo of colour. Begin with a white *Arenaria* and a group of irises at the edge. Don't forget *Campanula carpatica*, which is a good ground cover combining white and blue. Following on and in the centre, plant a mixture of columbines that go well with the powdery blue of two or three clumps of *Veronica incana*. Next can come shades of pink, with *Lychnis flos-ovis* positioned immediately behind *Helianthemum* 'Wisley Pink'. An interesting contrast can be made between the flat flowers of *Salvia horminum* and the spikes of *Pyrethrum roseum*. This setting is rounded off perfectly with a background of *Dictamnus albus* combined with the blue of *Aconitum*.

—It is also quite fun to mix the colours together, taking care though to avoid the stronger reds and oranges. Lupins can have a prominent position as their colours are always soft and they can be positioned just behind *Pulsatilla*, which flower at the same time. (To keep it in proportion use three groups of *Pulsatilla* for every lupin.) Miniature roses grouped along the edge will flower throughout the summer if the dead blooms are removed regularly. *Lavandula* blends perfectly with this arrangement.

—*Cosmos* seeds can be sown directly *in situ*; the few reds there are among the pinks and whites will not detract from the overall pastel effect of the border.

—In this kind of border I like shrubs with delicate flowers such as *Deutzia, Spiraea* or *Buddleia alternifolia*, with its cascade of flowering branches. The *Ceanothus* 'Gloire de Versailles', with its delicate hint of blue, situated just behind a cluster of blue and white *Hesperis* will give off a wonderful scent in the summer evenings.

KEYS TO
SUCCESS

Your garden is shaded and has a clay soil. You dream of summer blossoms of pink and blue, shimmering green foliage in autumn and a beautiful and trouble-free garden. Yet you cannot spare much time for gardening.

You love cyclamens, stocks, irises and peonies, but you do not know if they will flourish in the habitat you can provide. The following tables will supply the answers to all the questions you may have.

□ ★ △ ■ ☆ ▲

To make the table easy to follow, we have given each variety one of the following six symbols (the symbols have no botanical significance in themselves):

The column on the left gives the Latin names.

A

	SOIL TYPES							CONDITIONS			FOLIAGE							FLOWERS									ANNUALS	
	PEATY	SANDY, LIGHT	POOR, DRY	DAMP, WELL-DRAINED	CLAY	DRY AND WARM	SHADED, SEMI-SHADED	SUNNY	MEDITERRANEAN	COASTAL	SILVERY	GOLDEN	VARIEGATED	RED	EVERGREEN	AUTUMNAL	WHITE AND GREEN	BLUE, MAUVE	VIOLET, BLACK	YELLOW, ORANGE	PINK	RED	GOOD CUT FLOWERS	SCENTED	LONG-FLOWERING	SOW THEN PLANT OUT	SOW DIRECT	SELF-SEEDING
Acaena buchananii		□			□		□	□	□		□				□						□							
Acaena microphylla		★				★		★	★	★				★	★						★							
Acaena novae-zelandiae		△				△		△	△	△				△	△						△							
Acanthus mollis		■		■	■	■	■	■	■								■	■			■							
Acanthus spinosus		☆		☆	☆	☆	☆	☆	☆								☆	☆			☆							
Achillea aurea		▲	▲		▲			▲								▲				▲			▲	▲	▲			
Achillea filipendulina		□	□		□			□		□										□			□	□	□			
Achillea millefolium		★	★		★			★		★	★						★				★	★	★	★				★
Achillea ptarmica		△	△		△			△		△							△				△		△	△				
Acidanthera		■						■	■								■						■					
Aconitum arendsii				☆	☆		☆											☆			☆		☆					
Aconitum napellus				▲	▲		▲											▲			▲		▲					
Aconitum wilsonii				□	□		□											□			□		□					
Actaea rubra				★			★										★											
Adiantum pedatum	△			△			△		△						△													
Adonis amurensis		■		■			■	■										■			■							
Adonis vernalis		☆				☆	☆											☆										
Aethionema		▲	▲			▲	▲	▲	▲					▲			▲				▲						▲	
Aethionema 'Warley rose'		□				□	□	□	□					□							□				□			
Agapanthus campanulatus		★			★			★	★	★							★	★			★		★					
Agapanthus umbellatus		△			△			△	△	△							△	△			△		△					
Agave americana				■	■		■		■	■					■			■			■							
Ageratum houstonianum							☆	☆									☆	☆	☆					☆				
Ajuga reptans				▲	▲		▲	▲				▲	▲		▲		▲				▲				▲			
Alchemilla alpina					□	□	□														□							□
Alchemilla mollis				★	★	★	★	★									★				★							★
Allium caeruleum		△	△					△	△								△				△	△	△					
Allium cirrhosum			■					■	■											■		■	■	■				
Allium christophii		☆	☆					☆	☆		☆						☆				☆	☆	☆					☆
Allium cowanii		▲	▲					▲	▲								▲				▲	▲	▲	▲				
Allium giganteum		□	□					□	□		□							□			□	□	□					
Allium karataviense		★						★	★								★				★	★	★					
Allium molly		△	△					△	△											△		△	△	△				
Allium oreophilum		■	■					■	■								■				■	■	■					
Allium schoenoprasum			☆					☆	☆									☆		☆	☆	☆	☆	☆				
Allium schubertii			▲					▲	▲											▲	▲	▲	▲					
Allium ursinum			□					□	□								□				□	□	□					□
Alstroemeria aurantiaca		★						★	★											★	★		★		★			
Alstroemeria ligtu		△						△	△											△	△		△		△			
Althaea rosea		■	■		■	■		■	■	■							■	■		■	■	■			■			■
Alyssum saxatile			☆			☆		☆	☆	☆	☆									☆	☆	☆		☆				
Amaranthus caudatus						▲		▲	▲	▲		▲				▲	▲			▲		▲	▲		▲		▲	▲
Amaryllis belladonna		□						□		□							□				□	□	□	□				
Anacyclus depressus		★	★					★	★	★	★						★				★							
Anagallis linifolia		△	△					△	△	△											△				△			
Anaphalis triplinervis		■					■		■	■	■						■	■										
Anchusa azurea								☆	☆	☆														☆				
Androsace carnea			▲					▲			▲										▲							
Androsace sarmentosa			□					□			□										□							
Anemone blanda								★										★	★		★	★	★					
Anemone coronaria			△				△	△	△	△								△	△		△	△	△					

360

FLOWERING-SEASON | **DECORATIVE USES** | **OTHER USES** | **PROBLEMS**

Column headers:

FLOWERING-SEASON:
- DECEMBER, JANUARY
- FEBRUARY, MARCH
- APRIL, MAY
- JUNE, JULY, AUGUST
- SEPTEMBER, OCTOBER
- NOVEMBER

DECORATIVE USES — FLOWERS:
- GROUND-COVER
- AROUND ROSE BUSHES
- GOOD COVER FOR OPEN GROUND
- GOOD UNDERGROWTH COVER
- GIANT
- FOR DRIED FLOWERS

DECORATIVE USES — PLANTS:
- HAS DECORATIVE FRUITS
- FOR POTS AND TUBS ON THE PATIO IN THE SUN
- FOR POTS AND TUBS ON THE PATIO IN THE SHADE

OTHER USES:
- BULBS REMAIN IN GROUND
- OLDER VARIETIES

OTHER USES — GROUND COVER:
- GROW IN SHADE
- GROW IN SUNNY POSITIONS
- ESTABLISH QUICKLY
- FOR SLOPES AND BANKS
- FOR NOOKS, WALLS, ROCKERIES AND PAVING

OTHER USES — PLANTS:
- CLIMBING ANNUALS
- GROWN FROM SEED
- ATTRACT BEES AND BUTTERFLIES
- EASY FOR THE WEEKEND GARDENER
- FLOURISH IN WATER
- CARNIVOROUS
- ATTRACTS RABBITS
- VERY INVASIVE
- POISONOUS OR ALLERGENIC

PROBLEMS:
- ATTRACTS SLUGS
- TOLERANT OF POLLUTION
- PRONE TO FROST

361

Species	PEATY	SANDY, LIGHT	POOR, DRY	DAMP, WELL-DRAINED	CLAY	DRY AND WARM	SHADED, SEMI-SHADED	SUNNY	MEDITERRANEAN	COASTAL	SILVERY	GOLDEN	VARIEGATED	RED	EVERGREEN	AUTUMNAL	WHITE AND GREEN	BLUE, MAUVE	VIOLET, BLACK	YELLOW, ORANGE	PINK	RED	GOOD CUT FLOWERS	SCENTED	LONG-FLOWERING	SOW THEN PLANT OUT	SOW DIRECT	SELF-SEEDING
Anemone hupehensis				□	□		□	□									□	□			□		□		□			
Anemone nemorosa				★	★		★	★									★	★			★							
Angelica archangelica				△	△		△	△									△							△				△
Antennaria dioica		■	■		■		■	■	■	■							■				■	■						
Anthemis cupaniana		☆	☆		☆		☆	☆	☆	☆							☆			☆				☆				
Anthemis nobilis			▲		▲		▲	▲							▲		▲			▲				▲				
Anthemis tinctoria			□		□		□										□			□	□							
Antirrhinum majus			★		★	★		★	★	★							★			★	★					★	★	
Aponogeton distachyus				△			△	△									△			△								
Aquilegia flabellata				■	■		■	■									■	■		■	■	■						
Aquilegia vulgaris				☆	☆		☆	☆									☆	☆		☆	☆	☆	☆					☆
Arabis albida		▲			▲		▲	▲	▲	▲							▲				▲	▲	▲					▲
Arctotis grandis	□	□			□		□	□	□									□	□				□	□				
Arenaria balearica	★			★	★		★	★							★		★											
Argemone mexicana	△	△			△		△	△	△	△							△			△			△			△	△	
Arisaema candidissimum				■	■	■		■									■	■		■						■		
Arisaema sikokianum				☆	☆	☆		☆					☆				☆			☆								
Armeria maritima	▲	▲			▲		▲	▲	▲	▲					▲		▲				▲	▲						
Artemisia absinthium	□	□			□			□	□	□									□		□	□						
Artemisia dracunculus	★				★		★	★	★								★				★	★						
Artemisia ludoviciana	△				△		△	△	△	△							△				△	△						
Artemisia schmidtiana	■				■		■	■	■	■											■	■						
Arum italicum 'Pictum'				☆	☆		☆	☆	☆				☆				☆						☆	☆				
Aruncus dioicus				▲	▲		▲										▲						▲		▲			
Asarum canadense				□	□		□																	□				
Asclepias cornutii				★	★			★	★	★										★	★		★	★				
Asclepias tuberosa	△	△			△			△	△	△										△	△		△		△			
Asperula odorata			■	■			■	■									■							■				
Asphodeline liburnica							☆		☆											☆				☆				
Asphodeline lutea	▲	▲						▲	▲	▲										▲			▲	▲				
Asplenium adiantum-nigrum				□			□								□								□					
Asplenium trichomanes				★			★								★								★					
Aster alpinus								△	△								△	△		△	△	△						
Aster amellus								■		■								■										
Aster datschii								☆										☆					☆					
Aster diffusus horizontalis								▲									▲	▲					▲					
Aster ericoides								□									□	□					□					
Aster farreri								★										★					★					
Aster novae-angliae					△			△									△			△	△	△						
Aster novi-belgi					■			■									■	■		■	■	■						
Aster tongolensis				☆				☆										☆					☆					
Aster tradescantii								▲									▲	▲					▲					
Aster yunnanensis								□										□					□					
Astilbe arendsii				★													★			★	★	★	★	★	★			
Astrantia major				△			△										△				△				△			
Athyrium filix-femina				■			■		■														■					
Athyrium goeringianum				☆			☆		☆				☆										☆					
Aubrieta deltoidea								▲	▲						▲		▲	▲			▲	▲		▲				
Ballota pseudodictamnus		□						□	□	□							□							□				
Baptisia australis				★				★	★									★				★	★					
Begonia evansiana				△			△	△					△				△				△							△

Garden Plant Selection Guide

	FLOWERING-SEASON						DECORATIVE USES			FLOWERS		PLANTS					OTHER USES — GROUND COVER					PLANTS							PROBLEMS				
	DECEMBER, JANUARY	FEBRUARY, MARCH	APRIL, MAY	JUNE, JULY, AUGUST	SEPTEMBER, OCTOBER	NOVEMBER	GROUND-COVER AROUND ROSE BUSHES	GOOD COVER FOR OPEN GROUND	GOOD UNDERGROWTH COVER	GIANT	FOR DRIED FLOWERS	HAS DECORATIVE FRUITS	FOR POTS AND TUBS ON THE PATIO IN THE SUN	FOR POTS AND TUBS ON THE PATIO IN THE SHADE	BULBS REMAIN IN GROUND	OLDER VARIETIES	GROW IN SHADE	GROW IN SUNNY POSITIONS	ESTABLISH QUICKLY	FOR SLOPES AND BANKS	FOR NOOKS, WALLS, ROCKERIES AND PAVING	CLIMBING ANNUALS	GROWN FROM SEED	ATTRACT BEES AND BUTTERFLIES	EASY FOR THE WEEKEND GARDENER	FLOURISH IN WATER	CARNIVOROUS	ATTRACTS RABBITS	VERY INVASIVE	POISONOUS OR ALLERGENIC	ATTRACTS SLUGS	TOLERANT OF POLLUTION	PRONE TO FROST
					□									□										□				□	□				
	★								★				★											★				★	★	★			
		△								△					△																△		
		■								■		■				■			■											■		
		☆	☆									☆								☆									☆			
		▲	▲					▲				▲				▲							▲						▲		
			□									□											□						□		□
			★								★		★									★						★			
			△																					△						△		
		■	■									■											■							■		
		☆	☆					☆				☆											☆						☆		
	▲	▲					▲					▲			▲	▲	▲		▲	▲					▲			▲		
			□									□											□						□	□	
	★	★	★												★	★													★		
			△																					△	△				△		
		■	■							■																			■	
		☆	☆						☆			☆																	☆		
		▲	▲									▲			▲		▲						▲						▲		
			□						□			□			□		□						□		□	□				
			★								★	★		★					★	★			★	★	★ ★ ★			★	★	
			△									△	△							△	△	△		△	△	△		△	△	
	■							■			■			■ ■						■					■					
		☆																													
		▲																										▲		
																				□								□		
		★																										★		
		△							△							△	△				△	△					△		
		■													■				■	■							■		
		☆																		☆	☆									
		▲																		▲	▲									
		□																		□	□									
		★																		★	★									
		△																		△	△									
		■																		■	■									
		☆											☆							☆	☆									
		▲																		▲	▲									
		□																		□	□									
		★																		★										
		△					□	△																						
			■					■			■		■			■		■										■ ■		
								☆					☆						☆									☆		
		▲									▲				▲	▲ ▲		▲										▲		
		□			□						□							□				□						□		
		★																		★										
		△																									△	△	△	

363

	SOIL TYPES						CONDITIONS				FOLIAGE						FLOWERS									ANNUALS		
	PEATY	SANDY, LIGHT	POOR, DRY	DAMP, WELL-DRAINED	CLAY	DRY AND WARM	SHADED, SEMI-SHADED	SUNNY	MEDITERRANEAN	COASTAL	SILVERY	GOLDEN	VARIEGATED	RED	EVERGREEN	AUTUMNAL	WHITE AND GREEN	BLUE, MAUVE	VIOLET, BLACK	YELLOW, ORANGE	PINK	RED	GOOD CUT FLOWERS	SCENTED	LONG-FLOWERING	SOW THEN PLANT OUT	SOW DIRECT	SELF-SEEDING
Begonia semperflorens							□	□	□					□			□				□	□		□	□			
Begonia tuberhybrida		★					★										★			★	★	★		★				
Bellis perennis								△								△	△				△	△		△				
Bergenia ciliata							■	■		■						■	■				■	■					■	■
Bergenia cordifolia				☆	☆		☆	☆		☆					☆	☆	☆				☆	☆	☆	☆				
Bergenia purpurascens				▲	▲		▲	▲		▲				▲	▲	▲	▲				▲	▲	▲	▲				
Bergenia stracheyi							□	□		□				□	□	□	□				□	□		□				
Beta vulgaris				★	★			★			★			★													★	
Bletilla hyacinthina		△		△			△	△	△								△				△							
Borrago officinalis		■	■		■		■											■										■
Brachycome iberidifolia		☆	☆					☆	☆	☆							☆	☆			☆			☆	☆		☆	☆
Briza maxima			▲				▲	▲	▲											▲							▲	▲
Browallia speciosa							□	□									□	□						□				
Brunnera macrophylla				★	★		★											★										
Calamintha alpina			△				△	△	△	△							△											
Calamintha nepetoides							■	■																■				
Calandrinia umbellata		☆	☆					☆	☆	☆	☆										☆							
Calceolaria darwinii	▲						▲	▲												▲								
Calceolaria herbeo-hybrida	□	□					□	□									□			□	□	□		□	□			
Calceolaria integrifolia	★	★			★		★	★	★	★										★				★	★			
Calendula officinalis			△		△			△	△	△										△					△		△	△
Callistephus chinensis		■						■									■	■	■	■	■	■	■	■	■	■		
Calluna vulgaris	☆	☆						☆	☆		☆			☆	☆	☆	☆	☆			☆	☆		☆	☆			
Caltha palustris				▲	▲		▲										▲			▲								
Camassia cusickii				□	□		□										□	□					□					
Camassia leichtlinii				★	★		★										★	★					★					
Camassia quamash				△	△		△											△					△					
Campanula alliariifolia							■		■								■											■
Campanula carpatica								☆		☆							☆	☆										☆
Campanula cochlearifolia								▲		▲							▲	▲										
Campanula glomerata								□		□							□	□						□				□
Campanula latifolia								★		★							★	★					★					★
Campanula medium								△		△							△	△			△		△				△	△
Campanula portenschlagiana							■	■		■							■	■						■				■
Campanula poscharskyana								☆		☆							☆	☆						☆				☆
Campanula pyramidalis								▲		▲							▲	▲			▲			▲				▲
Campanula trachelium								□		□							□	□										
Canna hybrida								★	★	★				★	★					★	★	★		★				
Cardiocrinum giganteum				△			△																△					
Catananche caerulea		■	■		■	■	■	■	■	■								■			■		■					
Catharanthus roseus				☆			☆	☆	☆								☆	☆						☆				
Celosia argentea		▲						▲	▲											▲		▲			▲	▲		
Centaurea cyanus		□						□	□	□							□	□			□	□				□	□	□
Centaurea dealbata		★			★			★	★	★	★	★									★	★	★		★			
Centaurea macrocephala		△			△			△	△											△			△					
Centaurea montana		■			■			■	■								■	■					■					
Centranthus ruber			☆		☆			☆	☆	☆											☆	☆		☆				☆
Cerastium tomentosum			▲					▲	▲	▲	▲						▲							▲				▲
Ceratostigma plumbaginoides		□						□	□							□		□							□			
Cheiranthus cheiri			★					★	★	★							★	★	★	★	★	★	★	★		★	★	
Chelone obliqua							△														△	△	△					

364

	FLOWERING-SEASON						DECORATIVE USES									OTHER USES														PROBLEMS			
							FLOWERS							PLANTS					GROUND COVER				PLANTS										
	DECEMBER, JANUARY	FEBRUARY, MARCH	APRIL, MAY	JUNE, JULY, AUGUST	SEPTEMBER, OCTOBER	NOVEMBER	GROUND-COVER	AROUND ROSE BUSHES	GOOD COVER FOR OPEN GROUND	GOOD UNDERGROWTH COVER	GIANT	FOR DRIED FLOWERS	HAS DECORATIVE FRUITS	FOR POTS AND TUBS ON THE PATIO IN THE SUN	FOR POTS AND TUBS ON THE PATIO IN THE SHADE	BULBS REMAIN IN GROUND	OLDER VARIETIES	GROW IN SHADE	GROW IN SUNNY POSITIONS	ESTABLISH QUICKLY	FOR SLOPES AND BANKS	FOR NOOKS, WALLS, ROCKERIES AND PAVING	CLIMBING ANNUALS GROWN FROM SEED	ATTRACT BEES AND BUTTERFLIES	EASY FOR THE WEEKEND GARDENER	FLOURISH IN WATER	CARNIVOROUS	ATTRACTS RABBITS	VERY INVASIVE	POISONOUS OR ALLERGENIC	ATTRACT SLUGS	TOLERANT OF POLLUTION	PRONE TO FROST
			□		□									□	□																□	□	□
			★												★																★	★	★
	△	△	△							△			△			△					△			△							△	
		■											■	■		■					■			■							■	
			☆	☆									☆	☆		☆					☆			☆							☆	
	▲	▲											▲	▲		▲					▲			▲							▲	
			□											□		□					□			□							□	
			★								★				★		★ ★								★						★		
		△														△															△		
		■	■													■									■						■		
			☆	☆																	☆												
			▲									▲													▲						▲		
			□											□																			□
		★	★							★				★			★					★			★						★		
			△										△				△					△	△								△		
			■		■												■								■						■		
			☆											☆								☆												
			▲											▲																	▲		▲
			□											□																	□		□
			★											★																	★	★	
			△							△			△			△															△	△	
			■																										■				
			☆	☆							☆		☆	☆		☆	☆	☆	☆	☆			☆	☆									
	▲															▲							▲		▲		▲						
			□			□									□									□					□			
			★					★							★									★						★		
			△			△									△									△						△		
			■										■											■							■		
		☆											☆				☆	☆	☆	☆				☆									
			▲										▲											▲						▲		
			□										□			□					□			□					□			
			★										★			★								★						★		
			△										△			△								△						△		
		■			■								■				■ ■ ■			■			■		■					■		
			☆		☆								☆			☆	☆ ☆			☆			☆										
			▲										▲											▲						▲		
			□										□											□						□		
			★										★											★					★	★		
			△					△	△						△													△		△		△
			■							■		■			■									■						■		
			☆																														
			▲							▲		▲																		▲		
			□																	□	□								□			
			★											★							★	★								★		
			△						△					△						△	△								△		
		■	■											■									■	■						■		
			☆	☆									☆			☆					☆			☆				☆		☆		
			▲			▲							▲			▲	▲ ▲ ▲		▲			▲	▲			▲			▲		
			□	□									□					□ □ □ □								□		□		
	★	★	★										★			★				★			★	★					★		
			△	△										△										△					△		

Column groups: **SOIL TYPES** (Peaty, Sandy Light, Poor Dry, Damp Well-Drained, Clay, Dry and Warm) · **CONDITIONS** (Shaded Semi-Shaded, Sunny, Mediterranean, Coastal) · **FOLIAGE** (Silvery, Golden, Variegated, Red, Evergreen, Autumnal) · **FLOWERS** (White and Green, Blue Mauve, Violet Black, Yellow Orange, Pink, Red, Good Cut Flowers, Scented, Long-Flowering) · **ANNUALS** (Sow Then Plant Out, Sow Direct, Self-Seeding)

Plant	PEATY	SANDY, LIGHT	POOR, DRY	DAMP, WELL-DRAINED	CLAY	DRY AND WARM	SHADED, SEMI-SHADED	SUNNY	MEDITERRANEAN	COASTAL	SILVERY	GOLDEN	VARIEGATED	RED	EVERGREEN	AUTUMNAL	WHITE AND GREEN	BLUE, MAUVE	VIOLET, BLACK	YELLOW, ORANGE	PINK	RED	GOOD CUT FLOWERS	SCENTED	LONG-FLOWERING	SOW THEN PLANT OUT	SOW DIRECT	SELF-SEEDING
Chionodoxa gigantea		□				□		□										□			□							
Chrysanthemum carinatum		★				★		★	★	★							★	★		★	★	★	★		★		★	★
Chrysanthemum coccineum		△			△			△	△	△											△	△	△		△			
Chrysanthemum coreanum		■				■		■									■			■	■	■	■		■			
Chrysanthemum haradjanii		☆				☆		☆			☆									☆			☆	☆				
Chrysanthemum maximum		▲				▲		▲		▲							▲			▲			▲		▲			
Chrysanthemum paludosum		□				□		□									□						□					
Chrysanthemum ptarmicoefolium		★				★		★			★									★			★	★				
Chrysanthemum rubellum		△		△	△			△		△											△		△	△	△			
Chrysanthemum uliginosum		■		■		■		■									■						■		■			
Cimicifuga dahurica				☆			☆										☆						☆					
Cimicifuga racemosa				▲			▲										▲						▲					
Clarkia elegans		□						□	□	□											□	□		□		□		
Cleome spinosa		★						★	★	★							★				★		★	★	★			
Clivia miniata		△					△		△	△							△			△								
Cobaea scandens		■						■	■								■	■										
Codonopsis clematidea		☆						☆										☆						☆				
Colchicum autumnale				▲			▲	▲									▲											
Colchicum byzantinum				□			□	□													□							
Colchicum cilicium					★		★	★													★							
Colchicum luteum					△		△	△																				
Convallaria majalis				■			■	■									■				■		■	■				
Convolvulus cneorum			☆					☆	☆	☆	☆						☆	☆										
Convolvulus mauritanicus		▲						▲	▲	▲	▲						▲	▲										
Convolvulus tricolor								□	□	□	□						□	□								□		
Coreopsis drummondii	★	★			★			★		★										★		★	★		★			★
Coreopsis grandiflora		△			△			△		△										△			△		△		△	△
Coreopsis tinctoria		■			■			■												■	■	■		■			■	■
Coreopsis verticillata		☆			☆			☆		☆										☆				☆				☆
Cortaderia argentea			▲	▲				▲		▲							▲			▲		▲	▲					
Cortaderia rendatleri			□	□				□		□										□		□	□					
Corydalis cashmeriana	★	★		★			★											★						★				
Corydalis lutea		△		△			△													△				△				△
Cosmos atrosanguineus	■	■		■	■			■	■									■				■	■	■				
Cosmos bipinnatus		☆	☆		☆			☆	☆								☆			☆	☆	☆	☆				☆	☆
Cosmos sulphureus		▲	▲		▲			▲	▲								▲			▲		▲	▲				▲	▲
Crambe cordifolia		□						□									□											
Crepis aurea			★					★		★										★			★					
Crinum × powellii		△		△	△			△	△	△							△				△	△	△					
Crocosmia × crocosmiiflora		■		■	■			■	■	■				■			■			■	■	■	■	■				
Crocosmia masonorum		☆		☆	☆			☆	☆	☆										☆		☆	☆	☆				
Crocus chrysanthus		▲	▲		▲			▲	▲									▲		▲			▲					
Crocus ochroleucus								□	□								□	□										
Crocus pulchellus								★	★									★										
Crocus sativus		△						△	△									△		△		△		△				
Crocus vernus		■	■		■			■	■								■	■		■			■					
Cucurbita pepo				☆				☆	☆																			
Cuphea cyanea								▲	▲													▲			▲			
Cyclamen cilicium							□	□	□		□										□			□				
Cyclamen coum							★	★	★		★						★				★	★		★				
Cyclamen europaeum							△		△		△										△	△		△				

366

FLOWERING-SEASON
- DECEMBER, JANUARY
- FEBRUARY, MARCH
- APRIL, MAY
- JUNE, JULY, AUGUST
- SEPTEMBER, OCTOBER
- NOVEMBER

DECORATIVE USES

FLOWERS
- GROUND-COVER
- AROUND ROSE BUSHES
- GOOD COVER FOR OPEN GROUND
- GOOD UNDERGROWTH COVER
- GIANT
- FOR DRIED FLOWERS

PLANTS
- HAS DECORATIVE FRUITS
- FOR POTS AND TUBS ON THE PATIO IN THE SUN
- FOR POTS AND TUBS ON THE PATIO IN THE SHADE
- BULBS REMAIN IN GROUND
- OLDER VARIETIES

OTHER USES

GROUND COVER
- GROW IN SHADE
- GROW IN SUNNY POSITIONS
- ESTABLISH QUICKLY
- FOR SLOPES AND BANKS
- FOR NOOKS, WALLS, ROCKERIES AND PAVING

PLANTS
- CLIMBING ANNUALS
- GROWN FROM SEED
- ATTRACT BEES AND BUTTERFLIES
- EASY FOR THE WEEKEND GARDENER
- FLOURISH IN WATER
- CARNIVOROUS

PROBLEMS
- ATTRACTS RABBITS
- VERY INVASIVE
- POISONOUS OR ALLERGENIC
- ATTRACTS SLUGS
- TOLERANT OF POLLUTION
- PRONE TO FROST

367

D

Species	PEATY	SANDY, LIGHT	POOR, DRY	DAMP, WELL-DRAINED	CLAY	DRY AND WARM	SHADED, SEMI-SHADED	SUNNY	MEDITERRANEAN	COASTAL	SILVERY	GOLDEN	VARIEGATED	RED	EVERGREEN	AUTUMNAL	WHITE AND GREEN	BLUE, MAUVE	VIOLET, BLACK	YELLOW, ORANGE	PINK	RED	GOOD CUT FLOWERS	SCENTED	LONG-FLOWERING	SOW THEN PLANT OUT	SOW DIRECT	SELF-SEEDING
	SOIL TYPES					CONDITIONS					FOLIAGE						FLOWERS									ANNUALS		
Cyclamen hederifolium				□		□		□				□					□				□							□
Cyclamen neapolitanum							★		★			★					★			★	★							
Cyclamen persicum						△		△				△									△			△				
Cyclamen pseudo-ibericum						■		■				■						■			■			■				
Cynara cardunculus		☆	☆					☆	☆	☆	☆							☆					☆					
Cynoglossum nervosum		▲					▲	▲	▲	▲								▲					▲	▲	▲			
Cyperus eragrostis				□			□	□																				
Cyperus longus				★			★	★															★					
Cypripedium calceolus	△	△					△											△										
Cypripedium reginae	■	■		■			■										■			■								
Daboecia	☆	☆		☆			☆	☆									☆			☆			☆					
Dahlia cactus							▲	▲	▲								▲	▲	▲	▲	▲		▲					
Dahlia decorative							□	□	□								□	□	□	□	□	□	□					
Dahlia double-flowered							★	★	★								★	★	★	★	★	★	★					
Dahlia dwarf double-flowered							△	△	△								△	△	△	△	△	△	△					
Dahlia dwarf single-flowered							■	■	■								■	■	■	■	■	■	■					
Dahlia pompon							☆	☆	☆								☆		☆	☆	☆	☆	☆					
Datura metel		▲					▲	▲									▲			▲	▲	▲	▲					
Datura meteloides					□		□	□													□			□	□	□		
Delphinium ajacis							★	★	★								★	★	★	★	★	★	★	★			★	★
Delphinium belladonna							△	△									△	△	△	△	△		△					
Delphinium cardinale							■	■									■	■	■	■	■	■	■					
Delphinium grandiflorum							☆	☆									☆	☆	☆	☆	☆	☆		☆				
Delphinium nudicaule							▲	▲									▲	▲	▲	▲	▲	▲	▲					
Delphinium zalil							□	□									□	□	□	□	□	□						
Dianthus alpinus			★				★	★	★								★			★			★					
Dianthus arenarius							△	△	△	△							△						△					
Dianthus barbatus							■	■									■	■	■	■	■		■		■	■	■	
Dianthus caryophyllus							☆	☆									☆	☆		☆	☆		☆					
Dianthus chinensis							▲	▲		▲							▲			▲	▲				▲			
Dianthus deltoides							□	□									□			□		□						
Dianthus gratianopolitanus							★	★	★												★		★					
Dianthus knappii							△	△	△											△			△					
Dianthus plumarius							■	■	■								■	■	■	■	■		■				■	
Dianthus superbus							☆	☆									☆	☆		☆			☆					
Diascia barberae							▲	▲													▲				▲			
Diascia cordata		□					□	□													□			□				
Dicentra eximia		★	★		★												★				★							
Dicentra spectabilis		△	△	△		△				△							△				△			△				
Dichelostemma ida-maia		■			■																	■		■				
Dictamnus albus		☆				☆		☆	☆	☆							☆	☆		☆				☆				
Dierama pendulum		▲						▲		▲					▲		▲			▲		▲						
Dierama pulcherrimum		□						□		□					□		□				□	□	□					
Digitalis ambigua		★			★	★	★			★							★			★	★	★						
Digitalis ferruginea		△			△	△	△			△							△			△	△	△						
Digitalis mertonensis		■			■	■	■			■							■			■	■	■						
Digitalis purpurea		☆			☆	☆	☆	☆									☆			☆	☆	☆						☆
Dionaea				▲				▲									▲											
Dodecatheon meadia				□													□											
Doronicum caucasicum				★	★			★												★			★					
Doronicum plantagineum				△				△												△								

368

FLOWERING-SEASON
- DECEMBER, JANUARY
- FEBRUARY, MARCH
- APRIL, MAY
- JUNE, JULY, AUGUST
- SEPTEMBER, OCTOBER
- NOVEMBER

DECORATIVE USES

FLOWERS
- GROUND-COVER
- AROUND ROSE BUSHES
- GOOD COVER FOR OPEN GROUND
- GOOD UNDERGROWTH COVER
- GIANT
- FOR DRIED FLOWERS

PLANTS
- HAS DECORATIVE FRUITS
- FOR POTS AND TUBS ON THE PATIO IN THE SUN
- FOR POTS AND TUBS ON THE PATIO IN THE SHADE
- BULBS REMAIN IN GROUND
- OLDER VARIETIES

OTHER USES

GROUND COVER
- GROW IN SHADE
- GROW IN SUNNY POSITIONS
- ESTABLISH QUICKLY
- FOR SLOPES AND BANKS
- FOR NOOKS, WALLS, ROCKERIES AND PAVING

PLANTS
- CLIMBING ANNUALS GROWN FROM SEED
- ATTRACT BEES AND BUTTERFLIES
- EASY FOR THE WEEKEND GARDENER
- CARNIVOROUS
- FLOURISH IN WATER

PROBLEMS
- ATTRACTS RABBITS
- VERY INVASIVE
- POISONOUS OR ALLERGENIC
- ATTRACTS SLUGS
- TOLERANT OF POLLUTION
- PRONE TO FROST

369

E

	SOIL TYPES						CONDITIONS				FOLIAGE						FLOWERS										ANNUALS	
	PEATY	SANDY, LIGHT	POOR, DRY	DAMP, WELL-DRAINED	CLAY	DRY AND WARM	SHADED, SEMI-SHADED	SUNNY	MEDITERRANEAN	COASTAL	SILVERY	GOLDEN	VARIEGATED	RED	EVERGREEN	AUTUMNAL	WHITE AND GREEN	BLUE, MAUVE	VIOLET, BLACK	YELLOW, ORANGE	PINK	RED	GOOD CUT FLOWERS	SCENTED	LONG-FLOWERING	SOW THEN PLANT OUT	SOW DIRECT	SELF-SEEDING
Draba aizoides					□		□				□						□											
Dryas octopetala		★					★			★					★		★											
Dryopteris cristata						△	△			△																		
Dryopteris dilatata						■	■			■																		
Dryopteris filix-mas				☆			☆			☆																		
Eccremocarpus scaber		▲					▲	▲	▲											▲					▲			
Echinacea purpurea				□			□														□	□	□					
Echinops ritro		★			★	★		★	★	★	★							★					★		★			
Echinops sphaerocephalus						△		△	△	△	△							△					△		△			
Echium lycopsis							■	■	■								■	■			■				■		■	
Echium fastuosum							☆	☆	☆								☆	☆			☆				☆			
Echium vulgare		▲						▲	▲	▲							▲								▲		▲	▲
Epilobium angustifolium	□		□			□	□		□								□				□							□
Epimedium grandiflorum		★		★	★		★	★								★	★	★		★	★							
Epimedium rubrum	△		△				△	△						△		△				△	△							
Epimedium versicolor	■			■			■	■								■				■								
Eranthis hyemalis	☆			☆			☆													☆								
Eremurus himalaicus	▲						▲										▲				▲							
Eremurus robustus	□						□										□			□			□					
Eremurus stenophyllus bungei	★						★										★			★			★					
Erica carnea		△					△	△	△	△					△	△	△				△	△		△	△			
Erica cinerea	■						■	■	■		■				■		■				■	■		■	■			
Erica darleyensis		☆					☆	☆	☆	☆					☆		☆				☆			☆	☆			
Erica tetralix	▲						▲	▲	▲	▲	▲				▲		▲				▲			▲	▲			
Erica vagans							□	□	□	□					□		□				□				□			
Erigeron aurantiacus							★	★	★											★								
Erigeron karvinskianus							△	△	△								△	△		△	△	△			△			
Erigeron leiomerus							■	■	■									■										
Erigeron speciosus							☆	☆	☆									☆			☆		☆					
Erinus alpinus		▲			▲		▲									▲		▲			▲	▲		▲				▲
Erodium chamaedryoides		□					□	□													□							
Erodium manescavi							★	★		★											★			★				
Eryngium agavifolium						△		△	△	△	△							△					△					
Eryngium alpinum		■					■	■	■	■								■					■					
Eryngium bourgatii		☆				☆		☆	☆	☆	☆							☆					☆					
Eryngium maritimum							▲	▲	▲	▲								▲					▲					
Eryngium oliveranum		□					□	□	□	□								□					□					
Eryngium variifolium							★	★	★	★								★					★					
Erysimum		△					△	△	△									△					△	△				
Erythronium dens-canis				■		■							■				■				■							
Erythronium revolutum				☆		☆							☆				☆				☆							
Erythronium tuolumnense								▲												▲								
Eschscholzia californica		□	□				□	□	□								□			□							□	□
Eucomis bicolor		★					★	★	★		★						★			★				★	★			
Eucomis punctata		△					△	△	△				△				△							△	△			
Eupatorium purpureum				■			■														■		■	■	■			
Eupatorium rugosum							☆																☆	☆	☆			
Euphorbia characias		▲					▲	▲	▲						▲		▲						▲					
Euphorbia griffithii							□	□	□					□							□							
Euphorbia marginata		★	★				★	★	★				★				★						★				★	★
Euphorbia myrsinites		△	△				△	△	△	△					△		△			△								△

370

	FLOWERING-SEASON						DECORATIVE USES — FLOWERS							DECORATIVE USES — PLANTS				OTHER USES — GROUND COVER					OTHER USES — PLANTS								PROBLEMS			
	DECEMBER, JANUARY	FEBRUARY, MARCH	APRIL, MAY	JUNE, JULY, AUGUST	SEPTEMBER, OCTOBER	NOVEMBER	GROUND-COVER	AROUND ROSE BUSHES	GOOD COVER FOR OPEN GROUND	GOOD UNDERGROWTH COVER	GIANT	FOR DRIED FLOWERS	HAS DECORATIVE FRUITS	FOR POTS AND TUBS ON THE PATIO IN THE SUN	FOR POTS AND TUBS ON THE PATIO IN THE SHADE	BULBS REMAIN IN GROUND	OLDER VARIETIES	GROW IN SHADE	GROW IN SUNNY POSITIONS	ESTABLISH QUICKLY	FOR SLOPES AND BANKS	FOR NOOKS, WALLS, ROCKERIES AND PAVING	CLIMBING ANNUALS	GROWN FROM SEED	ATTRACT BEES AND BUTTERFLIES	EASY FOR THE WEEKEND GARDENER	FLOURISH IN WATER	CARNIVOROUS	ATTRACTS RABBITS	VERY INVASIVE	POISONOUS OR ALLERGENIC	ATTRACTS SLUGS	TOLERANT OF POLLUTION	PRONE TO FROST
																			□															
		★							★							★		★			★				★						★		
		△							△					△		△				△											△		
		■							■					■		■				■											■		
									☆					☆		☆				☆											☆		
		▲											▲																				▲
		□											□												□						□		
		★									★		★											★						★		
		△											△																		△		
		■											■												■								
		☆											☆																		☆		
													▲																				
			□				□	□					□			□									□		□			□		
		★												★	★																★		
		△												△		△				△											△		
		■												■	■					■											■		
	☆														☆				☆					☆			☆	☆		☆		
		▲													▲																		
		□								□					□																		□
		★								★					★																		★
△	△	△								△						△				△				△	△						△		
			■	■							■				■					■				■	■								
☆	☆	☆																		☆				☆	☆								
			▲																	▲				▲	▲								
			□	□																				□									
			★											★										★	★								
		△	△													△								△	△								
			■																					■	■								
			☆																	☆				☆	☆					☆			
		▲	▲																					▲	▲						▲		
			□		□							□					□	□	□						□						□		
		★			★							★					★	★	★						★						★		
			△							△		△												△	△						△		
			■							■		■								■				■	■						■		
			☆							☆		☆								☆				☆	☆						☆		
			▲							▲		▲			▲									▲	▲						▲		
			□							□					□									□	□						□		
			★							★					★									★	★						★		
		△										△			△					△				△	△						△		
		■						■				■	■	■						■											■		
		☆									☆		☆	☆	☆					☆											☆		
		▲											▲	▲	▲																▲		
			□									□			□		□								□						□		
		★										★			★									★	★			★			★		
		△										△			△									△	△			△			△		
		■		■			■		■		■													■	■						■		
			☆	☆																					☆						☆		
		▲	▲									▲												▲	▲			▲	▲		▲		
		□	□									□													□			□	□		□		
			★									★		★	★										★			★	★	★	★		
		△										△					△			△					△			△	△	△	△		

F

G

	SOIL TYPES						CONDITIONS				FOLIAGE						FLOWERS									ANNUALS		
	PEATY	SANDY, LIGHT	POOR, DRY	DAMP, WELL-DRAINED	CLAY	DRY AND WARM	SHADED, SEMI-SHADED	SUNNY	MEDITERRANEAN	COASTAL	SILVERY	GOLDEN	VARIEGATED	RED	EVERGREEN	AUTUMNAL	WHITE AND GREEN	BLUE, MAUVE	VIOLET, BLACK	YELLOW, ORANGE	PINK	RED	GOOD CUT FLOWERS	SCENTED	LONG-FLOWERING	SOW THEN PLANT OUT	SOW DIRECT	SELF-SEEDING
Euphorbia polychroma							□	□	□							□				□								
Euphorbia robbiae							★	★	★																			
Euphorbia wulfenii						△	△	△	△								△			△								
Euryops acraeus		■	■				■	■		■										■								
Felicia amelloides		☆	☆			☆		☆	☆	☆								☆			☆			☆				
Festuca glauca		▲	▲		▲		▲	▲	▲	▲				▲														
Filipendula hexapetala		□					□										□											
Filipendula rubra				★			★														★			★				
Filipendula ulmaria				△			△				△						△							△				
Foeniculum vulgare		■			■		■	■												■		■	■					■
Freesia × kewensis		☆						☆	☆								☆	☆	☆		☆	☆	☆					
Fritillaria imperialis							▲		▲											▲		▲		▲				
Fritillaria meleagris				□			□		□										□									
Fritillaria persica							★		★										★					★				
Fuchsia magellanica						△	△		△								△				△	△						
Gaillardia aristata		■			■		■													■		■	■					
Gaillardia pulchella		☆			☆		☆													☆		☆				☆		
Galanthus elwesii				▲	▲												▲				▲	▲						▲
Galanthus nivalis		□		□	□												□					□						
Galega officinalis				★	★			★	★	★							★	★		★		★		★				
Galtonia candicans		△						△	△	△							△					△		△				
Gaultheria procumbens	■	■		■			■	■							■					■								
Gaultheria shallon	☆	☆		☆			☆	☆							☆					☆								
Gaura lindheimerii		▲	▲		▲		▲	▲	▲								▲				▲							
Gazania hybrida			□		□		□	□	□											□	□	□	□		□	□		
Gentiana acaulis							★																					
Gentiana asclepiadea		△					△	△									△						△					
Gentiana farreri	■		■				■										■			■								
Gentiana lutea	☆		☆				☆										☆											
Gentiana septemfida		▲		▲	▲		▲	▲									▲					▲						
Gentiana sino-ornata	□		□				□										□											
Geranium endressii							★	★													★							
Geranium ibericum					△		△										△											
Geranium magnificum				■										■			■	■										
Geranium macrorrhizum			☆		☆		☆	☆								☆					☆			☆				
Geranium platypetalum							▲											▲										
Geranium pratense				□			□								□	□	□											
Geranium pratense 'Johnson's Blue'					★		★	★										★										
Geranium psilostemon							■														■							
Geranium renardii				☆			☆		☆							☆												
Geranium sanguineum							▲							▲							▲			▲				
Geranium subcaulescens							□														□							
Gerbera jamesonii		★					★	★									★			★	★	★	★		★			
Geum × borisii		△			△		△	△									△											
Geum chiloense		■			■		■	■														■						
Gilia capitata							☆		☆								☆				☆		☆	☆	☆	☆		
Gilia tricolor							▲		▲								▲	▲	▲	▲			▲			▲	▲	
Gladiolus byzanthinus		□					□	□	□								□		□	□	□	□						
Gladiolus colvillii		★					★	★	★								★		★	★	★	★						
Gladiolus hybride		△					△	△	△								△		△	△	△	△						

Plant Selection Chart

Column header groups (left to right):

- **FLOWERING-SEASON:** DECEMBER, JANUARY · FEBRUARY, MARCH · APRIL, MAY · JUNE, JULY, AUGUST · SEPTEMBER, OCTOBER · NOVEMBER
- **DECORATIVE USES — FLOWERS:** GROUND-COVER · AROUND ROSE BUSHES · GOOD COVER FOR OPEN GROUND · GOOD UNDERGROWTH COVER · GIANT · FOR DRIED FLOWERS
- **DECORATIVE USES — PLANTS:** HAS DECORATIVE FRUITS · FOR POTS AND TUBS ON THE PATIO IN THE SUN · FOR POTS AND TUBS ON THE PATIO IN THE SHADE · BULBS REMAIN IN GROUND · OLDER VARIETIES
- **OTHER USES — GROUND COVER:** GROW IN SHADE · GROW IN SUNNY POSITIONS · ESTABLISH QUICKLY · FOR SLOPES AND BANKS · FOR NOOKS, WALLS, ROCKERIES AND PAVING
- **OTHER USES — PLANTS:** CLIMBING ANNUALS · GROWN FROM SEED · ATTRACT BEES AND BUTTERFLIES · EASY FOR THE WEEKEND GARDENER · FLOURISH IN WATER · CARNIVOROUS
- **PROBLEMS:** ATTRACTS RABBITS · VERY INVASIVE · POISONOUS OR ALLERGENIC · ATTRACTS SLUGS · TOLERANT OF POLLUTION · PRONE TO FROST

Symbol key: ★ filled star · ☆ open star · ■ filled square · □ open square · ▲ filled triangle · △ open triangle

Dec/Jan	Feb/Mar	Apr/May	Jun–Aug	Sep/Oct	Nov	Ground-cover	Rose bushes	Open ground	Undergrowth	Giant	Dried	Fruits	Pots sun	Pots shade	Bulbs	Older	Shade	Sunny	Quick	Slopes	Nooks	Climb	Seed	Bees	Easy	Water	Carniv.	Rabbits	Invasive	Poison	Slugs	Pollution	Frost
	□													□			□				□				□			□		□		□	
		★						★						★											★			★	★			★	
	△	△						△						△											△			△		△		△	
		■												■						■													
		☆																		☆												☆	☆
		▲								▲				▲						▲										▲		▲	
		□					□			□						□				□	□									□			
		★					★									★							★	★						★			
		△					△									△							△	△						△			
		■	■						■					■																■			
		☆												☆									☆	☆						☆			
▲															▲	▲								▲						▲			
□							□								□	□							□							□			
★															★									★			★			★			
		△	△																	△	△												
		■											■									■	■							■			
		☆											☆									☆	☆							☆			
▲										▲	▲									▲	▲		▲		▲		▲			▲			
□			□							□	□									□	□						□			□			
	★	★								★							★							★			★			★			
		△								△		△		△						△								△	△				
	■											■		■		■														■			
	☆										☆			☆		☆					☆									☆			
		▲																▲									▲			▲			
		□											□				□	□		□													
	★	★												★										★						★			
		△												△						△							△						
			■																	■							■						
		☆														☆											☆						
		▲											▲							▲							▲						
			□											□													□						
		★															★	★	★		★												
	△	△													△		△	△	△		△												
	■	■																							■								
	☆	☆						☆						☆			☆		☆		☆									☆			
		▲															▲	▲	▲		▲												
	□	□				□	□										□	□	□		□												
		★															★	★	★		★												
		■													■	■	■	■			■												
	☆	☆															☆	☆			☆									☆			
		▲															▲	▲	▲		▲									▲			
		□															□	□	□		□												
		★											★								★												
	△	△											△								△									△			
	■	■											■								■									■			
		☆									☆		☆								☆									☆			
		▲											▲								▲									▲			
		□													□						□											□	
		★																														★	
		△																														△	

373

Table groups: **SOIL TYPES** (Peaty, Sandy/Light, Poor/Dry, Damp/Well-drained, Clay, Dry and Warm, Shaded/Semi-shaded) · **CONDITIONS** (Sunny, Mediterranean, Coastal) · **FOLIAGE** (Silvery, Golden, Variegated, Red, Evergreen, Autumnal) · **FLOWERS** (White and Green, Blue/Mauve/Violet/Black, Yellow/Orange, Pink, Red, Good Cut Flowers, Scented, Long-flowering) · **ANNUALS** (Sow then Plant Out, Sow Direct, Self-seeding)

Species	PEATY	SANDY, LIGHT	POOR, DRY	DAMP, WELL-DRAINED	CLAY	DRY AND WARM	SHADED, SEMI-SHADED	SUNNY	MEDITERRANEAN	COASTAL	SILVERY	GOLDEN	VARIEGATED	RED	EVERGREEN	AUTUMNAL	WHITE AND GREEN	BLUE, MAUVE, VIOLET, BLACK	YELLOW, ORANGE	PINK	RED	GOOD CUT FLOWERS	SCENTED	LONG-FLOWERING	SOW THEN PLANT OUT	SOW DIRECT	SELF-SEEDING
Gladiolus primulinus								□	□								□		□	□	□						
Glaucium flavum		★	★			★		★	★	★	★								★							★	★
Gloriosa rotschildiana								△	△											△				△			
Godetia grandiflora		■						■	■	■							■			■	■				■		
Gomphrena globosa		☆						☆	☆	☆							☆		☆	☆	☆	☆		☆	☆		
Gunnera manicata				▲			▲	▲	▲																		
Gypsophila elegans								□	□								□			□		□				□	□
Gypsophila paniculata								★	★								★			★		★					
Gypsophila repens								△	△		△						△			△		△					
Haberlea rhodopensis				■			■										■						■				
Hedysarum coronarium								☆	☆											☆							☆
Helenium autumnale				▲	▲		▲										▲		▲		▲	▲					
Helianthemum nummularium	□	□			□			□	□								□		□	□	□						
Helianthus annuus		★			★			★		★									★		★	★			★		
Helianthus decapetalus		△			△			△		△									△			△					
Helianthus salicifolius		■						■		■									■			■					
Helichrysum angustifolium				☆	☆			☆	☆	☆							☆		☆	☆	☆		☆	☆			
Helichrysum bracteatum	▲	▲			▲			▲	▲	▲							▲		▲	▲	▲	▲		▲	▲		
Helichrysum petiolatum	□							□	□								□		□			□	□				
Heliopsis scabra		★			★			★		★							★		★		★						
Heliotropium × hybridum	△							△	△	△							△	△				△	△	△			
Helipterum manglesii	■	■						■	■	■							■			■	■		■		■		
Helleborus atrorubens							☆											☆			☆						
Helleborus foetidus				▲	▲		▲										▲			▲		▲	▲				
Helleborus lividus				□	□		□										□			□		□					
Helleborus niger				★	★		★		★								★			★		★	★				
Helleborus orientalis				△	△		△		△								△	△		△		△	△				
Helxine			■				■								■		■										
Hemerocallis citrina				☆	☆		☆	☆	☆										☆			☆					
Hemerocallis fulva				▲	▲		▲	▲											▲	▲	▲						
Hepatica triloba		□		□			□						□				□	□		□							
Heracleum mantegazzianum				★	★		★	★									★										
Hesperis matronalis		△			△		△	△	△	△							△	△				△	△				△
Heuchera x brizoides							■	■									■			■	■	■		■			
Heuchera sanguinea				☆			☆							☆			☆				☆	☆					
Hieracium aurantiacum	▲							▲											▲		▲		▲				▲
Hieracium pilosella	□			□				□									□										□
Hosta fortunei		★		★			★				★		★				★	★			★						
Hosta lancifolia		△		△			△						△					△			△						
Hosta plantaginea		■		■			■										■				■						
Hosta sieboldiana		☆		☆			☆				☆		☆				☆				☆						
Hosta ventricosa		▲		▲			▲											▲			▲						
Houstonia caerulea		□		□			□	□					□				□	□									
Houttuynia cordata				★			★	★								★	★				★						
Hyacinthoides hispanica		△		△			△	△									△	△		△		△					
Hyacinthoides non-scripta		■		■			■	■									■	■		■	■						
Hyacinthus orientalis		☆						☆	☆								☆		☆	☆	☆	☆	☆				
Hypericum calycinum		▲	▲		▲	▲	▲	▲	▲						▲				▲								
Hypericum citinum			□		□	□	□	□	□						□				□								
Hypericum olympicum		★				★	★	★	★	★							★		★								
Hypericum polyphyllum					△	△	△	△	△	△							△		△								

FLOWERING-SEASON

- DECEMBER, JANUARY
- FEBRUARY, MARCH
- APRIL, MAY
- JUNE, JULY, AUGUST
- SEPTEMBER, OCTOBER, NOVEMBER

DECORATIVE USES

FLOWERS
- GROUND-COVER
- AROUND ROSE BUSHES
- GOOD COVER FOR OPEN GROUND
- GOOD UNDERGROWTH COVER
- GIANT
- FOR DRIED FLOWERS

PLANTS
- HAS DECORATIVE FRUITS
- FOR POTS AND TUBS ON THE PATIO IN THE SUN
- FOR POTS AND TUBS ON THE PATIO IN THE SHADE

OTHER USES

GROUND COVER
- BULBS REMAIN IN GROUND
- OLDER VARIETIES
- GROW IN SHADE
- GROW IN SUNNY POSITIONS
- ESTABLISH QUICKLY
- FOR SLOPES AND BANKS
- FOR NOOKS, WALLS, ROCKERIES AND PAVING

PLANTS
- CLIMBING ANNUALS
- GROWN FROM SEED
- ATTRACT BEES AND BUTTERFLIES
- EASY FOR THE WEEKEND GARDENER
- FLOURISH IN WATER
- CARNIVOROUS

PROBLEMS

- ATTRACTS RABBITS
- VERY INVASIVE
- POISONOUS OR ALLERGENIC
- ATTRACTS SLUGS
- TOLERANT OF POLLUTION
- PRONE TO FROST

375

Column group headers: **SOIL TYPES** (Peaty, Sandy/Light, Poor/Dry, Damp/Well-drained, Clay, Dry and Warm) · **CONDITIONS** (Shaded/Semi-shaded, Sunny, Mediterranean, Coastal) · **FOLIAGE** (Silvery, Golden, Variegated, Red, Evergreen, Autumnal) · **FLOWERS** (White and Green, Blue/Mauve/Violet/Black, Yellow/Orange, Pink, Red, Good Cut Flowers, Scented, Long-flowering) · **ANNUALS** (Sow then Plant Out, Sow Direct, Self-seeding)

Margin index letters: **I** (Iberis–Ixia), **J K L** (Jasione–Lewisia)

Plant	PEATY	SANDY, LIGHT	POOR, DRY	DAMP, WELL-DRAINED	CLAY	DRY AND WARM	SHADED, SEMI-SHADED	SUNNY	MEDITERRANEAN	COASTAL	SILVERY	GOLDEN	VARIEGATED	RED	EVERGREEN	AUTUMNAL	WHITE AND GREEN	BLUE, MAUVE, VIOLET, BLACK	YELLOW, ORANGE	PINK	RED	GOOD CUT FLOWERS	SCENTED	LONG-FLOWERING	SOW THEN PLANT OUT	SOW DIRECT	SELF-SEEDING
Hyssopus		□	□		□			□	□									□					□				□
Iberis amara					★			★	★	★							★			★	★	★	★				
Iberis officinalis			△		△			△	△	△							△			△	△	△	△				
Impatiens balfouri			■	■			■										■	■		■	■		■		■	■	
Impatiens balsamina							☆										☆	☆	☆	☆	☆		☆	☆	☆		
Impatiens roylei				▲			▲										▲	▲		▲	▲	▲	▲		▲	▲	
Incarvillea delavayi		□						□											□	□							
Incarvillea mairei								★	★	★									★	★							
Inula ensifolia				△				△											△				△				
Inula helenium								■											■			■	■				
Inula hookeri					☆			☆											☆				☆	☆	☆			
Inula magnifica				▲				▲											▲			▲	▲				
Inula orientalis								□											□			□	□				
Ipheion uniflorum		★						★	★								★										
Ipomoea purpurea		△					△	△	△	△								△						△			
Ipomoea tricolor		■					■	■	■	■								■						■		■	
Iris bucharica		☆						☆	☆	☆							☆		☆								
Iris danfordiae		▲	▲					▲	▲	▲									▲			▲					
Iris ensata	□			□				□	□	□							□	□				□					
Iris foetidissima			★	★	★		★	★	★	★					★		★					★					
Iris germanica hybrid		△			△			△	△	△						△	△	△	△	△		△	△				
Iris kaempferi	■			■				■	■	■							■	■		■	■	■	■				
Iris laevigata	☆			☆				☆	☆	☆							☆					☆					
Iris louisiana	▲			▲				▲	▲	▲							▲	▲	▲			▲	▲				
Iris pseudacorus				□			□	□	□	□									□			□					
Iris reticulata		★						★	★	★							★	★				★					
Iris sibirica				△				△	△								△	△				△					
Iris spuria				■				■	■	■							■	■	■			■					
Iris unguicularis		☆	☆					☆	☆	☆					☆		☆	☆					☆	☆			
Iris versicolor				▲				▲	▲	▲								▲		▲	▲						
Iris xiphioides		□																□				□					
Iris xiphium		★						★	★	★							★	★	★	★		★					
Ixia hybrid		△						△	△	△							△			△	△	△					
Jasione perennis			■					■	■								■	■				■					
Kniphofia galpinii		☆		☆				☆	☆	☆							☆		☆		☆	☆					
Kochia scoparia		▲	▲	▲	▲			▲	▲	▲						▲									▲	▲	
Lagurus ovatus		□	□					□	□	□															□	□	
Lamium galeobdolon						★	★												★					★			
Lamium maculatum				△	△		△	△			△		△				△			△							
Lantana		■						■	■	■							■		■	■		■	■	■			
Lathyrus grandiflorus		☆		☆	☆			☆	☆								☆	☆	☆	☆			☆				
Lathyrus latifolius		▲		▲				▲	▲								▲	▲	▲	▲	▲		▲				▲
Lathyrus odoratus		□		□				□	□								□	□	□	□	□		□		□	□	
Lathyrus vernus				★				★	★								★	★		★	★		★				
Lavandula spica			△		△			△	△	△	△						△	△		△		△	△	△			
Lavandula stoechas			■		■			■	■	■	■						■	■				■	■	■			
Lavatera trimestris				☆	☆	☆		☆	☆	☆							☆			☆	☆	☆		☆			
Leontopodium		▲	▲		▲			▲			▲						▲										
Leucojum aestivum				□			□	□									□					□					
Leucojum vernum			★	★			★	★									★					★					
Lewisia cotyledon			△					△	△	△					△		△		△	△	△		△				

FLOWERING-SEASON						DECORATIVE USES									OTHER USES													PROBLEMS					
DECEMBER, JANUARY	FEBRUARY, MARCH	APRIL, MAY	JUNE, JULY, AUGUST	SEPTEMBER, OCTOBER	NOVEMBER	GROUND-COVER	AROUND ROSE BUSHES	GOOD COVER FOR OPEN GROUND	GOOD UNDERGROWTH COVER	GIANT	FOR DRIED FLOWERS	HAS DECORATIVE FRUITS	FOR POTS AND TUBS ON THE PATIO IN THE SUN	FOR POTS AND TUBS ON THE PATIO IN THE SHADE	BULBS REMAIN IN GROUND	OLDER VARIETIES	GROW IN SHADE	GROW IN SUNNY POSITIONS	ESTABLISH QUICKLY	FOR SLOPES AND BANKS	FOR NOOKS, WALLS, ROCKERIES AND PAVING	CLIMBING ANNUALS	GROWN FROM SEED	ATTRACT BEES AND BUTTERFLIES	EASY FOR THE WEEKEND GARDENER	FLOURISH IN WATER	CARNIVOROUS	ATTRACTS RABBITS	VERY INVASIVE	POISONOUS OR ALLERGENIC	ATTRACTS SLUGS	TOLERANT OF POLLUTION	PRONE TO FROST
		□																						□	□						□		
	★	★										★			★	★	★			★				★	★						★		
	△	△										△					△			△				△	△						△		
		■												■										■					■		■		
		☆												☆											☆						☆		
		▲	▲				▲							▲											▲				▲		▲		
		□										□												□							□		
		★										★											★										
		△					△					△				△									△								
		■					■																		■								
		☆					☆																		☆								
		▲					▲		▲	▲															▲								
		□					□																		□								
	★											★			★			★					★										
		△										△													△						△		
		■										■							■						■						■	■		
		☆										☆			☆			☆							☆						☆			
▲	▲											▲			▲									▲						▲			
		□										□			□									□						□	□		
									★		★	★			★	★								★						★	★		
		△										△			△	△							△	△						△	△		
		■													■	■								■	■						■		
		☆													☆	☆								☆						☆			
		▲										▲			▲									▲						▲			
		□										□			□	□						□		□						□			
	★											★			★			★						★						★			
		△					△					△			△	△								△						△	△		
	■														■									■						■	■		
☆	☆														☆			☆						☆						☆		☆	
															▲															▲			
		□													□															□			
	★						★					★			★	★		★												★	★		
		△										△			△			△	△	△										△			△
		■	■									■						■												■	■		
		☆																							☆						☆		
		▲										▲													▲						▲		
		□								□														□						□			
		★							★					★				★	★	★					★				★		★		
		△										△						△	△	△					△						△		
		■	■									■																			■	■		
		☆																							☆						☆		
		▲										▲			▲										▲						▲		
		□					□					□			□	□								□						□			
★	★						★								★			★	★									★		★			
	△											△						△															△

377

	SOIL TYPES						CONDITIONS				FOLIAGE						FLOWERS									ANNUALS		
	PEATY	SANDY, LIGHT	POOR, DRY	DAMP, WELL-DRAINED	CLAY	DRY AND WARM	SHADED, SEMI-SHADED	SUNNY	MEDITERRANEAN	COASTAL	SILVERY	GOLDEN	VARIEGATED	RED	EVERGREEN	AUTUMNAL	WHITE AND GREEN	BLUE, MAUVE	VIOLET, BLACK	YELLOW, ORANGE	PINK	RED	GOOD CUT FLOWERS	SCENTED	LONG-FLOWERING	SOW THEN PLANT OUT	SOW DIRECT	SELF-SEEDING
Liatris scariosa				□				□									□						□		□			
Liatris spicata				★				★									★	★					★					
Libertia formosa				△			△	△	△						△		△						△					
Ligularia clivorum				■									■							■			■	■				
Ligularia przewalskii				☆																☆			☆					
Ligularia wilsoniana							▲	▲												▲			▲					
Lilium auratum	□			□				□	□														□	□				
Lilium candidum		★			★			★	★	★							★						★	★				
Lilium hansonii		△		△	△	△	△	△	△											△			△	△				
Lilium henryi		■		■	■	■	■	■												■			■	■				
Lilium longiflorum	☆	☆				☆	☆	☆									☆						☆	☆				
Lilium martagon							▲	▲														▲	▲	▲				
Lilium pardalinum giganteum	□			□		□	□	□														□	□					
Lilium regale		★			★			★	★								★						★	★				
Lilium speciosum	△			△				△	△								△						△	△				
Lilium tigrinum	■	■			■			■	■											■			■	■				
Limnanthes douglasii		☆		☆				☆	☆	☆										☆			☆	☆			☆	
Limonium latifolium		▲						▲	▲	▲							▲	▲	▲	▲			▲	▲	▲			
Limonium sinuatum		□						□	□	□							□	□	□	□	□		□	□	□			
Limonium tataricum								★	★	★							★	★					★	★	★			
Linaria alpina								△	△	△								△										△
Linaria cymbalaria								■	■	■								■										■
Linaria maroccana		☆	☆			☆		☆	☆	☆							☆			☆	☆						☆	☆
Linaria polychroma								▲	▲	▲										▲								▲
Linaria purpurea								□	□	□								□										□
Linum flavum								★	★								★	★		★								
Linum grandiflorum								△	△	△							△	△									△	
Linum perenne								■	■								■	■										■
Linum usitatissimum								☆	☆								☆	☆										
Liriope muscari	▲	▲	▲				▲						▲		▲			▲						▲				
Liriope spicata	□						□		□				□				□							□				
Lithospermum	★	★						★	★	★	★							★						★				
Lobelia cardinalis				△				△	△					△								△		△				
Lobelia erinus		■						■	■								■	■						■	■			
Lobelia fulgens								☆														☆						
Lobelia syphilitica				▲				▲										▲										
Lobelia vedrariensis				□	□			□									□											
Lobularia maritima		★	★					★									★							★	★		★	
Lotus berthelottii		△						△	△		△													△	△			
Lotus corniculatus								■	■											■				■				
Lunaria annua		☆	☆		☆		☆	☆	☆	☆							☆			☆	☆		☆					☆
Lupinus arboreus								▲	▲								▲	▲	▲	▲	▲	▲	▲					▲
Lupinus polyphyllus		□			□			□	□	□							□	□	□	□	□	□	□					□
Lupinus tricolor								★	★								★	★	★	★	★	★	★				★	★
Lychnis alpina								△									△			△	△	△						
Lychnis chalcedonica				■				■	■								■			■	■							
Lychnis coronaria				☆	☆			☆	☆	☆	☆						☆				☆	☆						☆
Lychnis flos-cuculi					▲			▲	▲								▲				▲							
Lychnis flos-jovis					□			□	□	□											□	□						
Lychnis haageana		★					★	★	★											★	★							
Lysichiton americanum				△			△	△	△											△				△				△

FLOWERING-SEASON | DECORATIVE USES | OTHER USES | PROBLEMS

Column headers (left to right):

FLOWERING-SEASON
- DECEMBER, JANUARY
- FEBRUARY, MARCH
- APRIL, MAY
- JUNE, JULY, AUGUST
- SEPTEMBER, OCTOBER
- NOVEMBER

DECORATIVE USES
- GROUND-COVER
- AROUND ROSE BUSHES
- GOOD COVER FOR OPEN GROUND
- FLOWERS: GOOD UNDERGROWTH COVER
- GIANT
- FOR DRIED FLOWERS
- PLANTS: HAS DECORATIVE FRUITS
- FOR POTS AND TUBS ON THE PATIO IN THE SUN
- FOR POTS AND TUBS ON THE PATIO IN THE SHADE
- BULBS REMAIN IN GROUND
- OLDER VARIETIES

OTHER USES
- GROUND COVER: GROW IN SHADE
- GROW IN SUNNY POSITIONS
- ESTABLISH QUICKLY
- FOR SLOPES AND BANKS
- FOR NOOKS, WALLS, ROCKERIES AND PAVING
- CLIMBING ANNUALS
- GROWN FROM SEED
- ATTRACT BEES AND BUTTERFLIES
- PLANTS: EASY FOR THE WEEKEND GARDENER
- FLOURISH IN WATER
- CARNIVOROUS
- ATTRACTS RABBITS
- VERY INVASIVE

PROBLEMS
- POISONOUS OR ALLERGENIC
- ATTRACTS SLUGS
- TOLERANT OF POLLUTION
- PRONE TO FROST

Legend symbols used in grid: □ (open square), ■ (filled square), ☆ (open star), ★ (filled star), △ (open triangle), ▲ (filled triangle), ● (filled circle)

	SOIL TYPES					CONDITIONS				FOLIAGE						FLOWERS									ANNUALS		
	PEATY	SANDY, LIGHT	POOR, DRY	DAMP, WELL-DRAINED	CLAY	DRY AND WARM	SHADED, SEMI-SHADED	SUNNY	MEDITERRANEAN	COASTAL	SILVERY	GOLDEN	VARIEGATED	RED	EVERGREEN	AUTUMNAL	WHITE AND GREEN	BLUE, MAUVE	VIOLET, BLACK	YELLOW, ORANGE	PINK	RED	GOOD CUT FLOWERS	SCENTED	LONG-FLOWERING	SOW THEN PLANT OUT	SOW DIRECT	SELF-SEEDING
Lysimachia clethroides		□		□	□		□	□								□	□							□				
Lysimachia ephemerum							★	★			★						★											
Lysimachia nummularia		△		△	△	△	△					△								△								
Lysimachia punctata		■		■	■	■	■													■			■					
Lythrum salicaria				☆	☆			☆													☆	☆				☆			
Macleaya cordata				▲	▲		▲	▲												▲						▲		
Macleaya microcarpa				□	□		□	□			□									□		□				□		
Malcolmia maritima			★				★	★	★								★	★		★	★	★	★				★	★
Malope trifida				△			△	△									△			△	△	△					△	
Malva moschata			■	■	■		■			■							■				■		■		■			
Matteucia struthiopteris		☆		☆			☆																	☆				
Matthiola incana		▲	▲				▲	▲	▲	▲							▲	▲		▲	▲	▲	▲	▲	▲			
Maurandia		□					□	□					□							□	□							
Meconopsis betonicifolia	★	★		★			★										★	★										
Meconopsis cambrica		△		△	△	△											△			△								△
Meconopsis grandis	■	■		■			■											■										
Meconopsis napaulensis	☆	☆		☆			☆	☆									☆			☆	☆							
Mentzelia hispida							▲	▲	▲											▲				▲			▲	
Mentzelia lindleyi		□					□	□	□											□				□			□	
Mertensia virginica		★		★			★			★								★										
Mesembryanthemum criniflorum		△	△			△		△	△	△							△	△		△	△	△				△	△	
Mimulus cardinalis				■				■	■											■	■	■						
Minuartia laricifolia		☆		☆				☆	☆	☆							☆											
Mirabilis jalapa		▲	▲					▲	▲	▲							▲			▲	▲	▲		▲			▲	▲
Miscanthus		□		□	□		□		□				□															
Molucella laevis							★	★									★						★	★	★		★	★
Monarda didyma				△	△		△										△	△		△	△	△	△					
Moraea						■		■									■	■										
Morina longifolia		☆						☆	☆	☆											☆			☆				
Muehlenbeckia complexa										▲							▲											
Muscari armeniacum		□		□				□										□					□					
Muscari comosum		★		★				★										★					★					
Muscari latifolium		△		△				△										△					△					
Muscari moschatum				■				■										■					■					
Muscari tubergenianum		☆						☆										☆					☆					
Myosotis alpestris				▲			▲										▲	▲			▲					▲	▲	
Myrrhis odorata				□													□							□				
Narcissus bulbocodium				★	★			★									★			★			★					
Narcissus canaliculatus				△				△									△			△			△	△				
Narcissus juncifolius				■				■									■			■			■	■				
Narcissus poeticus				☆	☆			☆									☆			☆			☆	☆				
Narcissus pseudonarcissus				▲				▲									▲			▲			▲					
Narcissus tazetta		□		□			□	□									□			□			□	□				
Narcissus triandrus				★				★									★			★			★					
Nelumbo nucifera					△		△	△									△				△			△				
Nemesia strumosa		■						■	■								■			■	■				■			
Nemophila maculata		☆		☆			☆	☆									☆				☆						☆	☆
Nemophila menziesii		▲		▲			▲	▲										▲									▲	▲
Nepeta × faassenii		□	□					□	□	□								□						□	□			
Nerine bowdenii		★						★	★	★											★		★		★			
Nicandra physaloides		△	△		△		△	△	△								△										△	△

380

| | FLOWERING-SEASON | | | | | DECORATIVE USES | | | | | | | | OTHER USES | | | | | | | | | | | | | PROBLEMS | | | | | |
| | | | | | | FLOWERS | | | | | PLANTS | | | GROUND COVER | | | | | | | PLANTS | | | | | | | | | | | |
Plant	DECEMBER, JANUARY	FEBRUARY, MARCH	APRIL, MAY	JUNE, JULY, AUGUST	SEPTEMBER, OCTOBER	NOVEMBER	GROUND-COVER AROUND ROSE BUSHES	GOOD COVER FOR OPEN GROUND	GOOD UNDERGROWTH COVER	GIANT	FOR DRIED FLOWERS	HAS DECORATIVE FRUITS	FOR POTS AND TUBS ON THE PATIO IN THE SUN	FOR POTS AND TUBS ON THE PATIO IN THE SHADE	BULBS REMAIN IN GROUND	OLDER VARIETIES	GROW IN SHADE	GROW IN SUNNY POSITIONS	ESTABLISH QUICKLY	FOR SLOPES AND BANKS	FOR NOOKS, WALLS, ROCKERIES AND PAVING	CLIMBING ANNUALS	GROWN FROM SEED	ATTRACT BEES AND BUTTERFLIES	EASY FOR THE WEEKEND GARDENER	FLOURISH IN WATER	CARNIVOROUS	ATTRACTS RABBITS	VERY INVASIVE	POISONOUS OR ALLERGENIC	ATTRACTS SLUGS	TOLERANT OF POLLUTION	PRONE TO FROST
			□											□				□							□				□				
			★											★				★							★								
			△											△	△	△		△		△					△								
			■					■						■			■	■	■	■					■			■	■		■		
			☆					☆									☆								☆	☆					☆		
			▲							▲															▲						▲		
			□																						□						□		
			★									★								★			★	★							★		
			△									△													△								
			■					■								■									■								
			☆						☆				☆												☆								
	▲	▲											▲			▲				▲			▲	▲						▲		
			□									□																				
			★						★																		★	★				
			△						△			△								△				△				△	△	△		
			■	■					■																				■	■		
			☆									☆															☆		☆				
																	▲							▲								
			□																					□								
			★						★																★								
			△						△			△					△			△					△					△		
		■	■						■									■							■			■		■		■
			☆															☆							☆								
			▲	▲									▲										▲	▲						▲		
										□		□												□					□			
			★						★		★														★							
			△							△	△													△	△							
			☆															☆		☆												
			□						□					□			□			□	□			□							□	
			★									★		★			★			★	★				★						★	
			△									△		△			△			△	△			△	△						△	
			■									■		■			■			■	■			■							■	
			☆									☆		☆			☆			☆	☆										☆	
	▲	▲						▲				▲			▲	▲	▲		▲					▲				▲			▲	
			□																												□	
			★					★				★		★			★				★			★			★		★		★	
			△					△				△		△			△				△			△			△		△		△	
			■					■				■		■			■				■			■			■		■		■	
			☆					☆				☆		☆	☆		☆				☆			☆			☆		☆		☆	
	▲	▲						▲				▲					▲						▲	▲						▲		
□	□	□						□				□		□										□			□		□		□	
			★					★				★		★										★			★		★		★	
				△																					△				△			
				■																												
			☆											☆				☆						☆					☆			
			▲											▲										▲					▲			
			□			□						□				□	□		□					□								
				★								★		★										★					★	★	★	★
			△									△	△											△					△			

O

P

Plant	PEATY	SANDY, LIGHT	POOR, DRY	DAMP, WELL-DRAINED	CLAY	DRY AND WARM	SHADED, SEMI-SHADED	SUNNY	MEDITERRANEAN	COASTAL	SILVERY	GOLDEN	VARIEGATED	RED	EVERGREEN	AUTUMNAL	WHITE AND GREEN	BLUE, MAUVE	VIOLET, BLACK	YELLOW, ORANGE	PINK	RED	GOOD CUT FLOWERS	SCENTED	LONG-FLOWERING	SOW THEN PLANT OUT	SOW DIRECT	SELF-SEEDING
Nicotiana affinis				□			□	□									□				□	□	□		□			
Nicotiana sylvestris				★			★	★									★						★		★			
Nigella		△		△				△									△	△		△	△		△				△	△
Nymphea hybride								■									■			■	■	■						
Nymphea × marliacea								☆									☆				☆							
Oenothera biennis								▲		▲										▲				▲				▲
Oenothera lamarckiana								□	□								□											
Oenothera missouriensis								★		★										★								
Oenothera perennis			△					△		△										△								
Oenothera pumila								■		■										■								
Oenothera tetragona								☆		☆										☆								
Omphalodes verna		▲		▲			▲											▲										
Onoclea sensibilis				□		□																						
Onopordum bracteatum		★	★		★			★	★	★	★																	★
Ornithogalum arabicum		△			△			△	△	△							△				△			△				△
Ornithogalum magnum					■			■	■	■							■				■			■				
Ornithogalum nutans		☆		☆	☆			☆	☆	☆							☆				☆			☆				
Ornithogalum thyrsoides		▲			▲			▲	▲	▲							▲				▲			▲				
Ornithogalum umbellatum		□		□	□			□	□								□				□			□				
Osmunda regalis																				★								
Osteospermum auriantacum		△				△		△	△	△							△		△		△			△	△			
Osteospermum ecklonis		■				■		■	■	■														■	■			
Ourisia coccinea	☆			☆																		☆						
Ourisia macropylla				▲													▲											
Oxalis adenophylla	□	□						□	□	□							□				□							
Oxalis deppei		★			★			★	★	★							★				★							
Pachysandra terminalis	△						△								△								△					
Paeonia lactiflora		■			■			■	■								■			■	■	■	■					
Paeonia officinalis		☆			☆			☆													☆	☆	☆	☆				
Papaver alpinum								▲	▲								▲			▲	▲							
Papaver nudicaule		□						□	□								□				□							□
Papaver officinalis								★	★								★			★	★	★						
Papaver orientale		△						△	△								△			△	△							△
Papaver rhoeas		■	■					■	■	■							■				■	■					■	■
Papaver somniferum								☆	☆	☆							☆				☆						☆	☆
Paradisea liliastrum								▲									▲							▲				
Pelargonium graveolens		□	□			□		□	□												□	□		□	□			
Pelargonium peltatum		★	★			★		★	★	★							★				★	★		★	★			
Pelargonium regale		△	△			△		△	△	△							△				△	△		△	△			
Pelargonium tomentosum		■	■			■		■	■	■							■				■	■		■	■			
Pelargonium zonale		☆	☆			☆		☆	☆	☆							☆			☆	☆	☆		☆	☆			
Peltiphyllum peltatum				▲	▲			▲													▲			▲				
Pennisetum alopecuroides								□	□																□			
Pennisetum japonicum			★					★	★															★				
Pennisetum orientale			△					△	△																△			
Penstemon heterophyllus								■	■								■	■		■	■	■						
Penstemon pinifolius								☆	☆								☆	☆		☆		☆						
Petasites fragrans				▲			▲										▲							▲				
Petunia × hybrida		□	□					□	□								□	□		□	□			□		□		
Phacelia campanularia		★			★		★	★	★	★								★									★	★
Phacelia tanacetifolia				△			△	△	△	△								△									△	△

FLOWERING-SEASON · DECORATIVE USES · OTHER USES · PROBLEMS

Column key (left to right):

FLOWERING-SEASON
1. DECEMBER, JANUARY
2. FEBRUARY, MARCH
3. APRIL, MAY
4. JUNE, JULY, AUGUST
5. SEPTEMBER, OCTOBER
6. NOVEMBER

DECORATIVE USES
7. GROUND-COVER
8. AROUND ROSE BUSHES
9. GOOD COVER FOR OPEN GROUND
10. GOOD UNDERGROWTH COVER
— *FLOWERS*
11. GIANT
12. FOR DRIED FLOWERS
— *PLANTS*
13. HAS DECORATIVE FRUITS
14. FOR POTS AND TUBS ON THE PATIO IN THE SUN
15. FOR POTS AND TUBS ON THE PATIO IN THE SHADE
16. BULBS REMAIN IN GROUND
17. OLDER VARIETIES

OTHER USES
— *GROUND COVER*
18. GROW IN SHADE
19. GROW IN SUNNY POSITIONS
20. ESTABLISH QUICKLY
21. FOR SLOPES AND BANKS
22. FOR NOOKS, WALLS, ROCKERIES AND PAVING
— *PLANTS*
23. CLIMBING ANNUALS
24. GROWN FROM SEED
25. ATTRACT BEES AND BUTTERFLIES
26. EASY FOR THE WEEKEND GARDENER
27. FLOURISH IN WATER
28. CARNIVOROUS

PROBLEMS
29. ATTRACTS RABBITS
30. VERY INVASIVE
31. POISONOUS OR ALLERGENIC
32. ATTRACTS SLUGS
33. TOLERANT OF POLLUTION
34. PRONE TO FROST

#	3	4	5	Decorative & Other uses (symbols)	Problems (symbols)
1	□			14 □	24 □, 25 □(bees area), 27 □, 31 □
2	★			25 ★	29 ★, 31 ★, 32 ★
3	△			12 △, 13 △	34 △
4	■			26 ■, 27 ■	32 ■
5	☆			26 ☆	32 ☆
6	▲			29 ▲	
7	□		□	18 □, 19 □	29 □
8	★			19 ★	
9	△				
10	■				
11	☆				
12	(1 ▲, 2 ▲)			10 ▲, 13 ▲, 16 ▲, 19 ▲, 25 ▲	32 ▲
13	□			10 □	
14	★			11 ★	26 ★, 29 ★, 30 ★, 31 ★, 32 ★
15	△ (1 △)			13 △, 16 △, 19 △, 26 △	29 △, 31 △, 32 △
16	■ (2 ■)			13 ■, 16 ■, 19 ■, 26 ■	29 ■, 31 ■, 32 ■
17	☆ (4 ☆)	☆		10 ☆, 13 ☆, 16 ☆, 26 ☆	29 ☆, 31 ☆, 32 ☆
18	▲	▲		13 ▲, 16 ▲, 17 ▲, 26 ▲	29 ▲, 31 ▲, 32 ▲
19	□	□		13 □, 16 □, 26 □	29 □, 31 □, 32 □
20	★ (2 ★)				
21	△			13 △, 19 △, 26 △	34 △
22	■			13 ■, 19 ■, 26 ■	34 ■
23	☆			13 ☆	
24	▲			19 ▲	
25	□ (2 □)			13 □, 18 □, 19 □, 26 □	
26	★			13 ★, 16 ★, 18 ★, 19 ★, 26 ★	32 ★
27	△			15 △, 17 △, 18 △, 19 △, 27 △	
28	■ (1 ■)			26 ■	29 ■, 31 ■, 32 ■
29	☆ (5 ☆)			16 ☆	29 ☆, 31 ☆, 32 ☆
30	▲ (1 ▲)			13 ▲, 16 ▲, 26 ▲	32 ▲
31	□			13 □, 16 □, 20 □, 26 □	32 □
32	★			13 ★, 16 ★, 26 ★	32 ★
33	△			13 △, 16 △, 26 △	32 △
34	■ (2 ■)			13 ■, 16 ■, 26 ■	32 ■
35	☆			13 ☆, 26 ☆	32 ☆
36	▲			13 ▲, 26 ▲	32 ▲
37	□			13 □, 26 □	32 □, 33 □
38	★	★		13 ★, 26 ★	32 ★, 33 ★
39	△	△		13 △, 26 △	32 △, 33 △
40	■	■		13 ■, 26 ■	32 ■, 33 ■
41	☆	☆		13 ☆, 26 ☆	32 ☆
42	▲			13 ▲, 26 ▲	34 ▲
43	□ (2 □)	□		13 □, 19 □, 26 □	32 □
44	★	★		13 ★, 19 ★, 26 ★	32 ★
45	△	△		13 △, 26 △	
46	■			13 ■, 26 ■	
47	☆			13 ☆, 26 ☆	
48	▲			13 ▲, 26 ▲	30 ▲
49	□			13 □, 24 □	32 □
50	★			13 ★, 19 ★, 25 ★, 26 ★	32 ★
51	△			19 △, 25 △, 26 △	32 △
52	■				
53	☆				
54	▲				

Column groups: **SOIL TYPES** (Peaty, Sandy/Light, Poor/Dry, Damp/Well-Drained, Clay, Dry and Warm); **CONDITIONS** (Shaded/Semi-Shaded, Sunny, Mediterranean, Coastal); **FOLIAGE** (Silvery, Golden, Variegated, Red, Evergreen, Autumnal); **FLOWERS** (White and Green, Blue/Mauve, Violet/Black, Yellow/Orange, Pink, Red, Good Cut Flowers, Scented, Long-Flowering, Sow then Plant Out, Sow Direct, Self-Seeding) — last three = ANNUALS.

	Peaty	Sandy,Light	Poor,Dry	Damp,Well-Drained	Clay	Dry and Warm	Shaded,Semi-Shaded	Sunny	Mediterranean	Coastal	Silvery	Golden	Variegated	Red	Evergreen	Autumnal	White and Green	Blue,Mauve	Violet,Black	Yellow,Orange	Pink	Red	Good Cut Flowers	Scented	Long-Flowering	Sow then Plant Out	Sow Direct	Self-Seeding
Phalaris arundinacea				□			□	□	□				□				□											
Phlomis fruticosa		★						★	★	★										★								
Phlomis samia		△	△		△			△	△	△										△								
Phlox douglasii								■									■	■			■							
Phlox drummondii								☆									☆	☆		☆	☆	☆				☆		
Phlox maculata								▲									▲	▲			▲							
Phlox paniculata				□				□									□	□		□	□	□	□	□			
Phlox subulata								★									★	★			★	★						
Phormium tenax		△	△					△	△	△			△	△														
Phygelius aequalis		■	■					■	■	■										■		■			■			
Phygelius capensis		☆	☆					☆	☆	☆												☆			☆			
Phyllitis scolopendrium			▲	▲			▲	▲	▲	▲					▲													▲
Physalis franchetii		□	□	□	□			□	□																			
Physostegia virginiana				★				★									★				★	★		★				
Phytolacca americana		△		△				△	△							△					△	△						△
Pinguicula grandiflora				■			■	■										■										
Platycodon		☆			☆			☆									☆	☆			☆		☆		☆			
Plumbago capensis								▲	▲									▲										
Podophyllum	□			□			□										□											
Polemonium coeruleum				★			★	★										★										
Polemonium foliosissimum				△			△	△										△										
Polygonatum commutatum				■			■										■					■						
Polygonatum multiflorum						☆	☆										☆					☆						
Polygonum affine			▲	▲				▲							▲	▲					▲	▲						
Polygonum amplexicaule				□	□			□													□	□						
Polygonum bistorta				★	★			★														★						
Polygonum campanulatum								△									△				△	△						
Polygonum compactum 'Roseum'								■													■	■						
Polygonum vaccinifolium								☆													☆							
Polypodium vulgare		▲	▲	▲	▲		▲								▲								▲					
Polystichum aculeatum				□			□		□						□													
Polystichum falcatum				★			★		★						★													
Polystichum setiferum							△		△						△													
Pontederia cordata				■				■										■										
Portulaca grandiflora		☆	☆					☆	☆	☆										☆	☆	☆			☆	☆	☆	
Potentilla atrosanguinea								▲	▲	▲											▲	▲						
Primula acaulis				□			□										□								□			□
Primula auricula								★									★	★		★	★	★		★				
Primula beesiana								△										△										
Primula bulleyana	■							■												■								
Primula capitata								☆										☆										
Primula denticulata	▲							▲									▲	▲		▲	▲							
Primula florindae				□			□										□							□				□
Primula japonica				★			★										★				★	★						★
Primula juliae								△										△										
Primula pulverulenta								■														■						
Primula rosea								☆													☆	☆						
Primula sieboldii				▲				▲									▲	▲				▲						
Prunella grandiflora				□	□										□		□	□			□				□			□
Prunella webbiana				★	★													★			★			★				★
Pulmonaria angustifolia				△			△	△										△										△

FLOWERING-SEASON · DECORATIVE USES · OTHER USES · PROBLEMS

DEC, JAN	FEB, MAR	APR, MAY	JUN, JUL, AUG	SEP, OCT	NOV	GROUND-COVER	AROUND ROSE BUSHES	GOOD COVER FOR OPEN GROUND	GOOD UNDERGROWTH COVER	GIANT	FOR DRIED FLOWERS	HAS DECORATIVE FRUITS	FOR POTS & TUBS ON PATIO IN SUN	FOR POTS & TUBS ON PATIO IN SHADE	BULBS REMAIN IN GROUND	OLDER VARIETIES	GROW IN SHADE	GROW IN SUNNY POSITIONS	ESTABLISH QUICKLY	FOR SLOPES & BANKS	FOR NOOKS, WALLS, ROCKERIES & PAVING	CLIMBING ANNUALS	GROWN FROM SEED	ATTRACT BEES & BUTTERFLIES	EASY FOR THE WEEKEND GARDENER	FLOURISH IN WATER	CARNIVOROUS	ATTRACTS RABBITS	VERY INVASIVE	POISONOUS OR ALLERGENIC	ATTRACT SLUGS	TOLERANT OF POLLUTION	PRONE TO FROST
												□					□	□						□				□		□			
		★																															
		△															△							△				△	△	△			
	■											■					■			■				△									
		☆										☆												☆									
												▲												▲									
		□										□											□	□									
	★					★						★					★			★				★									
		△										△																					△
	■											■												■	■								
		☆										☆											☆	☆									
								▲	▲		▲		▲		▲						▲		▲							▲			
			□							□	□																	□		□			
	★											★											★	★									
		△							△		△																	△	△	△			
	■																■									■							
		☆										☆												☆					☆				
		▲										▲																			▲			
	□								□								□												□				
	★											★											★	★									
	△											△											△	△									
	■					■	■					■		■	■									■			■		■				
		☆					☆	☆				☆		☆	☆								☆				☆		☆				
		▲	▲			▲						▲		▲	▲	▲	▲	▲					▲				▲		▲				
		□	□			□						□		□	□	□	□					□				□		□				
		★	★			★						★		★	★	★	★					★				★		★				
		△	△			△						△		△	△	△	△					△				△		△				
		■	■			■						■		■	■	■	■					■				■		■				
		☆	☆			☆						☆		☆	☆	☆	☆					☆				☆		☆				
								▲				▲		▲				▲					▲				▲						
								□				□		□				□					□									□
								★				★		★	★			★					★									★
								△				△		△	△			△					△									△
	■																									■							
		☆										☆											☆										
	▲	▲										▲						▲					▲						▲				
															□								□										
★	★											★		★				★					★									
		△										△						△															
		■										■						■															
		☆										☆						☆															
		▲									▲	▲						▲															
		□									□	□						□					□									
★		★										★						★					★									
△	△											△						△					△									
		■										■						■															
☆	☆											☆						☆															
	▲							▲				▲						▲					▲									
		□					□					□		□	□			□					□									
	★					★						★		★	★			★					★									
	△						△					△	△	△	△			△					△						△			

385

	SOIL TYPES					CONDITIONS					FOLIAGE						FLOWERS										ANNUALS	
	PEATY	SANDY, LIGHT	POOR, DRY	DAMP, WELL-DRAINED	CLAY	DRY AND WARM	SHADED, SEMI-SHADED	SUNNY	MEDITERRANEAN	COASTAL	SILVERY	GOLDEN	VARIEGATED	RED	EVERGREEN	AUTUMNAL	WHITE AND GREEN	BLUE, MAUVE	VIOLET, BLACK	YELLOW, ORANGE	PINK	RED	GOOD CUT FLOWERS	SCENTED	LONG-FLOWERING	SOW THEN PLANT OUT	SOW DIRECT	SELF-SEEDING
Pulmonaria officinalis				□			□				□	□					□			□								□
Pulmonaria saccharata			★				★					★					★	★										★
Pulsatilla vulgaris						△				△							△	△			△							
Puschkinia scilloides		■		■	■		■	■										■					■					
Ramonda pyrenaica				☆			☆										☆	☆			☆							
Ranunculus asiaticus		▲		▲				▲	▲								▲			▲	▲		▲		▲			
Raoulia australis	□		□	□			□	□	□	□										□		□		□				
Reseda alba		★	★					★		★							★						★	★			★	★
Reseda odorata																							△	△			△	△
Rheum palmatum		■		■	■			■						■							■		■					
Rhodohypoxis baurii		☆						☆	☆								☆				☆	☆		☆				
Ricinus communis		▲						▲	▲					▲												▲	▲	
Rodgersia aesculifolia				□	□		□							□			□			•			□					
Rodgersia pinnata				★	★		★							★						★	★		★					
Rodgersia tabularis				△	△		△										△				△		△					
Romneya coulteri		■						■	■	■							■				■		■					
Rudbeckia bicolor		☆		☆				☆		☆										☆	☆	☆			☆			
Rudbeckia fulgida		▲		▲				▲		▲										▲	▲	▲		▲				
Rudbeckia laciniata		□		□				□		□										□	□	□		□				
Rudbeckia nitida		★		★				★												★	★	★		★				
Ruscus aculeatus				△		△			△					△		△					△			△				
Ruta graveolens		■	■	■	■			■	■	■				■									■					
Sagina subulata		☆		☆				☆							☆		☆											
Sagittaria sagittifolia				▲	▲												▲											
Salpiglossis sinuata		□						□	□	□								□		□	□	□				□		
Salvia argentea		★						★	★	★							★							★				★
Salvia coccinea								△	△	△							△							△				
Salvia farinacea		■						■	■	■							■	■						■				
Salvia grahamii								☆	☆	☆							☆							☆	☆	☆		
Salvia haematodes								▲	▲	▲							▲							▲				
Salvia horminum								□	□	□							□	□					□				□	□
Salvia involucrata 'Bethellii'								★	★	★											★			★				
Salvia officinalis			△					△	△	△	△	△					△				△			△				
Salvia patens		■						■	■	■								■						■				
Salvia sclarea			☆					☆	☆	☆	☆						☆						☆	☆				☆
Salvia splendens								▲	▲	▲											▲			▲				
Salvia superba								□	□								□									□	□	
Sanguinaria canadensis			★			★				★							★							★				
Sanguisorba obtusa			△	△		△											△				△							
Santolina chamaecyparissus		■	■		■			■	■	■	■				■					■			■					
Santolina virens		☆	☆		☆			☆	☆	☆					☆					☆			☆					
Sanvitalia procumbens								▲	▲											▲							▲	
Saponaria ocymoides								□	□								□				□	□						
Sarracenia			★				★		★					★						★	★							
Saxifraga aizoon							△		△	△							△											
Saxifraga caespitosa							■		■								■											
Saxifraga cochlearis							☆		☆	☆							☆											
Saxifraga cortusifolia							▲		▲								▲											
Saxifraga decipiens							□										□				□	□						
Saxifraga hypnoides		★			★		★		★						★		★											
Saxifraga linguaeformis							△		△								△											

FLOWERING-SEASON					DECORATIVE USES — FLOWERS					DECORATIVE USES — PLANTS						OTHER USES — GROUND COVER				OTHER USES — PLANTS							PROBLEMS					
DECEMBER, JANUARY	FEBRUARY, MARCH	APRIL, MAY	JUNE, JULY, AUGUST	SEPTEMBER, OCTOBER, NOVEMBER	GROUND-COVER	AROUND ROSE BUSHES	GOOD COVER FOR OPEN GROUND	GOOD UNDERGROWTH COVER	GIANT	FOR DRIED FLOWERS	HAS DECORATIVE FRUITS	FOR POTS AND TUBS ON THE PATIO IN THE SUN	FOR POTS AND TUBS ON THE PATIO IN THE SHADE	BULBS REMAIN IN GROUND	OLDER VARIETIES	GROW IN SHADE	GROW IN SUNNY POSITIONS	ESTABLISH QUICKLY	FOR SLOPES AND BANKS	FOR NOOKS, WALLS, ROCKERIES AND PAVING	CLIMBING ANNUALS	GROWN FROM SEED	ATTRACT BEES AND BUTTERFLIES	EASY FOR THE WEEKEND GARDENER	FLOURISH IN WATER	CARNIVOROUS	ATTRACTS RABBITS	VERY INVASIVE	POISONOUS OR ALLERGENIC	ATTRACTS SLUGS	TOLERANT OF POLLUTION	PRONE TO FROST
	□						□						□		□				□				□							□		
	★						★						★		★				★				★							★		
	△						△				△	△		△					△				△				△		△	△		
■							■					■							■				■						■	■		
	☆													☆					☆											☆		
	▲	▲										▲											▲						▲	▲		
	□											□							□													
	★	★										★			★							★								★		
	△											△			△							△										
	■							■																						■	■		
	☆	☆										☆		☆					☆				☆							☆		
	▲											▲											▲			▲		▲		▲		
	□						□																□									
	★						★																★										
	△						△															△											
	■											■																					■
	☆	☆										☆											☆							☆		
	▲											▲											▲						▲			
	□							□				□											□							□		
	★	★										★											★							★		
△	△						△		△	△		△		△								△							△		
	■											■					■						■		■					■		
	☆											☆				☆	☆						☆							☆		
	▲													▲									▲	▲		▲				▲		
	□											□											□							□		
	★											★					★						★							★		
	△											△											△							△		
	■											■											■							■		
	☆											☆											☆							☆		
	▲											▲											▲							▲		
	□											□											□							□		
	★	★										★											★							★		
	△											△							△				△							△		
	■	■										■							■				■							■	■	
	☆											☆											☆							☆		
	▲											▲											▲							▲		
	□											□											□							□		
	★						★						★										★							★		
	△						△																△									
	■				■							■				■			■				■									
	☆			☆								☆				☆			☆				☆							☆		
	▲											▲																		▲		
	□											□					□						□				□	□		□		
	★																							★							★		
△	△																													△		
■																■													■		
	☆	☆										☆				☆													☆		
	▲											▲				▲													▲		
	□											□				□													□		
	★										★					★							★							★		
	△															△													△		

387

Plant	PEATY	SANDY/LIGHT	POOR/DRY	DAMP/WELL-DRAINED	CLAY	DRY AND WARM	SHADED/SEMI-SHADED	SUNNY	MEDITERRANEAN	COASTAL	SILVERY	GOLDEN	VARIEGATED	RED	EVERGREEN	AUTUMNAL	WHITE AND GREEN	BLUE/MAUVE	VIOLET/BLACK	YELLOW/ORANGE	PINK	RED	GOOD CUT FLOWERS	SCENTED	LONG-FLOWERING	SOW THEN PLANT OUT	SOW DIRECT	SELF-SEEDING
Saxifraga oppositifolia							□		□								□			□	□							
Saxifraga stolonifera				★			★						★				★											
Saxifraga umbrosa				△	△		△			△			△								△							
Scabiosa atropurpurea								■		■							■	■			■	■	■				■	
Scabiosa caucasica								☆		☆							☆	☆			☆			☆	☆			
Scabiosa ochroleuca										▲										▲			▲	▲				
Schizanthus pinnat		□						□	□								□			□	□	□	□			□	□	□
Schizostylis coccinea		★		★				★	★											★	★	★		★				
Scilla campanulata							△	△	△								△	△					△					
Scilla sibirica		■		■				■	■	■							■	■										
Scilla tubergeniana							☆	☆	☆								☆	☆										
Scutellaria indica								▲								▲	▲	▲										
Sedum acre		□	□					□	□	□						□				□								□
Sedum aizoon								★	★	★																		
Sedum lydium								△	△	△																		
Sedum spathulifolium		■						■	■	■	■			■	■	■	■			■								
Sedum spectabile		☆						☆	☆	☆	☆									☆	☆			☆				
Sedum spurium		▲	▲	▲	▲			▲	▲	▲				▲	▲	▲	▲			▲	▲							
Sedum telephium								□	□	□											□							
Sempervivum arachnoideum			★					★	★	★	★				★		★			★	★							
Sempervivum tectorum			△					△	△	△					△		△											
Senecio cineraria		■						■	■		■						■	■			■	■		■		■		
Senecio greyi		☆						☆	☆	☆	☆						☆			☆								
Shortia galicifolia	▲			▲			▲										△			▲								
Shortia uniflora				□			□									△	□											
Sidalcea malvaeflora				★				★		★							★			★	★	★		★				
Silene acaulis								△		△							△			△	△		△	△				△
Silene armeria								■		■							■			■	■			■				■
Silene schafta								☆		☆							☆			☆				☆				☆
Silene pendula								▲		▲							▲			▲				▲			▲	▲
Silybum marianum		□	□	□				□	□	□			□								□			□				□
Sisyrinchium striatum		★						★	★		★						★			★								★
Smilacina racemosa		△		△			△																	△				
Solanum capsicastrum		■						■	■						■		■											
Solanum crispum										☆					☆				☆									
Solanum jasminoides															▲					▲								
Soldanella alpina	□			□													□											
Sodanella montana	★			★													★											
Solidago canadensis		△			△			△		△										△			△	△	△			
Sparaxis tricolor		■						■	■	■										■	■	■						
Sprekelia formosissima		☆						☆	☆	☆												☆						
Stachys lanata		▲	▲			▲		▲	▲	▲	▲						▲											
Stachys macrantha			□	□	□		□	□	□								□				□			□				
Stachys officinalis			★			★		★	★	★	★						★							★				
Sternbergia clusiana								△	△	△										△				△				
Sternbergia lutea		■			■			■	■	■										■								
Sternbergia fischeriana								☆	☆	☆										☆								
Stipa calamagrostis		▲						▲		▲					▲		▲			▲				▲				
Stipa gigantea		□						□			□				□		□			□								
Stokesia laevis		★		★				★	★									★					★	★				
Symphytum caucasicum				△	△		△	△										△										

The table below records flowering season, decorative uses, other uses and problems for a series of garden plants. Symbols used: □ ★ △ ■ ☆ ▲

	FLOWERING-SEASON					DECORATIVE USES											OTHER USES														PROBLEMS		
									FLOWERS				PLANTS				GROUND COVER				PLANTS												
	DEC, JAN	FEB, MAR	APR, MAY	JUN–AUG	SEP–NOV	Ground-cover	Around rose bushes	Good cover for open ground	Good undergrowth cover	Giant	For dried flowers	Has decorative fruits	Pots/tubs patio sun	Pots/tubs patio shade	Bulbs remain in ground	Older varieties	Grow in shade	Grow in sunny positions	Establish quickly	For slopes and banks	Nooks, walls, rockeries and paving	Climbing annuals	Grown from seed	Attract bees and butterflies	Easy for weekend gardener	Flourish in water	Carnivorous	Attracts rabbits	Very invasive	Poisonous or allergenic	Attracts slugs	Tolerant of pollution	Prone to frost
1		□											□							□					□						□		
2		★						★					★							★					★						★		
3			△	△									△					△		△					△						△		
4			■																						■								
5			☆										☆											☆	☆								
6			▲										▲											▲	▲								
7			□	□									□											□						□			
8			★	★									★		★			★		★					★						★		★
9	△		★	★									△	△	△			△		△					△				△	△	△		
10	■								□	■			■	■	■			■		■					■				■	■	■		
11	☆												☆	☆	☆			☆		☆					☆				☆	☆	☆		
12		▲																▲															
13			□										□				□		□	□					□						□		
14			★										★				★		★					★						★		
15			△										△				△		△					△						△		
16			■										■				■		■					■						■		
17				☆									☆				☆		☆			☆	☆							☆		
18			▲										▲				▲	▲	▲			▲	▲							▲		
19			□										□				□		□			□								□		
20			★										★						★				★							★		
21			△												△			△		△										△		
22			■		■								■					■			■		■							■	■	
23			☆		☆								☆					☆			☆		☆									
24	▲							▲					▲					▲												▲		
25	□							□					□					□												□		
26		★		★									★												★					★		
27		△	△								△		△					△		△			△	△						△		
28		■	■										■					■		■			■	■						■		
29		☆	☆	☆									☆					☆			☆		☆	☆						☆		
30		▲	▲										▲					▲			▲		▲							▲		
31			□										□			□		□			□		□							□		
32			★										★					★												★		
33			△					△					△					△			△	△								△		
34			■							■		■	■					■					■			■				■			
35			☆										☆					☆												☆		
36			▲	▲									▲					▲												▲		
37	□																□											□		□		
38	★																★											★		★		
39			△	△				△									△	△		△	△						△			△		
40			■										■					■													■	
41			☆										☆		☆			☆									☆			☆		
42			▲										▲			▲		▲		▲	▲									▲		
43			□										□		□			□			□									□		
44			★										★					★			★									★		
45				△									△		△			△			△									△		
46				■									■		■			■										■		■		
47				☆			☆						☆		☆													☆		☆		
48			▲					▲		▲		▲						▲			▲									▲		
49			□							□		□									□									□		
50			★										★					★			★									★		
51			△					△	△									△	△					△				△		△		

389

T

	SOIL TYPES						CONDITIONS				FOLIAGE						FLOWERS											ANNUALS
	PEATY	SANDY, LIGHT	POOR, DRY	DAMP, WELL-DRAINED	CLAY	DRY AND WARM	SHADED, SEMI-SHADED	SUNNY	MEDITERRANEAN	COASTAL	SILVERY	GOLDEN	VARIEGATED	RED	EVERGREEN	AUTUMNAL	WHITE AND GREEN	BLUE, MAUVE	VIOLET, BLACK	YELLOW, ORANGE	PINK	RED	GOOD CUT FLOWERS	SCENTED	LONG-FLOWERING	SOW THEN PLANT OUT	SOW DIRECT	SELF-SEEDING
Symphytum orientale							□										□											□
Symphytum rubrum							★											★										
Symphytum × uplandicum							△											△										
Tagetes erecta							■		■											■		■	■	■	■	■		
Tagetes patula								☆		☆										☆		☆	☆	☆	☆	☆		
Tellima grandiflora		▲		▲	▲		▲	▲							▲	▲	▲											▲
Teucrium chamaedrys							□		□												□							
Teucrium crispum								★		★																		
Teucrium polium								△		△	△						△	△										
Thalictrum adiantifolium							■																■					
Thalictrum aquilegifolium			☆				☆										☆	☆			☆	☆	☆					
Thalictrum kiusianum							▲																▲					
Thalictrum speciosissimum			□				□				□									□			□					
Thermopsis lanceolata								★		★										★								
Thermopsis montana		△						△		△							△											
Thunbergia alata		■					■	■									■								■	■		
Thunbergia grandiflora								☆																				
Thymus cilicicus			▲					▲	▲						▲			▲						▲				
Thymus × citriodorus		□						□	□						□			□						□				
Thymus hirsutus doerfleri			★					★	★						★			★						★				
Thymus serpyllum			△					△		△	△				△			△						△				
Tiarella cordifolia	■			■			■	■							■	■	■							■				■
Tiarella trifoliata							☆								☆	☆	☆							☆				
Tiarella wherryi							▲								▲	▲	▲							▲				
Tigridia pavonia		□						□	□	□							□			□	□	□						
Tolmiea menziesii		★		★			★	★									★											
Torenia fournieri		△						△	△																△			
Tradescantia × andersoniana		■		■			■	■									■	■			■	■						
Tricyrtis hirta				☆			☆											☆		☆				☆				
Tricyrtis macropoda				▲			▲											▲		▲				▲				
Trillium erectum	□			□			□										□			□	□							
Trillium grandiflorum	★			★			★										★			★	★							
Trillium ovatum				△			△										△			△	△							
Trillium sessile				■			■						■				■			■	■							
Trillium undulatum	☆						☆										☆											
Trollius chinensis								▲												▲		▲						
Trollius cultorum				□				□												□		□						
Trollius europaeus				★				★												★								
Tropaeolum majus			△			△		△	△	△										△	△	△		△	△		△	△
Tropaeolum peregrinum		■				■		■	■	■				■						■					■		■	
Tropaeolum polyphyllum		☆	☆			☆		☆	☆	☆	☆									☆					☆			
Tropaeolum speciosum	▲	▲	▲	▲		▲	▲	▲	▲	▲										▲		▲			▲			
Tropaeolum tuberosum		□				□		□	□	□										□					□			
Tulipa acuminata			★			★		★		★							★			★		★	★					
Tulipa clusiana			△			△		△	△	△							△			△		△	△					
Tulipa **Darwin**			■			■		■		■							■		■	■	■	■	■					
Tulipa **double early**			☆			☆		☆		☆							☆			☆		☆	☆					
Tulipa **double late**			▲			▲		▲		▲							▲			▲		▲	▲					
Tulipa **fleur de lis**			□			□		□		□							□			□		□	□					
Tulipa fosteriana			★			★		★	★	★							★			★	★	★	★					
Tulipa greigii			△			△		△	△	△				△								△	△					

390

Column headers (reading diagonally, left to right):

- DECEMBER, JANUARY
- FEBRUARY, MARCH
- APRIL, MAY
- JUNE, JULY, AUGUST
- SEPTEMBER, OCTOBER
- NOVEMBER
- GROUND-COVER
- AROUND ROSE BUSHES
- GOOD COVER FOR OPEN GROUND
- GOOD UNDERGROWTH COVER
- GIANT
- FOR DRIED FLOWERS
- HAS DECORATIVE FRUITS
- FOR POTS AND TUBS ON THE PATIO IN THE SUN
- FOR POTS AND TUBS ON THE PATIO IN THE SHADE
- BULBS REMAIN IN GROUND
- OLDER VARIETIES
- GROW IN SHADE
- GROW IN SUNNY POSITIONS
- ESTABLISH QUICKLY
- FOR SLOPES AND BANKS
- FOR NOOKS, WALLS, ROCKERIES AND PAVING
- CLIMBING ANNUALS
- GROWN FROM SEED
- ATTRACT BEES AND BUTTERFLIES
- EASY FOR THE WEEKEND GARDENER
- FLOURISH IN WATER
- CARNIVOROUS
- ATTRACTS RABBITS
- VERY INVASIVE
- POISONOUS OR ALLERGENIC
- ATTRACT SLUGS
- TOLERANT OF POLLUTION
- PRONE TO FROST

Sub-headings: FLOWERS / PLANTS (under DECORATIVE USES); GROUND COVER / PLANTS (under OTHER USES)

391

	SOIL TYPES					CONDITIONS					FOLIAGE						FLOWERS									ANNUALS		
	PEATY	SANDY, LIGHT	POOR, DRY	DAMP, WELL-DRAINED	CLAY	DRY AND WARM	SHADED, SEMI-SHADED	SUNNY	MEDITERRANEAN	COASTAL	SILVERY	GOLDEN	VARIEGATED	RED	EVERGREEN	AUTUMNAL	WHITE AND GREEN	BLUE, MAUVE	VIOLET, BLACK	YELLOW, ORANGE	PINK	RED	GOOD CUT FLOWERS	SCENTED	LONG-FLOWERING	SOW THEN PLANT OUT	SOW DIRECT	SELF-SEEDING
Tulipa kaufmanniana		□				□		□	□	□							□			□	□							
Tulipa **Mendel**		★			★			★		★							★				★	★						
Tulipa marjoletti		△				△		△		△							△			△	△	△	△					
Tulipa parrot		■				■		■		■							■			■	■	■	■					
Tulipa single early		☆				☆		☆		☆							☆			☆	☆	☆	☆					
Tulipa single late		▲				▲		▲		▲							▲			▲	▲	▲	▲					
Tulipa sprengeri		□				□		□	□	□										□		□	□					
Tulipa sylvestris		★				★		★	★	★										★			★	★	★			
Tulipa tarda		△				△		△		△							△						△					
Tulipa **Triomphe**		■				■		■		■							■			■	■	■	■					
Tunica saxifraga										☆							☆				☆							
Typha angustifolia				▲				▲																				
Typha minima				□				□																				
Veratrum nigrum		★						★											★									
Veratrum viride								△									△											
Verbascum bombyciferum		■	■					■	■	■										■					■			
Verbascum chaixii		☆	☆					☆	☆	☆										☆					☆			
Verbascum phoeniceum		▲	▲					▲	▲								▲	▲		▲	▲				▲			
Verbascum thapsus			□					□	□											□		□						
Verbena bonariensis		★						★	★									★			★		★	★				★
Verbena hastata								△	△									△			△		△		△	△		△
Verbena venosa								■	■	■							■	■		■	■		■	■	■			■
Veronica gentianoides			☆					☆										☆					☆					☆
Veronica incana								▲	▲	▲					▲		▲				▲			▲				
Veronica longifolia								□										□			□		□					
Veronica spicata								★		★							★	★			★				★			
Veronica virginica								△									△	△					△					
Vinca major	■	■	■	■	■		■						■		■		■	■						■				
Vinca minor	☆	☆	☆	☆	☆		☆						☆		☆		☆	☆	☆									
Viola cornuta							▲										▲	▲	▲					▲	▲	▲	▲	▲
Viola labradorica							□							□	□		□	□						□				□
Viola papilionacea							★										★	★										★
Viola odorata							△										△	△						△				△
Viola wittrockiana							■										■	■		■		■		■	■	■		
Zantedeschia aethiopica			☆	☆				☆	☆								☆			☆			☆	☆				
Zantedeschia elliottiana				▲	▲			▲	▲				▲				▲			▲			▲					
Zantedeschia rehmanii				□	□			□	□											□	□		□					
Zauschneria californica		★	★			★		★	★	★	★											★	★		★			
Zinnia elegans		△			△	△		△	△								△			△	△	△				△		

V

Z

FLOWERING-SEASON						DECORATIVE USES			FLOWERS		PLANTS			OTHER USES				GROUND COVER				PLANTS					PROBLEMS					
DECEMBER, JANUARY	FEBRUARY, MARCH	APRIL, MAY	JUNE, JULY, AUGUST	SEPTEMBER, OCTOBER	NOVEMBER	AROUND ROSE BUSHES	GOOD COVER FOR OPEN GROUND	GOOD UNDERGROWTH COVER	GIANT	FOR DRIED FLOWERS	HAS DECORATIVE FRUITS	FOR POTS AND TUBS ON THE PATIO IN THE SUN	FOR POTS AND TUBS ON THE PATIO IN THE SHADE	BULBS REMAIN IN GROUND	OLDER VARIETIES	GROW IN SHADE	GROW IN SUNNY POSITIONS	ESTABLISH QUICKLY	FOR SLOPES AND BANKS	FOR NOOKS, WALLS, ROCKERIES AND PAVING	CLIMBING ANNUALS	GROWN FROM SEED	ATTRACT BEES AND BUTTERFLIES	EASY FOR THE WEEKEND GARDENER	FLOURISH IN WATER	CARNIVOROUS	ATTRACTS RABBITS	VERY INVASIVE	POISONOUS OR ALLERGENIC	ATTRACTS SLUGS	TOLERANT OF POLLUTION	PRONE TO FROST

INDEX

C

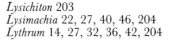

R

S

Achevé d'imprimer sur les presses de Maury-Imprimeur S.A., 45330 Malesherbes

Imprimé en France

01.23.4254.92